The Arabs and Zionism before World War I

The Arabs and Zionism before World War I

by

NEVILLE J. MANDEL

UNIVERSITY OF CALIFORNIA PRESS

Berkeley Los Angeles London

University of California Press
Berkeley and Los Angeles, California
University of California Press, Ltd.
London, England

ISBN 0-520-02466-4
Library of Congress Catalog Card Number: 73-78545
Printed in the United States of America

For Susan, Ronen, Shai and David Yakir

Contents

Preface

This book began life as a doctoral thesis, submitted at Oxford in 1965. At that time, it had the pedantic title of "Turks, Arabs and Jewish Immigration into Palestine: 1882–1914." It was lengthy, written in that special language reserved for doctoral theses, and although I would not have admitted it, designed for just two specialist readers—my examiners. In editing it, I have tried to remedy these and other defects. The text has been shortened, the style lightened, and the content, I hope, made accessible to a somewhat wider reading public. A limited amount of new material has also been added.

By preparing my thesis in Oxford and Jerusalem and returning to both those centres of learning to edit it some years later, I was able to draw on the talents of a wide range of scholars. I am deeply in their debt, and if I were to mention every one of them by name, the list would be exceedingly long. I have no alternative therefore but to express my sincere appreciation to them all collectively.

There are some, however, who cannot go unmentioned, and perhaps I will be forgiven if I single them out. While writing my doctorate, I was extremely fortunate to be guided by Mr. Albert Hourani of St. Antony's College, Oxford. While gathering source material in Israel in 1963, I was supervised by Professor Mayir Vereté of the Hebrew University of Jerusalem. Dr. Michael Heymann (the Director of the Central Zionist Archives) and Dr. Jacob Ro'i, who was then preparing a Master's thesis on "The Attitude of the New Yishuv to the Arabs, 1882–1914," were also invaluable counsellors in Jerusalem. Back in Oxford, Dr. Mustafa Badawi, Dr. Geoffrey Lewis and Dr. David Patterson helped me over technical problems in Arabic, Turkish and Hebrew. Miss Elizabeth Monroe, after examining the thesis, gave me sound advice about editing it. Professor David Vital of the University of Haifa, Mr. David Farhi of the Hebrew University, and the anonymous reader of the University of California Press brought their very specialised knowledge to bear on the manuscript once it was complete. And then Mr. Max Nurock of Jerusalem, who for over fifty years has been improving other people's style, helped me to improve mine too. If, after all this generous guidance, errors of fact and judgement remain—as, no doubt, some do—the fault is entirely mine.

Before concluding this preface, it is only proper that I also thank the Scottish Department of Education, the Carnegie Trust and St. Antony's College, Oxford, who together financed my research; my typists, Mrs. Marjorie Edwards, Mrs. Pat Kirkpatrick and Mrs. Malka Rome, who worked wonders with my drafts; and my brother Edwin who, in a very different way, made it all possible.

Note on Transcriptions

Turkish has been transcribed on the basis of standard Turkish orthography; Arabic on the basis of the system in the second edition of the *Encyclopaedia of Islam,* with minor modifications which will be obvious to the expert, and without vowel quantities being marked; Hebrew on the basis of the system in the Funk & Wagnalls *Jewish Encyclopedia,* also with minor modifications, mainly to adapt it to "modern Hebrew" pronunciation.

The transliteration of proper names posed special problems. In general, all Ottoman subjects—with the exception of Arabs and of Jews *with Hebrew surnames*—have had their names transliterated as if they were Turks, irrespective of the origin of their names: thus, Abdülhamid (a Turk with an Arabic name); Kosmidi (an Ottoman Greek); and Noradungiyan (an Ottoman Armenian). Arabs have had their names transliterated from Arabic, and Jews with Hebrew surnames from Hebrew. This system has been maintained even when it produced the occasional incongruity: thus, Nisim Ruso (an Ottoman Jew with a Hebrew forename which would have been transliterated "Nissim" if he had had a Hebrew surname).

Accepted English spellings of place names have been used; other place names have been transliterated as appropriate from Turkish, Arabic or Hebrew. Ottoman administrative terms and titles have been transliterated from Turkish: thus, vilâyet, sancak and efendi (rather than the slightly more familiar "vilayet," "sanjak," and "effendi"). Muslim religious terms have been transliterated from Arabic: thus, shaykh and waqf.

Certain concessions have been made in these rules for the sake of the reader who is not a specialist. For example, when a person wrote almost exclusively in a European language, the way he spelt his name was usually retained: thus, Négib Azoury and Albert Antébi; and a few composite terms, which have been accepted into the literature, have also been retained: thus, First Aliya and New Yishuv.

Abbreviations

AIU	Alliance Israélite Universelle
AIU	Alliance Israélite Universelle Archive
APC	Anglo-Palestine Company
Consple.	Constantinople
CUP	Committee of Union and Progress
CZA	Central Zionist Archives
CZA (A)	Central Zionist Archives (Austro-Hungarian material)
Damas.	Damascus
Enc.	Enclosure
FO	Foreign Office
ISA (G)	Israel State Archive (German material)
ISA (T)	Israel State Archive (Ottoman material)
JCA	Jewish Colonization Association
JCA	Jewish Colonization Association Archive
Jerus.	Jerusalem
JNF	Jewish National Fund
Kay.	Kaymakam
Min.	Minister
Mutas.	Mutasarrıf
OFM	Ottoman Foreign Ministry Archive
PJCA	Palestine Jewish Colonization Association Archive
Pres.	President
PRO	Public Record Office
PRO (G)	Public Record Office (German material)
Q d'O	Quai d'Orsay Archive
SP	Sublime Porte
US (T)	State Department Archive (material on Turkey)
ZAC	Zionist Actions Committee
ZCO	Zionist Central Office

* Italicised abbreviations are for archives which are described in the Note on Sources.

OTTOMAN PALESTINE: 1914

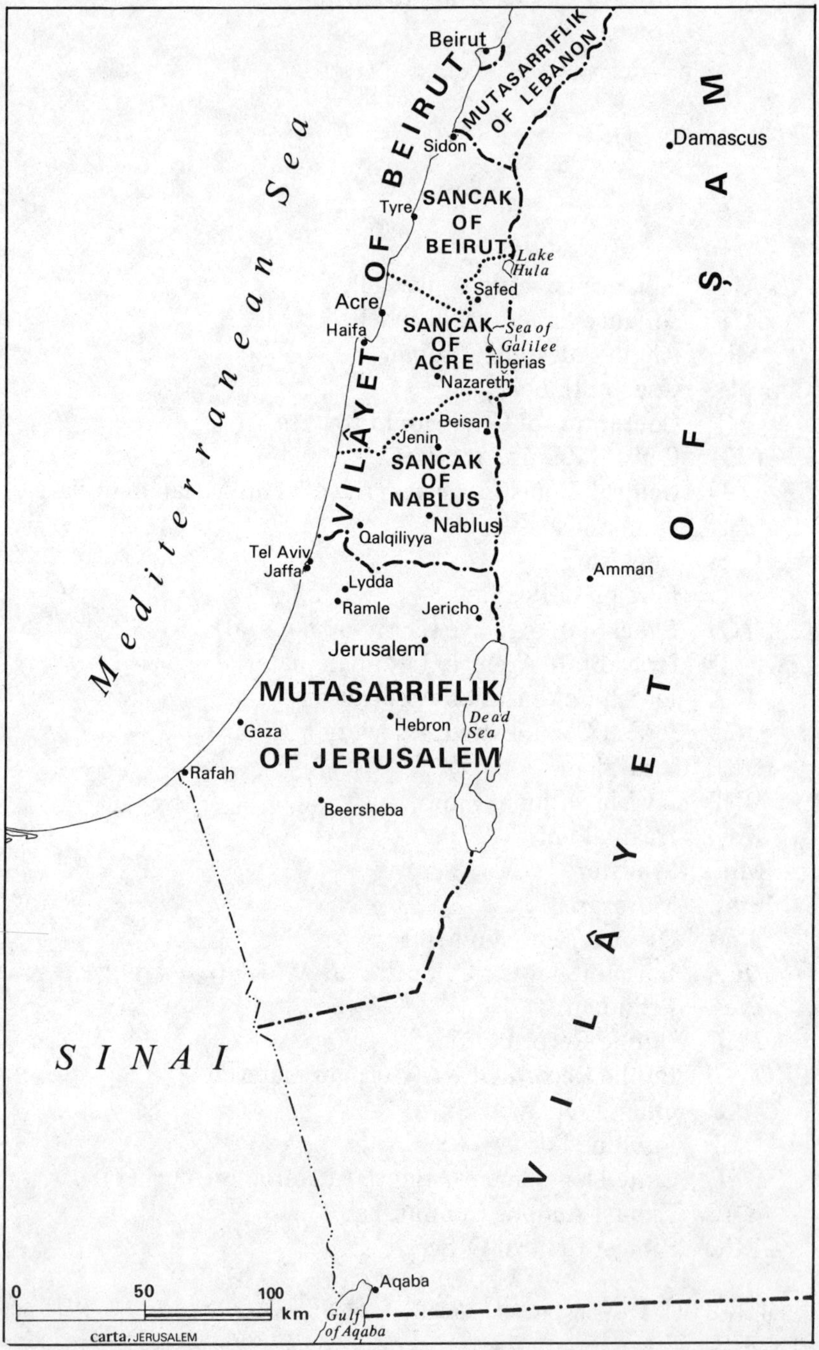

Beirut
MUTASARRIFLIK OF LEBANON
VILÂYET OF BEIRUT
Mediterranean Sea
Sidon
Damascus
SANCAK OF BEIRUT
Tyre
Lake Hula
Safed
Acre
Haifa
SANCAK OF ACRE
Sea of Galilee
Tiberias
Nazareth
Beisan
Jenin
SANCAK OF NABLUS
Nablus
Qalqiliyya
Tel Aviv
Jaffa
Amman
Lydda
Ramle
Jericho
Jerusalem
MUTASARRIFLIK OF JERUSALEM
Gaza
Hebron
Dead Sea
Rafah
Beersheba
VILÂYET OF ŞAM
SINAI
0
50
100
km
Aqaba
Gulf of Aqaba
carta, JERUSALEM

JEWISH SETTLEMENT IN PALESTINE: 1914

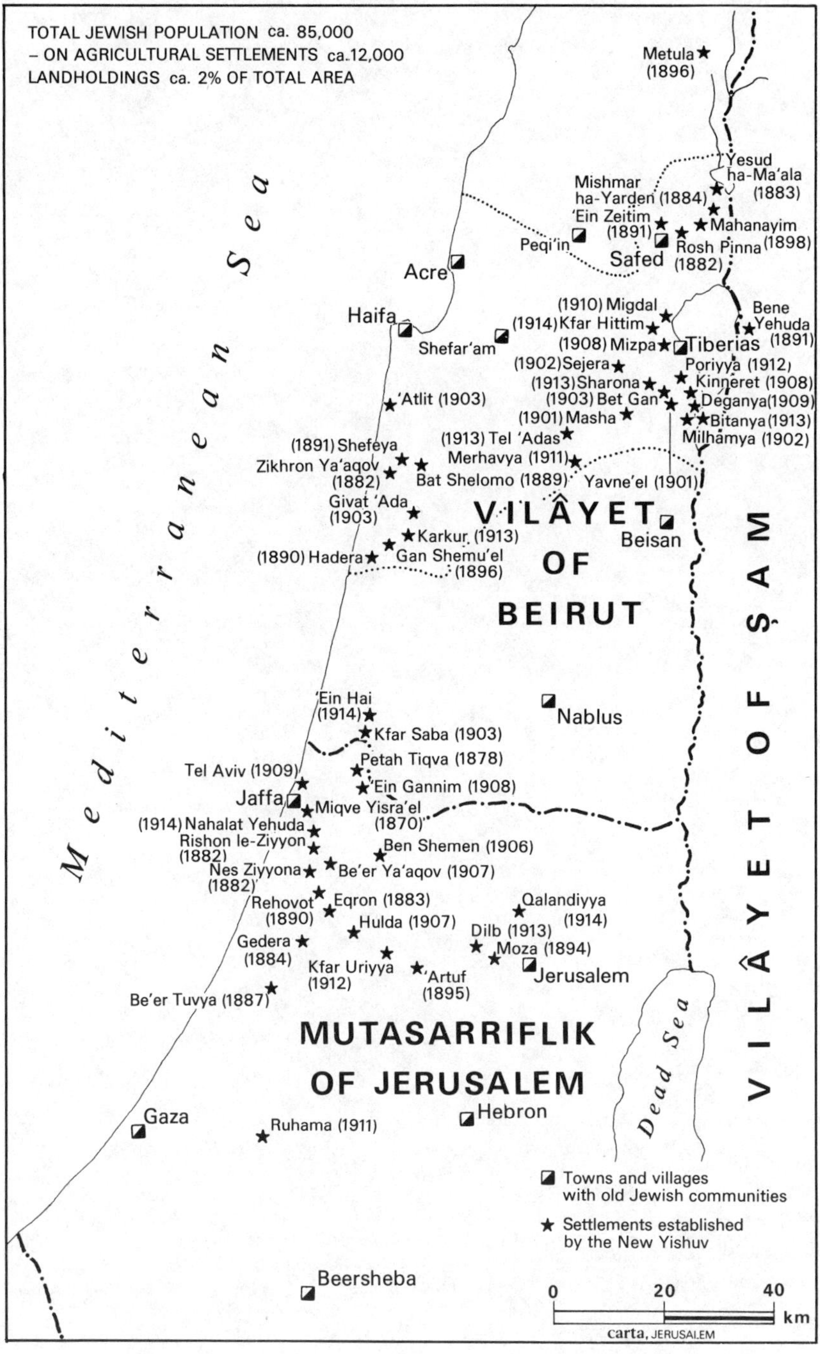
TOTAL JEWISH POPULATION ca. 85,000
– ON AGRICULTURAL SETTLEMENTS ca.12,000
LANDHOLDINGS ca. 2% OF TOTAL AREA
Mediterranean Sea
Metula (1896)
Yesud ha-Ma'ala (1883)
Mishmar ha-Yarden (1884)
'Ein Zeitim (1891)
Mahanayim
Peqi'in
Safed
Rosh Pinna (1898)
(1882)
Acre
Haifa
Shefar'am
(1910) Migdal
(1914) Kfar Hittim
(1908) Mizpa
Tiberias
Bene Yehuda (1891)
(1902) Sejera
Poriyya (1912)
(1913) Sharona
Kinneret (1908)
(1903) Bet Gan
Deganya (1909)
(1901) Masha
Bitanya (1913)
'Atlit (1903)
(1913) Tel 'Adas
Milhamya (1902)
(1891) Shefeya
Merhavya (1911)
Zikhron Ya'aqov (1882)
Bat Shelomo (1889)
Yavne'el (1901)
Givat 'Ada (1903)
VILÂYET OF BEIRUT
Beisan
Karkur (1913)
(1890) Hadera
Gan Shemu'el (1896)
VILÂYET OF ŞAM
'Ein Hai (1914)
Nablus
Kfar Saba (1903)
Petah Tiqva (1878)
Tel Aviv (1909)
'Ein Gannim (1908)
Jaffa
Miqve Yisra'el (1870)
(1914) Nahalat Yehuda
Rishon le-Ziyyon (1882)
Ben Shemen (1906)
Nes Ziyyona (1882)
Be'er Ya'aqov (1907)
Rehovot (1890)
Eqron (1883)
Qalandiyya (1914)
Hulda (1907)
Dilb (1913)
Gedera (1884)
Moza (1894)
Kfar Uriyya (1912)
'Artuf (1895)
Jerusalem
Be'er Tuvya (1887)
Dead Sea
MUTASARRIFLIK OF JERUSALEM
Hebron
Gaza
Ruhama (1911)
Towns and villages with old Jewish communities
Settlements established by the New Yishuv
Beersheba
0 20 40 km
carta, JERUSALEM

Introduction

In this book I set out to explore the Arab reactions to Zionist aims and activities in Palestine before 1914. To do so, I have had to cover the pre-Zionist period from the beginning of the 1880s, because those years form the essential background to what happened after 1897, the year in which the Zionist Movement was founded. I have also had to examine in depth the Ottoman Government's policies towards all Jewish settlement in Palestine, both Zionist and non-Zionist, because the Arab reactions can only be understood in the light of those policies.

At the same time, I have had to keep my subject within certain bounds. As a result, I have concentrated almost entirely on the reactions of the political élite among the Arabs to Zionism, because in the long run it was their response, and not that of the peasant masses, which was significant. Then, although Zionist reactions to the Arabs in Palestine are the other side of my particular coin, I have not entered into them, except where necessary to explain the Arab position. Fascinating as the Zionist side is, it is an independent topic, meriting full and separate treatment in its own right. Finally, I have not gone beyond the entry of the Ottoman Empire into World War I—for two main reasons. First, the prewar period can be regarded as an almost self-contained phase of the Arab-Zionist confrontation (with the war years of 1914–18 belonging to the next phase). Second, and more important, Arab opposition to Zionism had emerged by 1914. This fact, which is not without powerful implications for the history of what is now the Arab-Israel conflict, stands out in sharpest relief if a line is firmly drawn at the outbreak of World War I.

Broadly speaking, the conventional view is that all was well between Arab and Jew in Palestine before World War I. The Jews, it is said, were too few and the Arabs too inarticulate for discord to manifest itself. Among the Arabs there was, at most, only rudimentary opposition to Jewish settlement in Palestine and only a vague awareness of Zionist aims. A corollary of this view is that the Arabs only discovered the "challenge" of Zionism when the Balfour Declaration was issued by the British Government in 1917.

This view persists for a number of reasons. Events since 1917 have tended to eclipse the earlier period. Historians have been mainly concerned with the British conduct of the Mandate in Palestine from 1922 to 1948, and with Jewish progress to statehood over those years. Others, who lived through the events, have memories of undeniably close and amicable contact between Arabs and Jews in Palestine, on an individual and non-political basis, before—and long after—1914. But more fundamentally, the view survives because no systematic investigation, utilising primary source material, has been made into the Arab response *on the political level* to the first three decades of modern Jewish settlement in Palestine from 1882 to 1914.

The sources yield a picture which does not tally with the conventional one. In 1882 an increased flow of Jewish immigrants on their way to Palestine did not pass unnoticed in Beirut. In 1891 Arab notables in Jerusalem sent a telegram to the Ottoman Government asking it to put an end to Jewish immigration into Palestine and land sales to Jews. In 1899 a former President of the Municipal Council in Jerusalem wrote to the Chief Rabbi of France, urging that Zionism "in the geographic sense of the word" should stop. After the Young Turk Revolution of 1908 there was a relatively free press in the Ottoman Empire, in which the Arabs expressed their views on Zionism. There was also a parliament in which Arab deputies and others raised the issue. By 1914, Arabs beyond the limits of Palestine were well informed about Zionist activities in the country, and the essentials of the Arab anti-Zionism had been worked out. Arab nationalists had met Zionist leaders, and small anti-Zionist societies had been formed in Jerusalem, Jaffa, Nablus, Haifa, Beirut, Constantinople and Cairo.

Hence the conclusions to this book suggest that the conventional view of Arab reactions to Zionism before World War I requires modification, perhaps radical modification. It seems clear that the *political élite* among the Arabs in Palestine and the surrounding areas had responded to Zionism to a greater extent than has been recognised, and that Arab antagonism to Zionism had emerged well before the Balfour Declaration was issued. It follows therefore that, from the point of view of the present-day Arab-Israel conflict, the period before 1914 should be viewed in a new light, for the roots of Arab hostility to Israel extend back to it.

Although it is easy enough to state the purpose of this study and its main conclusion, conducting the research for it was another matter. The major methodological problem encountered was the paucity of source material in Arabic. A few contemporary Arabic newspapers and periodicals survive, but by no means all the relevant Arabic press is extant. The private papers of Arabs who lived through the period are generally inaccessible, and the records of the early Arab nationalist societies have been lost—if they ever existed.

In these circumstances there was no alternative but to approach the subject mainly through non-Arab sources. Fortunately these are abundant, and they are described in some detail in the Note on Sources. Diplomatic reports from Palestine and Constantinople contain much useful information, and Jewish archives are extremely valuable, even if the material in them needs to be treated with especial care. Unexpected mines of information are to be found in these archives. For instance, numerous copies of official Ottoman documents relating to Jews in Palestine are contained in the files of the Jewish Colonization Association, and the Central Zionist Archives possess the monitoring of the Arabic press conducted by the Zionist Office in Jaffa from December 1911 onwards. This particular collection offers reliable translations of literally hundreds of Arabic articles on Zionism which are not otherwise available. While this relative wealth of diplomatic and Jewish material to supplement the somewhat limited Arabic sources, my task proved far from fruitless.

The terms "Palestine" and "Arabs" need a few words of explanation.

This study deals with Palestine at the end of the Ottoman period, and under the Ottomans Palestine was never a single administrative unit. In the latter half of the nineteenth century it was part of the large *vilâyet* of *Şam* ("Syria"); and that area, which is the centre of gravity for this book—west of the River Jordan—was divided into the three *Sancaks* of Jerusalem, Nablus and Acre (see Map 1). Each of these sancaks was governed by a *mutasarrıf,* and subordinate to him were *kaymakams* (sub-governors) in the main towns, such as Jaffa, Gaza, Tiberias and Safed. In the 1880's the Vilâyet of Şam was reorganised. In 1887, the Sancak of Jerusalem was made an independent mutasarrıflik, whose mutasarrıf was responsible directly to the various ministries and departments of state at Constantinople. In 1888, the new Vilâyet of Beirut was formed, and the two Sancaks of Nablus and Acre in the north of Palestine were transferred to it. Thus, for most of the period under consideration, the south of Palestine was governed from Jerusalem, and the north from Beirut.

Despite these administrative divisions and changes, the concept of a *geographic* area called "Palestine" was used by the three main parties figuring in this book: the Ottoman Government, the Arabs and the Jews. The Ottoman Government employed the term "Arz-i Filistin" (the "Land of Palestine") in official correspondence, meaning for all intents and purposes the area to the west of the River Jordan which became "Palestine" under the British in 1922. The Arabs used the term "Filasṭin" to designate an area whose limits had varied at different historical periods, and thus their notion of its precise dimensions was necessarily vague, especially in the decades before World War I, given the recent administrative changes which had taken place. The Jews' use of "Palestine" was equally imprecise, because for them it was a translation of "'Ereẓ Yisra'el" (the "Land of Israel"), the dimensions of which had also varied at different stages of Jewish history. Nonetheless, the Zionist Movement's programme, adopted in 1897, spoke (in German) of a home "in Palestine" for the Jewish people, and the first Zionist institution established in the country was the "Anglo-Palestine Company."

For the sake of simplicity, therefore, "Palestine" is used in this book to mean the area which was so designated under the British Mandate from 1922 to 1948. Moreover, in order to avoid a lot of periphrastic inconvenience, that geographic area is also referred to as the "country" of Palestine. And when mention is made of "the surrounding provinces," the adjacent areas of the Vilâyets of Beirut and Şam are meant.

Scholars differ over the population figures for Palestine during the period under discussion, because reliable statistics simply do not exist. In 1895, Vital Cuinet, a noted French geographer of the

Ottoman Empire, put the total population of Palestine—Arab and Jewish—at rather less than half a million.[1] Other authorities put it higher, approaching seven hundred thousand in 1914.[2] Perhaps it would be wisest, therefore, to regard these figures as no more than orders of magnitude and, whilst accepting them as some sort of parameters, to allow fairly generous margins of error for them. According to Cuinet, more than three-quarters of the population were concentrated in the Mutasarrıflık of Jerusalem, where there was more arable land than in the rough, mountainous north.[3] Most were Sunni Muslims, and only about 16 per cent of the total were Christian Arabs, many of whom lived in Jerusalem, Bethlehem, Jaffa, Nazareth and Haifa. In the north of the country there were also small numbers of Druze and Mutawalis (Shiite Muslims). Bedouin were to be found in various parts of the country.

The social structure of Palestine was similar to that of other Arab provinces in the Ottoman Empire. The majority of the population were peasants ("fellahin"), living in villages and working the land. Illiteracy, poverty and ignorance were commonplace, both in the villages and in the towns.

In the early nineteenth century the village shaykhs enjoyed considerable power and independence, primarily because they acted as tax-farmers for the authorities, usually on a hereditary basis. In the middle of the century, however, various fiscal and administrative reforms (*tanzimat*) were instituted. The system of collecting taxes was changed, and at the same time steps were taken to cut down the traditional privileges of the village shaykhs. The effect of these reforms was to consolidate the already strong position of the urban élite, so much so that by the end of the century almost all political power had passed to a handful of great Muslim families, who lived in the larger towns.

This small group of families was landowning and wealthy. The most influential of them were those in Jerusalem (with names like al-Ḥusayni, al-Khalidi and al-Nashashibi), not merely because they came from the Holy City but because their city was the

1. Cuinet, *passim* (computed from the figures given for the Mutasarrıflık of Jerusalem and the Sancaks of Nablus and Acre).
2. Barron, p. 3, gives the population in 1914 as 689,275 (based on Ottoman sources, which he notes are "not strictly accurate"). Part of the discrepancy between Cuinet's figures and Barron's is to be explained by the twenty-year gap between them, during which time Jewish immigration was proceeding—see below.
3. Cuinet, *passim*.

administrative centre of an independent mutasarrıflık, ranking with Damascus, while Nablus and Acre were dependent on Beirut. They, and their counterparts in other towns, owed their allegiance firmly to the Ottoman Empire, and developed an interest in maintaining the new status quo. They took over the tax-collecting functions and sat on the newly formed administrative councils—and, in so doing, were able to increase their land holdings and wealth still further. Forming an educated élite, they provided the Arabs in Palestine with their intellectuals and men of letters, both spiritual and secular. They filled all the key religious posts in the country (*Muftis* of Jerusalem and other towns, the religious courts and so forth), and entered the local administration. As a result, they came to dominate all aspects of life in Palestine.

Besides these notables and the village shaykhs (who, though deprived of political power, still enjoyed social prestige), one other group should be mentioned: the wealthier of the Christian Arabs in the towns who, from a Western, secular point of view, were often better educated than the Muslims. It was they, for example, who edited the first newspapers in Palestine, as elsewhere in the Arab provinces. They were frequently merchants, tradesmen and officials; some of them owned land and a few were professional men.

Nationalism in the European sense was almost unknown among the Arabs at the end of the nineteenth century. Personal loyalties were therefore to family and religion and, at another level, either to the Ottoman Empire (probably a somewhat abstract concept for most) or to the much more concrete framework of town or village. In the years before 1914 a discrete Palestinian "patriotism" (rather than a full nationalism) emerged, in large part as a reaction to Zionism. But, as Joshua Porath has pointed out in his work on the nationalist movement in Palestine after 1918, there were also historical, religious and social factors, which furnished local Arabs with a basis for identifying in wider terms than their immediate towns and villages.[4] When, for example, the Muslim armies first conquered the area in the seventh century, the southern and central sectors of the country became "Jund Filasṭin," the military district of Palestine. That district—the larger part of the country—functioned for four centuries, until the coming of the Seljuks (1072–99). Thereafter, it was not formed again, but under the Ottomans the

4. Porath, pp. 4–7.

Sancak of Nablus, in the centre of the country, was at times governed from Jerusalem, and the military garrisons in both areas regularly shared their duties. To illustrate the religious plane, both Islam and Christianity speak of a "Holy Land," conceptually similar to the Land of Israel, with Jerusalem at its centre. The Muslim *Qaḍi* (religious judge) of Jerusalem had jurisdiction over a larger area than the Mutasarrıflık of Jerusalem, and on occasion his influence extended as far as Haifa. Similarly, the Greek Orthodox Patriarch of Jerusalem, head of perhaps the most venerable Christian institution in the country, had authority over the whole of Palestine and beyond. Finally, on the social plane, much of the Muslim population was divided between the rival clans of "Qays" and "Yaman," which traced their origins back to the north and south of Arabia respectively. Paradoxically, the centuries of feuding between these clans had some cohesive effect on Palestine, for on both sides it brought together Arabs from all over the country and gave them a sense of unity and purpose transcending their separate towns and villages.

To sum up: The fellahin formed the majority of the population of Palestine. But they were inert, socially and politically, and by the end of the nineteenth century their shaykhs had lost most, if not all, their political power. Thus, while their reactions to the Jewish colonies set up in their midst are interesting, they are not central to this book. The focus is on that small but dominant segment of the population, which by the turn of the century controlled the country's political, economic and intellectual life: the urban notables. In Arabic, they were called *aʿyan*—literally, "eyes"—and bearing in mind the special historical, religious and social factors associated with Palestine, they were the "eyes" of the country in a very real sense.

Small numbers of religious Jews, mainly from Europe, had been making their way into Palestine for centuries. In the 1880s, however, the volume and nature of this flow changed. A large exodus of Jews from Russia was in progress, and while most of the emigrants travelled westwards, towards America, a tiny proportion headed for Palestine. More often than not, the latter were Jewish nationalists, belonging to the "Lovers of Zion" Movement, who, after a false start in 1878, established their first agricultural settlements in Palestine in 1882. Fifteen years later, Theodor Herzl gave more concrete form to Jewish national aspirations by founding the Zionist Movement which, as noted above, sought a home for the Jewish people in Palestine.

As a result of this immigration, the Jewish population of Palestine rose from about twenty-four thousand in 1882 to approximately eighty-five thousand in 1914.[5] More than half of the newcomers were nationalists, who were dedicated to rebuilding their nation's patrimony in Palestine and constituted the "New Yishuv," the modern Jewish community. In 1914 the New Yishuv numbered some thirty-five thousand, of whom about twelve thousand lived on agricultural settlements. The remainder were not confined to the four "Holy Cities" of Jerusalem, Hebron, Tiberias and Safed (where almost all Jews lived in 1882), but also resided in fair numbers in Jaffa and Haifa.

The reactions of the Arabs to the Zionist Movement and the New Yishuv only came clearly to the surface after the Young Turk Revolution in 1908. But the process to which they were reacting had been going on for over twenty-five years. When their reactions are examined, it becomes evident that they were responding to the policies of the Ottoman Government towards Jewish settlement in Palestine since the 1880s, just as much as to the activities of the Jews themselves. Hence the point of departure for this book is a brief survey of the Ottoman policies and practice in question.[6]

5. For these figures, or rather estimates, see *ha-Enziklopedya ha-ʿivrit,* vol. vi, cols. 666–74, "Demography" (R. Bachi). Since as many as one in every two immigrants may have departed again, the total number of Jews actually entering Palestine from 1882 to 1914 may have been anything up to 100,000.

6. For more detailed treatment of this subject, see my articles in *Middle Eastern Studies.*

1

Ottoman Policy and Practice: 1881–1908

MODERN Jewish immigration into Palestine in significant numbers began in 1882. The Ottoman Government at the Sublime Porte in Constantinople was aware of this influx from the outset, and indeed decided to oppose Jewish settlement in Palestine in autumn 1881, some months before the increased flow of Jews got under way.

On examination, the Sublime Porte's alertness is not as remarkable as it may seem at first sight. Tsar Alexander II was assassinated in 1881. His death was followed by pogroms against the Jews of Russia and then, in 1882, by the notorious "May Laws" which stiffened the existing economic discrimination against the Jews. The stirring of the Jewish community, physical and intellectual, was heightened. Many more than before began to leave Russia, mainly for America, and not a few began thinking in practical terms about Jewish nationalism—an idea which had been spreading in recent years among Jews not only in Russia but also in Austro-Hungary and Rumania.

Given the aggressive intentions of Russia and Austro-Hungary towards the Ottoman Empire throughout the nineteenth century, the Porte had good reason to try and keep abreast of events in those rival Empires. *Inter alia,* therefore, its diplomatic representatives in St. Petersburg and Vienna sent regular reports and press cuttings about Jewish affairs to Constantinople, and in the catalogues of the Ottoman Foreign Ministry there is even a separate file, listed under Russia, entitled "Situation of the Jews; Question of their immigration into Turkey: 1881," covering settlement in the Ottoman Empire as a whole.[1] Moreover, there had been direct approaches to the Porte on this question in recent years—for example, by such strange figures as the English traveller and mystic Laurence Oliphant, who in 1879 had submitted a scheme to settle Jews on the east bank of the River Jordan,[2] and by more solid gentlemen, like an Anglo-German group, who in 1881 presented the Porte with proposals to settle Jews along a railroad which they wanted to build from Smyrna to Baghdad.[3] It may also be assumed that individual Jews enquired about the possibility of settling in the Empire as well.

Thus in November 1881, ostensibly in response to the Anglo-German group's approach, the Ottoman Government announced that:

> [Jewish] immigrants will be able to settle as scattered groups throughout the Ottoman Empire, excluding Palestine. They must submit to all the laws of the Empire and become Ottoman subjects."[4]

This, in a nutshell, was the Ottoman Government's policy towards Jewish settlement in the Empire from 1881 onwards. In April 1882, it was repeated in a notice posted outside the Ottoman Consulate-General at Odessa, where growing numbers of Russian Jews were applying for visas to enter Palestine,[5] and again in June by the Ottoman Foreign Minister in conversation with the American Minister at the Porte.[6] In brief, Jews could settle in the Empire, but not in Palestine; they were to become Ottoman subjects, not to live in concentrated groups, and not to seek any special privileges.

The specific exclusion of Palestine took the Jews by surprise, and various theories were advanced to explain it. Oliphant, who was in close contact with Jews in Austro-Hungary and Rumania, suggested that it derived from Muslim sentiments over Palestine, anti-Jewish

1. *OFM* Cartoon 208, Dossier 139. Although catalogued, this file cannot be found.
2. Oliphant, pp. 502–10.
3. *Jewish Chronicle,* no. 650 (9.9.1881).
4. *Ḥavaẓẓelet,* xii, 41 (1.9.1882Z(: CF. *Levant Herald,* iii, 444 (24.11.1881).
5. *Ha-Meliẓ,* xviii, 16 (9.5.1882).
6. State Dept., *Papers,* 1882, pp. 516–19, no. 319 (11.7.1882) and encs., L. Wallace (Consple.) to F. T. Frelinghuysen (Washington).

influences in Constantinople, and the crisis between the Ottoman Empire and Great Britain over Egypt.[7] Jews in Palestine, on the other hand, put the blame variously on the influence of local Sephardi (Oriental) Jews, who were unsympathetic to Ashkenazi (European) Jews;[8] on Jews living on alms in Jerusalem, who feared that the newcomers would encroach upon their own meagre income;[9] and on the Mutasarrif, Rauf Paşa, who was thought to be personally ill-disposed to Jews.[10] For its part, the Porte, when pressed by foreign governments, talked of the penury prevalent in Jerusalem, and also claimed that Jewish immigrants were a threat to public order and hygiene in the city.[1] But none of these explanations is convincing and some of them are demonstrably false. For instance, the crisis over Egypt in 1882 only began *after* the Porte had formulated its policy at the end of the previous year.

The real reasons lay elsewhere. They were principally two. First, the Ottoman Government feared the possibility of nurturing another national problem in the Empire. Second, it did not want to increase the number of foreign subjects, particularly Europeans and nationals of the Great Powers, in its domains.[12]

Towards the end of 1882, Ottomans ministers told Isaac Fernandez, a leading Jewish figure in Constantinople, of the first of these reasons. They were determined "to resist firmly the immigration of Jews into Syria and Mesopotamia, as they [did] not wish to have another nationality established in great numbers in that part of the Empire."[13] In the light of their misfortunes with national minorities throughout the nineteenth century (which had resulted in considerable territorial losses in the Balkans) and only

7. Druyanow, *Ketavim,* i, 37-38 (24.6.1882), L. Oliphant (Consple.) to D. Gordon [Lyck].
8. *Ibid.* i, 318-23 (13.11.1884), J. Rivlin and Y. M. Pines (Jerus.) to Gordon.
9. Druyanow, *Pinsker,* p. 191.
10. Druyanow, *Ketavim,* i, 321 (13.11.1884); cf. Yaᶜari, pp. 174, 238 and 240.
11. *PRO* FO 195/1581, no. 9 (5.3.1887), N. T. Moore (Jerus.) to Sir W. A. White (Consple.); cf. State Dept., *Papers,* 1888, ii, 1559-60, no. 57 (28.1.1888), O. S. Straus (Consple.) to Secy. of State Bayard; and *ISA(T)* no. 47 (15.12.1887), Ministry of Internal Affairs (SP) to Mutas. (Jerus.).
12. The six "Great Powers" represented at the Sublime Porte at the end of the nineteenth century were Great Britain, France, Russia, Austro-Hungary, Germany and Italy. But for the purposes of this book it will seldom be necessary to differentiate between them and other Powers of lesser rank (including the United States) also represented at Constantinople.
13. *PRO* FO 78/3394, no. 1155 (30.12.1882); H. Wyndham (Consple.) to Earl Granville (FO).

four years after the Congress of Berlin (which in 1878 had confirmed Rumania's independence and created a semi-independent Bulgaria), the ministers' fears were understandable. As they told Fernandez in 1883, Jewish settlement in Palestine was a political issue, and they simply did not want another Rumanian or Bulgarian question on their hands.[14]

Second, the Ottoman Government apparently did not warm to the prospect of the European immigrants flowing in relatively large numbers into the Empire. By the nineteenth century the European was disliked and distrusted by the Turk—and, it should be added, by most Arabs as well. Under the system of "Capitulations," Europeans enjoyed extensive extra-territorial privileges, including the right to trade, travel, and hold property freely throughout the Empire. Thanks to the Capitulations, they were also largely exempt from Ottoman taxes and dues, and beyond the reach of Ottoman courts. By the middle of the nineteenth century, the Powers were exploiting the Capitulations in order to deepen their influence in the Empire, while the Ottoman Government was trying to abolish them. In these circumstances, Ottoman ministers must have asked themselves why, of all things and of all places, let European numbers and influence mount in Palestine. Presumably they only had to recall that, while the Crimean War (1854–56) had nominally been fought over the Christian Holy Places in Jerusalem, a broader issue had been the attempt by Russia to distort the Capitulations and so extend her protection over all Greek Orthodox subjects of the Ottoman Empire. What would happen now if European Jews were allowed to flood into Palestine?

Two subsidiary considerations probably reinforced the Porte's opposition to Jewish settlement in Palestine. Many of the prospective immigrants belonged to the "Lovers of Zion" Movement, which had taken roots among Jews in Eastern Europe, particularly in Russia and Rumania, from the late 1860's onwards. The Lovers of Zion called for a Jewish national revival, through settlement in Palestine, which they conceived as their nation's homeland, and through the renascence of Hebrew as a living language. They themselves had given the Ottoman Government the impression that their movement was larger and more powerful than it actually was. They

14. Letter of 20.12.1883, I. Fernandez and S. Bloch (Consple.) to S. Hirsch Miqve Yisraʿel), published in Margalith, p. 204.

exaggerated its numbers in the European Jewish press,[15] and in the summer of 1882 sent various delegations to Constantinople, one of which—from Rumania—bore a petition speaking of the "hundreds of thousands" of potential Jewish immigrants.[16] They contacted prominent Ottoman Jews,[17] not to speak of the American Minister at the Porte,[18] and the Ottoman Ministers of the Interior and of War.[19] And within a short while, they moved Baron Edmond de Rothschild of Paris to use his influence on their behalf as well.[20] Little wonder that the Government became apprehensive of what was afoot.

The other subsidiary consideration was that most of the Jews in question were Russian subjects, and Russia was the arch-enemy of the Ottoman Empire. During the nineteenth century alone, there had been four Russo-Turkish wars, the last as recently as 1877-78. Moreover, the Ottoman Government held Russia responsible for Balkan nationalism and the resultant losses to its Empire in Europe. The Lovers of Zion were Jewish nationalists, and the Porte could have had no wish to have another Russian-educated and possibly Russian-inspired, nationalist movement to contend with, especially in the heart of the Arab provinces or the Empire, which were still free of the "canker" of European nationalism.

This opposition was quickly translated into practice by official restrictions, first on Jewish entry into Palestine and then on land purchase in the country. Again, the Porte's alertness is striking. On 29 June 1882, a tiny group of Lovers of Zion, calling themselves the Biluyim (after the Hebrew initials for the biblical phrase "House of Jacob, come ye and let us go") and numbering all of fourteen souls, set sail from Constantinople for Jaffa. On the very same day, the Porte sent a telegram to the Mutasarrıf of Jerusalem, forbidding Russian, Rumanian, and Bulgarian Jews to land at Jaffa or Haifa.[21] They were to disembark at some other Ottoman port and not set foot in any of the four "Holy Cities" (Jerusalem, Hebron, Safed and Tiberias), where most of the Jews in Palestine were concentrated.

15. Yavneʿeli, i, 66; Klausner, pp. 137-39; WJissotski, p. 62 (5.4.1885).
16. State Dept., *Papers,* 1882, pp. 517-18, enc. 1 to no. 319; Rumanian petition.
17. Yavneʿeli, i, 214-15.
18. State Dept., *Papers,* 1882, pp. 516-17, no. 319 (11.7.1882).
19. Chissin, p. 9 (24.7.1882).
20. Wissotski, p. 55 (2.4.1885), and pp. 74-75 (4.4.1885).
21. *Ha-Maggid,* xxvi, 28 (19.7.1882).

This directive was contrary to one of the Capitulations, which assured Russian subjects of the right of unrestricted travel throughout the Ottoman Empire (except Arabia).[22] The Mutasarrıf, therefore, sought guidance from the Porte, and in the exchange which followed that summer clearer instructions were worked out,[23] which were also sent to the Governor of the Vilâyet of Şam (embracing the north of Palestine).[24] From these instructions and the way in which they were enforced, two things stood out. One was the Porte's concern to prevent Jewish imigrants from *settling* in Palestine—thus Jewish *pilgrims* and *businessmen* were still allowed to visit the country for short periods. The other was that the restrictions were primarily aimed against *Russian* Jews; Jews from other countries, who in any event were arriving in much smaller numbers, were of less concern.

Irregularities were not long in arising. For instance, in Constantinople Russian Jews could obtain permits for internal travel within the Empire and thus would arrive in Palestine with valid papers. Although efforts were made in the spring of 1883 to seal this loophole and tighten the restrictions generally,[25] Jews from all countries—including Russia—could always enter Palestine as pilgrims or businessmen,[26] and then outstay their welcome. The Mutasarrıf of Jerusalem recognized that this did not accord with the Porte's real purpose and so again turned to Constantinople for advice. A correspondence ensued; the Ministries of Internal and Foreign Affairs conferred; the opinions of the Porte's legal advisers were sought; and the Council of State considered the question in March 1884.[27] After a further exchange with Jerusalem,[28] it was

22. There were no Capitulations with Rumania (independent 1882) or Bulgaria (still nominally tributary to the Ottoman Empire in 1882).
23. *ISA (G)* A III 9, no. 858 (12.7.1882), von Tischendorf (Jerus.) to Reichskanzler (Berlin); cf. *Ḥavaẓẓelet,* xii 35 (7.7.1882).
24. *PRO* FO 195/1410, no. 86 (24.10.1882), G. J. Eldridge (Beirut) to Lord Dufferin (Consple.); and enc. 1 to no. 97 (29.11.1882), N. Vitale (Latakia) to Eldridge.
25. *PRO* FO 78/3506, enc. to no. 48 (22.1.1883), Wyndham to Granville: *"Notification officielle"* (n.d.); cf. *PRO* FO 195/1447, no. 3 (16.1.1883) Eldridge to Dufferin; *Times* (London) no. 30,730 (30.1.1883), letter from Oliphant (Haifa), enclosing order (26.12.1882) Vali (Şam) to Kay. (Haifa); and *Ḥavaẓẓlet,* xiii, 9 (16.2.1883).
26. *Ḥavaẓẓelet,* xiii, 9 (16.2.1883); cf. *ibid.* 15 (6.4.1883) and 16 (15.4.1883).
27. *ISA (T)* no. 89 (4.3.1884): minutes of this meeting (copied to Jerusalem).
28. *ISA (T)* no. 84 (8.4.1884), Ministry of the Interior (SP) to Mutas. (Jerus.).

decided to close Palestine to all Jewish businessmen, on the grounds that the Capitulations, which permitted Europeans to trade freely within the Empire, applied exclusively to areas "appropriate for trade"—the Council of State did not consider Palestine such an area.[29] Henceforth, only Jewish *pilgrims* could enter Palestine. Their passports were to be properly visaed by Ottoman consuls abroad; on arrival they were to hand over a deposit guaranteeing their departure, and they were to leave after thirty days.[30]

In all this, the role of the Powers was crucial. If the entry restrictions were to be effective, they had to be accepted by the Powers, on whose nationals they fell. And, broadly speaking, the Powers did not accept them, being intent on preserving their privileges under the Capitulations. There were, of course, certain differences in the positions taken by the various Powers, depending to some extent on the state of their relations with the Ottoman Empire. For example, from the 1880s onwards, Germany was actively trying to befriend the Empire and on occasion seemed inclined to fall in with the entry restrictions.[31] But in general the Powers refused to acquiesce in them, and so, in 1888, after adopting a strong stand,[32] they were able to extract an important concession from the Porte permitting Jews to settle in Palestine, provided that they arrived singly, and not en masse.[33]

The only major exception among the Powers during the 1880s was Russia, which at first did accept the restrictions and was even suspected by some of having gone so far as to invite them.[34] The reasons for Russia's attitude are not entirely clear—she may have feared that a larger Jewish community in Palestine could endanger the status quo over the Holy Places in Jerusalem, or her position may merely have been an extension of the Tsarist Government's

29. *ISA (T)* no. 89 (4.3.1884).
30. *Ḥavaẓẓelet,* xiv, 23 (2.5.1884).
31. *PRO* FO 195/1612, no. 15 (29.5.1888), Moore to White.
32. Texts of American, French, and British *Notes* in State Dept., *Papers,* 1888, ii, 1588–91, dated 17, 23, and 24 May 1888 respectively.
23. *Ibid.* p. 1619 (4.10.1888), translation of *Note Verbale* from SP to American Embassy (Consple.) ; cf. *PRO* FO 195/1607 (6.10.1888), White to Moore.
34. Klausner, p. 138; Straus, p. 80; cf. Wissotski, pp. 71–72 (2.4.1885); report of conversation with Haham Başı (Consple.); *ibid.* p. 62 (5.4.1885), K. Z. Wissotski (Consple.) to L. Pinsker (Odessa); and Druyanow, *Ketavim,* i, 280 (26.5.1885), A. Veneziani (Consple.) to Pinsker.

hard attitude to its Jews at home. At the beginning of the 1890s, however, Russia changed her position and joined the other Powers in resisting the restrictions. Consequently, the Porte was unsuccessful when, for a brief moment in 1891, it tried to close the entire Ottoman Empire, first to Russian Jews (who were seeking to enter Palestine in increasing numbers),[35] and then to all foreign Jews.[36] It was similarly unsuccessful when over the next two years it urged Russia to prevent shipping companies from giving Jews passage into the Empire.[37] Presumably Russia had come to share the view that the preservation of her privileges under the Capitulations was more important than worrying about an enlarged Jewish presence in Palestine—which anyhow could be used to increase Russian influence in the country.

With individual Jewish settlers allowed to enter Palestine in addition to pilgrims, and with none of the Powers accepting the Porte's position, the entry restrictions were fatally flawed. The Ottoman Government therefore turned its attention to another aspect of Jewish settlement in Palestine, namely, the question of land sales to Jews, which were so brisk in the early 1890s that the price of land had shot up and speculation in land by Ottoman subjects as well as foreigners was not unknown.[38]

In November 1892 the Mutasarrıf of Jerusalem was ordered to stop the sale of *miri* land (state land requiring official permission for transfer) to Jews, even if they were Ottoman subjects.[39] As most of the land in Palestine (like land throughout the Arab provinces) was miri, there were loud protests from foreigners—both Jewish and Gentile—who had invested in land.[40] The embassies in

35. *OFM* A/346, no. 101693/170 A (18.8.1891), Said Paşa (SP) to Hüsni Paşa (St. Petersburg).
36. *OFM* A/346, *Note Verbale,* no. 701718/82 (19.10.1891), SP to Foreign Missions (Consple.): cf. (26.20.1891), Said Paşa to Ottoman representatives (European capitals and Washington).
37. *OFM* A/346, many despatches and telegrams between Said Paşa and Ottoman representatives in Russia from end 1891 to end 1893; finally, evasive reply in *Note Verbale,* no. 836 (29.11.1893), Russian Embassy (Consple.) to SP.
38. Cf. Ginsberg, "Emet me-ereẓ yisraᶜel" (1891), *Kol kitve,* p. 26.
39. *PRO FO* 195/1765, no. 35 (30.12.1892Z(, J. Dickson (Jerus.) to Sir F. C. Ford (Consple.).
40. E.G. *PRO FO* 195/1765, no. 35 (30.12.1892), enc. (22.12.1892); *PRO FO*

Constantinople took up their cause, protesting a "manifest breach" of the Capitulations[41]—even though the Capitulations were not strictly relevant in this case and it would have been more appropriate to put greater emphasis on the Ottoman Land Code of 1867, which did make provision for foreigners to acquire real estate in the Empire. However, as with the entry of individual Jewish settlers, the Powers were able, in 1893, to extract a concession from the Porte regarding land purchase. Foreign Jews, legally resident in Palestine, would be permitted to buy land, on condition that they could prove their legal status in the country and undertook not to let "illegal Jews" live on their land (if urban) or set up a colony on it (if rural).[42]

Ottoman policy on Jewish settlement in Palestine, and the restrictions that it entailed, were thus well established by the early 1890s and were probably not subjected to any review until Theodor Herzl published his famous pamphlet, *The Jewish State,* in February 1896. In this pamphlet, Herzl gave more concrete expression to Jewish national aspirations, arguing (as the title indicates) that the "Jewish problem" could only be solved by establishing a Jewish state, possibly in Palestine but possibly elsewhere, in which persecuted Jews could live in freedom and dignity. This pamphlet led directly to the formation of the Zionist Movement in 1897, with Herzl at its head.

It is not generally realised that Herzl brought himself and his ideas to the Porte's attention one year *before* the Zionist Movement was founded. He did so by visiting Constantinople in June 1896 and making contact not only with senior officials in person but also with the Sultan through an intermediary. Displaying impressive ignorance of Ottoman sensitivities, Herzl's ideas were not calculated to

195/1806, encs. 1 and 2 (22. and 23.3.1893) to no. 19 (29.4.1893), Dickson to Ford; and *ISA (G)* A III 14 (16.12.1892), I. Frutiger & Co. (Jerus.) to von Tischendorf.

41. *CZE (A)* (25.1.1893), *Note Verbale,* Italian Embassy (Consple.) to SP; and (7.2.1893), *Note Verbale,* Austro-Hungarian Embassy (Consple.) to SP.

42. *ISA (G)* A XXII 18 (3.4.1893), *Note Verbale,* SP to German Embassy (Consple.); cf. *PRO* FO 195/1789, enc. (3.4.1893) to no. 278 (23.7.1893): copy of *Note* from SP to Italian Embassy (Consple.).

43. T. Herzl, *Der Judenstaat* (Vienna, 1896); references are to S. d'Avigdor's translation: *The Jewish State.*

appeal to the Porte. At a time when the Government's grip on its remaining territories in the Balkans was far from secure, and when the Sultan was under attack from Young Turks abroad for the "dismemberment" of the Empire, Herzl asked that Palestine should be granted to the Jews with official blessing in the form of what he called a "charter." And at a time when the Government had had its fill of heavy European interference in its internal affairs, including control of the Public Debt from 1881 onwards, Herzl hoped that his "Jewish State" would enjoy Great Power protection. In exchange for Palestine, he somewhat nebulously offered "to regulate the whole finances of Turkey" for "his Majesty the Sultan."[44]

These ideas were not well received in Constantinople. The Grand Vezir was averse to Herzl's scheme, and although some leading figures—ᶜIzzat Paşa al-ᶜAbd (the Sultan's Second Secretary and an Arab from Damascus), Mehmed Nuri Bey (Chief Secretary at the Foreign Ministry), and Ibrahim Cavid Bey (the Grand Vezir's son and a member of the Council of State)—were perhaps more favourably inclined, each was not without his reservations.[45]

Herzl's main aim, however, was to gain the Sultan's approval for his plan, judging correctly that the Ottoman monarch held final sway in the Empire's affairs. The Sultan was that enigmatic personality, Abdülhamid II, a man not lacking in shrewdness, whatever else his contemporaries and historians may have said about him (which, on the whole, has not been kind). He probably knew about the increased flow of Jewish immigrants into Palestine from very early on. He is said to have received a delegation of Lovers of Zion from Rumania in 1882.[46] There is harder evidence to show that in 1891 he was unhappy about granting Ottoman nationality to Jewish immigrants as he feared that "it may in the future result in the creation of a Jewish government in Jerusalem"; he therefore ordered Jewish immigrants to be shipped to America.[47] Similarly,

44. Herzl, *Jewish State,* pp. 29–30.
45. Herzl, *Diaries,* i; for Grand Vezir's opposition, pp. 375–76 (19.6.1896), p. 383 (21.6.1896), pp. 400–401 (29.6.1896); ᶜIzzat Paşa al-ᶜAbd was "bluntly negative" at first, p. 371 (18.6.1896), but later warmed to the idea in a modified form, p. 383 (20.6.1896) and pp. 394–95 (26.6.1896), cf. p. 400 (29.6.1896); Ibrahim Cavid's interest and reservations, pp. 371–72 (18.6.1896), and then "categorically . . . in favour," p. 401 (29.6.1896).
46. Klausner, pp. 110–11.
47. Farhi, "Documents on the Attitude of the Ottoman Government," p. 2, quoting C. R. Atilham, *31 Mart Faciası* (Istanbul, 1956), pp. 43–44. As far as is known, this order was not acted upon.

he was disturbed in 1892 by an abortive attempt to settle Jews on the east coast of the Gulf of Aqaba.[48]

On Herzl's proposals he was emphatic. One day after Herzl's arrival in Constantinople in June 1896, he told Herzl's aide, Philipp Michael de Newlinski,

> If Mr. Herzl is as much your friend as you are mine, then advise him not to take another step in this matter. I cannot sell even a foot of land, for it does not belong to me, but to my people. My people have won this empire by fighting for it with their blood and have fertilized it with their blood. We will again cover it with our blood before we allow it to be wrested away from us. The men of two of my regiments from Syria and Palestine let themselves be killed one by one at Plevna. Not one of them yielded; they all gave their lives on that battlefield. The Turkish Empire belongs not to me, but to the Turkish people. I cannot give away any part of it. Let the Jews save their billions. When my Empire is partitioned, they may get Palestine for nothing. But only our corpse will be divided. I will not agree to vivisection.[49]

Abdülhamid accordingly refused to meet Herzl on this occasion. Nonetheless, there were elements in Herzl's ideas which attracted his interest. Hence, on the day of Herzl's departure from Constantinople, Abdülhamid sent him an Ottoman decoration and a message requesting that he should work to improve the Empire's image in the European press and obtain a loan of T£2,000,000.[50] Abdülhamid was willing to explore Herzl's worth—or so it seemed.

Over the next year support for Herzl's ideas grew, particularly in Jewish student circles and among Lovers of Zion in Eastern Europe and in Palestine itself. This did not pass unnoticed by the Ottoman authorities.[51] Nor did a visit to Palestine by a group of distinguished British Jews in April 1897,[52] or news of a rally in New York in May in favour of the forthcoming Zionist Congress. In June the Mutasarrıf of Jerusalem reported a conversation he had on these subjects with the local German Consul, who did not entirely dismiss the

48. *PRO* FO 78/4450, no. 34 (9.2.1892), Sir E. Baring (Cairo) to Lord Salisbury (FO).
49. Herzl, *Diaries,* i, 378 (19.6.1896).
50. *Ibid.,* i, 401 (29.6.1896).
51. *PRO (G)* K 692/Türkei 195, no. 49 (19.6.1897), von Tischendorf to Reichskanzler (Berlin).
52. The group did not travel to Palestine as supporters of Herzl—see Herzl, *Diaries,* ii, 513 (29.1.1897).

possibility of a Jewish state being established[53]—and the restrictions against the Jews in Palestine were promptly renewed, a month before the first Zionist Congress at Basel in August.[54] Even though Zionist aims, as elaborated by that Congress, spoke equivocally of a Jewish "home" in Palestine "secured by public law" (rather than a Jewish "state," protected by the Great Powers), the Ottoman Government was alarmed. So that there should be no mistaking its attitude, the Grand Vezir accordingly asked Isaac Fernandez, as a prominent Jew in Constantinople, to make it known that the Porte had not given Herzl any encouragement whatsoever in his ideas.[55] Clearly, then, the Government and Abdülhamid took the Zionist Movement seriously from its inception. Over the next years Ottoman representatives not only in Eastern Europe but also at Washington, London, Vienna and Berlin reported on the Movement's progress,[56] and even used special funds to obtain their information.[57] Moreover, according to the President of the Commission of Immigrants at the Porte, Abdülhamid had made the "Jewish question" a personal one by 1900, and would not entertain any suggestion from ministers or officials which might advance Jewish interests, especially in Palestine.[58]

Despite rebuffs, Herzl still set a meeting with the Sultan as a major objective. After considerable efforts (and expense), he obtained his audience in May 1901, and it lasted over two hours. In excitement, Herzl recorded in his diary that he "got everything in."[59] True, Abdülhamid had made encouraging noises, but a colder look at the diary suggests that it was Herzl who had, in fact, been taken in. Only in subsequent months, after all the letters and memoranda detailing his proposals for the consolidation of the Ottoman Public Debt were ignored, did Herzl sense that something was amiss. And although he was summoned to Constantinople twice

53. *PRO (G)* K 692/Türkei 195, no. 49 (19.6.1897).
54. *JCA* 279/No. 26 (5.8.1897), J. Niégro (Miqve Yisraʿel) to Pres., JCA (Paris).
55. *AIU* I G I (29.10.1897), Fernandez to AIU (Paris).
56. E.G. *OFM* 332/17, no. 9550/63 (29.4.1898), Ali Ferruh Paşa (Washington) to Tevfık Paşa (Consple.); no. 23598/216 (8.6.1898), Antopulos (London) to Tevfık Paşa; nos. 28858/74 and 28859/96 (both 9.7.1898), Tevfık Paşa to Mahmud Nedim Paşa (Vienna) and Ahmed Tevfık Paşa (Berlin); nos. 23600/182 (21.7.1898) and 23612/189 (28.7.1898), both Mahmud Nedim Paşa to Tevfık Paşa.
57. E.G. *OFM* 332/17 telegram no. 58 (21.4.1898), Ali Ferruh Paşa to Tevfık Paşa.
58. *JCA* 280/[unnumbered] (13.2.1900), Niégo (Smyrna) to Pres., JCA.
59. Herzl, *Diaries,* iii, 1110 ff. (19.5.1901).

in 1902 to communicate with the Sultan through officials,[60] Herzl only recognized how Abdülhamid had used him to his own advantage when a French project for the consolidation of the Public Debt was approved in the summer of 1902.[61]

At another level also, Herzl's audience with Abdülhamid in May 1901 was ill-starred. The restrictions on Jewish entry and land purchases in Palestine had been consolidated in the winter of 1900 and had gone into effect in new form in January 1901—four months before Abdülhamid received Herzl.

Throughout the 1890s, administrative difficulties had arisen in Palestine over the restrictions. They arose partly because the Porte was under pressure from the Powers, which refused to cooperate, and partly because of bureaucratic confusion within the Porte itself, which led to a multiplication of often conflicting orders from the various departments of state involved—the Grand Vezirate, the Ministries of Foreign and Internal Affairs, and the Cadastre (the department of dealing with land questions). The land purchase restrictions of 1892-93 soon proved unsatisfactory, and by 1898 the Mutasarrıf of Jerusalem was pressing for more precise instructions.[62] Related questions were raised over what buildings could be constructed on Jewish land and colonies to accommodate the needs of a growing population and agriculture.[63] But by far the biggest difficulties resulted from the entry restrictions. In 1898, shortly before the second Zionist Congress at Basel, the Mutasarrıf of Jerusalem was ordered to revert to the unambiguous instructions of 1884: only Jewish *pilgrims* could visit Palestine—for up to thirty days. As the Porte had ruled a decade earlier that individual Jewish settlers could enter Palestine, the Administrative Council in Jerusalem asked the Grand Vezir what was to be done with foreign Jews now legally resident in Palestine and, for that matter, with the considerable body of Jews illegally resident there.[64]

60. *Ibid.*, iii, 1215-33 (15-18.2.1902); and *ibid.*, iv, 1313-42 (25.7-2.8.1902). Galanté, "Abdul Hamid II" produces some evidence to show that Abdülhamid received Herzl a second time in 1902, but this meeting is otherwise unknown.
61. Herzl, *Diaries,* iii, 1256 (14.3.1902); iv, 1319 (27.7.1902); iv, 1331 (13.7. 1902); and iv, 1341 (2.8.1902).
62. *JCA* 263/enc. 2 to no. 9 (14.7.1899), Mutas. (Jerus.) to Grand Vezir (SP).
63. *JCA* 263/enc. to no. 26 (14.11.1899): Resolution of Admin. Council (Jerus.), sent on 16.11.1899 to Min. of the Interior, seeking guidance and referring to two similar inquiries dated 15.8.1898 and 17.12.1898.
64. *ISA (T)* no. 86 (9.7.1898), Admin. Council (Jerus.) to Grand Vezir and Min. of the Interior (Consple.), referring to order of 17.5.1898 from latter to Mutas. (Jerus.)

The Porte was slow to face up to the recurrent enquiries of this nature which it received from the authorities in Palestine. But it could not ignore other aspects of the problem making themselves felt in Constantinople itself. For example, in 1898 various embassies made representations to the Foreign Ministry in view of the attempt to revert to the 1884 instructions and of obstacles put in the way of their nationals reaching Palestine.[65] Ottoman representatives abroad reported a continued demand by Jews for visas for Palestine. Jewish emigrants from Eastern Europe were to be seen in Constantinople. Bad harvests and anti-Semitic outbreaks in Rumania in 1899, together with rumours that the Ottoman Government was making land available to Jews in Anatolia,[66] led to more pressure on the Porte. It reacted in various ways during this period. In October 1899, the local authorities in Palestine were ordered to take a record of the details in the visas of Jewish pilgrims on entry.[67] In May 1900 the Mutasarrıf of Jerusalem was reminded that only Muslim immigrants were allowed to settle in the province.[68] And in June 1900 the Porte tried to stop Jews from disembarking at Constantinople, requesting the Powers to invite their respective shipping companies not to take aboard Jews intending to settle in the Empire.[69] But the Powers rejected this appeal in the same way as they had disposed of a similar request ten years earlier,[70] and the Porte's problems remained.

Meanwhile, the authorities in Palestine continued to write about their administrative difficulties, and thus, pressed on all sides, the Porte sent a commission of enquiry, made up of three senior officials, to Palestine in June 1900.[71] Officially the commission came to investigate questions concerning land purchases and building at

65. E.G. *PRO* FO 78/5479, no. 542 (13.10.1898), Sir N. O'Conor (Consple.) to Salisbury; and State Dept., *Papers,* 1898, p. 1093, no. 25 (22.11.1898), Straus to J. Hay (Washington).

55. *JCA* 280/[unnumbered letter], (13.2.1900), Niégo to Pres., JCA.

67. *Ikdam,* no. 1898 (16.10.1899).

68. *AIU* IV E 11 (3.7.1900), A. Antébi (Jerus.) to Pres., AIU (Paris), enclosing copy of *"ordre viziriel"* (18.5.1900) to Mutas. (Jerus.).

69. *PRO* FO 78/5479, enc. to no. 230: *Note Verbale* (27.6.1900), SP to British Embassy (Consple.).

70. Powers' *Notes* of rejection in *OFM* A/346.

71. *PRO* FO 195/2075, enc. to no. 51 (1.7.1900), J. H. Monahan (Haifa) to Sir R. Drummond-Hay (Beirut).

the Jewish colony of Zichron Yaʿaqov, but Aaron Aaronsohn, the agronomist, was perturbed at the commissioners' tendency to interest themselves in wider aspects of Jewish settlement in Palestine.[72] That autumn the Council of Ministers consolidated the restrictions with a view to solving all the problems of recent years.[73]

As from 28 January 1901,[74] Ottoman and foreign Jews "long resident" in Palestine and those "whose residence is not prohibited" were to enjoy the same rights as other Ottoman subjects. They could buy miri land and build on it under the provisions of the Land Code. Thus, by this simple step, the status of illegal *settlers* long resident in Palestine had been regularized. They were to be treated as Ottoman subjects and, like all Ottomans, might buy land and build on it. Similarly, the land purchase disabilities previously suffered by Ottoman Jews on account of the recent immigrants had been removed. At the same time, property owners were still forbidden to assist new Jewish arrivals to remain in Palestine.

There were changes in the regulations concerning Jewish *pilgrims* as well. Henceforth, they were no longer required to pay a cash deposit as a guarantee that they would depart after one month. Instead, all Jews, including Ottoman subjects, were to surrender their papers on entry and, in exchange, were to receive a residence permit allowing them to stay in Palestine for three months. This permit, costing one piastre, was to differ in form from other documents issued to visitors entering Palestine and, because of its colour, it soon became known as the Red Slip. It was to be handed back by the pilgrims on departure so that a check could be kept on Jews visiting Palestine. Detailed statistics were to be compiled every month to enable the authorities to expel pilgrims whose permits had expired. Officials who failed to enforce these orders would be severely punished.

Consequently, Herzl's audience with Abdülhamid did not achieve anything. On the contrary, an officer from the secret police was

72. Letter (2.7.1900) A. Aaronsohn (Zikhron Yaʿaqov) to Dr. H. Joffe, in Samsonow, pp. 261-63.
73. *JCA* 264/enc. to no. 76 [n.d.]; Min. of the Interior to Provincial Governors—*ISA (T)* no. 30 gives date as 29.11.1900.
74. *ISA (G)* A XXII 18; circular (9.1.1901), Mutas. (Jerus.) to Consuls (Jerus.); cf. *PRO* FO 78/5479, enc. to no. 34: *Note Verbale* (21.11.1900) SP to Missions (Consple.), giving notice of the new entry regulations.

sent to Palestine after it to set up a branch of the service there,[75] and Jewish newspapers in Salonika were prohibited from publishing articles about Zionism, even though the articles were critical of the Movement.[76] In spite of this, Herzl refused to give up hope that Abdülhamid could be won over, and, until he died in 1904, Herzl kept on elaborating—to no avail—new financial schemes which, he argued, held out to the Ottoman Empire its last opportunity of redemption before he concluded alternative schemes with Great Britain for Jewish colonisation in the Sinai Peninsula and East Africa.

In 1905, a year after Herzl's death, the seventh Zionist Congress debated the issue of whether or not Zionist attentions should be exclusively directed at Palestine. After heated discussion, the Congress came out in favour of Palestine, to the renewed alarm of the Porte.[77] The Movement's new President, David Wolffsohn, was less precipitate than his predecessor and did not come to Constantinople to negotiate with officials until 1907.[78] But his efforts were no more successful than Herzl's, and Ottoman policy, together with the restrictions flowing from it, remained without prospect of change until the Young Turk Revolution of 1908.

Under Abdülhamid (1876–1908), things could hardly have been otherwise. The basic reasons underlying Ottoman opposition to Jewish settlement in Palestine had been greatly reinforced by developments both within the Empire and beyond since the early 1880s. Ottoman territories in the Balkans had become a prime focus of European diplomacy, and Balkan nationalism had risen to more dangerous proportions. Crete, after a series of revolts, had gained its independence in 1898. The Armenians had caused serious disturbances, which were cruelly put down. There had been upheavals in the Hauran (to the north-east of Palestine) and in the Yemen. Moreover, for the European Powers this was an era of new alliances and alignments which, in sum, put less and less of a premium on the continued existence of the Ottoman Empire.

75. *AIU* IV E 12 (17.6.1901), Antébi to Pres., AIU.
76. *AIU* I G I (2.7.1901), A. Eskénazi (Consple.) to same.
77. *JCA* 267/no. 129 (25.8.1905) Antébi to Pres., JCA; and *CZA* Z2Z598 (4.9. 1905), D. Levontin (Jaffa) to D. Wolffsohn (Cologne).
78. *CZA* W 35/4 (Wolffsohn's incomplete diary of his visit to Constantinople, for 25.10–3.11.1907); and *CZA* W 35/5 (notes by Wolfssohn and his companion, Dr. N. Katzenelsohn).

Russia's interest in influence and, if possible, presence south of the Bosphorus was as pronounced as ever, and Austro-Hungary still held Bosnia and Herzegovina in her grasp under the terms of the Treaty of Berlin (1878). It was also an era of great imperialistic expansion on the part of Europe, which did not leave the Ottoman Empire's one-time provinces in North Africa untouched. Egypt, by then only tenuously attached to the Empire, became a British protectorate in 1882. Tunis, also nominally tributary to the Empire, became a French protectorate in 1883. The Anglo-French incident at Fashoda in 1898-99, the Franco-German crisis over Morocco in 1905, and Anglo-Russian rivalry in Persia, culminating in the 1907 Convention between those Powers, were probably disquieting to the Porte, even though all these events took place outside the Empire. In this disturbing political climate, both at home and internationally, Abdülhamid was in no position to relinquish any part of his Empire, autocrat as he was. That the Zionists were careful to request a limited form of autonomy in Palestine and at all times asserted Jewish loyalty to the Sultan was of little consequence.

Abdülhamid had still other reasons to frown on the Zionists' proposals for Palestine. He knew full well that he reigned over a discontented Empire, and he was nervous. *Inter alia,* he was concerned about the loyalty of his Arab subjects and consciously pursued policies which he hoped would enhance his popularity among them. He also posed as a champion of Pan-Islamism in an effort to maintain the support of his own Muslim subjects and to rally to his side Muslims beyond the Empire's borders. He therefore claimed to be Caliph (spiritual ruler of the Muslims) as well as Sultan (temporal ruler of the Empire). With an eye to his Arab subjects and as the would-be Caliph of all Muslims, Abdülhamid could scarcely deliver Jerusalem, the third city of Islam, to the Jews.

Finally, Herzl's "golden egg"—his plans to consolidate the Ottoman Public Debt—lacked substance, attractiveness, and practicality. First, Herzl and the Zionists simply did not command the immense funds necessary for the task. Second, although the Empire had been virtually bankrupt when Abdülhamid came to power, its financial situation had improved over the years under the supervision of the European Powers. Their control was exercised through the "Council for the Public Debt," and it is inconceivable that they would have surrendered the administration of the Debt (and the leverage it offered to interfere in the Empire's internal affairs), let alone tolerate its consolidation by a Jewish group to be recompensed with a foothold in a part of the Empire which was still, at the turn of the century, of undeniable interest to the Powers themselves.

Herein lies a paradox. The Ottoman Government was opposed to modern Jewish settlement in Palestine from the outset. It had solid reasons for its opposition, and these reasons grew stronger with the passage of time. It knew of Herzl's ideas well before the Zionist Movement was founded. Abdülhamid, too, was personally involved and allergic to them. Ottoman policy was thus clear and constant. It was quickly backed up with restrictions on Jewish entry into Palestine and land purchase there. Yet, for all that, it failed.

But the paradox was more apparent than real. Important defects in the Government's policy have been mentioned. Moreover, there were discrepancies between the way the policy, and the restrictions accompanying it, were formulated in Constantinople and the way they were administered in Palestine.

In the period before the Zionist Movement was founded, the Mutasarrıflık of Jerusalem—then the main focus of Jewish settlement in Palestine—was governed successively by three men. The first of the three, Mehmed Şerif Rauf Paşa (1877–89), was by far the most competent and zealous.[79] He tried earnestly to enforce the entry restrictions against Jews,[80] and he made difficulties for foreign Jews already residing in the Mutasarrıflık who wished to become Ottoman subjects.[81] He also tried to prevent land sales to Jews and building operations on their land, even though the land purchase restrictions were only promulgated some years after he left Jerusalem.[82]

But, for all his efforts, Jewish settlers managed to enter the Mutasarrıflık and establish themselves. Even when the entry restrictions were at their most severe and when Rauf Paşa prodded the port authorities to enforce them strictly, Jews of all nationalities

79. Cf. Whitman, pp. 95–98; Chissin, p. 84 (14.5.1886); and Cohn-Reiss, p. 151.
80. E.G. *Ḥavaẓẓelet,* xii, 35 (7.7.1882); xiii, 1 (27.9.1882); xiii, 28 (3.8.1883); xiv, 23 (2.5.1884); xiv, 40 (12.9.1884); xv, 44 (20.8.1885); etc.
81. Druyanow, *Ketavim,* iii, 690 (31.1.1885), E. M. Altschuler (Suwalki) to S. Mohilewer (Bialystok); cf. Palestine Exploration Fund, *Quarterly Statement,* 1888, p. 21.
82. Druyanow, *Ketavim,* iii, 690-1 (31.1.1885); Chissin, p. 75 (9.12.1885); and Druyanow, *Ketavim,* i, 848 (21.9.1886), E. Roqaḥ (Jaffa) to Pinsker.

could always enter as pilgrims. If the police attempted to expel them after the expiry of their allotted time, they turned to their consuls for protection. Since the Powers (except Russia during the 1880s) did not accept the entry restrictions, consular protection was readily granted and there was little the local authorities could do when the Capitulations were invoked. And if Rauf Paşa held firm, say in a determined effort to put an end to illegal building on a Jewish colony (as building on miri land always required official permission), the consul could refer the issue to his embassy at Constantinople, where pressure was frequently brought to bear on the Porte to make the Mutasarrıf relent.[83]

But usually the Jews did not need to go as far as their consuls. Bribery ("baksheesh") was part of life in the Ottoman Empire, and the Jews could bribe any official, short of Rauf Paşa himself, who ventured to block their way.[84] Everything had its price: entry and release of baggage at the ports, permits to buy land and build on it. As the officials put it, "If it's a question of your interests and the Empire's—yours come first."[85] The Jewish immigrants from Russia were familiar with these conventions and fell in with them easily. The colonists could afford to be liberal, since from 1882 onwards they were backed by Baron Edmond de Rothschild of Paris, and Ottoman officials, with their miserable salaries, could scarcely afford to refuse.

In time, the Jews found other ways of circumventing the restrictions. They could enter Palestine overland via Egypt. They could buy land in the names of Ottoman Jews long established in the country, or (for a consideration) in the names of local Arabs,[86] and even of consuls or consular-agents.[87] As for building, "temporary structures" had a way of becoming permanent, and if buildings could not be put up above ground level, "dug-outs" were an alternative.[88]

After Rauf Paşa left Jerusalem, he continued to have a distinguished career in the Ottoman provincial service, was Minister of

83. Cf. Yaʿari, pp. 227-43.
84. References to Ottoman officials taking bribes are numerous. For a few contemporary references see, e.g., Chissin, p. 77 (9.12.1885); Druyanow, *Ketavim*, i, 847, (21.9.1886); and *AIU* I C 3 (4.10.1887), Hirsch to Pres. AIU.
85. Lewin-Epstein, p. 261.
86. Yellin, pp. 171-72.
87. Yellin, pp. 31-33; and Levontin, p. 56.
88. Chissin, p. 75.

Internal Affairs for a short while after the Young Turk Revolution, and was appointed Ottoman High Commissioner in Egypt in 1909. His successors were men of lesser calibre. Reşad Paşa (1889–90) was removed from Jerusalem in response to protests from local Arabs that he was granting too many building permits to foreigners, both Jewish and Christian.[89] He was replaced by Ibrahim Hakki Paşa (1890–97), a decent but, it seems, unintelligent fellow, who among Arabs in Jerusalem earned the nickname of "Ibrahim al-Ṭays"—"Ibrahim the Fool."[90] What Rauf Paşa could not do, his successors certainly could not do. And, it need only be added, the situation in the north of the country (governed until 1888 from Damascus and therefore from Beirut) was much the same regarding Jewish entry and land purchase.

The net result was that the Jewish community of Palestine continued to grow, despite the restrictions. Reliable statistics are impossible to obtain, but the following give the broad picture. In 1882, the total Jewish population of Palestine was about twenty four thousand. By 1890, it had almost doubled to some forty seven thousand.[91] Five agricultural colonies were successfully established in the south of the country in the 1880s, and four in the north. In the early and mid-1890s four more were set up in the south, and five in the north. Thus, by the time the Zionist Movement was founded in 1897, there were already about fifty thousand Jews in Palestine and eighteen new settlements.

Shortly after the first Zionist Congress, Abdülhamid sent a member of his own Palace staff to be Mutasarrıf of Jerusalem. He maintained this practice until the Young Turk Revolution in 1908, presumably because he wanted to tighten his personal control on developments in the province. But the move appears to have been counter-productive. His Palace staff were often less experienced administrators than members of the regular provincial service, and some of them, by all accounts, were more venal.[92] Moreover, the consolidated regulations, which went into force in

89. *ISA (G)* A III 14 (24.5.1890), Murad (Jaffa) to von Tischendorf; cf. *ha-Meliẓ,* xxx, 27 (13.2.1890).
90. Literally "Ibrahim the Goat"—see Cohn-Reiss, p. 177.
91. *Ha-Enẓiqlopedya ha-ʿivrit,* vol. vi, col. 674.
92. *JCA* 263/no. 17 (23.10.1899), Antébi to Pres., JCA; *JCA* 265/no. 119 (7.7.1901), same to same; *JCA* 265/no. 10 (31.3.1902), same to same; *PRO* FO 195/2225, no. 54 (27.12.1906), J. G. Freeman (Jerus.) to G. Barclay (Consple.); and *L'Indépendence Arabe,* i, 2 (1907), pp. 27–28.

1901, did not achieve their purpose. Jews could still enter Palestine as pilgrims. Certain classes of formerly illegal Jewish settlers obtained the right to buy land. And besides, these regulations had been unceremoniously rejected by all the Powers, including Russia, shortly after they were issued.[93]

This is not to say that the restrictions and the efforts of the authorities in Palestine were totally ineffectual. Whilst they did not succeed in preventing Jews from entering the Mutasarrıflık, they curtailed land purchases by Jews and also inhibited official Zionist activities. Since both these aspects—land purchases and Zionist activities in Palestine—are central to later events, they warrant detailed treatment at this stage.

In 1897, the year of the first Zionist Congress, a commission was set up in Jerusalem to scrutinise land sales to Jews. It was headed by the Mufti of Jerusalem, Muḥammad Ṭahir al-Husayni (father of Ḥajj Amin al-Ḥusayni, the Mufti of Jerusalem during the Mandate). Muḥammad Ṭahir, it appears, had already exhibited some opposition to Jewish settlement in Palestine during the 1880s and early 1890s.[94] Under his chairmanship, the commission effectively halted land sales to Jews in the Mutasarrıflık for the next few years.[95]

Thus, when the Jewish Colonization Association (JCA—an organisation founded by Baron Maurice de Hirsch in 1891 and unconnected with the Zionist Movement) began to interest itself in Palestine in 1896, it very quickly discovered that the possibilities of buying land were wider in the north of the country. As David Haym, JCA's first full-time official in Palestine, explained in 1899, the authorities in the Sancak of Acre were more flexible than those in the Mutasarrıflık of Jerusalem and were prepared to present their

93. *CZA (A), Note Verbale* no. 784/61 (10.12.1900), Italian Embassy (Consple.) to SP; and *ISA (G)* A XXII 18, *Note Verbale* (16.1.1901) German Embassy (Consple.) to SP; cf. State Dept., *Papers,* 1901, pp. 517-18, no. 354 (28.2.1901), and *Documents Diplomatiques Français,* 2nḍ series, i, 187, no. 146 (19.3.1901), Hay and T. Delcassé (Paris), instructing their respective embassies at Constantinople not to comply with the latest directives.

94. E. Yellin, *Le-ẓeʿeẓaʿai* (Jerusalem, 1938), p. 77; and *ISA (G)* A XXII 18 [n.d. (*ca.* March, 1893)] I. Frutiger & Co. to von Tischendorf.

95. *ISA (G)* A XXII 18 [n.d. (1897)], unsigned minute concerning Mufti's prevention of land sales to Jews; *ISA (T)* no. 100 (28.12.1905), Mutas. (Jerus.) to Grand Vezir and Min. of Internal Affairs (SP); *AIU* VIII E 21 (8.11.1906), Antébi to Pres., AIU; and *JCA* 261/enc. to no. 338 (30.8.1904), Antébi to JCA (Beirut).

superior, the Vali of Beirut, with *faits accomplis.*[96] Accordingly, JCA's attentions were turned northwards, and in 1900 an office was opened in Beirut.

However, land purchase in the north of Palestine was still by no means simple. Although Arab landowners were willing to sell land to JCA, they were mindful of the Ottoman authorities. As Haym observed: "Everyone tells you the same thing. 'Here are my title-deeds; you do the necessary; make the arrangements yourselves with the authorities for their transfer to the name of whom you wish and, when the time comes, I shall declare that I have sold you my land.' "[97]

The breakthrough, from JCA's point of view, came in 1901 when the Council of Ministers ruled that JCA's President, Narcisse Leven, could, as a foreigner, buy land in the Vilâyet of Beirut under the Ottoman Land Code of 1867, provided that he undertook not to install foreign Jews on it.[98] The very fact that this concession could be granted shortly after the 1901 regulations went into force points to another weakness in the Government's handling of its own policy. Under this concession, JCA acquired 31,500 dunams of land near Tiberias in the early part of 1901, mainly from the Sursuq family of Beirut (a dunam equals about one quarter of an acre).[99] These large purchases, together with a rumour that the new regulations entitled Jews to enter Palestine freely,[100] alarmed Arab peasants in the Tiberias region. Fellahin from several villages (including Lubiyya, ᶜAbbadiyya, Dalaᶜika, and ᶜArab al-Subayh) molested JCA's surveyor on a number of occasions when he came to measure lands for sale.[101] When villagers at Kafar Kama heard that JCA was negotiating for land at Umm Jubayl which they had rented for fifteen years, they tried, unsuccessfuly, to obtain a first option on the property through the court at Tiberias.[102] The peasants were supported by the Kaymakam of Tiberias, Amir Amin Arslan Bey,

96. *JCA* 255/[no number] (22.1.1899) and no. 79 (16.2.1899), both D. Haym (Miqve Yisraᶜel) to Admin. Council, JCA (Paris).
97. *JCA* 255/no. 93 (11.4.1899), Haym and Niégo (Miqve Yisraᶜel) to Admin. Council, JCA.
98. *PRO* FO 195/2097, enc. to no. 33 (26.4.1901), Drummond-Hay to O'Conor.
99. *CZA* Z2/635, enc. to letter of 28.5.1911.
100. *PRO* FO 195/2097, no. 19 (7.3.1901), Monahan to Drummond-Hay.
101. *JCA* 258/no. 57 (3.7.1901), S. I. Pariente (Beirut) to Pres., JCA; and *JCA* 259/no. 85 (30.8.1901), C. Dreyfuss (Beirut) to same.
102. *JCA* 262/no. 56 (9.6.1901), S. Sonnenfeld and E. Meyerson (Paris) to Pariente.

who later served as a deputy in the Ottoman Parliament for a period after the Young Turk Revolution and, although a Druze, supported the Arab nationalist cause.[103] In view of the prevailing disquiet, the Porte abrogated the Leven concession at the end of 1901.[104] However, from 1898 to 1901, JCA managed to acquire enough land in the north of Palestine to establish six colonies from 1899 to 1904.

After the Leven concession was cancelled, the Valis of Beirut saw to it that the land purchase regulations were enforced more diligently in the north of Palestine.[105] On the other hand, three particularly corrupt Palace secretaries governed the Mutasarrıjflık of Jerusalem from 1901 to 1906, and opportunities for land purchases by Jews there opened up once again.[106] Thus, despite the fact that the Porte regularly tried to make the land purchase regulations more stringent during that period, the older colonies in the Mutasarrıflık continued to expand and two new ones were founded in 1906 and 1907.

A bank, called the Anglo-Palestine Company (APC), was the first Zionist institution properly speaking, to be established in Palestine. The Porte had known of its connection with the Zionist Movement from the moment that its parent company, the Jewish Colonial Trust, was registered at London in 1898.[107] Hence when David Levontin (a founder of Rishon le-Ẓiyyon in 1882, who had returned to Russia to become a banker) arrived at Jaffa in 1903 to open the APC's first branch, the local authorities put a series of obstacles in his way, on orders from Constantinople.[108] Since the APC was an English company, Levontin turned for assistance to the British Consul,[109] and—as often happened in such situations—it was the British Embassy at Constantinople which was able to ease matters. In December 1903, the British Consul informed Levontin that the APC could engage in business in Palestine "so long as it confined its operations to commercial matters."[110]

103. Kalvarisky, pp. 53–54.
104. *JCA* 265/no. 134 (11.11.1901), Antébi to Pres., JCA.
105. *JCA* 261/no. 292 (2.1.1905), Pariente to Admin. Council, JCA.
106. *JCA* 266/no. 50 (17.3.1903), Antébi to Pres. JCA; *ISA (T)* no. 33 (9.7. 1907), Kay. (Jaffa) to Mutas. (Jerus.).
107. *OFM* 332/17, no. 23598/216 (8.6.1898), Antopulos to Tevfık Paşa; and no. 23612/189 (28.7.1898), Mahmud Nedim Paşa to same.
108. *PRO* FO 195/2149, no. 46 (1.9.1903), Dickson to O'Conor.
109. *PRO* FO 195/2149 (20.8.1903), APC (Jaffa) to Dickson; and *CZA* W/124/I (24.8.1903), Levontin, "Report II."
110. *CZA* W/124/I (26.12.1903), Dickson to Levontin.

Almost immediately, the Mutasarrıf of Jerusalem, Osman Kâzim Bey, applied for a loan of T£1,000 in favour of the Mutasarrıflık.[111] This was the first of several advances to the local administration, which amounted to T£56,000 by the end of 1904.[112] The borrowing was against uncollected taxes and promises from Kâzim Bey of an *irade* (imperial decree) sanctioning it.[133] Later, Kâzim also talked of a *ferman* (imperial charter) "in which the Turkish Government would recognize that [the APC] has rendered it services and contributed to the prosperity of the country."[114] Levontin's interest in such credentials was understandable but, predictably, they never materialized. The only benefits the APC gained were ones in Kâzim's gift to confer—which was not inconsiderable. By lending to the Mutasarrıflık, the APC's status was enhanced, and no difficulties were met over land purchases.[115] But in June 1904 land sales to all foreigners were prohibited unless authorised by the Porte,[116] and a month afterwards Kâzim was transferred to Aleppo. He told Levontin that the Jews had brought the latest prohibition on themselves by publicising conditions in Jerusalem in their periodicals, especially in the official Zionist journal, *Die Welt* (which Kâzim himself received).[117]

His successor was Ahmed Reşid Bey. One of his first acts was to remind the consuls in Jerusalem of the restrictions on land purchase by foreign Jews.[118] But, within a month, when pressed by the Porte for the immediate payment of revenues due, he found it expedient to take a short-term loan from the APC—and the relationship between the company and the Mutasarrıf of Jerusalem was reestablished.[119] In place of irades and fermans, Levontin now (with Reşid Bey's encouragement) explored the possibility of obtaining commercial concessions from the Government as a means of strengthening the APC's position in Palestine.[120] But

111. *CZA* W/124/I (4.1.1904), Levontin to Wolffsohn; cf. Levontin, ii, 56.
112. *CZA* W/ 124/II, Levontin, "Palestine Report" (1904).
113. *CZA* Z1/531 (7.2.1904), Levontin to T. Herzl (Vienna); and W/124/I (16.2.1904), Levontin to Wolffsohn.
114. *CZA* Z1/531 (29.5.1904), Levontin to O. Kokesch (Vienna).
115. *CZA* W/124/II, Levontin, Report for Jan.-Jun. 1904.
116. *AIU* VI E 16, enc. to letter of 13.6.1904: no. 7 (12.5.1904) Min. of Cadastre (SP) of Directors of Cadastre.
117. *CZA* W/124/II (1.7.1904), Levontin to Wolffsohn.
118. *ISA (G)* A XXII 18 (15.9.1904), Mutas. (Jerus.) to Consuls (Jerus.).
119. *CZA* W/124/II (13.10.1904), Levontin to Wolffsohn.

no such concessions were ever granted,[121] and Reşid Bey could do no more than help it by unofficially relaxing—to his personal advantage—the existing restrictions, especially regarding land purchases.[122]

As with Kâzim Bey before him, this eventually led to Reşid's removal from Jerusalem.[123] He was replaced at the end of 1906 by Ali Ekrem Bey, son of Namıl Kemal, the famous Turkish essayist, poet, and Young Ottoman ideologue. Ekrem Bey, though also a Palace secretary, was a man of different stamp from his immediate predecessors, and he set about enforcing the regulations resolutely. He also reopened a question shelved by previous Mutasarrıfs concerning the tax on land at the Miqve Yisraᶜel agricultural school which had never been paid;[124] he stopped all planting and building operations in Jewish colonies;[125] and levied higher taxes on their crops.[126]

Not satisfied with that, he also made a thorough investigation of the situation regarding the restrictions, on the basis of memoranda which he commissioned from his subordinates and of documents in the archives of the Mutasarrıflık.[127] His report, submitted in the summer of 1907 to the Sultan's Second Secretary for transmission to the Grand Vezir "if appropriate,"[128] gave a lucid, uncompromising account of the Porte's instructions since 1884.[129] He attributed the inconsistencies in them, and their ineffectiveness, to the Porte's lack of resolution in standing up to the Powers. The 1901 regulations were still in force, but had not been and never could be applied.

120. *CZA* W/124/II (6.12.1904), same to same; and cf. copies of tenders in *CZA* L5/11/II.
121. Levontin, ii, 171.
122. *CZA* W/125/I [n.d. (May, 1905)], Levontin to Wolffsohn.
123. *ISA (T)* no. 36 (11.7.1906), Reşid Bey to Grand Vezir.
124. *AIU* VII E 22 (22.5.1907), S. Loupo (Miqve Yisraᶜel) to Antébi; plus many subsequent letters in *AIU* VIII E 23 and VIII E 24.
125. *AIU* VIII E 23 (3.7.1907), Antébi to Loupo.
126. *CZA* Z2/598 (25.6.1907), Levontin to Wolffsohn; and *AIU* VIII E 23 (3.7. 1907), Antébi to Pres., AIU.
127. *ISA (T)* no. 91, i (29.6.1907), Passport Officer (Jaffa) to Ekrem Bey; no. 24 (30.6.1907), Chief of Police (Jaffa) to same; no. 91, iii (10.7.1907), Director of Registry Office (Jerus.) to same; nos. 33 (9.7.1907), 25, (25.7.1907), 56 (29.7. 1907), and 107 (29.8.1907), all Kay. (Jaffa) to same; and nos. 28 and 101 (14.7.1907), both Director of Cadastre (Jerus.) to same.
128. *ISA (T)* no. 92 (29.8.1907), Ekrem Bey to [confidant (SP)].
129. *ISA (T)* no. 21 [n.d. (mid-August, 1907)]: first part of Ekrem Bey's report.

The Jews welcomed the Red Slip given to them on arrival because it guaranteed their entry into Palestine, whereas their expulsion, without the cooperation of the consuls, was impossible. Moreover, the Minister of the Interior had himself deprived the directives of all force in 1904, when he instructed the Mutasarrıf of Jerusalem "not to permit a situation in which problems arise with foreign embassies."[130]

The report reached Constantinople at the same time as a long dispatch from the Ottoman Consul at The Hague about the eighth Zionist Congress in August 1907.[131] Before the month was out, the British Consul in Jerusalem suspected that Ekrem Bey had received "secret instructions" to hamper the APC's business in Palestine and the Zionists' activities generally.[132] At the beginning of September, an order arrived from Constantinople prohibiting transfers of miri land to Ottoman Jews.[133] As a result of this order (and Ekrem Bey's efforts beforehand) the APC managed to acquire only sixteen hundred dunams of land near Lyda in 1907,[134] in contrast with over nineteen thousand dunams acquired throughout Palestine under Kâzim and Reşid in 1904.[135] At the end of 1907 the authorities began to withhold permission for land transfer formalities to proceed even when the buyer and seller were both foreign nationals; this, according to the British Consul in Jerusalem, was a "new departure."[136]

Ekrem Bey was energetically seconded by the Kaymakam of Jaffa, Asaf Bey.[137] Like Ekrem Bey, he also prevented further building in Jewish colonies,[138] and imposed "incredibly heavy" taxes on them.[139]

This clamp-down on Jewish activities throughout the Mutasarrıflık was interrupted on 16 March 1908 by an accident in Jaffa,

130. *ISA (T)* no. 34 (8.9.1904), Min. of the Interior to Reşid Bey.
131. *OFM* 332/17, no. 1205/30 (26.8.1907), Nisak Efendi (Hague) to Tevfık Paşa.
132. *PRO* FO 195/2255, no. 35 (27.8.1907), E. C. Blech (Jerus.) to O'Conor; cf. *PRO* FO 195/2287, no. 1 (11.1.1908), same to same; and no. 18 (25.3.1908), same to Barclay.
133. *AIU* VIII E 23 (11.9.1907), Antébi to Fernandez.
134. *CZA* W/126/I (19.1.1908): Levontin, Report for December 1907.
135. *CZA* W/124/II (15.1.1905): Levontin, Annual Report for 1904.
136. *PRO* FO 195/2287, no. 1 (11.1.1908), Blech to O'Conor; cf. *CZA* W/125/III [n.d. (received 8.12.1907)], Antébi to Levontin.
137. Cf. *Revue du Monde Musulman, v, 7 (1908), 517.*
138. Cf. *ISA (T)* no. 46 (24.10.1907), Asaf Bey to Ekrem Bey.
139. *CZA* W/125/III (27.12.1907), Levontin to Wolffsohn.

in which one Muslim and thirteen Jews were wounded. It merits brief description here mainly on account of others (of a different sort) that were to occur the next spring in the Tiberias region. Arab,[140] Jewish, and official[141] accounts of what happened—and why—differ significantly, but they generally agree on the following factual outline. A day before the Jewish festival of Purim, some Jews and Arabs were involved in a brawl, in the course of which a Muslim was badly hurt. The Jews fled to a nearby Jewish hotel, Hotel Baruch, and the police were called. About an hour later, the police appeared at the hotel escorted by a *kavas* (guard) from the Russian Vice-Consulate as required under the Capitulations, since Hotel Baruch belonged to a Russian subject. The police entered, and with the kavas's permission arrested five Jews. They then proceeded with the kavas to a second Jewish hotel, Hotel Spector, where a large Purim celebration was being held, but no arrests were made there. About a quarter of an hour later, Hotel Spector was raided by the local military commandant with soldiers and some Muslim Arabs. Shots were heard and thirteen Jews were injured, some of them badly.

The British Consul in Jerusalem, Edward Blech, reported that there had been growing bitterness in Jaffa against the influx of Jews in recent years.[142] Both Blech and the German Vice-Consul in Jaffa, Rössler, believed that the Russian Jews were themselves partly at fault because they were "turbulent and aggressive, saturated with socialistic ideas."[143] David Levontin was prepared to put the blame squarely on some of the recent Jewish immigrants for walking around armed and publishing indiscreet articles in their magazine, *Ha-Poʿel ha-Ẓaʿir,* which was read in translation by Ottoman officials and Christian Arab intellectuals.[144] But Rössler agreed with Jewish observers in associating the particular tension between Arabs and Jews in Jaffa with Asaf Bey's appointment in June 1907. According to Rössler, Asaf Bey had openly voiced anti-Jewish sentiments and had influenced his subordinates

140. *Al-Ahram,* no. 1,282 (10.4.1908).
141. *PRO* FO 195/2287, encs. to no. 18: accounts by Jewish leaders and Ottoman authorities in Jaffa.
142. *PRO* FO 195/2287, no. 18 (25.3.1908), Blech to Barclay.
143. *PRO* FO 195/2287, no. 16 (19.3.1908), Blech to O'Conor.
144. *CZA* Z2/599 (7.4.1908), Levontin to Wolffsohn.

and some of the Arab population.[145] Blech, likewise, had little doubt that "when the affray and the arrest of the guilty Jews were reported to [Asaf Bey], he expressed strong resentment against the Jews; his hearers [the commandant and his men] thereupon took this as an authority to go and give [the Jews] a good lesson."[146] Asaf Bey later claimed that he had sent the soldiers to the scene because the Jews were plotting a revolution; the soldiers had merely returned the Jews' fire. Rössler discounted that claim, pointing out that there were only six thousand Jews in Jaffa in a total population of forty four thousand and that only Jews had been wounded in the affair.[147]

Asaf Bey was summoned to Constantinople about two weeks later, and Ekrem Bey in Jerusalem appears to have been very put out by the whole incident.[148] Told plainly how much he was disliked by Jews in the Mutasarrıflık, he reversed some measures he had taken, in an effort to show that he was not an anti-Semite. He denounced Asaf Bey in public, ordered land transfers to Jews to be expedited "during these critical moments,"[149] and had a Jew co-opted onto the Administrative Council in Jerusalem.[150]

Ekrem Bey's "conversion" did not last long enough to make itself felt in the Mutasarrıflık; three months later the Young Turk Revolution took place in Constantinople and Ekrem Bey was transferred to Beirut. But in terms of subsequent developments, it did not matter. By 1908, the Government's policy was irreparably breached. Relatively large numbers of Jews had entered the country, and the New Yishuv had come into existence.

On the eve of the Young Turk Revolution, the Jewish population of Palestine had risen to between seventy and eighty thousand,[151] three times its number in 1882 when the first entry restrictions were imposed. Of this total, perhaps thirty thousand belonged to

145. *PRO (G)* K 692/Türkei 195, no. 32/369 (20.3.1908), Rössler (Jaffa) to Reichskanzler.
146. *PRO* FO 195/2287, no. 18.
147. *PRO (G)* K 692/Türkei 195, no. 32/369; cf. *AIU* I C 3 (27.3.1908), E. Astruc (Jaffa) to Pres., AIU.
148. *AIU* VIII E 24 (3.4.1908), Antébi to H. Frank (Jaffa).
149. *AIU* VIII E 24 (5.4.1908), same to same.
150. *AIU* VIII E 24 (7.4.1908), same to same.
151. Cf. Bein, p. 47, quoting report (1907) by A. Ruppin, giving the upper figure of 80,000.

the New Yishuv, but at the same time it should be borne in mind that from seventy to a hundred thousand Jewish immigrants had entered Palestine during the quarter of a century under review, since probably as many as one in two of them departed again in view of the difficult local conditions (besides the efforts of the authorities). Put differently, the Jews of Palestine, having been less than 5 per cent of the total population in 1882 (about twenty four thousand out of, say, five hundred thousand) had grown to over 10 per cent in twenty five years (seventy to eighty thousand out of a population which also appears to have been on the rise and, together with the New Yishuv, was probably nearing six hundred fifty thousand in 1908).

Furthermore, by 1908 by no means all the Jews were concentrated in the four "Holy Cities" of Jerusalem, Hebron, Safed and Tiberias, as in 1882. As well as the six thousand Jews in Jaffa, there was now a new community of over two thousand at Haifa. In addition, the Jews had acquired some 400,000 dunams of land (out of a total area of about 27 million dunams)[152] and set up twenty six colonies, or more accurately, agricultural villages. By 1908 approximately ten thousand settlers lived on the colonies. In the older ones, they concentrated on growing grapes and oranges, and there were large wine-cellars at Rishon le-Ẓiyyon and Zikhron Yaᶜaqov. On the colonies established from about 1900 onwards (mainly in the north), wheat and cereals were the principal branches of farming.

Over the period, the Jewish community had become more diversified. Before 1882, there were two broad categories of Jews in Palestine. First, there were Sephardi (Oriental) Jews, who were generally Ottoman subjects and Arabic-speaking and who also enjoyed a fair degree of internal autonomy in running their own religious affairs under the Ottoman "millet" system. Then, there were Ashkenazi Jews, a somewhat larger group, who were generally European subjects and members of the deeply religious communities in the Holy Cities. After 1882, numbers of Jews still came from Europe to join the old, pious communities, but over half of the fifty thousand newcomers who remained in Palestine by 1908 were Jewish nationalists. They had come in waves—the "First Aliya" from 1882 onwards, and the "Second Aliya" from 1903 onwards (following renewed pogroms in Russia). The First Aliya was mainly

152. *Bein*, p. 47.

made up of supporters of the Lovers of Zion Movement, while many of the Second Aliya, besides being Zionists, had been affected by the Russian revolutionary movement and were imbued with a mixture of romantic, socialist, and anarchist ideologies. A few of these Jewish nationalists became Ottoman subjects, but the majority by far did not, so that they could continue to enjoy the privileges and immunities granted to Europeans under the Capitulations.

The New Yishuv received outside backing from various quarters, and after a shaky start, its colonisation efforts were bearing fruit by 1908. The Lovers of Zion in Eastern Europe sent contributions in the 1880s and 1890s, but the sums involved were small. Fortunately for the early colonies, Baron Edmond de Rothschild supported them almost from the beginning and invested large sums of money in them.

The Jewish Colonization Association began to interest itself in the colonies in Palestine in 1896, and in 1900 it took under its wing the colonies supported by Baron Rothschild as well. Although founded in 1897, the Zionist Movement did not begin operating in Palestine immediately, mainly because Herzl's "political Zionism" aimed at gaining official Ottoman approval before large-scale Jewish settlement proceeded. It therefore devoted most of its energies to spreading the Zionist idea among the Jews of the Diaspora and forming a large network of Zionist groups in their midst. The Anglo-Palestine Company, the first Zionist institution in Palestine, only opened its doors in Jaffa at the end of 1903. It was not until early in 1908 that a Zionist Office (called the Palestine Office) was set up in Jaffa, responsible for Zionist affairs in the country and reporting regularly to the Movement's Head Office in Germany.

But if the Zionist Movement was cautious, not all its protagonists in Palestine were—especially among the ranks of the Second Aliya. These young men and women (mainly from Russia) injected dynamism, intellectual vitality, and a sense of renewed purpose and direction into the weak New Yishuv which they found when they began to arrive in 1903. They formed two political parties, one marxist in orientation, and the other, also socialist, holding the "conquest of labour" (meaning physical labour on the land) as its highest ideal. They debated vigorously among themselves, arguing the need for a "conquest of soil", and for "Jewish labour" to replace the many Arabs who had found work on the new colonies. Some of them, having belonged to small Jewish self-defence units in Russia, began to replace Arab guards on the colonies. They spoke more Hebrew than their predecessors in the First Aliya and produced their own journals in that language. Those who did not join the colonies engaged in trade and commerce. Others were artisans. Still others fostered modern Jewish educational and cultural work. Benefiting doubly from the millet system on the one hand and the Capitulations on the other, they quite consciously set about laying the basis for an independent Jewish existence in Palestine.

The relations between the different segments of the Jewish community, and between that community as a whole and the Arab majority in Palestine, were complicated and diverse, reflecting the divisions within the Jewish group itself. The Sephardi Jews, being Ottomans and speaking Arabic, were well integrated into general society. They were sensitive to the mood of the Muslim and Christian Arabs, and in time many of them began to worry that their place in society might be damaged by the influx of Jewish nationalists from Europe (although some younger Sephardim were prepared to support the Zionists). The Ashkenazi Jews of the older communities in the Holy Cities also had an established place in general society (though they can scarcely have been called integrated). Many of them knew Arabic and broadly speaking, their relations with the Arabs were correct, if not close. They were affronted by the godlessness of some of their new immigrant coreligionists (particularly among the Second Aliya) and if, as seemed likely, these immigrants were liable to unsettle relations between the Arabs and *all* Jews in Palestine, this was another reason to deplore their arrival.

Most members of the New Yishuv were genuinely taken aback to find Palestine inhabited by so many Arabs (roughly 95 per cent of the population in 1882).[153] Given that they believed that they were coming to a barren, empty land, their surprise was understandable. Moreover, lacking a knowledge of Arabic, establishing their own colonies and institutions, and moving very much within their own environment, they perceived only slowly what the local population thought of them. The Arabs, on the other hand, observed the growth of the New Yishuv, noted the failure of the official restrictions on Jewish entry and land purchase—and began to react.

153. See unpublished M.A. thesis by Jacob Roʿi, *"Yaḥas ha-yishshuv el ha-aravim: 1880–1914" (Jerusalem, 1964).*

2

Early Arab Responses: 1882–1908

IN THE SUMMER of 1882, when increased numbers of Jews began passing through Beirut on their way to Palestine, the Christian editors of *al-Muqtaṭaf* (an important literary and scientific journal published in Beirut) received a letter from a reader who asked, "Were the Jews called Syrians at the time of Christ and before him?" The editors' reply was "Yes; Herodotus had already called them thus."[1] A simple question and a simple answer; things gradually grew more complicated.

Before entering into the complications, one inescapable fact must be noted at the outset. The immigrants who came to Palestine from the early 1880s onwards were not helped by being European and Jewish at one and the same time. In general, and subject to qualification, the attitudes of most Muslim and Christian Arabs were unfavourable to Europeans and Jews. Europeans were disliked for much the same reasons as the Turks disliked them. They were foreigners, often nationals of Powers which entertained designs on parts of the Ottoman Empire. Nonetheless they enjoyed extensive privileges under the Capitulations, in areas such as trade and taxation which sometimes gave them a considerable advantage over Ottoman subjects. Jews were treated with disdain because both Islam and Eastern Christianity predisposed their respective adherents in that way.

1. *Al-Muqtaṭaf*, vii, ([July], 1882), p. 47 [= 49].

Islamic attitudes to Jews stem from the manner in which Muḥammad referred to them in the Quran and the place he allocated them in Islamic society. At the start of his mission, Muḥammad, recognising that the Jews were monotheists, hoped that they would embrace the new religion he proclaimed, and certain aspects of Judaism were adopted by him (the direction of prayer, for example, was oriented towards Jerusalem). But after some months, when Jews did not convert en masse to Islam, Muḥammad's attitude to them changed (and indicative of that change, the direction of prayer was reoriented towards Mecca). References to Jews in the Quran become angry and derogatory, sometimes in the extreme. They are said to hate Muslims, to have broken their Covenant with God, and to have falsified their scriptures. God has cursed them and will mete out terrible retribution to them on the Day of Judgement. But for all that, they are *ahl al-kitab*—possessors of a divine book, and as such are permitted to live and practise their religion in the *dar al-islam,* the domain of Islam. Their status is that of *dhimmi,* that is, "protected persons." This status is not in any sense equal to that of the believing Muslims. It is distinctly inferior and carries with it obligations to pay a special poll-tax and to deport themselves as held appropriate for people tolerated by the true believers.

Christian Arabs were divided among a number of denominations of Eastern Christianity, and whilst there was often no love lost between them, they had in common a deep religious prejudice against Jews. *Inter alia,* this sentiment manifested itself in the "blood libel," the empty charge, which probably originated in Europe, that Jews use Christian blood for ritual purposes. The best known instance of the "blood libel" in the Arab provinces in the nineteenth century was at Damascus in 1840. But it was also raised on at least nine other occasions in the Vilâyet of Şam in the nineteenth century alone. The Christian Arabs' distaste for Jews was heightened by the fact that they, too, were *dhimmis* living in a Muslim empire. In theory, the interests of the two groups might be expected to have been similar, but in practice they found themselves, and their interests, at odds.[2] They competed with each other for the goodwill and favours of the dominant Muslim majority, on which they were both dependent. And, they vied with one another, since they often engaged in the same areas of economic life, as traders, merchants,

2. See Landau and Maʿoz, "Jews and non-Jews."

clerks, translators, and the like. In the latter half of the nineteenth century these tensions were very real in the Arab provinces, especially as there was a tendency for Muslims to take a somewhat kinder view of local Jews than Christians, since the latter were occasionally suspected of sympathising with European Powers, such as France and Russia, which were in the process of deepening their influence in the area—partly, if not largely, by means of contacts developed with local Christians.

Against this background, let us first look briefly at the reaction of Arab peasants to the Jews who came to settle among them, bearing in mind that these settlers were a minute element within Palestine's total population. Their exact numbers cannot be precisely known. In the mid-1880s they perhaps comprised between five hundred and a thousand souls. In 1893 the combined population of the nine colonies founded in the 1880s was a fraction over two thousand.[3] In 1898, there were over four thousand settlers in eighteen colonies;[4] and a decade later, in 1908, there were about ten thousand settlers in twenty six colonies. In the light of these figures, only a limited number of Arab villagers and a few passing Bedouin could have directly felt the presence of the Jewish settlers during the years before 1908.

In certain respects, the early settlers were unexceptionable to the fellahin. At the beginning, they seemed to have been objects of curiosity: in their clothing, language, and bearing they were quite unlike any other Jews whom the peasants may have seen. The dedication with which they worked is said to have caused surprise;[5] their "newfangled" machinery evoked interest;[6] and their strange methods (or, more often, their inexperience) could be amusing—as, for example, when colonists at Rishon le-Ẓiyyon tried to coax camels into pulling carts like horses.[7]

But there were other aspects to the newcomers which rankled with the fellahin and led to friction. They caused offence because

3. Dalman, pp. 199–200.
4. Computed from *Jewish Encyclopedia,* vol. i, col. 251.
5. Druyanow, *Ketavim,* i, 744 (n.d. [March, 1886]), J. Ossovetcky and J. Herzenstein (Rishon le-Ẓiyyon) to S. Hirsch (Miqve Yisraʿel).
6. *Miyyamin rishonim,* vol. i (1934–35), p. 9: (19.6.1885), I. Belkind (Rishon le-Ẓiyyon) to Z. Dubnow [address not given].
7. Chissin, p. 41 (17.12.1882).

they were ignorant of Arabic and of Arab ways; inadvertently they flouted local custom. For example, usage had it that everyone shared natural pasture lands, which the fellahin regarded as "God-given" (*hadha min Allah*). The Jews, unfamiliar with this custom and fearing for their first small crops, looked upon the incursions of Arab shepherds with their flocks as trespass, and used force to expel them. Alternatively, they rounded up the offending animals and either fined their owners or took a strong arm to them.[8] The colonies were a temptation to the Arabs to steal and, again, the settlers were forthright in restraining them.[9] Accidents, misunderstandings, and quarrels over matters of no great import also led to brushes between Arabs and Jews from time to time.[10]

As altercations of this kind were commonplace in Palestine (among the local population as well), they probably had little lasting effect. However, graver incidents also occurred, and these call for some discussion. The reasons for them usually went deeper than their immediate causes, and almost in the nature of things the most serious incidents arose over questions related to land. It will suffice to describe in detail the first major collision of this kind which took place in March 1886 at Petaḥ Tiqva (the oldest Jewish colony, founded in 1878, then abandoned and resettled in 1882).

The Muslim village of al-Yahudiyya, about four miles south of Petaḥ Tiqva, did not have sufficient pasture of its own and used to send its animals to graze on Petaḥ Tiqva's land.[11] The settlers offended the fellahin when they tried to put an end to this practice. The fellahin, for their part, also created a source of friction, by ploughing up a road to the north of the colony and demanding that the settlers use other routes to reach their outlying fields. Inconvenienced, the settlers felt that they could not comply, and so when one of them rode down the old road on 28 March, he was relieved of his horse by the fellahin. On the same day, the Jews

8. E.G. *Miyyamin rishonim,* vol. i (1934-35), pp. 7-8; Levontin, i, 75-78; and Haviv-Lubman, p. 15.

9. Samsonow, pp. 68-69.

10. E.g. *ha-Maggid,* xxvii, 6 (7.2.1883); Shuv, pp. 86 ff., and 101-2; *Miyyamin rishonim,* vol. i (1934-35), p. 39; (2.9.1885), Belkind to Dubnow; Haviv-Lubman, pp. 20-22; and Samsonow, p. 101.

11. The following analysis is based on Yaʿari, p. 345: entry for 29.3.1886 in A. L. Frumkin's diary; Druyanow, *Ketavim,* i, 746-54 (4.4.1886), Hirsch to L. Pinsker (Odessa); *ibid.,* i, 761-65 (12.4.1886), E. Roqaḥ (Jaffa) to Pinsker; *ha-Maggid,* xxx, 16 (29.4.1886); and *ha-Ẓevi,* ii, 35 (2.7.1886).

rounded up ten mules belonging to the fellahin which they found grazing on their land. On 29 March, it poured with rain and most of the colonists went to Jaffa for the day instead of working in the muddy fields. Fifty to sixty villagers from al-Yahudiyya, seeing the colony virtually empty, attacked it and did considerable damage. They injured five settlers (including a woman who later died from her wounds) and led away all the cattle and mules on the colony to the court in Jaffa, alleging that these had been found on their land and demanding compensation. When the Kaymakam of Jaffa heard of the incident, he dispatched soldiers to the colony with the public prosecutor and a local doctor. Under pressure from several consuls, more soldiers and a commission of inquiry were sent to Petaḥ Tiqva the following day. A day later thirty-one Arabs from al-Yahudiyya were arrested.

The immediate causes of this incident were, therefore, disputes over grazing rights and rights of access. But the deeper, underlying reasons were connected with the land which had been bought by the settlers at Petaḥ Tiqva and on which their colony stood. At one stage, much of the land had belonged to villagers from al-Yahudiyya, but they had forfeited it in vexing circumstances—partly to two Arab moneylenders in Jaffa for defaulting on their debts, and partly to the local authorities for failing to pay the taxes on it for five years. The settlers' land purchases from the moneylenders were unfortunate because they had sold the Jews more land than was actually theirs to sell. And acquisition of land sequestered by local authorities was ill-considered because, with more experience, the settlers would have known that the former owners of that kind of land were likely to try to regain it by various strategems and so would almost always prove troublesome.

Consequently, disputes over large parts of Petaḥ Tiqva's land were to be expected. They did not occur straightaway, because the settlers could not tend all their land at first and so they rented some of it back to peasants from al-Yahudiyya. But in 1884 they began taking up more of their land, and for the first time some peasants were confronted with the fact that they no longer owned the land. It was then that the first real clashes took place. Then, as the settlers continued to take up more of their land, they unwittingly aggravated the situation. Local usage, for example, had it that the man who prepared a piece of land for the summer crop automatically acquired a right to the land for the winter one. By denying the peasants this prerogative, further disputes were provoked.

Lacking a central administrator, the settlers made other mistakes, so that tempers at al-Yahudiyya were eventually aroused over the next year and a half, and the incident just described took place in spring 1886. But there was scarcely a Jewish colony which did not come into conflict at some time with its Arab neighbours, and more often than not a land dispute of one form or another lay behind the graver collisions. For example, Reuben Lehrer bought the first two thousand dunams of land at Nes Ẓiyyona (founded 1883) while still in Russia, only to lose over a quarter of it in a court case with peasants on arrival.[12] The settlers at Gedera (founded 1884) were harassed for years by peasants from nearby Qaṭra who hoped to recover land they had lost to an Arab moneylender.[13] In 1892 about a hundred fellahin from Zarnuqa raided Reḥovot (founded 1890) in circumstances reminiscent of the attack on Petaḥ Tiqva.[14] Ḥadera (founded 1891) had still not solved problems relating to the demarcation of its boundaries by 1902.[15]

Once the fellahin reconciled themselves to the fact that a Jewish colony could not be dislodged and had overcome whatever initial resentments they may have had, a *modus vivendi* was struck. Day-to-day relations between peasants and settlers were generally close and good, especially as most colonies employed from five to ten times as many Arabs as Jews,[16] and paid them relatively well for their labour.[17] The peasants also profited from the colonies in other ways. The settlers bought their produce, sometimes at "Arab markets" within the colony itself;[18] the discarded heaps of manure outside Arab villages, used by the Jews as fertiliser, became sources of income;[19] and as the colonies grew in size, local Arabs were

12. Smilanski, *New Ẓiyyona,* pp. 18–19.
13. Druyanow, *Ketavim,* i, 670–1 (15.11.1885), A. Muyal (Jaffa) to Pinsker; and *ibid.* for many subsequent documents.
14. *Ḥavaẓẓelet,* xxii, 24 (22.4.1892); Lewin-Epstein, pp. 246–51; and Smilanski, *Reḥovot,* p. 31.
15. *JCA* 259/no. 116 (8.4.1902), S. I. Pariente (Beirut) to Pres., JCA Paris.
16. Braslawski, pp. 73, 81, and 168.
17. Kalvarisky, pp. 52–53.
18. Chissin, p. 96 (18.10.1886).
19. *Ibid.,* pp. 90–91 (10.8.1886).

engaged on a permanent basis to help in guarding them.[20] Fellahin were accordingly attracted to the vicinity of the colonies. For example, by 1889 there were forty Jewish families at Rishon le-Ẓiyyon (founded 1882) and, in addition, over four hundred Arab families had come to settle in the neighbourhood. "The Arab village of Sarafand which stands to the south of [Rishon le-Ẓiyyon] used to be a complete ruin. . . . Now it has become a big, expansive village, because many families who had deserted the village have settled in it [again], since [now] there is work for all of them . . . and for their wives, sons and daughters."[21] According to this Jewish source, the same held true for several other Arab villages in the area.

In 1899, a representative of the Jewish Colonization Association inspected the colonies which Baron Edmond de Rothschild had supported in Palestine since 1883. It is abundantly clear from his report and subsequently from the annual reports of the JCA administrators in Palestine who took over responsibility for the older colonies that these had been accepted by the neighbouring peasants.[22] The colonies founded between 1899 and 1907 by JCA and the Zionist Movement were treated by the fellahin in much the same way as the earlier ones. Hence, if one dares to summarise the whole period until 1908, a rough pattern—of initial resentment, suppressed or open hostility, giving way in time to acceptance of the situation and generally good day-to-day relations—was discernible on the part of the peasants, even in the north of Palestine where initial tensions tended to be greater because of the presence of a more mixed Arab population and the relative scarcity of arable land.

In the towns, the picture was different, even though it took a few years for feeling to express itself. In the decade between 1881 and 1891, the Jewish population of Jerusalem almost doubled, from 13,920 to 25,322 souls.[23] In Jaffa the rate of increase was even higher, for in 1893 the Jewish population had reached 2,500, having been virtually non-existent in 1880.[24] Moreover, in Jaffa an

20. Druyanow, *Ketavim,* ii, 660 (5.3.1889), Y. M. Pines (Jerus.) to Pinsker.
21. Druyanow, *Ketavim,* iii, 66–7 (18.12.1889), J. Grazowski (Rishon le-Ẓiyyon) to J. Eisenstadt (Odessa).
22. *JCA* 273/[no number], (5.10.1899), E. Meyerson to Pres., JCA; many annual reports for 1900 to 1912 in *JCA* 256, 261, and 276.
23. Dalman, p. 196.
24. Trietsch, pp. 41–44.

exaggerated impression of the numbers of Jews coming to settle in Palestine must have been created. As the main point of entry into the Mutasirrıflık of Jerusalem, the town was now always full of Jews coming and going, for, as was mentioned earlier, many new arrivals departed after a short while. The Jews themselves heightened the illusion of great numbers by assembling in large crowds to greet every ship reaching Jaffa,[25] by the self-assertiveness of the immigrants on disembarkation,[26] and by the many representatives they sent ahead to buy land for them. The Jews expected the Arabs to be pleased at the demand for land. Those who owned land probably were, but others appear to have been alarmed at the Jews' willingness to buy land at apparently any price.[27] The activities of the settlers in the new colonies did not pass unnoticed by Arabs in the towns either. In 1891, the concessionnaire of the Régie des tabacs in Jaffa, Muḥammad Efendi, told Elijah Lewin-Epstein, one of the founders of Reḥovot, that the Jews were beginning to incur ill-will among the Arabs because

> we [the Lovers of Zion] have come to [Palestine] and are doing everything that occurs to us as if we did not know at all that there is a government in [Palestine], or that there are certain laws prevailing in the country which we are all obliged to respect. Thus we build our houses without permits, and plant vineyards without asking the Government if it is permitted for us to do so, and in general we do everything our heart desires without asking permission.[28]

It will be recalled that Rauf Paşa, the Mutasarrıf of Jerusalem from 1877 to 1889, conscientiously tried to enforce the Government's restrictions against the Jews. It was not until he left Jerusalem to become Vali of Beirut that there were signs of disquiet among the urban population in the Mutasarrıflık at the rapidly growing Jewish community. In 1891 news reached Jerusalem that still larger numbers of Jews were to be expected from Russia.[29] And on 24 June, the first Arab protest against modern Jewish settlement in Palestine was made in the form of a telegram from Jerusalem, asking the Grand Vezir to prohibit Russian Jews from entering

25. *Ḥavaẓẓelet,* xxi, 38 (17.7.1891).
26. *Ibid.,* xx, 45 (14.9.1890).
27. Ginsberg, "Emet me-ereẓ yisraʿel" (1891), *Kol kitve,* p. 27.
28. Lewin-Epstein, p. 255.
29. *PRO* FO 195/1727, no. 25 (16.7.1891), J. Dickson (Jerus.) to E. Fane (Consple.).

Palestine and from acquiring land there.[30] It should be noted that this protest was lodged less than a decade after modern Jewish immigration into Palestine began, and several years before the Zionist Movement was founded.

Contemporary observers were not in complete agreement over who signed the telegram. The British Consul in Jerusalem reported that it was sent by "leading Moslems",[31] and the German Vice-Consul in Jaffa (a local Arab) also noted that local Muslims were concerned at the rising number of Jews.[32] On the other hand, *ha-Or,* a Hebrew newspaper in Jerusalem, wrote that the telegram was sent by both Muslims and Christians, and observed that certain Muslim notables had refused to sign it, since they recognised "all the benefit which the Jews are bringing the country."[33] But there was no disagreement about the reason for the telegram. Local merchants and craftsmen feared the economic competition which would almost certainly follow if Jewish immigration continued.[34]

Three points of interest emerge from this first Arab protest against Jewish settlement in Palestine. It was initiated by Muslims (even if some refused to sign the telegram). Their fears were economic. And they spelt out the two basic demands which the Arabs never abandoned thereafter: a halt to Jewish immigration into Palestine, and an end to land purchase by them.

At the end of 1895, *al-Muqtaṭaf* reported that a "Dr. Mendes" had told an American newspaper that the only way to put an end to war in the world was to restore Palestine to the Jews.[35] *Al-Muqtaṭaf* did not suggest that Dr. Mendes should also consult the Arabs in Palestine about his idea. But if it had occurred to *al-Muqtaṭaf* to raise this point, the fears of the business community in the towns suggest that certain Arabs in Palestine may also have had reservations about a Jewish return to the country.

The Arabs, no less than the Turks, knew of the Zionist Movement from its inception. In Jerusalem Albert Antébi (the JCA

30. *PRO* FO 195/1727, no. 25; and *ha-Or,* vii, 34 (3.7.1891).
31. *PRO* FO 195/1727, no. 25.
32. *ISA (G)* A III 14 (10.8.1891), Murad (Jaffa) to von Tischendorf (Jerus.).
33. *Ha-Or,* vii, 34 (3.7.1891); cf. Manuel, pp. 71–72.
34. *Loc. cit.; PRO* FO 195/1727, no. 25; and *ISA (G)* A III 14 (10.8.1891).
35. *Al-Muqtaṭaf,* xix, 10 (1895), p. 795, "Dr. Mendes" may have been Henry Pereira Mendes, or his brother, Frederick de Sola Mendes, both rabbis in New York.

representative in the city and, from 1900, director of the Alliance Israélite Universelle school there) observed that the Zionist Congress's formulation of its aim—"a home in Palestine"—soon affected relations in the towns between Arabs and the Jewish immigrants.[36] The major issue was Jewish immigration into Palestine. In 1897, a local commission was set up in Jerusalem to see how the entry restrictions were being enforced and in September 1899 it submitted a report to the Administrative Council. After elaborating the difficulties of enforcement (described in Chapter One), it recommended that either the authorities invest more resources in tightening up the restrictions or, alternatively, Jews be allowed to settle in Palestine—provided that they become Ottoman subjects.[37] When this report was placed on the Administrative Council's agenda, the Mufti of Jerusalem (whose opposition to Jewish settlement was also noted in the previous chapter) proposed that the new arrivals be terrorised prior to the expulsion of all foreign Jews established in Palestine since 1891.[38] The Mutasarrıf was against this proposal, and supported the suggestion that Jews be allowed to settle, on condition that they be obliged to become Ottomans. The local notables who sat on the Administrative Council presumably accepted the commission's report as it stood, since a summary of it was sent to the Grand Vezirate in April 1900, and no more was heard of the Mufti's extreme proposal.

There were other Arabs who felt that Jewish settlement should not be encouraged. For example, certain locally born officials in Jerusalem considered that the 1901 regulations on Jewish entry and land purchase were an advance for the Jews, precisely because they regularised the status of long-resident illegal immigrants and gave them the same rights as Ottoman subjects to buy miri land. They therefore began collecting signatures to protest to the Porte.[39] Officials in the Vilâyet of Beirut also appeared reluctant to disclose the terms of the regulations,[40] perhaps because they too were dissatisfied with them.

36. *JCA* 263/no. 17 (23.10.1899), A. Antébi (Jerus.) to Pres., JCA.
37. *ISA (T)* enc. (30.9.1899) to no. 93 (28.4.1900) Mutas. (Jerus.) to Grand Vezir (SP).
38. *JCA* 263/no. 17.
39. *JCA* 264/no. 75 (17.12.1900), Antébi to Pres., JCA.
40. *PRO* FO 195/2097, no. 19 (7.3.1901), J. H. Monahan (Haifa) to Sir R. Drummond-Hay (Beirut).

As will be recalled, shortly after the regulations were issued, a concession was granted to Narcisse Leven, the President of the Jewish Colonization Association, to buy land in the Tiberias region. In 1901 Antébi tried to have this concession extended to the Mutasarrıflık of Jerusalem.[41] A "tempestuous" session of the Administrative Council, at which "the Qaḍi and the Mufti were very violent," was held in May 1901 to consider the matter.[42] After further consultations, the Council accorded Leven the right to purchase land in Jerusalem. However, protests from Jerusalem cannot have ceased because, when the Porte abrogated the Leven concession for the Tiberias region, it annulled all transfers made to his name in Jerusalem during 1901.[43] And early in 1902 Antébi noted that rancour against the Jews was spreading in the Administrative Council, the law-courts and government officials.[44] He was too familiar with local conditions to be discounted when he added explicitly that "the ill-will of the local population coincides with the creation of Zionism."[45]

These feelings were not confined to official circles (to which Arab notables were privy). In 1900, the Zionists were reported to be making the general Muslim population ill-disposed to all Jewish achievements in Palestine.[46] There also seem to have been hints of uneasiness, even among uneducated Arabs, about Zionist intentions. In 1901, illiterate Muslim peasants asked Antébi, "Is it true that the Jews want to retake this country?"[47] A year and a half later,

41. *JCA* 265/no. 113 (26.5.1901), Antébi to Pres., JCA.
42. *JCA* 265/enc. to no. 115: minutes of Administrative Council meeting (26.5.1901).
43. *JCA* 265/no. 134 (11.11.1901), Antébi to Pres., JCA.
44. *JCA* 265/no. 4 (28.2.1902), same to same.
45. *JCA* 265/no. 4. As will be seen, Antébis reports are relied on heavily throughout this book. Born in Damascus and educated in Constantinople and Paris, he came to Jerusalem in 1896, speaking fluent Arabic, Turkish and French. His strong personality, his languages, and the prestige of being both JCA representative and director of the Alliance school in Jerusalem enabled him to befriend many Arab notables and the principal Turkish officials in the city. He was particularly close to Bishara Ḥabib Efendi, the secretary to successive Mutasarrıfs of Jerusalem before 1914. Through Bishara he obtained copies of many official documents relating to Jewish affairs in Palestine. Well informed, of independent mind, and with relatively large funds at his disposal, he favoured Jewish immigration into Palestine, but had mixed feelings about the Zionist Movement, whose methods and representatives he often criticised.
46. *JCA* 263/no. 37 (8.1.1900), Antébi to Pres., JCA.
47. *JCA* 265/no. 114 (27.5.1901), same to same.

a young (and, it was noted, not very extreme) Muslim told a Jew in Jerusalem: "We shall pour out everything to the last drop of blood rather than see the Dome of the Rock fall into the hands of non-Muslims."[48] On a more sophisticated level, an excellent article, entitled "The Jewish Colonies and Settlements in Syria and Palestine," by Dr. Lamec Saad, the Chief Quarantine Officer in Jaffa, shows that by 1903 certain Christian Arabs in Palestine were well informed about Zionism.[49]

In 1905 an incident occurred in Jaffa which, although petty, was revealing. A member of the prominent Ḥusayni family asked David Levontin of the Anglo-Palestine Company to extend his credit. When Levontin refused, al-Ḥusayni became offensive. Levontin snapped back, "You are an educated man, yet you deal with us like a fellah from a village."[50] Al-Ḥusayni was so wounded that he complained, in English, to the President of the APC in London. He introduced himself as a member of the best and most respected family of Jerusalem and also as one of the few individuals who had tried to smooth down "the 'Anti-juife' [sic] feeling in this country."

> I have been working with Ïka [JCA] for three years with the most sincere and honourable intentions.
>
> But in face of my loyalty to the sons of Israïl I am very sorry to say that yesterday I was, with all my race, the Arabes, insulted by your representative M*r* Leventine, in your bank and before your employees.
>
> So as you see that M*r* Leventine thus abused, painfully, our welcome and sincerity to the Jews. Such a sad behaviour, that could not come out but of a man like M*r* Leventine, shall never [sic] be forgotten by me nor by my friends.[51]

These reactions to the Zionists, and to Jewish settlement in Palestine in general, give some notion—in a highly impressionistic way—of the changing mood among different segments of the local Arab population in the years prior to the Young Turk Revolution. Although too isolated to admit of generalisation, it seems clear that Arab anti-Zionism as such had not yet emerged. On the other

48. *AIU* I G 2 (1.3.1903), H. Calmy (Jerus.) to Pres., JCA.
49. *Dr. A. Petermanns Mitteilungen,* xlix, 11 (1903), pp. 250–54; Lamec Saad was born in al-ʿAbbadiyya (in present-day Lebanon) in 1852.
50. *CZA* W/125/I (13.3.1905), D. Levontin (Jaffa) to D. Wolffsohn (Cologne).
51. *CZA* W/125/I (10.2.1905), H. H. el-Husseini (Jaffa) to Pres., APC (London). "H. H. el-Husseini" cannot be identified.

hand, anti-Jewish feeling—specifically mentioned by al-Ḥusayni in Jaffa—was growing. Moreover, in view of the reference made by al-Ḥusayni to "all my race, the Arabes," faint traces of early Arab nationalism also appear to have been in the air. It will be necessary to return to the questions of anti-Jewishness (as distinct from anti-Zionism) and to Arab nationalism, but first the views of representatives of three important Arab groups must be discussed: those of Christian Arab intellectuals, of a leading Islamic thinker, and of a member of the political élite in Jerusalem.

Christian intellectuals were a small but important element in Arab society at the end of the nineteenth century. Because of their secular education and contacts with Europe, they were one of the main channels for the flow of Western ideas into the Arab world. Among the more influential of Christian Arabs of this type were Yaᶜqub Sarruf and Faris Nimr, the editors of *al-Muqtaṭaf,* who in 1884 had moved to Cairo where they were beyond the reach of the Ottoman censor and freer to express themselves through the columns of their highly didactic journal.

Six months after the first Zionist Congress, they were asked by a reader in Frankfurt what the Arabic press had to say about Zionism and also what *al-Muqtaṭaf* thought of it.[52] They replied that the Arabic press had simply mentioned the Zionist Congress among its other news items, without paying special attention to it. They went on to claim that the Jews who had settled to date had already taken over most of the trade and commerce in Palestine; if their numbers increased, they would monopolise business there. The editors did not think that the Jews would concentrate on agriculture, because they had never been farmers. Although there was room in Palestine for many times its present population, the mass transfer of poor Jews to the country and land purchase there would not be easy, even for wealthy men like Baron de Hirsch (through the Jewish Colonization Association). The Ottoman Empire "for its own good" was not content to let the Great Powers interfere and protect Jewish immigrants under the Capitulations; this was a great obstacle in the way of the Zionist Movement. "Therefore we believe the success of the Zionists is remote"; it would be easier to try to ameliorate the condition

52. *Al-Muqtaṭaf,* xxii, 4 (1898), pp. 310–11. Name and origin of questioner not given.

of Jews in Russia, Rumania and Bulgaria.

Apart from the intrinsic interest of this article, it was noteworthy in that it provoked a strong reaction from a leading Islamic thinker, Rashid Riḍa. Like the editors of *al-Muqtaṭaf,* Riḍa was also an Arab from the Vilâyet of Beirut, who published an important journal in Cairo. But instead of disseminating Western culture, his journal, *al-Manar,* was dedicated to propagating the religious ideas of Muḥammad ʿAbduh, one of the great Islamic teachers of the last century and Mufti of Egypt from 1899 until his death in 1905. Riḍa was his devoted disciple but, coming from what is today Lebanon, he was more involved than ʿAbduh in the politics of the Ottoman Empire. After 1908, he cooperated for a while with the Young Turks, but from 1912 onwards he was a moving spirit behind the Decentralisation Party, an Arab nationalist group based in Cairo, of which more will be said in later chapters.

A fortnight after the editors of *al-Muqtaṭaf* addressed themselves to the query on Zionism from their reader in Frankfurt, Riḍa reprinted their reply in *al-Manar* and took the opportunity to comment on it.[53] He was indignant at the national revival of the Jews, yet, at the same time, inspired by it. He also deplored the indifference and disunity of his compatriots (*rijal biladina*).

> You complacent nonentities . . . look at what peoples and nations do. . . . Are you content for it to be reported in the newspapers of every country that the penniless of the weakest of peoples [the Jews], whom all governments are expelling, have so much knowledge and understanding of civilisation and its ways that they can take possession of your country, establish colonies in it, and reduce its masters to hired labourers and its rich to poor men? Think about this question, and talk about it . . . Then, when it is clear to you that you are restricted in the rights of your homeland (*ḥuquq awṭanikum*) and in the service of your nation (*umma*) and co-religionists (*milla*), . . . examine and discuss . . . matters like this. It is more worthy of consideration . . . than slandering your brothers and accusing them of sinning.

The germs of Rashid Riḍa's Arab nationalism and, more generally, of his political ideas were already in evidence in this early rejoinder to *al-Muqtaṭaf.*[54] They were more fully developed in a

53. *Al-Manar,* i, 6 (1898), pp. 105–8.
54. For Riḍa's political ideas, see Hourani, *Arabic Thought,* pp. 227–30.

long article on Zionism, entitled "The Revival of a Nation after its Death" ("Ḥayat umma baᶜd mawtiha"), which appeared in *al-Manar* in January 1902,[55] shortly after the fifth Zionist Congress at Basel, at which Herzl reported on his audience with Abdülhamid.

Riḍa began with a plea, supported by a verse from the Quran, that Muslims should become politically aware. We fear, he wrote, that we may become as abject as the Jews, but we do not recognise the advantages we have over them—they have been dispossessed, whereas some of our land is still under the control of our leaders. But we should scrutinise our leaders' behaviour and take note of the Jews. They do not languish in the "blessing of the Torah" in order to succeed. They have preserved their language and religious unity despite their dispersion, they have supported one another, mastered modern arts and sciences and amassed capital which, Riḍa asserted, is the basis of power and strength in present times. Nothing prevents them from becoming the mightiest nation on earth except statehood (*mulk*), and they are striving towards this in "the natural way"—through great national organisations (*jamᶜiyatt milliyya*). "And nations do not succeed except through organisations."

At this point Riḍa stated his objection to the Zionist Movement. Originally it appeared that the Zionists only desired a refuge for persecuted Jews under the Sultan's protection; but now (in 1902), with a stronger movement, they sought national sovereignty in Palestine. "Israel Zangwill" had recently gone to Constantinople to negotiate the purchase of Jerusalem and was received warmly by Abdülhamid.[56] "Zangwill" had told the Zionist Congress that by the end of the twentieth century two million Jews will have returned to their ancient kingdom, which would be an example and guide to all nations. The Zionists, "Zangwill" was alleged to have said, had already collected a million dollars from poor Jews alone for the purchase of Palestine. There were as many Muslims in Egypt as Jews in the world, but—asked Riḍa, taking his readers to task—what interest did they show in their own welfare by raising a million piastres for a university in Egypt? He then printed a Zionist circular calling on Jews in Alexandria to attend a Zionist meeting.

55. *Al-Manar,* iv, 21 (1902), pp. 801–9.
56. Riḍa mistook Herzl for Zangwill.

By way of comment, he reprinted the passage from his first article on Zionism quoted above, adding that if that was his view four years ago, then *a fortioti* today. He concluded as he began, urging Muslims to keep a close watch on their leaders' behaviour and acquire technical skills and capital, so that they might become a true nation (*umma ḥaqiqiyya*) with public opinion bound by Islamic law and a process of consultation (*al-shariʿa wal-shura*). This was precisely the political doctrine which Rashid Riḍa regularly propounded through the columns of *al-Manar*.

The editors of both *al-Muqtaṭaf* and *al-Manar* were Arabs from the Vilâyet of Beirut living in Cairo. About a year later, however, a leading member of one of the outstanding Muslim families in Jerusalem was impelled by "a sacred duty of conscience" to put his feelings about Zionism on paper and address a carefully reasoned letter in French to Zadok Kahn, the Chief Rabbi of France and an acquaintance of Theodor Herzl. He was Yusuf Ḍiya Paşa al-Khalidi, who, at seventy years of age, had a long record of public service, having been an Ottoman vice-consul at the Russian Black Sea port of Poti, a deputy in the first Ottoman Parliament (1877–78), and a President of the Municipal Council in Jerusalem.[57] He had travelled in Europe and taught Arabic in Vienna for some time. He was an eloquent speaker, fluent in French and English as well as Turkish and Kurdish; he held liberal views and was known for his religious toleration.[58] He was critical of Abdülhamid's régime, and his forthright speeches in Parliament had led to expulsion from Constantinople when the second session was prorogued in 1878.[59]

His letter to Chief Rabbi Kahn was a unique, and in some ways a prophetic, document.[60] It was written by a well-meaning and responsible man of mature judgement, who was in no way bitter or disparaging. In theory, wrote Yusuf al-Khalidi, the Zionist idea was "completely natural, fine and just."

> Who can challenge the rights of the Jews on Palestine? Good Lord, historically it is really your country.

57. Al-Zirakli, ix, 310.
58. Amery, i, 69–70.
59. Devereaux, pp. 247–48.
60. *CZA* H III d. 14 (1.3.1899), Youssuf Zia Alkhalidy (Consple.) to Chief Rabbi Zadoc Kahn (Paris).

But the "brutal force" of reality had to be taken into account. Palestine was an integral part of the Ottoman Empire and was inhabited by non-Jews. What "material forces" did the Jews possess to acquire the Holy Places which were also common to "390,000,000 Christians" and "300,000,000 Muslims"? Yusuf al-Khalidi feared that, despite Jewish finance, the Holy Places could not be acquired without other, more formidable forces, "those of cannons and battleships." He doubted whether even Britain or America, the two nations "most favourably inclined towards the Jews," would be willing to fight for such a cause. In general, the Turks and Arabs were well disposed to Jews, but there were also some of them who were infected with racial hatred against the Jews, just as among the "most civilised nations." Moreover, in Palestine there were Christian "fanatics," especially among the Catholics and the Orthodox, who resented recent Jewish progress and "do not overlook any opportunity to excite the hatred of Muslims against the Jews." He predicted a popular movement against the Jews which the Ottoman Government, with "the best intentions in the world," could not quell. Even if Abdülhamid's consent were gained, it was folly on Herzl's part to think that the day would come when the Zionists would become masters of Palestine.

> It is necessary, therefore, for the peace of the Jews in Turkey that the Zionist Movement, in the geographic sense of the word, stops. . . . Good Lord, the world is vast enough, there are still uninhabited countries where one could settle millions of poor Jews who may perhaps become happy there and one day constitute a nation. That would perhaps be the best, the most rational solution to the Jewish question. But in the name of God, let Palestine be left in peace.[61]

Again, these early reactions to Zionism on the part of representatives of three élite groups among the Arabs are too isolated to admit of generalisation. But some aspects are noteworthy. The Christian editors of *al-Muqtaṭaf* asserted that Jews might monopolise trade. Rashid Tiḍa, a future Arab nationalist, had concluded

61. It is not known why Yusuf al-Khalidi chose to write to Kahn rather than directly to Herzl. However, Kahn passed his letter to Herzl, who replied to him on 19.3.1899, suggesting that the Jews could live peaceably in the Ottoman Empire, discounting the difficulties likely to arise with the Arabs, and indicating that if Abdülhamid did not accept the Zionists' offer to regulate the Empire's finances, they would in fact go elsewhere. See Herzl, *Kol kitve Herzl* (Jerusalem and Tel Aviv, 1957), iii, 309–10.

that the Zionists sought national sovereignty in Palestine (even though their programme spoke only of a "home" in Palestine). And Yusuf al-Khalidi, concerned about the future of Palestine, wished to avert unpleasantness, and even violence, between Arabs and Jews, sparked off by Christian extremists.

The case of Négib Azoury is therefore of special interest, because he had the distinction of combining both Arab nationalism and opposition to Zionism with anti-Semitism. A Maronite Christian from the Vilâyet of Şam or of Beirut,[62] he studied at l'Ecole des sciences politiques in Paris before going to Constantinople to enter the Ottoman civil service school.[63] In 1898, at the age of about twenty five, he was sent to work in the administration in Jerusalem, where, according to the French Consul, he did not distinguish himself.[64] Through marriage, he became a brother-in-law of Bishara Ḥabib Efendi, the Mutasarrıf's secretary and interpreter, to whose post he is reported to have aspired. Failing to obtain it, he tried to be appointed concessionnaire of the Régie des tabacs in Jaffa.[65] Unsuccessful in that as well, he began to intrigue against both the Mutasarrıf Kâzim Bey (1902–04), and Bishara Efendi.[66] Kâzim Bey was incensed, and Azoury, taking fright, fled to Cairo in May 1904,[67] where he attacked Kâzim Bey in a newspaper called *al-Ikhlas* for his corruption (and, apparently, for his deference to Albert Antébi).[68] From Cairo he travelled to Paris, where he founded his "Ligue de la Patrie arabe," only to be condemned to death *in absentia* on 31 July "for having left his post without permission and having proceeded to Paris where he has devoted himself to acts compromising the existence of the Empire."[69] In December 1904 and January 1905, Azoury's "Ligue" (which seems to have consisted only of himself and one other associate) issued two manifestos in French and Arabic, both headed "The Arab Countries for the Arabs." The first was addressed to "All the Citizens of the Arab Homeland Subjected to the Turks," and the second to the "Enlightened and Humanitarian Nations of Europe and North

62. *Q d'O* N.S.109, no. 14 (8.2.1905), F. Wiet (Jerus.) to T. Delcassé (Paris).
63. Jung, i, 10–11.
64. *Q d'O* N.S.109, no. 14.
65. *Ibid.*
66. *AIU* VII E 18 (16.2.1905), Antébi to Pres., AIU (Paris).
67. *AIU* VII E 18 (16.2.1905); and *Q d'O* N.S. 109, no. 14.
68. *AIU* VII E 16 (22.6.1904), Antébi to Pres., AIU; and *Q d'O* N.S. 131, no. 39 (30.6.1904), A. Boppe (Jerus.) to Delcassé.
69. *L'Indépendence Arabe,* i, 7–8 (1907), p. 97.

America."[70] A month later, Azoury published *Le Réveil de la Nation Arabe,* a book which has become a minor classic in Arab nationalist literature. In it, he called for the complete detachment of the Arab provinces from the Ottoman Empire.[71]

The largest part of *Le Réveil* dealt with the Ottoman Empire's relations with the Great Powers. However, in his first chapter, Azoury described the "political geography" of Palestine, which, he said, constituted "a complete miniature of the future Arab Empire."[72] In doing so, he discussed Jewish activities in Palestine. His statistics were not always accurate: there were, he claimed, only two hundred thousand Arabs in Palestine, plus an equal number of Jews (in 1905).[73] He was at pains to prove from the Bible that the Hebrews never conquered the whole of Palestine and so their kingdom, being vulnerable, was destroyed.[74] The Zionists, he alleged, wanted to avoid that error by occupying the "natural frontiers" of the country—Mount Hermon, the Suez Canal, and the Arabian Desert.[75] Circumstances favoured the Zionists, because they could take advantage of the local authorities' corruption and the consuls' ignorance of local conditions.[76]

Azoury was violently attacked a year later by Farid Kassab, a young Greek Orthodox Arab from Beirut, then studying dentistry in Paris.[77] Kassab's pamphlet is not so much a logical refutation of the call to Arab independence as a defence of life in the Ottoman Empire, coupled with invective against Azoury, the Catholic Church, and the Jesuits.[78] Kassab reserved special praise for the Jewish settlers in Palestine—they were peaceable and inoffensive, belonging to the same race as the Arabs; they were no more commercially minded than their neighbours, whereas they were more

70. *ISA (G)* A III 1, i: copies of these manifestos.
71. For Azoury's place in the Arab nationalist movement, see Hourani, *Arabic Thought,* pp. 277–79.
72. Azoury, p. IV.
73. *Ibid.,* p. 22.
74. *Ibid.,* pp. 3–6.
75. *Ibid.,* pp. 6–7.
76. *Ibid.,* pp. 44–47.
77. F. Kassab, *Le nouvel Empire Arabe: La Curie Romaine et le Prétendu Péril Juif Universel—Réponse à M. N. Azoury bey.* Little is known about Farid Kassab; he wrote another pamphlet three years later entitled *Palestine, Hellenisme et Clericalisme* (Constantinople, 1909), also from a staunchly Ottomanist point of view, in which the Jews are not mentioned.
78. Kassab, *Empire Arabe, Passim.*

devoted to industry and agriculture than anyone else; they did immense good in reviving their own barren land, thereby benefiting the Empire as well as themselves; moreover, they were not foreigners either "morally or politically"; they became loyal Ottoman subjects, without ambitions of national independence in Palestine.[79] Kassab challenged the existence of an "Arab nation" and Azoury's definition of it.[80] Azoury was a "Catholic bigot, a member of the Society of Jesus," believing that the Jews are deicides and therefore eternally damned.[81] Azoury was "not only anti-Jewish from the religious point of view, but also anti-Semitic."[82]

There is substance to this last indictment. As Albert Hourani has pointed out, the Ligue de la Patrie arabe "clearly echoes . . . the anti-Dreyfusard *Ligue de la Patrie française.*"[83] Moreover, in the preface to *Le Réveil,* Azoury announced that his book was intended to complement a larger work to be published shortly, *Le Péril juif universel, Révélations et études politiques*[84]—those who had dealt with the Jewish question until then had not taken its universal character sufficiently into account.[85] Azoury anticipated and dismissed possible charges of exaggeration, asserting that he had based himself on Jewish sources, though he added that he only accepted his own Church's interpretation of the Bible, which was infinitely superior to "the material and literal interpretation made by the Jews [which] renders [the Bible] dangerous and immoral and constitutes the most terrible condemnation of them."[86] Thus, beyond its significance as an Arab nationalist work, Azoury's book represents a departure from other writings by Arabs at this time: *Le Réveil de la Nation Arabe* is permeated by European anti-Semitism.

Moreover, Azoury's experience as an Ottoman official in Palestine enabled him to be the first Arab publicist to predict that Zionist and Arab nationalist aspirations were likely to come seriously into conflict. He had worked in Jerusalem at a time when two particularly corrupt Palace secretaries (Cavid Bey and Kâzim

79. *Ibid.*, pp. 38 ff.
80. *Ibid.*, pp. 28-29.
81. *Ibid.*, p. 40.
82. *Ibid.*, p. 39.
83. Hourani, *Arabic Thought,* p. 277.
84. Azoury, p. III.
85. *Ibid.*, p. VI.
86. *Ibid.*, p. VII.

Bey) had governed the Mutasarrıflık. He had witnessed the ineffectiveness of the restrictions against Jewish immigrants and land purchases, and the opening of a Zionist bank in Jaffa (the APC), which had gone on to establish branches in Jerusalem and Haifa.[87] Possibly, in trying to carry out his official duties, he had been frustrated by the Jews' reliance on their consuls and the Capitulations. Not enough is known about why Azoury chose to write his book in French or whom he was aiming it at.[88] But putting these questions aside, it is tempting to suggest that Azoury's experience in Jerusalem embittered him and led him to the conclusion that continued allegiance to the Ottoman Empire would deprive the Arabs of parts of their homeland,[89] with the result that he came to advocate total Arab independence of the Turks.

Of the potential Arab-Zionist conflict he warned:

> Two important phenomena, of the same nature but opposed, which have still not drawn anyone's attention, are emerging at this moment in Asiatic Turkey. They are the awakening of the Arab nation and the latent effort of the Jews to reconstitute on a very large scale the ancient kingdom of Israel. Both these movements are destined to fight each other continually until one of them wins. The fate of the entire world will depend on the final result of this struggle between these two people representing two contrary principles.[90]

There is reason to believe that other Arabs in Palestine, less articulate than Azoury, shared his attitudes and were also affected by that distinctive type of anti-Jewish prejudice usually thought to have been confined to Europe at the time. Azoury probably picked up his anti-Semitism as a student in Paris during the Dreyfus Affair, but the question remains how European anti-Semitism reached other Arabs during this period. Sylvia Haim and Moshe Perlmann believe that it entered the Arab world through the "anti-Dreyfusard clergy so well represented among the missionaries."[91] But this theory puts the blame too squarely on just one of the several foreign elements present in Syria and Palestine, all of them capable of conveying European prejudices to the Arabs. It is more probable that these

87. Cf. *L'Indépendence Arabe,* i, 1 (1907), p. 3.
88. Cf. Kedourie, "The Politics of Political Literature."
89. Cf. Azoury, pp. 44–47.
90. *Ibid.*, p. V.
91. Haim, "Arabic Antisemitic Literature"; and Perlmann; "Comment on Sylvia G. Haim's Article."

elements, none of which may have had much individual influence, combined to infect the Arabs, consciously or otherwise, with modern anti-Semitism.

As early as 1899, Eli Sapir, an Arabic-speaking Jew from Palestine, could write that foreign missionaries and priests were heightening Arab feeling against the Jews. Protestant missionaries, aiming at conversion, indirectly spread anti-Semitism. Sapir cites as evidence *Ben Hur,* an evangelical novel containing a passage about the death of Jesus at the hands of the Jews, which was translated into Arabic in 1897 by Dr. Cornelius van Dyke, an influential missionary and educator at the Syrian Protestant College.[92] Much more damage, Sapir said, was being done by Catholics, especially Jesuits, through their literature and in their schools. He mentions three books and also implicates *al-Bashir,* the important Jesuit periodical published in Beirut.[93]

These publications in themselves are meagre proof of what Haim and Perlmann call the activities of the "anti-Dreyfusard clergy." However, weightier evidence is to be found in writings by Père Henri Lammens, the Belgian scholar who taught at the Jesuit University of Beirut. In 1897 an article by him, entitled "Zionism and the Jewish Colonies," appeared in *Etudes,* the Jesuit journal.[94] Its tone, which is as anti-Jewish as it is anti-Zionist, was set in the opening paragraph, describing the first Zionist Congress: "As at an ordinary meeting of *'goyim,'* almost all the delegates were in evening dress and white tie; rabbinical cloaks seemed very sparse." According to Lammens, the Jews of Jerusalem were "recognisable . . . by their repulsive grubbiness and above all by that famous Semitic nose, which is not, like the Greek nose, a pure myth."[95]

Sapir says that among the Greek Orthodox Arabs a dislike for the Jews was not noticeable.[96] By 1909, however, it had become

92. Sapir; pp. 228-29.
93. *Ibid.,* p. 231. Sapir gives the titles of two of the three books he has in mind as *Ṣawt al-bariyya* and *Aṣḥab al-ukhdud;* neither of them can be readily identified. He did not name the third book.
94. *Etudes,* vol. lxxiii (1897), pp. 433-63.
95. *Ibid.,* p. 440; cf. also pp. 443, 450-1, and 452. A shortened version of this article appeared in *al-Mashriq,* vol. ii (1898), pp. 1089-94; cf. *ibid.,* pp. 406-8, another article by Lammens, "al-Yahud al-taʿih." His mixed anti-Semitism and anti-Zionism are also apparent in "Le Sionisme et la Turquie," *Etudes,* vol. lvi (1919), pp. 438-58.
96. Sapir, p. 230.

apparent—as Yusuf al-Khalidi had warned that it would. To some extent, the Russian Imperial Orthodox Palestine Society, which began to function in 1882, must be held responsible for this. The Society supported over a hundred Greek Orthodox institutions (mainly schools) in Syria and Palestine, and its attitude to the Jews was a projection of that of the Tsarist government in Russia. Thus, for example, the Society's clinics were open to all sections of the local population—save the Jews.[97]

Moreover, some members of the consular corps in Jerusalem and Jaffa were not above passing on European prejudices to the local Arabs and the Ottoman authorities. In 1905, David Haym reported that "the Austrian Consulate at Jaffa has permitted itself to transmit to the local Turkish authorities a denunciation of the Jewish population emanating from an Austrian protégé."[98] The Russian Vice-Consul was reported in 1908 to be an anti-Semite by his German colleague, who considered him partly to blame for the Purim incident in Jaffa that year.[99] Foreign banks and merchants, such as the Crédit Lyonnais and the Deutsches Palästina Bank, did not welcome Jewish incursions into their fields, and so the British Consul in Jerusalem believed that the Mutasarrıf's unease in 1903 about the Anglo-Palestine Company had "no doubt been further excited . . . by rival bankers and traders already doing business at Jaffa."[100] Nor did the thousand or so "Templers" (Protestants from Germany settled in Palestine) welcome the Jews. They too feared economic rivalry and also the possibility that they might eventually be included in the restrictions against the Jews.[101] In 1900, Antébi wrote to Paris that "Jerusalem already possesses its German anti-Semitic club."[102]

It is impossible to measure in any precise way how much these foreign elements influenced first the Christian Arabs in the towns and then other segments of the local population. But once again in retrospect, it can be sensed that their concerted influence was real and extended beyond the Christian community. In Jaffa, two Roman Catholic landowners (both of whom sold land to Jews)

97. *Otchet,* vol. i (1896), p. 39.
98. *CZA* Z1/545 (6.6.1905), D. Haym (Jaffa) to S. E. Soskin [Berlin?].
99. *PRO (G)* K 692/Türkei 195, no. 49 (19.6.1897), von Tischendorf to Reichskanzler.
102. *JCA* 263/no. 37 (8.1.1900), Antébi to Pres., JCA.

were named in connection with anti-Jewish approaches to the mutasarrıfs of Jerusalem during this period. After the seventh Zionist Congress in 1905, one of them, Anṭun Qaṣṣar, is reported to have denounced the Jewish immigrants to Reşid Bey;[103] and in 1907, both he and the other one, Iskandar Rok, are said to have helped to sway Ekrem Bey against the Jews.[104] Of much greater note was a tale about a saintly wizard and an impious Jew written in 1909 by a young Muslim in Jerusalem, Isᶜaf al-Nashashibi, who was at the beginning of a career in the Arab literary world. Al-Nashashibi prefaced his tale with an acknowledgement to the anti-Semitic writer, Edouard Drumont, and his followers—whom he described as "great Frenchmen," his "masters and teachers."[105] His real masters and teachers were surely the foreign missionaries and priests, the consuls and bankers, the German Templers and representatives of the Imperial Orthodox Palestine Society, who had injected a new and distinctive colouring into the changing climate of opinion in Palestine.

By the eve of the Young Turk Revolution, which took place in the summer of 1908, it is clear that Arab anti-Zionism had not yet emerged. On the other hand, there was unease about the expanding Jewish community in Palestine, and growing antagonism towards it.

From the outset, Arab fellahin, landowners and merchants responded to the Lovers of Zion in their different ways. The fellahin, generally speaking, found a *modus vivendi* with the early Jewish settlers, even if things were not always easy at first. Landowners were happy to sell land and receive high prices for it; only the official restrictions described in the previous chapter made it difficult for Jews to acquire more land than they actually bought. Merchants watched the Jewish influx with concern, and in 1891 some in Jerusalem expressed their fears of economic competition in a telegram to the Porte. These fears were therefore the first grounds for Arab opposition to modern Jewish immigration into Palestine.

103. *CZA* Z2/598 (4.9.1905), Levontin, to Wolffsohn.
104. *AIU* VIII E 22 (23.5.1907), Antébi to Pres., AIU; *CZA* W/125/III (18.12.1907), Levontin to Wolffsohn; and *AIU* I G 2 (17.8.1908), H. Frank (Jaffa) to Antébi.
105. *Ha-Ẓevi,* xxv, 129 (15.3.1909), reporting that this story, "The Wizard and the Jew," had appeared in *al-Aṣmaᶜi* (Jaffa).

After the Zionist Organisation was founded, there were indications of some deterioration in relations between Arabs and Jews. In 1899 the Mufti proposed that Jewish newcomers be terrorised and expelled; and two years later, officials in Beirut, as well as Jerusalem, showed that they were displeased with the 1901 regulations on Jewish entry and land purchase.

There were also signs that the unfavourable attitudes to Jews, traditionally held by Muslims and Chrtstians, were being sharpened and that European anti-Semitism was making itself felt. In 1902, rancour against Jews was said to be spreading in two areas of official life where urban notables were influential, namely, the Administrative Council and the law-courts. In 1905, a member of the Ḥusayni family wrote about the anti-Jewish feeling in the country. In the same year, Négib Azoury predicted a clash between the Arab and Jewish national movements, but in the present context his book, *Le Réveil de la Nation Arabe,* was equally remarkable for the anti-Semitism which it contained and which was reaching Arabs in Palestine through a number of channels.

At the upper level of the intellectual and political élites, the Christian editors of *al-Muqtaṭaf* were reserved about Zionism on economic grounds; Rashid Riḍa, an Islamic thinker, was opposed to the Zionist Movement for seeking Jewish national autonomy in Palestine; and Yusuf Ḍiya al-Khalidi, a prominent notable in Jerusalem, was deeply disturbed by Zionism "in the geographic sense."

Thus, to the extent that Arab attention had been drawn to the Jewish newcomers by 1908, the issue was probably still seen in terms of immigration rather than Zionism. And in the light of later expressions of opinion, one can speculate that the majority view was close to that contained in the report submitted by local notables in Jerusalem in 1899—that either the entry restrictions be made to work, or Jews be allowed to settle in Palestine, provided that they become Ottoman subjects.

The trouble with this view was that it was impracticable. On the one hand, the restrictions could not, in the final analysis, be made to work as long as the Powers did not accept them. And on the other hand, besides the major disincentives of giving up foreign nationality and the privileges accompanying it, there was no legal framework for Jewish newcomers in Palestine to become Ottoman subjects. Except in special cases, Ottoman nationality could only be acquired after five years' residence in the Empire, and although the 1901 regulations regularised the status of foreign Jews long resident in Palestine, they forbade all others to stay in the country for longer than three months. The Government only took steps to correct this anomaly in 1914.

Finally, although Arab notables seem to have been prepared for Jews to settle in Palestine if they became Ottomans, it cannot be said that there was any real enthusiasm for them. Indeed the only Arab found to have come out openly in favour of them was Farid Kassab; and without doubting his sincerity, he was to a large extent reacting to Négib Azoury. But that aside, in the absence of similar expressions of sympathy for the Jewish newcomers, his views can scarcely have been representative.

3

The New Régime: 1908–1909

THE YOUNG TURK Revolution took place on 24 July 1908. Under pressure, Abdülhamid restored the Constitution, which he had granted in 1876 and suspended less than two years later. Press censorship was lifted, the Sultan's network of spies was abolished, old-régime officials were dismissed, and arrangements were put in hand to reconvene Parliament for the first time in thirty years. For the peoples of the Empire, including the Arabs, the Revolution held promise of great changes. It took some time, however, for them to discover what these changes were to be. But it quickly became clear that the Young Turks' attitude to Zionism and Jewish settlement throughout the Empire in general was essentially the same as Abdülhamid's and that the new régime was not going to deviate from established policy on those issues.

When the Young Turks came to power, they were not a cohesive political group with a well-defined programme on which all were agreed. They were made up mainly of Ottoman Turks, but they were also supported by several groups representing other national elements within the Ottoman Empire, including certain Armenians, Albanians, Greeks and even Arabs. All shared the common aim of seeking to regenerate the Empire by reinstituting the Constitution and parliamentary processes. But they differed over the nature of the rehabilitated Empire they were striving for. The Turkish Young Turks, concentrated in the Committee of Union and Progress, envisaged—officially, at least—a strong, unified Empire in which the non-Turkish elements would be fused with the Turks. "Our Christian compatriots shall be Ottomanised citizens. We shall no longer be conquerers and slaves, but a new nation of freemen."[1] The non-Turkish elements, on the other hand, were not entirely happy with this approach. They tended to group themselves behind Prince Sabaheddin, a nephew of Abdülhamid, who had joined Young Turk exiles in Paris with his father in 1899. Through his League for Private Initiative and Decentralisation, Sabaheddin called for an Empire in which ethnic and religious groups would govern their own provinces on a decentralised basis. Much of the political strife which racked the Empire after the Revolution can be traced to the struggle between these two conflicting points of view.

In the years before the Revolution many Young Turks went abroad, where they could express their views more openly. As Paris was one of their centres, some of them came to know of the Zionist Movement not only through the general European press but also through the French *Echo Sioniste.*[2] A few of their leaders also met Zionists. Dr. Abdullah Cevdet Bey, an early Young Turk who after leaving the Empire had accepted a post as physician to the Ottoman Embassy at Vienna, met Theodor Herzl in 1903.[3] Ahmed Rıza, the leader of the Committee of Union and Progress, and others talked in Paris with Dr. Max Nordau, one of Herzl's closest collaborators.[3] Ahmed Rıza's journal, *Meşveret,* spoke of the Jews in the same terms as the Armenians: persecuted Jews were welcome to settle in the Empire as loyal Ottoman subjects—but if they sought autonomy, they would be opposed.[5] "Autonomy," Ahmed Rıza said in 1906, "is treason."[6]

Logic dictated that the Young Turks would view the Zionists with suspicion, if not hostility. In the light of what had happened in the Balkans, all nationalist movements were branded as secessionist, and therefore in direct conflict with the Young Turks' aim of preserving the integrity of the Empire. Furthermore, nationalist move-

1. Ramsaur, p. 93, quoting J. Macdonald, *Turkey and the Eastern Question* (London, 1913), p. 55.
2. *Ha-Ẓevi,* xxv, 6 (3.9.1908).
3. Herzl, *Diaries,* iv, 1417–18 (16.2.1903).
4. Nordau and Nordau, p. 193; cf. Netanyahu, ii, 238.
5. Rabinowitz, p. 456.
6. Ramsaur, p. 93, quoting Macdonald, p. 55.

ments, by definition, seek to develop specific national identities, and this ran counter to the philosophy of the Committee of Union and Progress, which aimed at creating a common Ottoman personality as a means of unifying the Empire. For both these reasons, members of the Committee—rather like Ottoman ministers in the 1880s—must have questioned the wisdom of exposing the Arabs, who were still among the most loyal elements of the Empire, to a nationalistic movement such as Zionism. Only Prince Sabaheddin's League for Private Initiative and Decentralisation could theoretically contemplate granting the Zionists some measure of administrative autonomy in Palestine, if it were to come to power. But, given the strength of the opposing group, the Committee of Union and Progress (the CUP), it was highly unlikely that Sabaheddin's group would gain the upper hand, in the early days of the Revolution at least.

The logic of the situation was soon confirmed. After the Revolution the Young Turk leaders preferred to operate behind the scenes rather than assume Cabinet Posts. They therefore remained somewhat elusive, but this did not prevent their views from becoming known. By the end of 1908 authoritative accounts of the new régime's attitude to Zionism had been given by well-placed Ottoman Jews to Dr. Victor Jacobson, the Zionist Organisation's representative in Constantinople, who came to the Ottoman capital in autumn 1908, nominally as managing director of the Anglo-Levantine Banking Company, an affiliate of the APC. His contacts included Emanuel Karasu (an important member of the CUP from Salonika), Hayim Nahum (the Haham Başı, or Chief Rabbi, of the Empire), Nisim Mazliah (a deputy in Parliament from Smyrna), and Nisim Ruso (secretary to the Minister of the Interior). As Jacobson reported: "[The Young Turks] consider us as separatists, if not today, then at any rate tomorrow. And they do not wish to let people enter [Palestine] who 'will create a new Armenian question' for them."[7]

On the other hand, the Young Turks were not opposed to Jewish immigration into the Empire at large. Dr. Namım Bey, an influential member of the CUP, told Max Nordau in Paris in November 1908 that arrangements had been made with the Jewish Colonization Association and the Alliance Israélite Universelle (a French organisation founded in 1860 for the "emancipation and moral

7. *CZA* L2/34/I (13.10.1908), V. Jacobson (Consple.) to A. Ruppin (Jaffa).

progress of the Jews") to settle up to a hundred thousand Jews in each of the Empire's thirty two provinces. But, he emphasised, these Jews must live in scattered groups. They were not to become a majority anywhere or form another national entity in the Empire.[8] That is to say, the new régime's policy was to be precisely the same as its predecessors' since 1881.

International events did not help the Zionists. In the autumn of 1908 Bulgaria declared its independence of the Ottoman Empire, Austro-Hungary annexed Bosnia and Herzegovina, and Crete announced its union with Greece. With parts of the Empire slipping away so quickly after the Revolution, the Young Turks could scarcely be sympathetic to any nationalist movement they suspected of separatist tendencies.

In the spring of 1909 the CUP, which soon emerged as by far the most dominant wing of the Young Turk Movement, tightened its control of the Government. On 13 February it ousted the Grand Vezir, Kâmil Paşa, who had served on many occasions both in that capacity and as Foreign Minister under Abdülhamid. The next day it installed Huseyn Hilmi Paşa, the liberally-minded Inspector-General of Rumelia from 1903 to 1908, whom the CUP regarded as more amenable to its views. Jacobson and his contacts spoke separately with Ahmed Rıza (now President of the Chamber—the lower house of Parliament), Talât Bey (Vice-President, and a powerful member of the CUP), Dr. Nazım and Enver Bey (another leading member of the CUP).[9] All thought Jewish immigration into the Empire desirable, but not into Palestine where, in Nazım's opinion, a large body of Jews could and would be a political danger.[10] With the CUP imposing its views directly on the Government, it was evident that no concessions to the Zionists were likely.

A fortnight after the Revolution, the Mutasarrıf of Jerusalem, Ali Ekrem Bey, put in a bid for a responsible post in Constantinople.[11] Though not recalled to the capital, he was made Vali of Beirut in August and shortly afterwards transferred elsewhere. Before leaving Jerusalem he submitted a report reiterating the dangers

8. *CZA* W/96 (25.11.1908), M. Nordau (Paris) to D. Wolffsohn (Cologne). Nordau recognised that this large figure, totalling 3,200,000 Jews, was inflated.
9. *CZA* Z2/7 (8. and 15.2.1909), both Jacobson to Wolffsohn.
10. *CZA* Z2/7 (8.2.1909).
11. *ISA (T)* no. 8 (6.8.1908), Mutas. (Jerus.) to Grand Vezir (SP).

of Jewish immigration into the Mutasarrıjflık as he saw them.[12] He was replaced in September by Subhi Bey who, unlike his predecessors since 1897, had not been a member of Abdülhamid's Palace staff but had held a post in the Ottoman civil service.[13] He had read Ekrem Bey's final report from Jerusalem, and when Isaac Fernandez and Victor Jacobson called on him in Constantinople before he set out, he cautiously reserved his position on the grounds that the new régime had not yet studied the whole question of Jewish activities in Palestine.[14]

At the end of 1908, Dr. Jacobson learned that the legal advisers at the Foreign Ministry were in fact considering the question of Zionism and Jewish settlement in Palestine.[15] Moreover, in March 1909, two senior officials from the Ministry of Justice were sent to Palestine to investigate the Jewish affairs there,[16] while Subhi Bey was ordered to comply with a decision taken in 1904 prohibiting sales of land to foreign Jews, even if they lived in Palestine.[17] After coming to Jerusalem, Subhi Bey appears to have been impressed by the Jewish colonies,[18] and, according to Albert Antébi, he made up his mind to discuss this order personally when he went to Constantinople on leave in the near future.[19] Until then he decided—apparently on his own authority—first, to allow land sales to Ottoman Jews to continue,[20] and second, to dispense with the need for foreign Jews purchasing land to undertake not to settle Jewish immigrants on it.[21]

Disturbances in the Orthodox Church in Jerusalem prevented Subhi Bey from going to Constantinople, and so he took up in writing the question of Jewish land purchase and its implications in Palestine.[22] In Constantinople, Nisim Ruso spoke to Hüseyn Hilmi Paşa (the new Grand Vezir) about Zionism.[23] At the end of

12. *ISA (T)* no. 11 [n.d., résumé], same to Min. of the Interior (SP).
13. *AIU* VIII E 25 (7.9.1908), A. Antébi (Jerus.) to H. Frank (Jaffa).
14. *CZA* Z2/7 (10. and 23.9.1908), both Jacobson to Wolffsohn.
15. *CZA* Z2/7 (29.12.1908), Jacobson to Wolffsohn.
16. *AIU* IX 3 26 (3.3.1909), Antébi to Pres., AIU (Paris).
17. *AIU* IX E 26 (10.3.1909), Antébi to I. Fernandez (Consple.), enclosing copy of instructions (11.2.1909), Min. of the Interior to Mutas. (Jerus.), repeating Grand Vezir's orders of 11.10.1904.
18. Cf. *ha-Ẓevi,* xxv, 74 (8.1.1909).
19. *AIU* IX E 26 (10.3.1909), Antébi to Fernandez.
20. *AIU* IX E 26 (10.3.1909).
21. *AIU* IX E 26 (5.4.1909), Antébi to Pres., AIU.
22. *AIU* IX E 26 (2.5.1909), same to same.
23. *CZA* Z2/8 (16.3.1909), Jacobson to Wolffsohn.

March, Hilmi Paşa replied to Subhi Bey. He agreed that Jewish settlement in Palestine would bring certain advantages to the local population and the Treasury. But he also pointed to the difficulties that would arise from the "constant intervention of a foreign government such as Russia" on behalf of its protégés in the Mutasarrıflık.[24] He ended by suggesting that, if Subhi could submit a plan which safeguarded the rights of Ottoman Jews and at the same time checked Jewish immigration from Russia and Rumania, "we shall willingly encourage the economic development of Ottoman Jews [in Palestine] and abolish the restrictions."[25] Thereupon, Subhi Bey set about preparing an appropriate scheme, with Antébi's help.[26]

Although the news of the Revolution was not believed in Palestine at first, it did not take long before a jubilant mood broke out among all sections of the local population.[27] On the plane of Arab-Jewish relations, *ha-Poᶜel ha-Ẓaᶜir* (a journal of the Second Aliya) reported in September that the atmosphere in Jaffa was greatly improved—"there is not the same cold attitude which was felt after the incident [last] Purim."[28] In Jerusalem, Muslims, Christians and Jews joined together to found a branch of the CUP and also a literary, political club called the Jerusalem Patriotic Society.[29] David Yellin, a Palestinian-born teacher in Jerusalem, indicated how much the atmosphere had changed when he noted that "we see for the first time in these societies Muslims (and of the upper class) associating with Jews and Christians."[30] Notables in Jerusalem encouraged fellahin in the region to create a society to look after their interests, which Jewish settlers also joined.[31] According to Yellin, the fellahin were "very content" to draw on the Jews' experience.[32] At the end of 1908, Albert Antébi formed La Société Commerciale de Palestine, a joint-stock company with

23. *CZA* Z2/8 (16.3.1909), Jacobson to Wolffsohn.
24. *AIU* IX E 26 (5.4.1909), quoting extracts from Hilmi Paşa's letter to Subhi Bey; cf. *CZA* Z2/8 (16. and 22.4.1909), both Jacobson to Wolffsohn.
25. *AIU* IX E 26 (5.4.1909), Antébi to Pres., AIU.
26. *AIU* IX E 26 (5.4.1909).
27. Rabinowitz, p. 280.
28. *Ha-Poᶜel Ha-Ẓaᶜir,* i, 12 (1908).
29. *Ha-Ẓevi,* i [xxv], 6 (3.9.1908).
30. *CZA* A/153, i (7.9.1908), D. Yellin (Jerus.) to P. Nathan [Berlin].
31. *CZA* A/153, i (6.10.1908), same to same.
32. *CZA* A/153, i (22.11.1908), same to same.

the APC as its bankers, in which five thousand of the six thousand subscribed shares were held by non-Jews, including the two newly elected deputies from Jerusalem in the Ottoman Parliament, Ruḥi Bey al-Khalidi and Saᶜid Bey al-Ḥusayni.[33]

But not everything went smoothly. In Jaffa, Arabs were provoked by the indiscreet behavious of some recent immigrants, who paraded a Zionist flag in the streets during the celebrations after the Revolution. These newcomers, members of the Second Aliya, also declared that political Zionism must be the basis of Jewish activity in Palestine and that the Jews must elect Zionist deputies to the Ottoman Parliament to press their claim to the country. The Arabs were reported to have restrained their feelings, and merely remarked: "Demand what you wish; we shall not grant your wish. Indeed, you are not capable of achieving what you want, so we shall not spoil our celebration, even by debating with you."[34]

The founders of the CUP branch in Jerusalem invited four Jews to join them—on condition, however, that they made conciliatory statements about their attitude to Zionism and that they did not hold the *sheqel* (membership and voting rights in the Zionist Movement).[35] In effect, this made them the first Arabs known to have drawn a clear distinction between "Jew" and "Zionist." And like the Committee's leaders in Constantinople: "These Young Turks conceive Zionism only as a political movement which aims at placing Palestine under an exclusively Jewish autonomy."[36]

General Elections to Parliament were held in the autumn of 1908. In the Mutasarrıflık of Jerusalem, three deputies were to be elected. Under the amnesty for political crimes granted by the Young Turks, Négib Azoury returned from Paris to stand as a candidate in Jaffa. It was symptomatic of the times that, after a Revolution which aimed at preserving the unity of the Empire and proclaimed "fraternity" as one of its slogans, Azoury avoided all reference in his public speeches to his Arab nationalist ideas and to the "universal Jewish peril."[37] Most candidates called for economic and administrative reforms; some also talked of helping the

33. *CZA* W/126/II (17.1.1909), D. Levontin (Jaffa) to Wolffsohn.
34. *CZA* W/126/II (25.8.1908), same to same.
35. *CZA* Z2'632 (24.8.1908), Ruppin to Wolffsohn.
36. *CZA* W/126/II (21.8.1908), Levontin to Directors, APC (London).
37. *CZA* Z2/632 (29.9.1908), Ruppin to Wolffsohn; cf. *al-Muqaṭṭam*, no. 5,943 (12.10.1908), cited by Harran, p. 75.

fellahin. But these ideas and the concept of voting for the nominees of a political organisation such as the CUP were foreign to the voters, who were taking part in modern elections for the first time in their lives. As their primary loyalties were to family and religion, the large Muslim majority in the Mutasarrıflık ensured that three Muslims, all from leading families, were elected: Ruḥi Bey al-Khalidi, Saᶜid Bey al-Ḥusayni, and Ḥafiẓ Bey al-Saᶜid.

Ruḥi Bey al-Khalidi was a grandson of Yusuf Ḍiya Paşa al-Khalidi, and also a man of distinction. He was forty-five years of age and had studied in Paris at l'Ecole des sciences politiques and the Sorbonne after an elementary education in Jerusalem, Beirut and Tripoli, and senior schooling in Constantinople.[38] He had returned to Jerusalem after the Revolution, somewhat a stranger to the city, having served for ten years as Ottoman Consul in Bordeaux, where he had been made an Officer of the Légion d'Honneur. He had written a history of literature entitled *Tarikh ᶜilm al-adab,* and, under the pen-name of *al-Maqdisi,* used to contribute to important Arabic journals such as *al-Manar* and *al-Hilal*. A member of the CUP, he was reputed to be a "liberal" in his political views.[39]

Saᶜid Bey al-Husayni was about thirty years old and was said by Zionists to be an "Arab nationalist."[40] He had been educated in Jerusalem and had studied for a time at the local Alliance Israélite Universelle school, where he appears to have acquired some knowledge of Hebrew, because under the old régime he had once acted as censor of a local Hebrew newspaper. In that capacity he had become a well-informed opponent of the Zionist Movement and Jewish immigration into Palestine.[41] His active opposition to the Zionists dated back at least to 1905 when, as President of the Municipal Council in Jerusalem, he had tried to prevent land sales to Jews at Moẓa, near Jerusalem.[42]

Ḥafiẓ Bey al-Saᶜid of Jaffa was in his sixties.[43] He had been the last Mufti of Gaza, and in 1905, during a campaign conducted by

38. For a short biography of Ruḥi Bey, see his *al-Muqaddima fi al-masᶜala al-sharqiyya* (Jerusalem, n.d. [published posthumously]), pp. 1–5; cf. Kaḥḥalah, iv, 174–175.
39. *Al-Hilal,* vol. xvii (1908), pp. 181–82.
40. *CZA* Z2/7 (13.11. and 5.12.1908), both Jacobson to Wolffsohn.
41. *CZA* Z2/632 (11.11.1908), Ruppin to Wolffsohn.
42. *JCA* 261/enc. to no. 338 (30.8.1905), Antébi to S. I. Pariente (Beirut).
43. *CZA* Z2/632 (11.11.1908).

the authorities against Négib Azoury's Arab nationalist manifestos, he had been put under house arrest while his papers were searched.[44] He did in fact come to take an active part in the Arab nationalist movement, but in 1908 the Jews considered him well disposed and accordingly supported his candidature. It was expected that he would be dominated by Ruḥi Bey and Saʿid Bey, since he was less educated and a poorer speaker than they.[45]

In the north of Palestine Shaykh Aḥmad Efendi al-Khammash of Nablus and Shaykh Asʿad Efendi Shuqayr of Acre were elected to represent their respective sancaks. The former was a very conservative Muslim; the latter, a Muslim scholar and father of Aḥmad Shuqayri (the Palestinian Arab leader until 1967), had been held in prison because, according to the *Revue du Monde Musulman,* the old régime had regarded him with suspicion.[46]

The Parliament was opened on 17 December 1908. Sixty of the 288 deputies in the Chamber were Arabs. Clearly even if the new régime was so disposed—which it was not—it could not afford to alienate the Arab deputies by treating the Zionists with special deference.[47]

A sequel to the widespread jubilation which greeted the Revolution was that public order deteriorated in parts of the Empire. In Palestine, the first disturbances took place in the north of the country. Even before the Revolution, security in the outlying sancaks of the Vilâyet of Beirut had been difficult to maintain, and the mixed population in the mountainous areas around Haifa, Nazareth, and Tiberias (which included Bedouin, Druze, and some recently settled Algerians and Circassians) was unruly. In 1908, these peasants called the new dispensation *ḥurriyya* ("liberty" or "political freedom"), and some of them seemed to think that it gave them licence to act as they liked. This led to attacks in the autumn on properties belonging to large Arab landowners to such an extent that landowners in Haifa and elsewhere made joint efforts to protect their estates.[48] Within this context, there were attacks in

44. *ISA (G)* A III 15, ii (25.5.1905), Rössler (Jaffa) to von Bieberstein (Consple.).
45. *CZA* Z2/632 (11.11.1908), Ruppin to Wolffsohn.
46. *Revue du Monde Musulman,* vol. vi (1908), p. 525–26. No details are given of why Asʿad Shuqayr was suspect or how long he was held in prison.
47. Cf. *CZA* Z2/7 (5.12.1908), Jacobson to Wolffsohn.
48. Harran, pp. 54–55.

November on Jewish settlements,[49] and in December villagers from Kafar Kanna tried to seize some land in the Kaza of Tiberias belonging to the Jewish Colonization Association.[50]

In the spring of 1909, after the CUP appointed Hüseyn Hilmi Paşa as Grand Vezir in place of Kâmil Paşa, a wave of disillusionment with the Revolution spread throughout the Empire. Strictly religious elements among the Muslims in the capital and beyond were offended by the CUP's secular attitudes, and several groups with vested interests in the old régime were disaffected. Eventually a Counterrevolution, inspired by the so-called Muhammadan Union, took place in Constantinople on 13 April 1909, but before it there were signs of unrest, particularly in Anatolia where thousands of Armenians were killed during the outbreaks. In this unsettled political climate, a series of serious incidents occurred around the JCA settlement and training farm at Sejera, halfway between Tiberias and Nazareth.

As in most cases of this kind, the events about to be described have to be viewed against a certain background of local tension between the colony and its Arab neighbours. JCA had bought eighteen thousand dunams of land for Sejera in 1899. Demarcation disputes with the four nearby villages of al-Shajara (Christians), Ṭurʿan (Muslims), Kafar Kanna (Muslims and Christians), and Kafar Sabt (Muslims from Algeria) persisted for years.[51] When the settlers began in 1903 to take up some of their land previously leased to the adjoining village of Lubiyya, the colony was raided on a number of occasions, and a settler was murdered in 1904 by the son of a shaykh from Lubiyya.[52] The colony was guarded by villagers from Kafar Kama, but in 1907 a group of Jewish workers from Russia who came to Sejera decided to take on that duty.[53] The former watchmen were disgruntled, and another source of friction had been created.

In February 1909, the Christian peasants at al-Shajara claimed some land that had been owned by the colony since 1899. Elie Krause (the manager of the training farm and for many years after

49. *AIU* VIII E 25 (8.11.1908), Frank to Antébi; cf. *al-Muqaṭṭam*, no. 5,973 (19.11.1908), cited by Harran, p. 37.
50. *AIU* IX E 26 (30.12.1908), Antébi to Frank.
51. *JCA* 255/[no number], (31.1.1900), D. Haym (Sejera) to Admin. Council, JCA; and *JCA* 270/no. 7 (24.11.1904), E. Krause (Sejera) to Pariente.
52. *JCA* 260/encs. to nos. 279 and 280 (25.8 and 8.9.1904), both Krause to Pariente.
53. Dinur, I, i, 205; cf. ben-Gurion, p. 18.

1914 director of the Miqve Yisraʿel agricultural school) reported that outside elements among the Arab population, who were dissatisfied with the new régime, had prompted the peasants into this action.[54] These outsiders were described as members of the Tiberias branch of the CUP, through which they worked to incite the Arab villages against the Jewish colonies.[55] In March, the settlers retaliated by refusing to employ peasants from al-Shajara or to buy their produce.[56] In April, the peasants dropped their claim on Sejera's land because the legal expenses were too high.[57] Peasants from al-Shajara harassed individual Jews,[59] burgled the colony, and on 3 April beat up some Kurdish Jews (who worked at Sejera but lived in al-Shajara).

In the midst of these tensions an Arab from Kafar Kanna was killed by a Jew. A conference of one of the Second Aliya's political parties was to be held at Sejera during the Jewish festival of Passover. On 5 April, the eve of the festival, a photographer, named Chaim Dubner, was attacked and robbed on his way to Sejera by four peasants shortly after passing through Kafar Kanna. Dubner shot back and wounded one of the peasants. By the next day it was clear that the wounded man, Raḍi Ṣaffuri (a well-known robber) was going to die, and his parents made him testify that he had been shot by two Jews from Sejera.[61] On 7 April, villagers from Kafar Kanna tried to steal animals from Sejera to avenge Ṣaffuri's death.[62] They demanded "blood money" for his death, which the officials at Sejera refused to pay. On 9 April, about fifty villagers from Kafar Kanna began to destroy plants in Sejera's fields, but were stopped by policemen from Tiberias.[63] Two days later, after spoiling more crops and stealing some cattle,[64] they gravely injured

54. *JCA* 271/no. 284 (7.2.1909), Krause to JCA (Paris).
55. *JCA* 271/no. 285 (19.2.1909), same to same.
56. *JCA* 271/no. 289 (25.3.1909), same to same.
57. *JCA* 271/no. 290 (12.4.1909), same to same.
58. *JCA* 271/no. 294 (7.6.1909), same to same.
59. *JCA* 271/[miscellaneous papers] (3.4.1909), Krause to Kay (Tiberias).
60. *JCA* 271/no. 290.
61. *JCA* 271/[misc. papers] (6.4.1909), Krause to Kay (Nazareth); and (8.4.1909), Krause to Antéti.
62. *JCA* 271/[misc. papers] (7.4.1909), Krause to Kay (Nazareth); and (7. and 8.4.1909), both Krause to Antébi.
63. *JCA* 271/[misc. papers] (10.4.1909), Krause to Kay (Tiberias).
64. *JCA* 271/no. 290; and *JCA* 271/ [misc. papers] (11.4.1909), Krause to Kay (Nazareth), and (11.4.1909), Krause to Antébi.

two Jews returning to Sejera from Tiberias.[65] Then, on the following day, two Jews were murdered, one by peasants from Kafar Kanna and the other by peasants from al-Shajara.[66]

Timely rains helped to calm the atmosphere.[67] The authorities at Nazareth recovered two mules which had been stolen from Sejera on 7 April, and arrested five villagers from Kafar Kanna.[68] Not long afterwards, half-a-dozen more villagers were arrested, and Dubner's photographic equipment was recovered. When an enquiry established Kafar Kanna's guilt, a delegation of priests from the village and from Nazareth came to Sejera to sue for peace.[69] But terms could not be agreed and the case was taken to court in Acre, where it dragged on for over two years.[70]

The incidents at Sejera were obviously different from the "Purim incident" in Jaffa twelve months earlier, and the differences went further than the simple contrast between their urban and rural settings. In Jaffa, the Ottoman authorities were mainly responsible for the incident. At Sejera, the local population were responsible. In Jaffa, such external influences as there were appear to have come from the Russian Vice-Consul. The peasants in the villages round Sejera were encouraged by members of the CUP branch at Tiberias. In Jaffa, a handful of Muslim Arabs joined the military Commandant when he raided Hotel Spector with his men. The fellahin from Kafar Kanna and al-Shajara were mostly Christians.

A more important question is whether there were undertones to the incidents at Sejera which marked them off from the disturbances in the north of Palestine in the autumn of 1908 when public security deteriorated, and also from the many instances of disenchantment with the new régime in the spring of 1909. Given that Krause believed that dissident elements in the CUP branch at Tiberias were responsible for inciting the peasants, the Sejera incidents

65. *JCA* 271/[misc. papers] (12.4.1909), Krause to Kay (Nazareth); and no. 290.
66. *JCA* 271/[misc. papers] (12.4.1909), Krause to Kay (Tiberias; and (12.4.1909), Krause to Antébi.
67. *JCA* 271/no. 291 (25.4.1909), Krause to JCA (Paris).
68. *JCA* 271/no. 292 (9.5.1909), same to same.
69. *AIU* IX E 26 (27.5.1909), Krause to Antébi; and *JCA* 271/no. 293 (28.5.1909), Krause to JCA (Paris).
70. *JCA* 271/no. 301 (12.2.1910), same to same; no. 306 (6.6.1910), same to same; no. 330 (20.11.1911), same to same; and cf. *CZA* L2/50/1 "Note sur l'état d'insécurité dont souffre la population israélite agricole dans les [sic] Caza de Tibériade" [undated and unsigned (ca. end 1911)].

should probably be seen in the first instance as part of a wider pattern. It was natural that in the early months after the Revolution certain Arabs who were unhappy with the aspects of the changed order of things should join branches of the CUP (which were often formed—as at Tiberias—on local initiative and not always recognised by the CUP's Central Executive). By so doing they provided themselves with a legal framework within which they could work to express their criticisms of the régime and try to influence policy. But, at the same time, there are grounds to suspect that some of those involved in the attacks on Sejera were also motivated by a desire to protest against Jewish colonisation in the Tiberias region (where there were already seven colonies)—feeble and inchoate as their protest may have been. This suspicion rests on two pieces of evidence. First, Krause specifically named Najib Naṣṣar as one of the principal outside instigators of the Sejera incidents.[71] Najib Naṣṣar was the editor of a Haifa newspaper called *al-Karmil,* and he emerged from 1909 onwards as the leading anti-Zionist publicist among the Arabs in Palestine. He came from Tiberias and was known to Krause as a former land-agent for the Jewish Colonization Association. As will be seen, his opposition to Jewish settlement in Palestine—even by 1909—was too pronounced to be ignored.

Secondly, there were reports that other Arabs who opposed Jewish settlement in Palestine were joining the CUP. For example, in May, Albert Antébi learned that some new members of the CUP in Jerusalem and Jaffa were demanding that the Committee pay heed to "the danger which menaces the country and the peasants from Jewish immigration." The branches most antagonistic to the immigration were in the north of Palestine, at Haifa, Nazareth and Tiberias; the branch at Beirut was also mentioned.[72] Similarly, an official of the Ottoman Bank told the director of the Alliance Israélite Universelle's Boys' School in Constantinople that the Committee's branches in "Syria" (meaning in this context the north of Palestine, Beirut and Damascus) intended to come out openly against Zionism and mass Jewish immigration into the area.[73]

And, in June, the question of Zionism was raised in the Ottoman Parliament for the first time by the deputy from Jaffa.

71. *JCA* 271/no. 294 (7.6.1909), Krause to JCA (Paris).
72. *AIU* IX E 26 (12.5.1909), Antébi to A. Bril (Jaffa).
73. *AIU* I G 1 (14.6.1909), A. Benveniste (Consple.), to Pres., AIU.

4

The Committee of Union and Progress in Power

THE COUNTERREVOLUTION of 13 April 1909 was quashed within two weeks, and by the end of the month public order in Constantinople and a government controlled by the Committee of Union and Progress were restored. Abdülhamid was deposed and a new Cabinet, again headed by Hüseyn Hilmi Paşa, took purposeful steps to prevent further insurrection. The CUP adopted a conscious policy of "Ottomanising" the Empire, the aim of which was to engender a strong, undivided loyalty to the Empire among its many national and ethnic groups, transcending any particularist tendencies that they may have had.

This policy was pursued energetically in various ways. Military service was introduced for non-Muslims; legislation was adopted to prevent nationalist societies from functioning; and dissident national groups, especially in Albania and Macedonia, were harshly repressed. The CUP even contemplated trying to encourage Muslim and Jewish immigration into Macedonia in order to neutralise Ottoman Greeks in that area, who were seeking union with Greece.[1]

Hence, in May and June, Ahmed Rıza Bey, the President of the Chamber, indicated to the Haham Başı that the Government would welcome large numbers of Jewish immigrants from eastern Europe in the Empire.[2] Newspaper reports of these approaches coincided

1. Cf. *Times* (London), no. 39,237 (4.4.1910).
2. *CZA* Z2/8 (17.5.1909), V. Jacobson (Consple.) to D. Wolffsohn (Cologne); and *ha-ᶜOlam*, iii, 22 (22.6.1909).

with the reports mentioned in the previous chapter that certain members of CUP branches in Palestine and surrounding areas were concerned about Jewish immigration into Palestine.[3] It comes as no surprise, therefore, that at the beginning of June Ḥafiẓ Bey al-Saᶜid, the deputy from Jaffa, raised the Zionist issue in Parliament for the first time. He did so in the form of a parliamentary question, in which he asked what Zionism implied and whether it was compatible with the interests of the Empire.[4] Giving a fair indication of his own view and possibly that of some other Arab deputies, he also demanded that the port of Jaffa be closed to Jewish immigrants.[5]

By way of reply, a commission of six deputies was set up to investigate the question.[6] However, according to the Mutasarrıf of Jerusalem, the Minister of the Interior wanted to expedite matters,[7] and so the whole matter of Jewish settlement in Palestine was reviewed in Cabinet on 20 June for the first time since the Revolution a year before.[8] The Cabinet had in front of it various reports from the Mutasarrıflık of Jerusalem and the Ministry of the Interior and also, one presumes, the views of the legal advisers at the Foreign Ministry and the report recently prepared by the Ministry of Justice (see p. 62).

The Cabinet appears to have recognised the complexity of the issue. On the one side, the Zionist Movement—as a nationalist movement backed up by relatively large-scale Jewish settlement in Palestine—was bound to be unacceptable to the CUP with its policy of "Ottomanising" the Empire. Moreover, some Arabs in and beyond Palestine were becoming more sensitive to the issue. On the other side, the constitutional rights of Ottoman Jews to acquire land in Palestine had to be considered, because one of the aims of the Revolution was to uphold the Constitution. The privileges of foreign Jews under the Capitulations and the Land Code of 1867 were also involved. Finally, the new régime's economic situation was not such that the financial implications of the question could be

3. *Jewish Chronicle,* no. 2,098 (18.6.1909); and *Revue du Monde Musulman,* viii, 6 (1909), p. 250. "L'Immigration juive en Turquie".
4. *CZA* Z2/8 (7.6.1909), Jacobson to Wolffsohn.
5. *AIU* IX E 27 (2.7.1909), A. Antébi (Jerus.) to H. Frank (Jaffa); cf. *Jewish Chronicle,* no. 2,098 (18.6.1909).
6. *AIU* IX E 27 (2.7.1909).
7. *AIU* IX E 27 (11.7.1909), Antébi to Pres., AIU (Paris).
8. Cabinet decision (20.6.1909), in Farhi, "Documents on the Attitude of the Ottoman Government," pp. 16–17.

lightly dismissed, since various Jewish groups, Zionist and non-Zionist alike, had recently expressed interest in purchasing extensive state (*miri*) and crown (*çiftlik*) lands in Palestine. In view of its complexity, the Cabinet decided to have a comprehensive paper on the question drawn up by the Director-General of the Cadastre in conjunction with all the relevant departments of state, and then to have a new law drafted by the Ministry of the Interior to prevent further Jewish settlement in Palestine.[9]

Subhi Bey, the Mutasarrıf of Jerusalem, was asked for his views and he replied by submitting the scheme which the Grand Vezir had invited him to prepare in March.[10] In it, he came out in support of limited Jewish immigration into Palestine, provided that the Jews became Ottoman subjects and settled on vacant lands so that they should not arouse "the apprehensions of the indigenous population."[11] At the beginning of July, Subhi Bey was summoned to Constantinople for consultations, apparently because of differences of opinion between the departments of state concerned.[12]

According to Subhi Bey, the Minister of the Interior sympathised with Arab opponents of Jewish settlement in Palestine.[13] Therefore, before the Minister gave up his position in August (after a disagreement with the CUP about the appointment of parliamentary deputies as under-secretaries of ministries), he formulated certain recommendations on the question. In essence, they were (1) that all Jews, Ottoman and foreign, should be prohibited from settling in Palestine, and (2) that foreign Jews should lose their right under the 1867 Land Code to acquire land.[14]

The issue did not rest while the draft law was being prepared. On 5 September, the Ministry of the Interior brought questions relating to land sales in Palestine to the attention of the Cabinet, which decided to suspend land transfers to Jews until the new law was adopted.[15] As an interim measure, Talât Bey, the new Minister of

9. *Loc. cit.*
10. *AIU* IX E 27 (2. and 16.7.1909), both Antébi to Frank.
11. Cf. *AIU* IX E 27 (11.7.1909), Antébi to Pres., AIU.
12. *AIU* IX E 27 (9.7.1909), Antébi to Pres., AIU; and *Q d'O* N.S. 132, no. 41 (27.1.1909), G. Gueraud (Jerus.) to S. Pichon (Paris).
13. *AIU* IX E 27 (9.7.1909).
14. *AIU* IX E 27 (18.10.1909), Antébi to Frank; cf. *CZA* W/16 (10.8.1909), Wolffsohn (Orient Express, Bulgaria) to J. Kann (The Hague).
15. Cabinet decision (5.9.1909), in Farhi, "Documents on the Attitude of the Ottoman Goivernment," p. 18.

the Interior and one of the most powerful members of the CUP, reinvoked the existing regulations. On 28 September, he informed provincial governors that, until the new law was ready (which, he said, would probably not be before the end of the current session of Parliament), "we consider that instructions communicated and the decisions taken [at earlier dates on Jewish immigration and land purchase] can well be put into practice now," especially as the matter was urgent and "since we now have capable officials."[16]

By the autumn of 1908 it had become clear that the old régime's policy on Jewish settlement in Palestine was going to be maintained. And by the summer of 1909, it was also clear that continued Zionist efforts to consolidate the New Yishuv in Palestine were liable to come into direct conflict with the CUP's policy of Ottomanising the Empire.

This point was well put by Dr. Rıza Tevfık Bey in July 1909 at a luncheon which Sir Francis Montefiore, the Honorary President of the English Zionist Federation, gave for five members of a delegation from the Ottoman Parliament visiting London. Rıza Tevfık was a highly respected Young Turk and a man of letters. As a child he had attended the Alliance Israélite Universelle school in Adrianople, where he acquired fluent Ladino (Judaeo-Spanish) and, it seems, a warm regard for Jews.[17] In 1908 he was elected a deputy for Adrianople, and in 1911 went on to help found the Liberal Union, a political party opposed to the CUP. In February 1909, he had identified himself enthusiastically with Zionism at a Jewish meeting in Constantinople.[18] But by July, when he addressed another Jewish gathering in Smyrna, his tone had changed. Still professing to be a "Zionist," he expressed the hope that persecuted Jews would find asylum in the Ottoman Empire. However, he cautioned his audience against translating Zionism into political terms.[19] In London, he repeated the substance of this speech to the *Jewish Chronicle,* emphasising that "the proper aim of Zionism is the happiness and welfare of the majority of the Jewish nation,

16. Circular (28.9.1909), Min. of the Interior to Vilâyet (Beirut), enclosed in *AIU,* IX E 27 (19.11.1909), Frank to Antébi.
17. *Jewish Chronicle,* no. 2,103 (23.7.1909); cf. *CZA* Z2/7 (12. and 22.2.1909), both Jacobson to Wolffsohn (Cologne).
18. *Times* (London), no. 38,905 (12.3.1909).
19. *L'Aurore,* i, 6 (16.7.1909); cf. a little earlier, *ha-ʿOlam,* iii, 22 (22.6.1909) quoting Rıza Tevfık, but not indicating the occasion of his remarks.

but there is a kind of Zionism which may defeat that object and achieve the opposite."[20] At Sir Francis Montefiore's luncheon, he repeated this message once again and warned that "the political aims of Zionism were not likely to evoke approval in the Turkish Empire, especially at the present moment, when there were so many internal political problems to solve."[21] Rıza Tevfık was politely telling his Zionist hosts that since the Counterrevolution in April, times had changed. The CUP was firmly reestablished in power and, coming from a Balkan province, Rıza Tevfık well knew what the CUP's policy of Ottomanising the non-Turkish elements in the Empire meant. Thus, with all his sympathy for Zionism, he advised caution.[22]

Throughout this period the Zionists were not left in any doubt about the Government's attitude. Days before Ḥafiẓ Bey's question in Parliament, the Grand Vezir had talked to Victor Jacobson, the Zionist representative in Constantinople, and was full of reserve about Zionism.[23] Immediately after Ḥafiẓ Bey's question, Jacobson secured interviews with the President of the Chamber, the Minister of the Interior and the Minister of Finance. All three staved Jacobson off with excuses that they were overworked and could not consider Zionism at the moment.[24] David Wolffsohn, the President of the Zionist Organisation, visited Constantinople in July and August and met many leading Ottoman personalities, including the Grand Vezir. Everyone told him that Jewish immigrants were welcome in the Empire, but not in Palestine, where a "Jewish problem" and "new complications" were feared.[25] The Grand Vezir was firm, asserting that Palestine was "closed" to Jewish immigrants and that the Government would not abolish the restrictions which had been in force "for twenty-five years."[26] That autumn, the Minister of Finance, Cavid Bey (who was a member of a Judaeo-Islamic syncretist sect called the Dönmes), told Jacobson that the Government did not trust the Zionists and that

20. *Jewish Chronicle,* no. 2,103 (23.7.1909).
21. *Jewish Chronicle,* no. 2,104 (30.7.1909).
22. Tâlat Bey and Ruḥi Bey al-Khalidi also attended the luncheon. Tâlat Bey associated himself with Rıza Tevfık's remarks; Ruḥi Bey is not reported to have spoken—*Jewish Chronicle,* no. 2,104 (30.7.1909).
23. *CZA* Z2/8 (30.5.1909), Jacobson to Wolffsohn.
24. *CZA* Z2/8 (7.6.1909), same to same.
25. *CZA* W/16 (10.8.1909), Wolffsohn (Orient Express, Bulgaria) to Kann.
26. *CZA* W/16 (10.8.1909).

negotiations between them were impossible.[27] A few days later, the Minister of Religious Endowments, Ḥammadah Paşa (who was an Arab), explained to Jacobson that the Zionists were suspected of seeking an independent Jewish state in the light of numerous declarations made by themselves.[28]

In December, the ninth Zionist Congress—the first since the Young Turk Revolution—was held in Hamburg. It resolved to retain, unamended, the Movement's original programme with its aim of a "home in Palestine" for the Jewish people "secured by public law." But, in view of the Young Turk Revolution, it also resolved to dispense with the objectives of a "Charter" and Great Power protection sought by Herzl while Abdülhamid was in power. Max Nordau, who took a leading part in the debates, counselled the Zionists to work patiently until "their elucidations, the effect of time, political developments, and greater maturity will have changed the attitudes of authoritative Turkish circles."[29]

Dr. Nazım Bey was angered by reports of the Congress shown to him by the Jewish editors of the *Journal de Salonique.* "Your Zionists frighten the Turkish masses. As for the élite, they will never permit a Jewish concentration in Palestine. Never, never ever, as long as we live, and I do not believe that we have a foot in the grave."[30] Jews would be welcome in Macedonia, but the Zionists, as Nordau said, must wait. The attitude of the CUP, and thus of the Government, towards the Zionist Movement had been stated unambiguously.

Not long after Ḥafiẓ Bey's question in Parliament on Zionism, the other two deputies from the Mutasarrıflık made their attitudes known through interviews with *ha-Ẓevi,* a Hebrew newspaper in Jerusalem. Both were clearly opposed to Jewish settlement in Palestine, with Ruḥi Bey al-Khalidi being more forthright and original than Saʿid Bey al-Ḥusayni.

Saʿid Bey took the position, which had been reiterated by the CUP and the Government, of favouring Jewish settlement in the Empire at large, but not in Palestine. Unlike the CUP, however,

27. *CZA* Z2/8 (26.10.1909), Jacobson to Wolffsohn (Cologne).
28. *CZA* Z2/8 (8.11.1909), same to same.
29. Quoted by Halpern, p. 269, from minutes of ninth Zionist Congress; cf. Laqueur, *History of Zionism,* p. 145.
30. Reprinted in *L'Aurore,* ii, 30 (14.1.1910).

he explained himself in terms not of opposition to nationalist movements, but of what came to be called after World War I the "absorptive capacity" of Palestine. He simply did not believe that the country could support large-scale Jewish immigration. Thus, in reply to a question, he conceded that small numbers of Jews would bring advantages to Palestine.[31]

On the other hand, Ruḥi Bey spoke in a very different voice: the Arabs were in Palestine as of right and they did not owe the Jews anything. After criticising European Jews in Palestine for holding aloof from the Arabs, and after saying that individual Jews should be allowed to enter the country freely, he declared:

> But to establish Jewish colonies is another question. The Jews have the financial capacity. They will be able to buy many tracts of land, and displace the Arab farmers from their land and their fathers' heritage. However, we did not conquer this land from you. We conquered it from the Byzantines who ruled it then. We do not owe anything to the Jews. The Jews were not here when we conquered the country.[32]

Ruḥi Bey's primary concern with Jewish land purchases and colonisation was not fortuitous. It represented a subtle but important change of emphasis. Before 1908, Arabs had related to the question of Jewish immigration into Palestine, rather than to Zionism as such. From 1909 onwards, they focussed much more on Jewish land purchase—and, with that, on Zionism and Zionist activities in Palestine (land purchase being at the heart of them).

The change did not take place in a vacuum. As was explained in Chapter One, the purchase of land on which to found new colonies was virtually halted in the Mutasarrıflık of Jerusalem for some years after 1897 and in the Vilâyet of Beirut from 1901 onwards. However, the situation in the Mutasarrıflık was relaxed under Kâzim Bey (1903–04) and Reşid Bey (1904–06); and quantities of land were acquired. In 1906, a children's village was established at Ben Shemen. In 1907, an agricultural training farm was set up at Ḥulda, and a colony at Beʿer Yaʿaqov. In 1908, another settlement was founded in the Mutasarrıflık, and two others made their appearance in the Vilâyet of Beirut. Two more followed in 1909, one in the Mutasarrıflık of Jerusalem, and the other in the Vilâyet of Beirut. Moreover, the Jewish suburbs outside the city walls of

31. *Ha-Ẓevi,* xxvi, 28 (1.11.1909).
32. *Ha-Ẓevi,* xxvi, 29 (2.11.1909).

Jerusalem were expanding, in view of the availability of freehold (*mülk*) land on the periphery of the city; and, in 1909, Tel Aviv was founded just north of Jaffa.

Besides Ruḥi Bey, there were other Arabs in the Mutasarrıflık who were concerned about Jewish land purchases. In October 1909, Albert Antébi reported that local "nationalistes Turcs," together with "les sectaires antisémites," were forming a group to oppose land sales to Jews.[33] Nothing more, however, was heard of this group until Antébi mentioned it again early in 1911, stating that the Nashashibi family of Jerusalem was behind it.[34] If it functioned as a group at all (and this seems doubtful), it probably confined itself to direct approaches to the authorities in Jerusalem to curb Jewish land purchases.

But whether or not it functioned as a group, the references to "nationalistes Turcs" and "les sectaires antisémites" are particularly interesting, as they may be regarded as the earliest categories of Arab anti-Zionists, properly speaking. By "Turkish nationalists," Antébi probably meant Arab notables among the political élite, who were deeply attached to the Ottoman Empire and who generally supported the CUP. Their opposition to Zionism derived from their fundamental loyalty to the Empire, and the belief that the Zionist Movement, as a nationalist, "secessionist" movement, might be a danger to the Empire as a whole, of which they—as Muslims—felt very much a part. In the following pages it will be convenient to describe this category of Arab anti-Zionists as "Ottoman loyalists." In 1909, Ḥafiz Bey al-Saʿid may have been representative of them for, as will be recalled, his parliamentary question inquired if Zionism was compatible with the interests of the *Empire* at large.

By "anti-Semitic sectarians," Antébi must surely have been referring to those Arabs—both Christian and Muslim—whose anti-Jewish sentiments had heightened over the previous quarter of a century and, as noted in Chapter Two, had been affected by European anti-Semitism. In June 1910 Antébi remarked that anti-Jewishness had become one's "daily bread in Palestine".[35] According to him, the attentions of those dispensing it were drawn to the Zionists, partly by the actions of the Zionists themselves (probably

33. *AIU* IX E 27 (18.10.1909), Antébi to Frank.
34. *AIU* X E 29 (4.1.1910 [= 1910]), Antébi to S. Loupo (Miqve Yisraʿel).
35. *AIU* IX E 28 (3.6.1910), Antébi to Pres., AIU.

a reference to the more assertive members of the Second Aliya),[36] and partly by the Ottoman authorities, whose official hostility to the Zionist Movement was being openly communicated to the local population.[37]

In addition to these two groups, three other trends gradually developed among Arab opponents of Zionism. The first was a direct response to the continuing Zionist work in Palestine, and was almost entirely confined to Arabs in the country. The other two emerged under the impact of wider political developments in the Ottoman Empire, and for the most part affected Arabs who lived outside Palestine.

The first trend, already making itself felt in 1910, was opposition to Zionism on grounds of what might be called local patriotism. That is to say, certain Arabs in Palestine began to perceive Zionist immigration and other activities as a direct threat to the position and well-being of the indigenous population. At first these local Arabs saw the "threat" to Palestine as additional to the alleged danger of the Zionist Movement to the Ottoman Empire as a whole. As a group, therefore, they were probably close to the Ottoman loyalists, and judging by his interview with *ha-Ẓevi*, Saʿid Bey al-Ḥusayni may have been representative of them. By 1911, however, this "threat" to Palestine was perceived as a separate danger, independent of whatever implications the Zionist Movement may have had for the Empire as a whole. On the basis not only of his interview with *ha-Ẓevi* but also of his subsequent actions, Ruḥi Bey al-Khalidi was representative of the trend. In time it also embraced local Arabs, Muslim and Christian, who were not necessarily supporters of the CUP or part of the traditional élite (like Ruḥi Bey).

As a result of its policies, the CUP soon acquired many enemies throughout the Empire. For reasons that will be explained, the Committee was vulnerable to attack on the Zionist issue. The attacks were unjustified, but the CUP's enemies were nevertheless quick to make whatever political capital they could out of this weak spot. In 1910, most of those involved in the campaign against the CUP were not Arabs but Turks and Ottoman Greeks. However, by

36. *AIU* IX E 28 (28.6.1910), Antébi to Pres., AIU.

37. Re Mutasarrıf of Jerusalem, *AIU* IX E 28 (3.7.1910), same to same; re Kaymakam of Jaffa (29.9.1910), same to same; also *ha-Or*, i, 121 (3.8.1910) and 122 (4.8.1910); re public prosecutor in Haifa and others, *ha-Mevasser*, i, 40 (18.10.1910).

the early summer of 1911, many Arabs, mainly Muslims living outside Palestine, had joined them. At first, their hostility to Zionism was "tactical," that is to say, subordinate to their wider opposition to the CUP and, it should be added, to things non-Muslim in general. But, by mid-1912, their antagonism to Zionism in its own right was hardening, and the first faint calls for "Muslim unity" to confront the Zionists were sounded in Beirut.

Christian Arabs appear to have lent the CUP their support for longer than the Muslims, but only a little longer. By the close of 1912, as a result of the first Balkan War and other factors, some Arab adversaries of the CUP, both Muslim and Christian, inclined towards Arab nationalism—either in its milder form of seeking "reform" in the Arab provinces or, in a minority of cases, in its more radical form of seeking complete independence of the Empire.

The Arab nationalists—ideologically important, though numerically a very small group—were not of one mind about Zionism. Partly because their early leaders came from areas outside Palestine and partly because they included Christian Arabs, they tended to view the question in a broader, almost "Pan-Arab" perspective. This allowed them in 1913 to contemplate the possibility of working with the Zionists and of seeking an agreement with them. But there were others among the nationalists who disagreed and who, by 1914, were opposed to Zionism on principle.

These three trends of Arab anti-Zionism—opposition on grounds of local patriotism, Muslim unity, and Arab nationalism—took some years to emerge. However, they were foreshadowed in the Arabic press, which, with the (temporary) removal of censorship, came to life after the Young Turk Revolution and almost at once interested itself in Zionist activities in Palestine.[38] More than one newspaper, in Palestine and beyond, had negative things to say about Zionism, particularly after the Counterrevolution of April 1909.[39] Three newspapers—*al-Aṣmaʿi, Nahḍat al-ʿArab,* and *al-Ḥaḍara*—can in retrospect be seen to have given early expression to the three trends outlined above. In so doing, they were in advance, sometimes very much in advance, of their readers. So what they wrote in the years 1908, 1909, and 1910 must be taken not as

38. *AIU* VIII E 25 (23.10.1908) Antébi to E. Saphir and M. Dizengoff (both Jaffa).
39. *Ha-Ḥerut,* i, 24 (23.7.1909); *CZA* L2/167 (5.8.1909), S. Muyal (Jaffa) to Zionist Office (Jaffa); *ha-Ẓevi* xxv, 240 (9.8.1909); and *ha-Ḥerut,* ii, 98 (25.5.1910).

reflecting an existing situation, but as an augury of forthcoming developments.

Before 1908 there was no Arabic press in Palestine, except for an official gazette—scarcely a newspaper—published in Jerusalem in Arabic and Turkish. Immediately after the Revolution, two small papers began to appear in the Mutasarrıflık: *al-Quds* in Jerusalem and *al-Aṣmaʿi* in Jaffa. A little later, *al-Karmil* (of which much will be said) was founded in Haifa. From the outset, *al-Aṣmaʿi* criticised the Jewish newcomers from a position of what has been called local patriotism. It was resentful of the privileges which the immigrants enjoyed under the Capitulations, and regarded the Jews as a threat to the local population.[40]

> They harm the local population and wrong them, by relying on the special rights accorded to foreign powers in the Ottoman Empire and on the corruption and treachery of the local administration. Moreover, they are free from most of the taxes and heavy impositions on Ottoman subjects. Their labour competes with the local population and creates their own means of sustenance. The local population cannot stand up to their competition.[41]

Al-Aṣmaʿi proposed various courses of action to counter this competition. Locally produced goods should be bought in preference to "foreign" (that is, Jewish) ones;[42] and wealthy Arabs should promote local commerce and industry.[43]

The paper was also concerned with the situation of the Arab peasant who, it suggested, should adopt the Jews' agricultural methods. To illustrate its point, *al-Aṣmaʿi* compared the low standard of living in large Arab villages with that in Jewish colonies, which were much smaller but supported the same number of people. The fellahin eked out a mean existence, mainly because they were ignorant and rotated their land among themselves. The Jewish settlers worked their land intensively and did well. The moral was that the younger generation of Arabs should learn Jewish techniques.[44]

The second trend—Arab opposition to Zionism on grounds of Muslim unity—evolved from a fabric of much wider opposition to

40. *AIU* VIII E 25 (21.10.1908), Antébi to Frank.
41. *Ha-Poʿel Ha-Ẓaʿir,* ii, I (1908), pp. 14–15.
42. *Loc. cit.*
43. *Ibid.,* ii, 3 (1908), p. 10.
44. *Ibid.,* ii, 1 (1908), pp. 14–15.

the CUP covering large parts of the Ottoman Empire. Among the reasons for the Counterrevolution in 1909 was the fear that the secular-minded members of the Committee were endangering the *shariʿa* (Islamic religious law) and even the Muslim character of the Empire. After the Counterrevolution, this fear took on a different form, and one of the more damaging accusations made against the CUP was that it was dominated by Jews and Freemasons.

With a little imagination and a willingness to disregard the facts for political purposes, this empty charge could be easily spun into an alarming plot along the following lines. Jewish influence among the Freemasons was said to be "frightening." The Freemasons had created the CUP to bring about the downfall of the Ottoman Empire. The end of this great but weak Muslim empire could be accelerated by undermining its Islamic institutions and imposing a Constitution and other European trappings on it. After the Empire had collapsed, the Jews, operating through the Freemasons in the CUP, would emerge and establish the "Kingdom of Israel" anew.

For all its transparency, this conspiratorial theory was presented in full to the Arabs as early as May 1909 in *Nahḍat al-ʿArab,* a periodical sponsored by the "Syrian Central Committee," an obscure (and probably minuscule) Arab group in Paris.[45] In its sixth number, it printed an unsigned letter alleging that the CUP's success derived from its links with Jews and Freemasons, and that the Jews' aim was to found a state in Palestine on the ruins of the Ottoman Empire.[46] The writer's reasoning was tortuous.

> The Jews say as follows: [Observant] Turkish and Arab Muslims will not be able in any circumstances to live in peace and quiet, and enjoy freedom and equality in a [constitutional] state based on a Muslim Caliphate. And what will happen then? The Turkish and Arab Muslims will rebel against the free-thinkers, disputes will break out between them, and then the Great Powers will intervene and protect Jewish interests. This will lead to conflicts and hatred between the different

45. Cf. *PRO* FO 371/561, enc. to F45494 (25.12.1908).
46. *Ha-Ḥerut,* i, 20 (14.7.1909), reprinting letter from *Nahḍat al-ʿArab.* From this point onwards *ha-Ḥerut,* the newspaper of Sephardi Jews in Jerusalem, is frequently cited as a source. Speaking Arabid, its editors were highly sensitive to changes in opinion among other segments of the local population towards the Jews. Thus they regularly reprinted in accurate Hebrew translation articles on Zionism from Arabic papers which are otherwise unavailable.

elements in the Empire. Order will break down; the rulers will be lost; and the Jews will finally achieve their desire.

To support his argument, the writer claimed, incorrectly, that most of the soldiers who had restored the CUP to power in April were Jews,[47] and that there had been two Jews in the delegation of four which informed Abdülhamid of his deposition.[48] The *New York Herald* and the *Berliner Tageblatt* had, he said, reported that all the leaders of the CUP were protégés of Emanuel Karasu, a Jew and a Freemason. Then, turning to his readers, he asked, "Do you not see that [the Jews] have already taken the reins of government in their hand, and that shortly they will unfurl the Jewish flag?" Therefore, "which Muslim is not bound to consider the danger threatening him from the Jews?"

Though often repeated, the myth of a dominant role played by Jews and Freemasons within the CUP has been disproved by Professor Bernard Lewis.[49] Before the Revolution, the Young Turks met in Masonic lodges to ensure secrecy. Jews had been members of the CUP, though not disproportionately so. In August 1908, a Young Turk named Refik Bey described in *Le Temps* the secret meetings held in Masonic lodges;[50] and in the same month Harry Lamb, the British Consul-General in Salonika, remarked that Emanuel Karasu, "as the introducer of freemasonry into Macedonia and head of the Salonika Masonic Lodge . . . has rendered important services to the Young Turk cause."[51] However, the letter in *Nahḍat al-ʿArab* is one of the earliest published instances where popular notions about Freemasons and Jews were brought together by the CUP's enemies to produce a double-edged indictment of the Committee. Freemasonry in Turkish (*farmasonluk*) implied "atheism of the most condemnable character"[52]—an accusation which had frequently been levelled against prominent Young Turks. And the image of the grasping, cosmopolitan Jew was not unfamiliar among the Turks and other peoples in the Empire.[53]

47. There was a Jewish volunteer unit in the "Corps of Operations" which quashed the Counterrevolution.
48. In fact, Karasu was the only Jew in the delegation.
49. Lewis, pp. 207–8, n. 4; cf. Ramsaur, p. 106.
50. Ramsaur, p. 107.
51. *PRO* FO 371/549/F 30972, no. 114 (24.8.1908), H. H. Lamb (Salonika) to Sir G. A. Lowther (Consple.).
52. Ramsaur, p. 111, quoting J. P. Brown, *The Darvishes* (London, 1927), p. 64.
53. See Galanté, *Le Juif dans le proverbe*, pp. 11–21.

Not long after the Counterrevolution, various anti-CUP groups began to exploit this charge, regardless of whether they believed it or not. But despite the letter in *Nahḍat al-ᶜArab,* these groups were not Arabs in the first instance and often not even Muslims. It was only after the spectre of Jewish domination had had an influence on Ottoman politics that certain Muslim Arab foes of the CUP made any significant use of this fantasy. And then it was only after it had gained some currency in the Arab provinces that a few of them began, in 1912, to call for Muslim unity against Jewish presence in Palestine.

The third trend of Arab anti-Zionism derived from Arab nationalism. Even though it was the last to emerge fully, expressions of it were to be found by the end of 1910 in *al-Ḥaḍara,* an Arabic newspaper appearing in Constantinople. In December of that year, this paper published a serious attack on the Zionists by an Arab who wrote under the evocative pseudonym of "Ṣalaḥ al-Din al-Ayyubi" ("Saladin") and who was subsequently identified as Shukri al-ᶜAsali, the Kaymakam of Nazareth.[54] Shortly afterwards, another article appeared in *al-Ḥaḍara,* by Rafiq Bey al-ᶜAẓm of Damascus, accusing the Zionists of disloyalty to the Empire and of seeking to reestablish the Kingdom of Israel.[55] The significant fact in the present context is not that certain Arab publicists should have taken their opposition to Zionism direct to the Ottoman capital by the end of 1910. It was that Shukri al-ᶜAsali, Rafiq al-ᶜAẓm, and one of *al-Ḥaḍara's* editors, ᶜAbd al-Ḥamid al-Zahrawi, were soon to emerge as prominent Arab nationalist leaders who were much concerned with the Zionist question and who dealt personally with Zionists in Palestine and elsewhere, especially in the years 1913 and 1914.

These different trends among Arabs hostile to Zionism evolved only gradually. In the process, the earlier categories of opposition—stemming from Ottoman loyalism and anti-Semitism—continued to exist alongside them. And since in part they were interrelated (for example, local patriotism beginning as an adjunct to Ottoman loyalism) or flowed from one another (anti-Semitism preceding apprehensions about Jewish influence in the CUP, preceding calls for Muslim unity), most Arabs who opposed Zionism did so for

54. *Ha-Ḥerut,* iii, 27 (23.12.1910).
55. *Ha-Ḥerut,* iii, 59 (1.3.1911).

a combination of reasons. In Palestine the most commonly held position was based on Ottoman loyalism coupled with local patriotism. To these could be added other elements which varied from group to group, depending on religion, occupation, political orientation, and so forth.

The man who best articulated this "mixed" stand was Najib al-Khuri Naṣṣar, editor of the Haifa newspaper, *al-Karmil,* whom Elie Krause had named as one of the instigators of the raids on Sejera in the spring of 1909. Without doubt, Naṣṣar proved himself the most active and vocal Arab anti-Zionist in Palestine before 1914. As well as attacking the Zionists violently through his newspaper, he rallied other newspapers to his cause, published the first book in Arabic on Zionism, and was responsible for organizing a variety of anti-Zionist activities. He therefore merits special attention.

Born in Tiberias, Naṣṣar was a Protestant of Greek Orthodox origin.[56] He had worked for fifteen years in a hospital run in Tiberias by Dr. David Torrance, the Free Church of Scotland's missionary[57] (under whose influence he may well have become a Protestant). He had also worked for some years with JCA as a land-agent.[58] According to two Jewish accounts, Naṣṣar founded *al-Karmil* at the end of 1908 after falling out with JCA (either over payment or terms of employment), with the express purpose "of writing against the Jewish newcomers in Palestine so that the Arabs would not continue to sell land to the Jews."[59]

The disagreement must have been very violent if it was the sole reason for founding *al-Karmil.* It would seem more probable that, in the course of his experience as a land-agent for JCA, Naṣṣar had reached the conclusion that over time the Jews were capable of buying up the whole of Palestine. As a supporter of the CUP, he regarded this possibility as a threat both to the Empire at large and to the position of the Arabs in Palestine in particular.

It was logical therefore that first Naṣṣar should direct his efforts principally against land sales to Jews, and by the beginning of 1910 it seems clear that his words were not falling on deaf ears. The British Vice-Consul at Haifa, for example, summing up the popular

56. *Q d'O* N.S. 132, no. 37 (20.9.1913), Grappin [?] (Haifa) to Pichon.
57. *Ha-Ḥerut,* iv, 158 (7.7.1912).
58. *AIU* I C 1–2 (8.8.1911), I. Nahon (Haifa) to Pres., AIU; and *CZA* L4/276/IIB (1.6.1919), C. Kalvarisky (notes).
59. Malul, p. 446; and *ha-Ḥerut,* iii, 6 (4.11.1910).

mood, reported that "the natives, chiefly the Christians, do not relish [the Jewish immigrants'] strengthening their hold on the land."[60]

Complaints by Jews against articles in *al-Karmil* resulted in its temporary suspension in the early summer of 1909,[61] and again in the winter of that year.[62] After an article entitled "Settlement or Devastation?" written by Naṣṣar in February 1910,[63] the Haham Başı in Constantinople demanded that Naṣṣar be brought to trial on charges of founding *al-Karmil* "solely to spread discord and sow dissension between the Jews and other Ottomans" and of "explaining the Torah as it suits [him]."[64] Naṣṣar was duly arraigned in Haifa, but on 30 May was acquitted on the grounds that he only had the best interests of the Empire at heart. Explaining the verdict, a court official commented that "he attacks Zionism alone, rightly so . . . all these trivial words in his articles are of no consequence."[65]

So Naṣṣar pressed on with his campaign. As a further argument against land sales to Jews, he alleged that many peasants were being forced to emigrate or live the life of bedouin.[66] In November he published an open letter from a Haifa notable urging Aḥmad al-Rimawi, the Muslim editor of *al-Najaḥ,* a short-lived newspaper in Jerusalem, to "look around and see what has happened."[67] Al-Rimawi acknowledged this call and in reply invited Naṣṣar to come to see how Jerusalem and the surrounding area were falling into the hands of the Jews and other foreigners. "We have no alternative but to accept your words, to adhere to your summons, to thank you for your alertness and to say to patriots [*waṭaniyyun*] in Jerusalem: 'Wake up, slumberers, wake up!' "[68]

By temperament, Naṣṣar appears to have been an activist, bent on taking his cause to a wider audience. In the months after the Young Turk Revolution, JCA had put in bids to acquire extensive crown

60. *PRO* FO 195/2342, enc. to no. 7 (12.2.1910), H. A. Cumberbatch (Beirut) to Lowther.
61. *Ha-Ḥerut,* i 13 (22.6.1909).
62. *Ha-Ḥerut,* ii, 57 (7.2.1910).
63. *Ha-Ḥerut,* ii, 60 (14.2.1910) re *al-Karmil,* no. 50; cf. *ha-Ḥerut,* ii, 89 (4.5.1910).
64. *Ha-Ḥerut,* ii, 98 (25.5.1910).
65. *Ha-Ḥerut,* ii, 103 (6.6.1910).
66. *L'Aurore,* ii, 58 (29.7.1910).
67. *Ha-Ḥerut,* iii, 26 (21.12.1910).
68. *Ibid.*

lands (çiftliks) in Iraq and the Jordan Valley[69] Baron Rothschild of Paris had also tendered for land in the Jordan Valley.[70] At the same time—though quite independently—an Arab from Beirut, called Najib al-Aṣfar, was negotiating with the Government for the purchase of all çiftliks in the Vilâyet of Şam ("Syria") and Palestine. In the middle of 1910, it was put about, wrongly, that al-Aṣfar was acting on behalf of the Jews.[71] Taking advantage of this rumour, Naṣṣar was able to persuade the editors of three newspapers in Beirut (*al-Mufid, al-Ḥaqiqa* and *al-Raʿy al-ʿAmm*) and one in Damascus (*al-Muqtabas*) to join his campaign against the Zionists.[72]

In terms of added weight to his campaign, this amounted to a considerable increment. At this stage, *al-Karmil* was a bi-weekly whose limited readership could scarcely have extended far beyond Haifa and the north of Palestine. Like most of the early Arabic newspapers to write against Zionism, it was edited by a Christian. On the other hand, the four newspapers which Naṣṣar enlisted to his cause in 1910 were relatively large and were edited by Muslims. They appeared in cities which were the administrative centres of the two provinces surrounding Palestine and where no anti-Zionist voices had previously been raised in the press. *Al-Muqtabas* in Damascus was the most important of them, being edited by Muḥammad Kurd ʿAli, who became a major literary figure in the Arab world. Moreover, with the exception of *al-Ḥaqiqa* (a bi-weekly), all were dailies.

A detailed discussion of the Arabic press *per se* (as distinct from referring to it as a guide to the future) will be presented in Chapter Six. Suffice to say here that, as more anti-Zionist articles were written in a widening circle of Arabic newspapers from 1910 onwards, more arguments against Zionism were worked out. In December 1910 many of them were marshalled by Shukri al-ʿAsali in an open letter addressed to Sami Paşa al-Faruqi, an Arab general in the Ottoman army, who was then engaged in putting down disorders in the Hauran.

69. *CZA* L2/34/I (24.10.1908), Jacobson to A. Ruppin (Jaffa); and *AIU* IX E 26 (15.3.1909), Antébi to Pres., AIU.
70. Cf. *Q d'O* N.S. 132, no. 41 (27.7.1909), Gueyraud to Pichon.
71. Cf. *CZA* Z2/9 (28.10.1910), Jacobson to H. Kann.
72. Malul, p. 446; cf. *ha-Ḥerut,* iii, 6 (4.11.1910); and *CZA* L2/50/I "Note sur l'état d'insécurité dont souffre la population israélite dans les [sic] caza de Tibériade" [undated and unsigned (ca. end 1911)].

Shukri al-ᶜAsali was a member of a distinguished Damascus family. After an early education at home and administrative training in Constantinople, he had entered the Ottoman provincial administration in his middle twenties, and had served as Governor of Latakia before taking up his post as Kaymakam of Nazareth in his early forties.[73] In January 1911, the British Consul in Damascus described him as a man "of superior intelligence. . . . He knows both Turkish and Arabic, and law remarkably well; and in the offices he has held, ever acted with justice and energy. His views are liberal and wide minded, . . . a man of high character, and of opinion strongly progressive and possibly even ultra-radical, but who has always gained for himself universal esteem and sympathy."[74]

It was a fair assessment of the man to suggest that his opinions were "possibly even ultra-radical" because, unknown to the Consul, al-ᶜAsali was a member of *al-Qaḥṭaniyya,* a secret Arab nationalist society founded in Constantinople in 1909.[75]

His open letter to Sami Paşa was published by *al-Muqtabas* in Damascus and then by *al-Karmil* in Haifa.[76] Writing under the pseudonym of "Saladin" (the name which he had used in *al-Ḥaḍara*), al-ᶜAsali began by quoting Jeremiah 32:44. "Men shall buy fields for money, and subscribe evidences, and seal them and take witnesses in the land of Benjamin, and in the places about Jerusalem, and in the cities of Judah, and in the cities of the mountains, and in the cities of the valley, and in the cities of the south: for I will cause their captivity to return, saith the Lord."

The Zionist Movement, in conjunction with the Jewish Colonization Association, the Alliance Israélite Universelle, the *faᶜulim* (sic, a colloquial Arabic form of *poᶜalim*—Hebrew for the Jewish workers) and others, was attempting to fulfil this prophecy by purchasing land in Palestine. According to al-ᶜAsali, Abdülhamid's régime had prevented Jewish settlement, but now, under the new régime, corrupt officials and treacherous Arab landowners had enabled the Jews to dominate wide expanses of territory. He

73. Al-Zirakli, iii, 250.
74. *PRO* FO 195/2370, no. 5 (25.1.1911), G. P. Devey (Damascus) to C. M. Marling (Consple.).
75. Antonius, p. 110, n. 2.
76. *Ha-Ḥerut,* iii, 26 (21.12.1910), translating in full the open letter from *al-Karmil* of 8.12.1910; cf. incomplete versions in *al-Muqtabas* [mohthly review], vi, 2 (1911), pp. 121–22; and M. Kurd ᶜAli, *Kitab khiṭaṭ al-sham* (Damascus, 1925–28), iii, 131–33.

described these areas—with undisguised exaggeration—as "three-quarters of the Kaza of Tiberias, half of the Kaza of Safed, more than half of Jerusalem and of the Kaza of Jaffa, as well as the most important part of Haifa itself plus some of its villages." And now, he contended, "they are trying to enter the Kaza of Nazareth to gain mastery over the Valley of Sharon and Jezreel." He continued:

They do not mix with the Ottomans, and do not buy anything from them. They own the Anglo-Palestine Bank which makes loans to them at a rate not exceeding 1 per cent *per annum.* Every village has set up an administrative office and a school, every kaza a central administration, and every district has a general administrator. They have a blue flag in the middle of which is a "Star of David," and below that is a Hebrew word meaning "Zion," because in the Torah Jerusalem is called the "Daughter of Zion." They raise this flag instead of the Ottoman flag at their celebrations and gatherings; and they sing the Zionist anthem. They have deceived the Government with lying and falsehood when they enrol themselves as Ottoman subjects in the registers, for they continue to carry foreign passports which protect them; and whenever they go to the Ottoman courts, they produce their passports and summon foreign protection; they settle their claims and differences amongst themselves with the knowledge of the administrator, and they do not turn to the Government. They teach their children physical training and the use of arms; you see their houses crammed with weapons, among them many Martini rifles. They have a special postal service, special stamps, etc., which proves that they have begun setting up their political aims and establishing their imaginary government. If the Government does not set a limit to this torrential stream, no time will pass before you see that Palestine has become a property of the Zionist Organization and its associates or of the nation mentioned above [the Jews].

Although the press was in advance of its readers, it is worth examining briefly some of these arguments and the way in which they were deployed, since they were used time and again by Arab publicists writing against Zionism. According to al-ʿAsali, the Jews claimed a divine right to Palestine, and the Zionists, hand in hand with other *non-Zionist* Jewish groups, were acting vigorously on it. They were disloyal to the Ottoman Empire. They took advantage of their privileges under the Capitulations. They had already acquired large tracts of land, and were trying to buy much more. They did not integrate with the local population. They had political aims. They had their own national symbols. They were creating their own institutions for self-government and self-defence. Abdülhamid had tried to prevent Jewish settlement in Palestine. The CUP, on the other hand, was facilitating it. Officials were venal, and Arab landowners treacherous. Unless action was taken, Palestine was lost.

There was some truth in a number of these arguments. The Zionists were interested in acquiring land, and were developing their own institutions. They were reluctant to become Ottoman subjects and give up the consular protection and other benefits they enjoyed as foreign nationals—privileges which were deeply resented by the local population, who had to pay heavier taxes, serve in the Ottoman army, and make do with the dubious justice of the Ottoman courts.

At the same time, many of al-ᶜAsali's arguments were clearly put in a very tendentious manner. For example, if he had wished to be fair, he should have said that the Anglo-Palestine Company offered loans, not at 1 per cent interest, but at rates customarily charged by banks in Europe, which were much lower than the usurious rates demanded by Arab moneylenders. Similarly, while it was true that the Jewish settlers were armed, so were their Arab neighbours. And it was slightly incongruous for a member of a secret Arab nationalist society to accuse the Jews of being disloyal to the Empire.

Moreover, much of what al-ᶜAsali said was not merely slanted but untrue. For example, the CUP were not facilitating Jewish settlement in Palestine. The Jews had not taken over the greater part of the Mutasarrıflık of Jerusalem or the Sancak of Acre. At the time of his writing, they were about 11 per cent of the total population of Palestine and they possessed less than 2 per cent of the land in the country (about 500,000 dunams out of a total of 27 million dunams).[77] Al-ᶜAsali was much nearer the mark when he accused the Ottoman officials of corruption and when he spoke out against Arab landowners who were very willing to sell land to Jews. According to al-ᶜAsali, they considered themselves part of the country's aristocracy, but to him they were criminals whom "God has denied all feelings of national honour and love of the homeland."

Al-ᶜAsali's open letter conveys very well the tone of much that was being written against the Zionists in the Arabic press by the end of 1910, though of course the emphasis varied from article to article.

77. *CZA* Z2/635 (31.3.1911), enclosing memorandum by Ruppin.

عدد ٢٣ — جريدة هزلية انتقادية فكاهية اسبوعية مصورة — السنة الاولى

صاحب الجريدة ومحررها
توفيق جانا

« اشتراك الحمارة »
في بيروت عن سنة مجيدي واحد
في الممالك الاجنبية عن سنة فرنك ١٠

الحمارة حرة في نشر وعدم نشر
ما يرد اليها من الرسائل

الاعلانات يتفق عليها مع الادارة

الحماره

المدير المسئول
نجيب جانا

« اشتراك الحمارة »
في الممالك المحروسة عن سنة مجيدي وربع
عن نصف سنة ثلاثة ارباع مجيدي

جميع المخابرات يجب ان تكون باسم
ادارة جريدة « الحمارة »
في بيروت

يا للحمائر ما احلى براذعها فكم امانت واحيت فيه من كدش * يرى الاديب بها علاً ومعرفة ولا تراها ذوات الاعين العمش

بيروت الجمعه في ٧ ربيع الثاني ١٣٢٩ وه٢ اذار سنة ١٣٢٧ ش و ٧ نيسان سنة ١٩١١

ص · — ابعد عن هذه القلعة يا خداع والا سلطت عليك جنود احفادي ولا تقرب قلعة فتحتها بدماء المسلمين ·

خ — وانا ماذا يهمني طالما في جيبي الباسابورط وورائي خمسة عشر مليونا من الليرات اشبع بها بطون اعيان البلاد الجائعة واداوي بها معدة كبار المأمورين من الجرب فكل يوم لي فوله ·

ص · — حيله كار تلكى بو قلعه يه ياقلاشمه يوقسه احفادمك عسكريني سكا مسلط ايدرم بو قلعه يى مسلمانلرك قانيله فتح ايتدم ·

خ · — بكا نه جيبمده پاسابورط ارقمده اون بش مليون ليرا وارايكن اعيان اهالينك آج قارنلرينى طويورر (واو يوزه) مبتلا اولان بيوك مأمورلرك معده لرينى تداوي ايده يلدكجه هر كون بر فوله اليرم

Al-Ḥimara, i, 23 (7.4.1911).

The caption reads, both in Turkish and Arabic:

"Ṣ[alaḥ al-Din] - 'Keep away from this fortress, you swindler, or else I shall set upon you the armies of my descendants and you will not come near a fortress which I conquered with Muslim blood.'

"H[ankin] - 'What does that matter to me, as long as [my foreign] passport is in my pocket and behind me [there are] fifteen million pounds with which I shall sate the hungry bellies of the notables of the country and with which I shall cure of the itch the high officials' stomach? And every day I'll have a Fula.' "

Al-ᶜAsali was an Arab nationalist and his views colour his words. Most other Arab publicists were not, so the main thrust of their attacks was that the Zionists were a danger to the Ottoman Empire or Palestine or both.

In spite of its tendentiousness and inaccuracies, not all the newspaper attacks on the Zionists were on the level of al-ᶜAsali's open letter, as can be seen from the cartoon shown above. The high rate of illiteracy among the Arabs and in the Empire in general led to the appearance of humorous reviews aimed at the less educated and presenting their political message pictorially.[78] One of these publications was *al-Ḥimara* of Beirut, which began lampooning the Zionists from its very first editions at the end of 1910.[79] In April 1911, after a public storm over the sale of some land at Fula (near Nazareth) to the Zionists, it printed the cartoon reproduced here. Saladin, the Muslim hero who drove the Crusaders out of the Holy Land, is threatening a grossly caricatured Jew pouring gold into the outstretched palm of either an Ottoman official or an Arab landowner. Saladin would be recognised as Shukri al-ᶜAsali and the Jew as Joshua Hankin, a Zionist land-agent. Between them are the emotive elements of the Hijaz Railway and a Crusader castle conquered by Saladin. The caption incorporates other elements used by Shukri al-ᶜAsali in his open letter to General Sami Paşa: the foreign passports and the financial resources of the Jews. The anti-Semitic aspect of the whole presentation cannot be overlooked.

78. Emin, p. 89.
79. *Ha-Ḥerut,* iii, 27 (23.12.1910).

5

Two Debates: March and May 1911

ZIONISM was discussed at length in the Ottoman Parliament on two occasions in the first half of 1911. Over the previous year uncertainty about the Zionist Movement had spread among various Ottoman circles, and the opponents of the Committee of Union and Progress took advantage of this during the first debate. Hence the issue was raised as part of a wider political assault on the CUP, and Arab deputies did not participate. The second debate was set against the background of protests in Palestine over land sales to Zionists. It was therefore an Arab occasion—and, given its objectives, an Arab defeat.

The attitude of CUP leaders and the Government to Zionism from the time of the Counterrevolution until the ninth Zionist Congress in December 1909 was described in the preceding chapter. Other Ottomans, beyond Government circles, would have heard the allegation that the CUP was dominated by Freemasons and Jews, but in the main they were probably ignorant of the Zionist Movement and its aims. Some of them—politicians, intellectuals, newspaper editors and the like—learnt more in January 1910 when Jacobus Kahn, a Dutch member of the Zionist Executive, sent them copies of the newly made French translation of his book, *Erets Israël—The Jewish Land.*

Although Kann had originally written this book before the

Young Turk Revolution in a private capacity, it was inevitably received as an authoritative statement of the Zionist Executive's position in 1910. It played down Palestine's commercial and strategic importance and called for a Jewish majority in the country, a Jewish army and police force, and an extension of the millet system to give Jewish secular leaders an autonomous government. Many of Kann's ideas were derived from Theodor Herzl, but as official Zionist policy since Herzl's death had moved away from "political Zionism" (that is, seeking an independent Jewish state) to "practical Zionism" (that is, consolidating the New Yishuv through immigration and settlement), Zionist representatives in Constantinople—not to speak of Ottoman Jews—thought that Kann's act was a major political blunder.[1]

The activities of other Jewish groups hoping to settle Jewish immigrants in the Empire also caused some confusion among influential Ottomans who were less informed than the Government about Zionism and its aims. The Jewish Colonization Association and the Alliance Israélite Universelle had maintained their interest in the possibility of acquiring lands on which to settle persecuted Jews and, in addition, Dr. Alfred Nossig, a one-time Zionist living in Berlin, spoke to leading Ottoman politicians in 1909 and again in 1910 about an organisation which he had set up himself, called the Allgemeine Jüdische Kolonisations-Organisation. Nossig explained that his organisation was not a Zionist society, that it did not seek national autonomy (implying that the Zionist Movement did), and that it aimed to settle Jews in Iraq.[2] Although JCA was permitted to survey certain lands in Asia Minor and Iraq,[3] the result of all these Jewish approaches to the Ottoman Government was to damage the Zionists' public image, and to make many prominent Ottomans wonder whether JCA and the other

1. *CZA* Z2/9 (29.1. and 15.2.1910), both V. Jabotinsky (Consple.) to D. Wolffsohn (Cologne); cf. *CZA* Z2/9 (12.2.1910), record of a meeting with the Haham Başı (Consple.).
2. *CZA* Z2/8 (8.11.1909), V. Jacobson (Consple.) to Wolffsohn; cf. *PRO* FO 371/992/177, no. 992 (27.12.1909), C. M. Marling (Consple.) to Sir E. Grey (FO); and *PRO* FO 371/992/32231, no. 621 (31.8.1910), Sir G. Lowther (Consple.) to Grey.
3. *AIX* IX E 27 (16.7.1909), H. Frank (Jaffa) to A. Antébi (Jerus.); *Q d'O* N.S. 132, no. 41 (27.7.1909), G. Gueraud (Jerus.) to S. Pichon (Paris); and *AIU* IX E 27 (15.9.1909), Antébi to Frank.

organisations involved were not Zionist organisations in disguise.[4]

Besides, there were Ottoman Jews who were opposed to the Zionist Movement and were actively working against it among leading Ottoman circles. Most of them lived in Salonika, where Jews and Dönmes formed the majority of the population and, equally important, where the CUP's headquarters were located. These Jewish anti-Zionists fell into three groups.[5] First, there were followers of the city's Haham Başı, who appears to have feared that the Zionists might compromise the position of the Jews in the Empire at large. Then, there were graduates of schools run by the Alliance Israélite Universelle, which was resolutely anti-Zionist during this period. And finally, there were members of the Club des Intimes, a Jewish society which supported the Government's Ottomanisation policy. They had made Dr. Nazım Bey of the CUP's Central Committee an honorary member of their club.

Moreover, the Zionist Movement was beginning to be dragged into the web of European power politics (in all probability unawares). By the time of the Young Turk Revolution, the Great Powers were divided between the Triple Alliance (Germany, Austro-Hungary and Italy) and the Triple Entente (Great Britain, France and Russia). Germany had not only become the strongest Power in Europe, but also was continuing to advance her influence in the Ottoman Empire, an influence which had been growing since the 1880s at the expense of Britain and France. The competition between these Powers was unremitting and was sometimes carried to extraordinary lengths. As Theodor Herzl had presided over Zionist affairs from his home in the Austro-Hungarian capital of Vienna, and as David Wolffsohn conducted Zionist business from Germany after Herzl's death, certain British and French representatives in the Ottoman Empire seem to have seen the possibility of portraying the Zionist Movement as yet another device to spread German influence. The Chief Dragoman at the British Embassy, G. H. Fitzmaurice (an Irish Catholic and an influential official in the Embassy by virtue of his knowledge of the Turkish language and Ottoman ways), apparently accepted the notion that the CUP was dominated by Freemasons and

4. *CZA* Z2/9 (1.8.1910) Jacobson to Wolffsohn; and (7.9.1910), same to J. Kann (The Hague).
5. *CZA* Z2/11 (14.2.1911), Jacobson to Wolffsohn.

Jews.[6] In 1911 the pro-CUP daily, *Tanin,* accused him of intriguing against the Ottoman Government and of alleging that it was pro-Zionist. The German Embassy also believed that Fitzmaurice was not above suspicion and that he was responsible for floating the idea that Germany supported Zionism in the Empire for her own purposes.[7] The Zionists likewise believed that British diplomats had taken this line to discredit the Germans and frighten the Turks.[8]

The French employed similar tactics against the Germans in Salonika early in 1911. In January of that year, Kâzım Nami, a writer in Salonika, told *Imparcial,* a local Ladino paper, that the CUP would never allow the Zionists to realise their projects in Palestine, whatever their aim might be.[9] The French Consul took this as an opening to supply Kâzım Nami with material for a series of anti-Zionist—and anti-German—articles in *Rumeli,* a CUP organ in Salonika.[10] The first four articles were essentially a historical description of Zionism. In the fifth, which appeared in the middle of February, Kâzım Nami attacked Zionism for being a political movement and a "front" for German advancement.[11] At the very least, he claimed, Zionism constituted a Jewish national renaissance, even if it did not have disloyal political aims—which he found difficult to believe. Since the object of "a home in Palestine secured by public law" had been retained by the ninth Zionist Congress, Kâzım Nami accused the Zionists of seeking Great Power interference in the internal affairs of the Empire. The Empire from large Jewish immigration into Palestine were offset by the dangers inherent in such an influx. "Our Zionists, whether unwittingly or unwittingly, are or will become the tools of foreign [in other words, German] politics."

It must be doubted whether these British and French representatives were acting on instructions—beyond, perhaps, general guidelines to try to counter the growth of German influence in the Empire. Whether these particular manoeuvres were detrimental to

6. Cf. Kedourie, "Young Turks, Freemasons and Jews."
7. *PRO* (G) Türkei no. 195, K 692/II, no. 57 (3.3.1911), von Marschall (pera) to Reichskanzler (Berlin); and no. 202 (26.7.1911), Miquel (Therapia) to Reichskanzler.
8. *Ha-Mevasser,* ii, 15 (1911), pp. 168–70. 9. Cf. *Osmanischer Lloyd* (6.1.1911).
10. *Q d'O* N.S. 137, no. 33 (10.2.1911), M. Choublier (Salonika) to Pichon, enclosing translations of first four articles.
11. *PRO* FO 371/1244/7151, no. 121 (22.2.1911), Lowther to Grey, enclosing translation of fifth article.

the Germans is also open to doubt. But they certainly could not have helped the Zionists in the eyes of the Ottoman public.

During 1910 opposition to the CUP grew in the Balkans and elsewhere because of its Ottomanist policies. Moreover, by February 1911, the Committee was itself in the throes of an internal crisis. Many of its supporters in Parliament felt that the Government had fallen into the hands of a "clique" from Salonika, represented in the Cabinet by Tâlat Bey, Cavid Bey, and Halaçyan Efendi (the Minister of Public Works). The dissident pro-CUP deputies in Parliament were grouped around Colonel Sadık, the leader of the Manastır branch of the CUP, and the non-CUP Minister of War, Mahmud Şevket Paşa, who had clashed with Cavid Bey in October 1910 and who, it was thought at that time, might have led a military coup d'état against the Salonika group.[12]

In the hope of appeasing the Committee's internal opposition, Talât Bey resigned on 10 February 1911. A few days later he was followed by Halaçyan Efendi and the Minister of Education, who was also close to the Salonika group. In the middle of the month Haci Adil Bey, the Secretary-General of the CUP, saw Dr. Jacobson and made no bones about the fact that the Committee would have none of Zionism. It could not afford to begin to favour the Zionist Movement lest its enemies charge it with being bribed or even bought over by the Jews.[13]

But given all the factors just described—the widening public knowledge and uncertainty about the Zionist Movement, the activities of anti-Zionist Jews and foreign diplomats, and the presence of the CUP's headquarters in a largely Jewish city—it was not difficult for the Committee's critics, whether internal or external, to make political capital of the Zionist issue. In particular, they harped on the theme that Jews were working through the CUP to realise their aims in Palestine. Hence, by March 1911 the British Ambassador at Constantinople could report that "Zionism has in fact become one of the main undercurrents of the political situation."[14]

The general budget debate began on 22 February, and the Minister of Finance, Cavid Bey, came under severe attack. On 27

12. *PRO* FO 371/1070/40442, no. 800 (2.11.1910), Lowther to Grey.
13. *CZA* Z2/11 (16.2.1911), Jacobson to Wolffsohn.
14. *PRO* FO 371/1245/9105, no. 146 (7.3.1911), Lowther to Grey.

February, Kosmidi Efendi, a Greek deputy from Constantinople, asserted that most commercial concessions in the Empire were being granted to Jews and spoke of the Cabinet acting like "wild beasts of prey."[15] After him, Lütfi Fikri Bey of Dersim, who later in the year was one of the founders of the Liberal Union, "all but openly charged the Minister of Finance with being a Zionist by referring to his relations with Jacques Menasche . . . , Me Salem and the Minister's 'chef de cabinet,' Nessim Rousso."[16]

Zionism *per se* was raised two days later by the leader of the People's Party, İsmail Hakkı Bey of Gümülcüne. Having taken issue with much of Cavid's policy, he tried to show that the Cabinet "beyond all possible doubt . . . followed the same course as Zionism."[17] İsmail Hakkı Bey declared that the Zionist aim was to found a Jewish state in Palestine once a Jewish majority was achieved there. After "protests from all sides" and interjections by two Jewish deputies, İsmail Hakkı Bey claimed that the Jews had acquired vast lands in Palestine. When he quoted some recent Zionist resolutions, Tâlat Bey interrupted to remark that the Zionist Congress was not a secret. İsmail Hakkı Bey then alleged that the Government was "not discouraging" the Zionists, who were trying to achieve their aim by "cornering" finance and industry in the Empire. To that end Sir Ernest Cassel had founded the National Bank of Turkey, and Emanuel Salem (a Jewish lawyer from Salonika) was one of his "agents."

With more protests from the floor at these imputations, the Grand Vezir urged the speaker to stop attempting to prove that the loyal Jewish population of the Empire could be deceived by the acts of some Zionist "fools" (*budala*).[18] But İsmail Hakkı Bey returned to the charge and claimed that the four French banks with which Cavid Bey had opened negotiations for a loan in 1910 were all Zionist organs, and that the Deutsche Bank, which had agreed to make the loan later in 1910, had done so at Zionist instigation through Jacques Menasche of Constantinople.

The Grand Vezir, presumably concerned about the distortions

15. *PRO (G)* Türkei, no. 195, K 692/II, no. 57 (3.3.1911), von Marschall (Consple.) to Reichskanzler; cf. *Stamboul,* xlv, 50 (28.2.1911); and *Levant Herald,* xl, 50 (28.2.1911).
16. *PRO* FO 371/1245/9105, no. 146 (7.3.1911), Lowther to Grey.
17. *Stamboul,* xlv, 52 (2.3.1911); *Levant Herald,* xl, 52 (1.2.1911); and *La Turquie,* vi 52 (2.3.1911); cf. *CZA* Z2/11 (2.3.1911), Jacobson to Wolffsohn.
18. *Stamboul,* xlv, 52 (2.3.1911).

in İsmail Hakkı Bey's charges and their implications for the CUP Government's standing in general, set about answering him point by point. He agreed that some European Jews wished to augment the Jewish population in Palestine and establish a Jewish state there. But most European Jews, and all Ottoman Jews, scoffed at the dreams of this group, who were a "handful of charlatans," incapable of establishing a Jewish government in Palestine. It was nonsense to implicate all Jews in this "apparition," for they were too realistic a people to let themselves be abused by such reverie. To illustrate the Government's attitude, the Grand Vezir repeated a remark made by Tâlat Bey while İsmail Hakkı Bey was speaking, to the effect that Dr. Nossig—whom he described as a *Zionist representative*—had recently been told that the Government could not accept the Zionists' demands and that Cavid Bey had refused to meet him.

The Grand Vezir demolished with ease İsmail Hakkı Bey's argument that the Government's contacts with foreign banks and financiers proved its complicity with the Zionists. Sir Ernest Cassel had enriched Egypt by creating the National Bank of Egypt and he had not installed a single Jew in it. After the Revolution, the Ottoman Government had invited Cassel to found a similar bank, and so the National Bank of Turkey was in no way connected with the Zionist Movement. Cassel himself could not be a Zionist, since he was a member of the English "High Church," and, as one of the biggest financiers in England, he was a precious friend of "Ottomanism."[19] Only one of the French banks approached by Cavid Bey in 1910, La Banque Louis Dreyfus, was a Jewish house, and the Deutsche Bank was the largest establishment of its kind in Germany—any Jews associated with it were motivated by business, and not by Zionist or religious, considerations. Neither of the Ottoman Jews mentioned by İsmail Hakkı Bey and Lütfi Fikri Bey was a Zionist "agent." Emanuel Salem was a director of La Banque de Salonique, and Jacques Menasche was acting on behalf of a French group which had tried to obtain commercial concessions in the Empire in 1910.

With the exception of a paper called *Tasvir-i Efkâr,* the Turkish press had seldom concerned itself with Zionism up to this point.

19. Sir Ernest Cassel was not a member of the Church of England; a Jew by birth, he had become a Roman Catholic.

Tasvir-i Efkâr was edited by Ebüzziya Tevfık, an Albanian, an influential journalist, a deputy in Parliament for Antalya—and an anti-Semite. In the 1880s, he had written a book entitled *Millet-i İsrailiye,* which so maligned the Jewish people that the Haham Başı had protested to the Grand Vezir when it first appeared and again, in 1898, when a second edition was being prepared.[20] In 1909, the British Embassy at Constantinople noted that Ebüzziya Tevfık suffered from anti-Semitic tendencies and had published a number of articles warning "against the dangers to be anticipated from the would-be exploitation of Turkey by unscrupulous Jewish financiers."[21]

Ebüzziya Tevfık's barbs also extended to the Zionists.[22] However, discussions of Zionism were rare in other papers, except for brief periods after Ḥafiẓ Bey al-Saᶜid's question in Parliament about Zionism in June 1909,[23] and after the ninth Zionist Congress in December of that year.[24] Only the debate in Parliament in the spring of 1911 stimulated greater press interest in Zionism. This in turn led the anti-CUP press to attack the Government for being not only pro-Jewish, but pro-Zionist. On 3 March, Hs̈eyn Cahid Bey (editor of *Tanin*) rallied to the Committee's defence in an editorial entitled "The Battle of Slander."[25] According to him, the "enemies of the Empire" presented themselves as its sincerest friends. Taking advantage of the masses' ignorance and political immaturity, they bandied about the "appalling" suggestion that the CUP was "selling the country to the Jews." Whenever a Jewish bank took part in a loan to the Government, or a minister appointed Jewish secretary, these "friends" claimed that their case was proven. The Government had no wish to sell Palestine to the Jews, any more than it wished to sell any part of the Empire to others, and those responsible for the idea were malicious troublemakers.

But the opposition press saw no reason to stop attacking the CUP over Zionism. *Yeni Gazete* took the Grand Vezir to task for

20. *Ha-Ẓevi,* xiv, 29 (10.5.1898).
21. *PRO* FO 371/992/177, no. 992 (27.12.1909), Marling to Grey.
22. *L'Aurore,* i, 19 (31.10.1909).
23. *CZA* Z2/8 (10.6.1909), Jacobson to Wolffsohn; and *AIU* I G 1 (17.6.1909), A. Benveniste (Consple.) to Pres., AIU (Paris).
24. *Ha-Ḥerut,* ii, 50 (21.1.1910).
25. Reprinted in *ha-Ḥerut,* iii, 67 (22.3.1911).

playing down the importance of the Zionist Movement and for calling its leaders "a handful of charlatans."[26] "Zionism," it wrote on 2 March, 'is widely spread, its strength is great, and it cannot be dismissed in this summary manner." Herzl had been a man of talent; Max Nordau is a great philosopher. In subsequent issues *Yeni Gazete* published a series of articles to warn its readers of the dangers allegedly inherent in Zionism.[27] Other papers, including *Tasvir-i Efkâr*[28] and the important daily, *İkdam,*[29] also printed anti-Zionist articles. Some of them quoted passages from Kann's *Erets Israël* to substantiate their objections.[30]

With all its other problems, the CUP was embarrassed by this offensive. At the beginning of April, Yunus Nadi, one of Dr. Nazım's aides and the editor of *Rumeli* in Salonika, wrote an article headed "Down with Zionism, Always and For Ever."[31] Instead of trying to laugh Zionism out of court, he took the other tack and conceded that it "is a real danger." Echoing the Grand Vezir and Talât Bey in Parliament on 1 March, he linked the proposals made by Nossig and others regarding Jewish settlement in Iraq with Zionist endeavours. He then claimed that he personally had always been against such proposals, for behind them "lurked the dream of forming an Israelite realm comprising the ancient states of Babel and Nineveh with Jerusalem as its centre." There was good reason to fear this dream pursued by certain foreign Jews because "behind them is the strongest power in the world—that of money." Moreover, Zionism was "a sort of advance guard of German influence in the East." He accordingly pledged himself to vigilance while the Empire's safety was at stake.

This article was revealing on three counts. Dr. Nazım's wing of the CUP was prepared to allow that the Zionists should be taken

26. *PRO* FO 371/1245/9103, no. 143 (4.3.1911), Lowther to Grey, enclosing an article from *Yeni Gazete* of 2.3.1911, entitled "The Storm over Zionism: Jewish Immigrants and the Policy of the Government."

27. *CZA* Z2/11 (21.3.1911), Jacobson to *Die Welt* (Cologne), enclosing a subsequent article from *Yeni Gazete,* without date.

28. *Ha-Ḥerut,* iii, 72 (31.3.1911). Two of the anti-Zionist articles from *Tasvir-i Efkâr* were reproduced in *al-Karmil*; *ha-Ḥerut,* iii 72, reprinted the second of these from *al-Karmil* of 25.3.1911.

29. *Ha-Ḥerut,* iii, 67 (22.3.1911).

30. *CZA* Z2/11 (15.3.1911), Jacobson to M. Bodenheimer (Cologne).

31. *PRO* FO 371/1245/16048, no. 271 (24.4.1911), Lowther to Grey, describing the immediate background to this article and enclosing a translation of it from *Rumeli* of 6.4.1911.

seriously. Secondly, the French Consul in Salonika had apparently had some success in manufacturing a German bogey. And finally, the Zionists, the Jewish Colonization Association, and Nossig had all been lumped together, to the extent that the Zionists were suspected—or at least accused—of being bent on establishing a state extending from Palestine to Iraq.

In mid-April Halil Bey, the new Minister of the Interior, gave what amounted to an official statement of the Government's position to a Jewish paper called *El Tiempo*:

> Whatever its form, the Government will not view Zionism in a favourable light. I cannot approve the least suggestion in this respect. Jews admit that they have never met in any [other] country the sympathy which one witnesses for them here. To follow the course of Zionism is for them to go counter to Ottomanism and the interests of Ottoman Jews. People who, being informed of these matters, combat Zionism, will always be assured of the approbation of those who desire the maintenance of the ties uniting the Jews to the Empire.
>
> Regarding Jewish immigration, it is the exclusive choice of Palestine which gives rise to doubts.
>
> It is because I know the discernment and patriotism of the Jews that I remain persuaded that they will not let themselves take to utopias.[32]

This statement left no doubts about where the Government stood, and soon found its way into the columns of other newspapers, such as *İkdam* and *Stamboul*.[33]

Before the second parliamentary debate on Zionism is discussed, pressures over the previous year from Arabs in Palestine to curb land sales to Jews must be surveyed. Not only do they form the background to the debate, but they also reflect currents of opinion of the local population more directly than the Arabic press described in the previous chapter.

It can be seen from these pressures that some Arabs in Palestine were beginning to perceive Zionist endeavours as a threat to their own position in the country. Most of them regarded this "threat" as supplementing the danger which the Zionist Movement allegedly represented to the Ottoman Empire at large. But a few Arabs in

32. *Stamboul,* xlv, 95 (24.4.1911).
33. Cf. *PRO* FO 371/1245/16048, no. 271.

Palestine were concerned about Zionism on exclusively local grounds, on the basis, that is, of local patriotism. They were prepared to agitate against Jewish land purchases, and furthermore, Arab deputies in Parliament were willing to make representations to the Government on their behalf.

In the spring of 1910 the Zionists opened negotiations with Ilyas Sursuq of Beirut for a tract of some of the best agricultural land in Palestine, embracing the villages of Fula and ᶜAfula, about halfway between Nazareth and Jenin. Sursuq's willingness to sell this land, totalling over ten thousand dunams, soon became public knowledte. Thus, at the beginning of May, he was criticised in the Arabic press,[34] and two telegrams against Jewish land purchases were sent from Haifa and Nazareth to the Government.

Copies of both telegrams reached the press in Constantinople, and the way in which each was framed was significant. The names of those who signed the telegram from Haifa did not appear in the newspapers. But it was written by Arab notables who may be described as both Ottoman loyalists and local patriots. They held that the press "of the West and of the East" bore witness to the Zionists' efforts since the Constitution to acquire lands in Syria and Palestine. Although there were, in fact, only about eighty thousand Jews in Palestine altogether, it was claimed that "about a hundred thousand Jewish immigrants" had arrived recently. These newcomers disrupted harmony in the country *and* exposed the Empire to political dangers. "Barely delivered from a régime of absolutism, we are becoming victims of the aspirations of Zionism which by making us mortgages ends by taking over our farms and fields."[35]

The second telegram was signed by the heads (*muhtars*) of all the religious communities in Nazareth. They viewed Jewish settlement in that area as a direct threat to themselves without, it should be noted, reference to any dangers to the Empire at large.

The arrival of Jewish immigrants in large numbers in this region coming from abroad is a cause of great political and economic injury. They have been forbidden in the past to settle here.

All the press is unanimous in recognising that the Zionists nourish the intention of expropriating our properties. For us these intentions are a

34. *Ha-Ḥerut,* ii, 97 (23.5.1910).
35. *La Turquie* (6.5.1910).

question of life and death. We draw the attention of the appropriate department to this.[36]

A few days after these telegrams were sent, Muslims said to be from "Aleppo, Beirut and its environs" petitioned the Government to stop Jewish immigration.[37] Then, in the middle of May, a group of Arab deputies demanded an assurance from the Minister of the Interior that Jews would not be permitted to take over the local population's land and that mass immigration of Jews would not be tolerated—"because they were a danger to the Empire."[38]

Thereupon instructions to that effect were cabled by the Ministry of the Interior to the authorities in Beirut and Jerusalem,[39] where the Government's position was described by the new Mutasarrıf, Azmi Bey:

We are not xenophobes; we welcome all strangers. We are not anti-Semites; we value the economic superiority of the Jews. But no nation, no government could open its arms to groups making proclamations everywhere and aiming to take Palestine from us. The political domination of the Jews in this country belongs to the realm of childish dreams, but as long as they even talk about it, we shall not tolerate their economic advancement. Were they to abandon these utopias and give proof of their [commitment to] Ottomanism, then all these difficulties and restrictions would fall away like magic.[40]

Within a few days, the British Consul in Jerusalem reported that foreign Jews long resident in Jerusalem were now being prevented from buying land.[41] At the beginning of June, David Levontin of the Anglo-Palestine Company wrote from Jaffa that it had become impossible for Ottoman Jews to acquire land as well.[42] Shortly afterwards, the British Vice-Consul in Haifa also informed his superior in Beirut that foreign Jews were finding great difficulty in purchasing land.[43] When a British Embassy official in

36. *Le Jeune-Turc* (7.5.1910); the editors had verified the text with the Ministry of the Interior.
37. *CZA* Z2/9 (11.5.1910), Jacobson to Wolffsohn.
38. *CZA* Z2/9 (1. and 7.6.1910), both Jacobson to Wolffsohn.
39. *CZA* L/2/34/I (8.6.1910), Jacobson to A. Ruppin (Jaffa).
40. *AIU* IX E 28 (16.5.1910), Antébi to Pres., AIU.
41. *PRO* FO 195/2351, no. 25 (21.5.1910), H. E. Satow (Jerus.) to Lowther; cf. (8.6.1910), same to same.
42. *CZA* W/127/I (2.6.1910), D. Levontin (Jaffa) to Wolffsohn.
43. *PRO* FO 195/2342, enc. to no. 31 (16.6.1910), H. A. Cumberbatch (Beirut) to Lowther.

Constantinople inquired about the renewed restrictions, the Minister of the Interior told him that they were "the outcome of complaints of the local inhabitants who feared a foreign Jewish invasion." Although the restrictions were originally imposed under Abdülhamid, "Constitutional Turkey" had not yet seen its way to remove them, and the whole question was under consideration by the Council of State.[44]

This was the second time in twelve months that the question had been reviewed at government level. But although the Cabinet had decided the previous June that the legislation against Jewish land purchases was required, none had been promulgated,[45] possibly because it was recognised that the constitutional rights of Ottoman Jews would be impaired.[46] The renewed pressure by Arab deputies in mid-1910 did not produce any more meaningful results, as the Council of State went no further than to reconfirm the existing regulations, underlining the restrictions on land sales to foreigners. Instructions in that sense were sent to the Vali of Beirut by the Ministries of Justice and of Foreign Affairs on 22 September and 3 October respectively.[47] The Minister of the Cadastre also issued orders that all mülk land on the periphery of Jerusalem was to be converted into miri, thereby strengthening central control on the land.[48] Predictably, the Powers saw in these orders a derogation from their privileges and in January and February 1911 they sent identical *Notes Verbales* to the Porte requesting that foreign Jews be allowed to acquire land in Palestine and Syria in accordance with the 1867 Land Code.[49] The porte rejected this plea with unusual firmness on 20 April, arguing that land transfer was a matter of internal administration and reserving its liberty of action.[50]

44. *PRO* FO 195/2351, minute (13.6.1910) by G. H. Fitzmaurice (Consple.) on folder to no. 25.
45. Talk of new legislation had continued till the end of 1909—see *ha-Ẓevi,* xxvi, 26 (29.10.1909); xxvi, 32 (5.11.1909); and *CZA* Z2/8 (6. and 13.12.1909), both Jacobson to Wolffsohn.
46. Cf. a letter from Hilmi Paşa to Subhi Bey, quoted in *AIU* IX E 26 (5.4.1909), Antébi to Pres., AIU; and *ha ᶜOlam,* iii, 40 (10.11.1909), giving the text of a draft law on Jewish immigration and reporting that it had been dropped because some of its clauses were unconstitutional.
47. *CZA* L2/24/VI (24.11.1910), E. Auerbach (Haifa) to Wolffsohn.
48. *Q d'O* N.S. 133, no. 44 (23.10.1910), Gueyraud to Pichon.
49. *OFM* A/346 for all these *Notes.*
50. *OFM* A/346, *Note Verbale,* no. 6787/37 (20.4.1911), SP to Foreign Missions (Consple.).

Despite these difficulties, the Zionists pressed on with their negotiations with Ilyas Sursuq for the land at Fula and ᶜAfula during the second half of 1910, partly because they regarded this purchase, to be made on the name of an Ottoman Jew, as tantamount to a test case with implications for all their work in Palestine.[51] The land in question fell within the Kaza of Nazareth, which was administered by Shukri al-ᶜAsali, the Arab from Damascus whose anti-Zionist articles were discussed in the preceding chapter. He was resolutely against the proposed sale.

The status of the land at ᶜAfula was particularly complicated. The Zionists and Sursuq accordingly agreed between themselves not to proceed with its transfer. However, terms were agreed for the Fula land, and its transfer should have taken place in October 1910. But Shukri al-ᶜAsali mounted a campaign against the sale, obliging his superiors in Beirut to consult the Ministry of the Interior.[52] The Porte's legal advisers ruled that Sursuq was entitled to dispose of his land to any Ottoman subject. This decision was sent to Beirut in November but, as the Vali was absent from the city, it did not become known until the end of December.[53]

Meanwhile, al-ᶜAsali made determined, but ultimately unsuccessful, efforts to stop the transfer, by trying first to prevent the peasants from vacating the land in the autumn, and then the Jewish settlers from starting work in the winter.[54] In a last-ditch attempt to frustrate the transfer, he withheld information in January 1911 relating to the land's tax liability and refused to accept certain fees due to him.[55] He also abused an employee of the Anglo-Palestine Company who came to pay them. The Zionists, he said, came to Palestine "solely to expel the poor Arab peasants from their land, and to set up their own government."[56] When the bank employee replied that the Jews were not disloyal to the Empire and remarked that he had a brother in the Ottoman army, al-ᶜAsali retorted that "he was sure [the Jew] had become a soldier only to acquire

51. *CZA* L1/102 (23.10.1910), Ruppin to JNF (Cologne).
52. *Ibid.*
53. *CZA* L1/102 (30.12.1910), Ruppin (Haifa) to JNF; cf. *CZA* L18/275;copy of decision from Ministry of the Interior (SP) to Vali (Beirut), dated 29.11.1910, with note of its transmission to Acre, dated 2.1.1911.
54. *CZA* L18/275 (25.12.1910), [Ruppin] to JNF.
55. *CZA* L18/275 (22.1.1911), [Ruppin] to JNF.
56. *CZA* L18/275 (22.1.1911).

proficiency in shooting, so that later he could shoot the Arabs."[57]

In the middle of January, al-ᶜAsali vacated his post to stand as a candidate in a by-election to the Ottoman Parliament held in Damascus following the death of Muḥammad al-ᶜAjlani. As a parting shot, al-ᶜAsali, again using his *nom de plume* of "Ṣalaḥ al-Din, published in a Beirut newspaper an article, entitled "The Fortress of Fula," in which he alleged that there was a fortress, built by Saladin, on the land to be sold to the Jews. Although this was false, the article provoked further protests against the sale. His departure, however, eased the transfer of the title deeds of Fula, and it was completed in February.

Such a stir had been caused in the Vilâyet of Beirut by this protracted affair that the Vali found it necessary to refute publicly the charges in al-ᶜAsali's article. On 21 February, an open letter, signed by the Vali, appeared in *Ḥadiqat al-Akhbar* in Beirut, setting out the steps which led to the transfer and emphasising its legality in terms of the constitutional rights of Ottoman subjects.[58]

Although public criticism over the sale of Fula continued for some months,[59] it was overtaken by the first debate on Zionism in the Ottoman Parliament. Over and above a foreseeable increase in articles on the subject in the Arabic press (some of which are discussed in the next chapter), the debate drew two immediate responses from Palestine.

In Jaffa, 150 Arabs sent a telegram to the President of the Chamber, the Grand Vezir and various newspapers, demanding that Parliament take measures against Jewish immigration and land purchase. With the Fula incident still fresh, they particularly protested against the purchase of land by Ottoman "men of straw" on behalf of the Zionists. They also protested against Jews who, they said, used their Ottoman and foreign papers interchangeably as it suited them.[60]

In Haifa, Najib Naṣṣar produced the first book in Arabic about Zionism: *al-Ṣihyuniyya—Zionism: Its History, Object and*

57. *Ha-Or,* ii [xxvii], 91/266 (5.2.1911).
58. *Ḥadiqat al-Akhbar* (21.2.1911), reprinted in *ha-Ḥerut,* iii, 60 (3.3.1911).
59. *Ha-Or,* ii [xxvii], 135/310 (4.4.1911).
60. *Ha-ᶜOlam,* v, 13 (12.4.1911); and Lichtheim, p. 193. The Zionist Office in Jaffa was inclined to dismiss this telegram as an intrigue by "a certain Nashashibi from Jaffa"—see *CZA* Z2/635 (31.3.1911), Ruppin to ZCO (Berlin).

Importance.[61] In large part, this was a personal reply by Naṣṣar to the Grand Vezir's rebuttal of the allegations made by İsmail Hakkı Bey during the first debate on Zionism. Naṣṣar's aim was to demonstrate that the "Zionist danger" was not imaginary and that Zionists leaders were not deranged (*mutahawwisun*), as was suggested by the Grand Vezir. In the course of trying to prove his point, the nature of Naṣṣar's opposition to Zionism came out clearly.

The first part of Naṣṣar's booklet was little more than a slanted translation of the article on Zionism in the *Jewish Encyclopedia* by Richard Gottheil, an American Zionist and a professor of semitic languages in New York. His heavy dependence on an encyclopedia was not accidental. Like Négib Azoury before him, Naṣṣar wished to disarm possible critics by assuring them that he had relied on authoritative sources. He therefore explained to his readers that an encyclopedia was a work edited by experts on which researchers could depend.[62] But he did not mention that the article in question had been written before the Young Turk Revolution, and that since then the Zionists, having moved away from "political Zionism," had dropped their demands for a "Charter" and Great Power protection. This omission was not, however, too recondite to escape the notice of the important literary journal in Cairo, *al-Hilal,* which noted that while *al-Şihyuniyya* dealt with the current situation in Palestine, it only covered the historical background until 1905 (the relevant volume of the *Jewish Encyclopedia* having been published in that year).[63]

After a short introduction, Naṣṣar set about translating Gottheil's article—after a fashion. All passages in which Gottheil mentioned opposition to Zionism or dissension within Zionist ranks were either heavily edited by Naṣṣar or omitted altogether.[64] Passages dealing with possible settlement schemes outside Palestine received similar

61. N. Naṣṣar, *al-ŞJihyuniyya: tarikhuha, gharaḍuha, ahammiyyatuha* (Haifa, 1911). Internal evidence suggests that this book was first published in serial form in *al-Karmil*—see *al-Şihyuniyya,* pp. 57 and 60; cf. also *ha-Ḥerut,* iii, 74 (5.4. 1911); and iii, 83 (3.5.1911).
62. Naṣṣar, p. 3.
63. *Al-Hilal,* xx, 1 (1911), p. 63.
64. Thus, Gottheil, p. 667, col. i: the paragraph on Reform Jews' rejection of Jewish "restoration to Zion" is omitted; pp. 672–74; the passage on opposition to the Zionist Movement is severely truncated; p. 676, col. ii: Zangwill's criticism of JCA at the fifth Zionist Congress is omitted; p. 679, col. ii: Gaster's criticism of Herzl and other opposition to the latter are omitted; p. 686, cols. i–ii: the passage on "Moral Zionism" (*"Aḥad ha-ʿAm"*) is severely cut; etc.

treatment.[65] Indications of the Movement's size and its resolutions concerning Palestine were highlighted.[66] Here and there, subtle changes of emphasis were introduced,[67] or suggestive asides, not in the English text, were added.[68] Gottheil had portrayed Zionism as an important but complex force in modern Jewish history; he had stressed that not all its supporters wanted a Jewish state and that many Jews rejected Zionism completely. Naṣṣar's version of the article suggested that every Jewish nationalist was striving for an independent state in Palestine *and in the surrounding lands*—and nowhere else. It also suggested that among Jews opposition to the Zionist Movement was negligible, and that many influential Christians supported the Zionists as well. This was a misrepresentation on both counts, because in the early 1900s there was considerable Jewish dissent from Zionism and little real Christian backing for it.

Gottheil had stated that since 1896 Zionism had been "dominating Jewish history." Exceptionally, Naṣṣar printed this observation in the original English, because he felt that it conclusively proved his thesis that Zionism could not be considered unimportant, or its leaders deranged.[69]

At a number of points in Gottheil's article, Naṣṣar inserted comments of his own. Having listed biblical references to a Jewish return to Zion, he commented—significantly, as it turned out a

65. Thus, Gottheil, p. 678, col. ii to p. 679, col. i: the passage on the East African scheme is omitted, except for one sentence stating that "Christian friends of the movement" bore most of the expenses incurred by the East African Commission; p. 680, cols. i-ii: the passage on the "Guas Ngishu Plateau" is omitted; and p. 685, cols. i-ii: the passage on Territorialism is much abridged, and the paragraph on Zangwill's "alliance" with Lucien Wolf is not included.

66. Thus, Gottheil, p. 676, col. i: the table of Zionist societies throughout the world is reproduced; p. 679, cols. i-ii: the account of the Zikhron Yaᶜaqov conference is given in full; pp. 680-1, the first half of the seventh Congress's resolution reaffirming the Basel Programme is reproduced, but the second half on the East African Commission is omitted; *loc. cit.* the seventh Congress's resolution about "proposed work in Palestine" is reproduced in full; and p. 684, col. i: the passage on the "wide spread of Zionism" is reproduced in full.

67. Thus, Gottheil, p. 671, col. ii: "Herzl suggested either Argentina or Palestine" reads in *al-Ṣihyuniyya,* p. 19, as "Herzl suggested either Palestine or Argentina"; and of course all the omissions, truncations, and careful reproduction of selected passages (as indicated in the preceding notes) distort the whole balance of Gottheil's article.

68. Naṣṣar, pp. 23 and 27, says that Gaster "banned the proclamation of Zionism in England"; in Gottheil's article there is no mention of this.

69. Naṣṣar, pp. 3-4.

few weeks later—that there were so many passages of this nature that the Jews did not confine their efforts to Palestine alone, but extended them to embrace Lebanon and Iraq. "Thus you see them adding the word 'Syria' to Palestine and in some instances 'Turkey in Asia and the East.' "[70]

The second, and more important, part of the book consisted of a short essay by Naṣṣar himself.[71] He began by drawing certain rather questionable conclusions from Gottheil's article. The Zionist Movement was powerful. It had ambitions on more than the land of Palestine itself. It possessed the money not only to realise its ambitions, but possibly to dominate the weak Ottoman Empire as well. The distinction between Zionists and non-Zionists was of no consequence, because all Jewish societies active in Palestine had the same objective in mind. The Zionist Movement had already set up a governmental framework through its congresses and committees, its financial and educational institutions, and its "para-military" associations for physical training.[72] Naṣṣar accepted wholeheartedly Gottheil's explanation that Zionism was partly a by-product of anti-Semitism. In his opinion, the nations of the world supported Zionism because they saw in it a means of divesting themselves of their Jews and the anti-Semitism bound up with them. He was far from happy at the prospect of the Ottoman Empire shouldering this burden.[73]

He then posed two questions which, as far as is known, had not been put before. He enquired, "What do we learn [from this exposé of Zionism]?" and also, "What do we need?"[74] As was mentioned in the preceding chapter, Naṣṣar objected to Zionism both as an Ottoman loyalist and as a local patriot. He accordingly was intent on showing that the Zionist Movement was a threat to the Empire as a whole. But, as a local patriot, he also held that the indigenous population of Palestine should look to its own interests—especially as, in his eyes, the Government was failing in its responsibilities.[75]

70. Naṣṣar, pp. 4-5.
71. *Ibid.*, pp. 58-64.
72. *Ibid.*, p. 60. By "para-military" societies Naṣṣar apparently meant the Maccabi sports associations affiliated to the Zionist Movement.
73. *Ibid.*, pp. 59-60. There are passages among Naṣṣar's comments which suggest that the anti-Semitism he feared would plague the East if the Jews settled in Palestine had already begun to grip him—see *ibid.*, pp. 12 and 17.
74. *Ibid.*, pp. 60 and 62.
75. *Ibid.*, p. 51.

Naṣṣar's "two-tiered" position was covered by his use of the first person plural in formulating his questions and by his loose use of ill-defined Arabic words such as *bilad* ("country"), *waṭan* ("homeland") and *shaʿb* ("people"). It was also reflected in the answers that he gave to his questions.

We learn, he said, that the Zionists' aim was to gain mastery "over our country (*biladina*) and the sources of our livelihood." The CUP did not hinder them, and Ottoman Jews were helping them.[76] Second, what was needed was strong leadership and bold, ambitious plans.[77] He took none other than Herzl as the foremost example of a leader who had propounded such plans and whose tenacity had welded a dispersed and divided people into unity.[78]

However, "we" are different from the Jews. We—*scilicet,* Ottoman subjects—have the Ottoman community (*jamiʿa*), of which the majority group (that is, the Muslims) has its spiritual leader, the Caliph. All Ottomans, including non-Muslims, are bound to respect the Caliphate because it is a force and a means to unity in the Empire, a medium required for the understanding of patriotism (*al-waṭaniyya*).[79]

Nonetheless, we—*scilicet,* Arabs in Palestine—"need to rely upon ourselves and to stop expecting everything from the Government."[80] We must defend ourselves "by ourselves"; this is legitimate under a constitutional régime. "Amongst us" there are many like Herzl, but they have to recognise "their own worth and moral courage" in order to take the first steps.

Let our men arise and let them begin by forming societies for Ottomans which will strive for Ottomanism and which will teach economy and implant the principle of not letting the capital of Ottomans enter the pockets of the settlers who will fight us for our existence and will not return [our money] to us. [Let them begin] by founding companies which will collect capital by the piastre so that the poor and the rich will participate in them, and which will purchase land and will carry out agricultural, industrial and commercial programmes. . . . Why do we, who have spent centuries suffering tragedy and misery, not become men and go on the way of

76. Naṣṣar, p. 61.
77. *Ibid.,* p. 62.
78. *Loc. cit.*
79. *Ibid.,* pp. 62–63. Cf. Dawn, "From Ottomanism to Arabism," p. 396, discussing Christian Arabs, who by about this time had come to regard Islam as part of their heritage; cf. also Hourani, *Arabic Thought,* pp. 251–52.
80. Naṣṣar, p. 63.

freedom and live for our patrimony (*waṭan*) and for ourselves, so that we shall not invoke upon ourselves the curses of our ancestors and our sons by losing the country (*bilad*) which [our] ancestors acquired with their blood?[81]

When Shukri al-ᶜAsali refused to accept the fees due to him for the transfer of Fula, he told the APC employee who had come to pay him that he would fight the purchase of the land by Jews "to his last drop of blood."[82] A few days later, in January 1911, he was elected a deputy for Damascus to the Ottoman Parliament, whither the Zionist question was conveyed in earnest. The first signs of this came during March and April when some Arab deputies,[83] led by Ruḥi Bey al-Khalidi from Jerusalem,[84] and including Riḍa al-Sulḥ (Beirut) and the newly arrived Shukri al-ᶜAsali,[85] lobbied for the new legislation against Jewish immigration into Palestine.

On 16 May the Chamber was engaged in examining the Ministry of the Interior's budget. Perhaps believing that a further discussion of Zionism would help the Arab deputies' efforts, Ruḥi Bey put himself down to speak.[86] Taking as his cue a remark that the national and religious beliefs of all groups should be respected, he began, somewhat self-consciously, by declaring that he was not an anti-Semite, but an anti-Zionist. He traced the history of the Jews in the Empire since the time of the Spanish Inquisition and, with the aid of biblical quotations, spoke at length about the intellectual origins of Zionism. He then picked up almost word for word the allegation in Yunus Nadi's article in *Rumeli,* which had been endorsed in Najib Naṣṣar's book. "The Zionists' aim," he declared, "is to settle numerous Jews in Iraq and Syria to form a Jewish kingdom having Jerusalem as its centre."[87]

81. Naṣṣar, pp. 63–64.
82. *CZA* L18/275 (22.1.1911). [Ruppin] to JNF.
83. *CZA* L2/34/I (13.3.1911), Jacobson to Ruppin.
84. *CZA* L2/34/I (12.4.1911), same to same.
85. *Ha-Or,* ii [xxvii], 120/295 (17.3.1911); and *ha-Mevasser,* ii, 11 (31.3.1911), pp. 131–32.
86. *CZA* Z2/11 (16.5.1911), Jacobson to Wolffsohn.
87. For reports of this discussion, on which the following account is based, see *PRO* FO 371/1245/19395, no. 346 (17.5.1911), Lowther to Grey; *Levant Herald,* xl, 115 and 116 (17. and 18.5.1911); *Stamboul,* xlv, 115 and 116 (17. and 18.5. 1911); *La Turquie,* vi, 115 and 116 (17. and 18.5.1911); and *L'Aurore,* iii, 126 (19.5.1911).

Ruḥi Bey was followed by the second deputy from Jerusalem, Saʿid Bey al-Ḥusayni, who outlined the main points in *Our Programme* by Menahem Ussishkin, a Zionist leader from Russia, which had come to the attention of the authorities in Jerusalem in 1905 while Saʿid Bey was President of the Municipal Council. He also revived a curious rumour, circulating at that time in Jerusalem, that Ussishkin was called "the Jewish Prince."[88] Like Ruḥi Bey, he too contended that "the Zionists' aim was to create a Jewish state extending from Palestine and Syria to Iraq."

In essence, however, Saʿid Bey's views had not changed since his interview with *ha-Ẓevi* in 1909. Immigrant Jews should go to other parts of the Empire, because Palestine could not hold them all. Even the Alliance Israélite Universelle (in one of whose schools he had spent some time) agreed with him in this. He too had nothing against Jews. They were active, industrious, and thrifty. He would be happy if they became Ottoman subjects and settled outside Palestine.

The next speaker, Nisim Mazliah from Smyrna, said that he did not want to take a stand on the Zionist issue, because he was a Jew. But he objected to the use of Zionism as a means of attacking the Government and felt that it was necessary "to clear the air." He therefore suggested that a commission should examine the question, as it touched on the honour of Ottoman Jews as well. This proposal was seconded by Vartkis Efendi, an Armenian deputy from Erzerum, who accused the Arab deputies of creating the one thing that the Empire lacked—a Jewish question. "Formerly, hatred of the Armenians was created; now you want to inculcate hatred of the Jews into the people."[89] When Ruḥi Bey pointed out that the Arabs were opposed only to foreign Jews, Vartkis Efendi retorted that the masses were incapable of making the distinction.

After a brief digression into Armenian affairs, the Chamber's attention was redirected to the Zionist question by Shukri al-ʿAsali, who distributed "Zionist stamps"[90] and spoke along lines close to his open letter to General Sami Paşa al-Faruqi of December 1910. He mentioned, for example, the Zionist flag and national anthem,

88. Cf. *CZA* Z2/598 (4.9.1905), D. Levontin (Jaffa) to Wolffsohn.

89. Jacobson had spoken to Vartkis about Zionism some time before this debate—see *CZA* Z2/12 (19.5.1911), Jacobson to Wolffsohn.

90. The "Zionist stamps" were stickers attached to envelopes by Zionists in Palestine and abroad as a form of contribution to the Jewish National Fund.

and the Zionist postal service. He had drawn the Government's attention to this—to no effect. The Jews were buying large tracts of land in the region of the Hijaz Railway (a rather dubious point he had raised in his campaign against the purchase of Fula, since the land in question was not far from the branch line connecting Haifa with the Hijaz Railway). Tâlat Bey commented that foreigners were legally entitled to acquire land anywhere in the Empire, except in the Hijaz itself. But al-ᶜAsali was not to be deflected. After taking possession of the land, he argued, the Jews would oppress the common people. "The Zionists intend to extend themselves towards Iraq and Syria to found a powerful state."

The Chamber, however, was growing impatient. Hafız Ibrahim Efendi, a member of the CUP's Central Committee and deputy from Ipek in Albania, complained that time was being wasted on "apparitions." The Empire had an army of a million men; it had nothing to fear from a hundred thousand Jews in Palestine.

On the following day, Dimitri Vlahov, a Bulgarian deputy from Salonika whom Victor Jacobson had befriended,[91] spoke at length in defence of Jewish immigration into Palestine.[92] Thereafter, the President of the Chamber accepted a motion from several deputies calling for closure, despite protests from Kosmidi Efendi, the Greek deputy who had first alluded to Zionism in the Chamber on 27 February, and from Saᶜid al-Ḥusayni on behalf of the Arab deputies.

Halil Bey, the Minister of the Interior, then replied to points raised in connection with his ministry's budget. On Zionism, he assured the Chamber that probably all Ottoman Jews were opposed to its political aims. The Government had no intention of modifying its attitude towards large concentrations of Jews anywhere in the Empire, and orders would be given to ensure the strict application of its regulations, which aimed at preventing such an eventuality in Palestine.

As will be recalled, the first discussion on Zionism in the Ottoman Parliament was really the pretext for an attack on the CUP and on the Minister of Finance in particular. In the main, it consisted of a dialogue between the leader of the People's Party and the Grand Vezir, who rose to defend the CUP Government and Cavid

91. *CZA* Z2/11 (16.5.1911), Jacobson to ZCO (Cologne).
92. *CZA* 13/23/Q: Draft memoirs of Dimitri Vlahov.

Bey. The second discussion was quite different. Although Arabs made up about one-fifth of the deputies in the Chamber, they seldom took an active part in the proceedings, possibly because they were unfamiliar with parliamentary procedures, and lacked both fluency in Turkish and cohesion as a group, coming from areas as far apart as North Africa, Yemen and Iraq. At best, the one potentially cohesive Arab group comprised the deputies from Syria, Palestine and Iraq, and indeed they had acted together on a previous occasion, during the "Lynch affair" over navigational concessions in Iraq in 1909.[93] On this second occasion, they put forward the three deputies most qualified to speak on their behalf. These three deputies came well prepared, and each tackled the Zionist issue from a different angle. The common denominator in their speeches was the unfounded charge that the Zionists entertained political and territorial ambitions which extended far beyond Palestine.

In winding up for the Arab deputies, Shukri al-ᶜAsali demanded the adoption of the draft legislation prepared in 1909 with a view to stopping Jewish settlement in Palestine. But he and his colleagues made little impact on the Government, and from their point of view the debate was a failure. All that they succeeded in extracting from the Minister of the Interior was an assurance that the existing restrictions against the Jews in Palestine would be resolutely enforced.

The Arab deputies failed to achieve more for perhaps two reasons. First, their three spokesmen were not very astute. Ruḥi Bey talked for too long and was too erudite. When pressed, he conceded that public order in the Jewish settlements was perfect. Saᶜid Bey also allowed that the Empire had much to gain from Jewish immigration. Shukri al-ᶜAsali made a similar tactical error in bringing up the Zionist postal service—it functioned, he said, in an exemplary fashion, which he wished the Ottoman postal service would emulate.

Second, and more important, the Arab deputies failed because, when *they* raised the Zionist issue, the Chamber was not concerned with the question. According to the Constantinople press, they were listened to amidst general indifference. At closure on 16 May, only about 50 of the 288 deputies remained in the Chamber. During the

93. Harran, pp. 128–32 and p. 147.

debate several deputies interrupted to complain that the Chamber's time was being wasted. The reason is not difficult to understand. Since the first discussion of Zionism in the Chamber, the CUP dissidents had attained most of their objectives. They had forced more members of the "Salonika Group," including Cavid Bey, to resign, and the differences within the Committee had been temporarily composed. The Turkish and Greek deputies who spoke in the first debate had never been genuinely worried about Zionism, and hence lent the Arab deputies no support when they raised the issue two months later.

Two points with wider implications for the Arabs ought to be noted at this stage. The notion that the CUP not only was dominated by the Freemasons and Jews, but also favoured the Zionists, had gained considerable ground during 1910. Turkish opponents of the CUP and members of various non-Turkish groups in the Balkans recognised that this canard had been put about to embarrass the CUP. But to certain Arabs in Palestine and beyond, seeing the continued flow of Jewish immigrants into the country and being less *au fait* with the workings of Ottoman politics in the capital, it must have seemed strangely plausible. And, as will be shown in the next chapter, it did not matter to many Arab opponents of the CUP whether this particular claim was true or false, because they had a political interest in promoting it.

Second, many Turks had been confused by the approaches of non-Zionist groups, such as the Jewish Colonization Association and the Allgemeine Jüdische Kolonisations-Organisation, seeking permission for Jewish immigrants to settle in the Empire, especially Iraq. Some of them went on to draw the erroneous conclusion that the Zionists wanted to found a state stretching from Palestine to Iraq. Najib Naṣṣar had purposely fostered this mistake in his book *al-Ṣihyuniyya*; and the three Arab speakers in the second debate had all levelled it against the Zionists as if it were an established fact.

6

The Liberal Union in Power

DURING the summer of 1911 the unpopularity of the CUP Government intensified, and the rifts within the Committee, which had been patched up in April and May, broke open again. Although the Turkish and Greek deputies had not supported the Arabs during the second debate on Zionism in Parliament, the discussion served to draw public attention to the subject again. As a result, the anti-CUP press, especially abroad, continued to allege that the Government was favouring the Zionists,[1] even though it was admitted that this charge was being maintained solely to embarrass the Government.[2]

The Government did its best to demonstrate that the allegation was unfounded. Thus, when a new mutasarrıf was appointed to Jerusalem in July, he arrived with strict instructions to check Jewish progress in Palestine.[3] At the same time, the Minister of Religious Endowments closed a loophole in the laws by forbidding the sale of any land belonging to a religious endowment (*waqf*) which had been wrongly registered with the Ministry of the Cadastre.[4]

1. E.G. Mècheroutiette, iii, 20 (July, 1911), pp. 37 ff.; 21 (Aug., 1911), pp. 20 ff.; 22 (Sept., 1911) pp. 57 ff.; 23 (Oct., 1911), pp. 29 ff.; and 24 (Nov., 1911), pp. 32 ff.
2. "X," "Les courants politiques dans la Turquie contemporaine," *Revue du Monde Musulman,* vol. xxi (1912), p. 211.
3. *AIU* X E 29 (2.8.1911), A. Antébi (Jerus.) to Pres., AIU (Paris).
4. *JCA* 268/enc. to no. 195 (21.6.1911), Antébi to J. Starkmeth (Jaffa).

Still under pressure at the end of the year, the Government disclosed its intention to enact new legislation against Jewish immigration and land purchase.[5] The draft law, prepared by the Ministry of the Interior, was in essence a recapitulation and stiffening of the existing restrictions. It put great stress on two points. First, Jewish immigrants were absolutely prohibited from settling in the Vilâyets of Beirut and Şam or in the Mutasarrıflık of Jerusalem; second, no large groups of Jews were to establish themselves *anywhere* in the Empire.[6]

It is possible to view this move as a response to the demands of the Arab deputies. After all, they had begun to press ministers for new legislation in the spring and had openly demanded it in the second debate. Moreover, when Ruḥi Bey al-Khalidi had returned to Jerusalem during the summer, he exhibited continuing concern over land purchases by Jews. Before he left Jerusalem for the reopening of Parliament in the autumn, he told the local director of the Cadastre to prevent any sales of land to Jews. He also let it be known that in Constantinople he was going to keep campaigning against Jewish land purchases in Palestine.[7]

But the real reason for the Government's move lay elsewhere. The Secretary-General of the CUP told Ahmed Agayev, a pro-Committee journalist close to Zionist representatives in the capital, that "the proposed legislation has only been elaborated for reasons of party politics."[8] The opposition was subjecting the CUP to "appalling attacks" in view of "its alleged friendliness with the Zionists"—and the draft law was the Committee's answer.

However, the CUP Government found itself caught on the horns of a dilemma. By responding to domestic political pressures, it exposed itself to external pressures from the European Powers, which had an ongoing interest in protecting their special privileges in the Empire. Members of the foreign missions at the Porte accordingly met in January 1912 and decided to deliver identical *Notes Verbales* to the Porte, rejecting the position taken in its *Note* of April 1911 that land transfer was a question of internal administration (see p. 105).[9]

5. *CZA* Z3/1447 (13.10.1911), A. Ruppin (Kaffa) to ZAC (Berlin).
6. *US (T),* Reel 62, file 867.55/16, no. 162 (27.3.1912), M. M. Rockhill (Consple.) to Secretary of State (Washington), enclosing a translation of the draft legislation.
7. *CZA* L/2/24/VI (9.11.1911), [Ruppin] to ZAC.
8. *CZA* Z3/43 (4.1.1912), V. Jacobson and I. Auerbach (Consple.) to ZAC.
9. *OFM* A/346 contains these *Notes,* all dated between 21.1. and 8.2.1912.

The Zionists too were unhappy with the Government's intention. Victor Jacobson wrote to Hüseynzade Ali Bey, a member of the CUP's Central Committee whom he knew, and went so far as to say that new legislation against Jewish immigration would be "a jolt to the press and finance of world Jewry."[10]

This remark has to be taken in the context of the Empire's international situation, which was not easy at the time. In September 1911, Italy had tried to take possession of Tripolitania. War was declared, and the Empire's finances, which had declined steadily since 1908, were put under extra strain. In the circumstances, the foreign missions' *Notes,* backed up by Jacobson's letter, had some impact. The Government, apparently reluctant to become embroiled with the Powers over an internal political gambit, decided to drop the issue. On 28 January, Jacobson was informed that his letter had been submitted to the CUP's Central Committee and that the Minister of the Interior had been instructed to withdraw the proposed legislation.[11] This retraction—which presumably disappointed the Arab deputies—was officially explained by the fact that the old restrictions were still in force and so, it was argued, additional legislation would be superfluous.[12]

In November 1911, a new political party, the Liberal Union,[13] had been formed in Constantinople. It brought together most of the opposition to the CUP, and its supporters composed a strong group in Parliament, discomfiting the Government. In December 1911, the Minister of the Interior, Memduh Bey, was defeated in a by-election in Constantinople by a Liberal Union candidate, Tahir Bey Hayreddin. And in January 1912, Kâmil Paşa, the old-regime statesman and a warm supporter of the Liberal Union, wrote a letter to the Sultan blaming the CUP for all the Empire's tribulations. At this, the Committee had Parliament prorogued and arranged for new General Elections.

In the city of Jerusalem, the CUP nominated candidates who were known locally for their anti-Zionist sentiments: Ruḥi al-Khalidi, ᶜUthman al-Nashashibi (a wealthy landowner who had failed to be elected in 1908), and Asaf Efendi (the president of the

10. *CZA* ZE/43 (29.1.1912), Jacobson and Auerbach to ZAC.
11. *Ibid.*
12. *CZA* Z3/44 (14.5.1912), I. Neufach (Consple.) to ZCO (Berlin).
13. So-called in English because of the party's official French name of Entente Libérale; in Turkish the party was called "Freedom and Association."

law-court). The Zionists interpreted this list as an attempt to rally support for the CUP, which had never been strong in Jerusalem.[14] (True, Tuḥi Bey was a member of the Committee and had been elected a vice-president of the Chamber when it reassembled in October 1911, but his two colleagues from the Mutasarrıflık, like many other Arab deputies, had joined the Liberal Union shortly after it was formed.)

Zionists in Constantinople conveyed their concern about the Jerusalem list to the CUP's Central Committee, again through Ahmed Agayev.[15] But on this occasion their representations could be of no avail because the CUP rigged the elections throughout the Empire to ensure the return of its own candidates. Despite the widespread antipathy towards the Committee, 269 CUP candidates were elected, while only half a dozen representatives of the opposition were successful. The deputies "elected" to represent Palestine were all CUP nominees: from Jerusalem, Ruḥi al-Khalidi and ᶜUthman al-Nashashibi and, from Gaza, Aḥmad ᶜArif Bey al-Ḥusayni (for the Mutasarrıfljık of Jerusalem); Shaykh Asᶜad Shuqayr and Ḥaydar Bey Ṭuqan (for the Sancaks of Acre and Nablus respectively). Aḥmad ᶜArif al-Ḥusayni had been Mufti of Gaza before his election and was thought by Jews in Jaffa to be well disposed towards them.[16] But in Constantinople he was known to have had differences with the CUP in the past and to have contributed anti-Zionist articles to anti-CUP organs in the capital.[17]

The CUP's blatant gerrymandering of the elections roused the anger of a number of army officers, who formed a group called the "Saviour Officers." Taking advantage of the general discontent, especially in the region of Albania, to put pressure on the Government, they forced the Cabinet to resign on 17 July. Their aim—to dislodge the CUP from power—was quickly achieved. A new Cabinet took office four days later, headed by Gazi-Ahmed Muhtar Paşa and including Kâmil Paşa and other prominent figures known to have disapproved of the CUP and its methods. Within a few weeks the Chamber, with its huge CUP majority, was dissolved. The Liberal Union was in power.

14. *CZA* Z3/1447 (22.2.1912), Ruppin to Jacobson.
15. *CZA* Z3/44 (22.3.1912), Auerbach to ZAC.
16. *CZA* Z3/1448 (7.5.1912), J. Thon (Jaffa) to ZAC; and *ha-Or,* iii [xxx], 169 [= 166] (5.5.1912).
17. *CZA* Z3/44 (20.2.1912), D. F. Marcus (Consple.) to ZCO; cf. *Q d'O* N.S. 134, no. 27 (4.5.1912), G. Gueyraud (Jerus.) to R. Poincaré (Paris).

What did the Arabs expect from the new Government? On the broadest level, in common with other non-Turkish groups in the Empire, they probably looked forward to a relaxation of the policy of Ottomanisation. Parallel with that, some of them hoped for administrative reforms, leading to a less centralised form of control and to greater autonomy in the provinces. On the very narrow level of the Zionist issue, Arabs in Palestine presumably expected the new Government to adopt a much firmer stand against Jewish activities since, in opposition, members of the Liberal Union had taken the lead in attacking the CUP for being pro-Zionist. On both levels, the Arabs were disappointed.

For the sake of continuity, it is necessary to return to the summer of 1911. Reports of the second debate on Zionism in Parliament swiftly reached the Arab provinces through the Arabic press. In general, there seems to have been approval of the stand taken by the Arab deputies,[18] coupled with keener awareness and greater distrust of the Zionists. For example, a Muslim in Haifa told the correspondent of a Hebrew newspaper that for eighteen hours a day he thought of the benefits which the Jews bring the country, and for six hours a day he suspected them of wanting to establish a Jewish state in Palestine.[19] Albert Antébi observed that as accounts of the speeches by Ruḥi Bey and Shukri al-ᶜAsali had circulated among the peasants, anti-Jewish feeling widened. A peasant had asked him if the Jews had really prepared a Jewish king for Jerusalem and if he would be a foreigner or speak Arabic.[20] "In all eyes the Jew is becoming the anti-patriot, the traitor prepared to plunder his neighbour to take possession of his goods. The Christian excels in these accusations, but the Muslim follows on his heels."[21]

One of the most important consequences of the debate was that by accident it revealed the existence of a group of "Ottoman loyalists" in Jaffa whose aim was to oppose the Zionists. The Ottoman News Agency's first telegraphic reports stated that "Hafız" had declared that the fear of the Zionists was imaginary. The deputy in question was Hafız Ibrahim Efendi from Ipek. But in Jaffa the report was taken to refer to Ḥafiẓ Bey al-Saᶜid, the town's deputy, who in fact does not appear to have taken part in the

18. *Ha-Or,* ii [xxvii], 186/361 (16.6.1911); and *ha-Ḥerut,* iii, 106 (19.6.1911).
19. *Ha-Or,* ii [xxvii], 204/379 (9.7.1911).
20. *JCA* 268/enc. to no. 195 (21.6.1911), Antébi to Starkmeth.
21. *AIU* X E 29 (21.6.1911), Antébi to Haham Bası (Consple.).

discussion at all. In protest, an open letter addressed to Ḥafiẓ Bey was published in *Falasṭin,* a paper newly founded in Jaffa. The Arab deputies who spoke against Zionism were praised, whereas Ḥafiẓ Bey was criticised for calling the Zionist danger "imaginary," especially as he was familiar with the question at first hand.

> [Zionism] is the danger which encompasses his homeland; [Zionism] is the awful wave which beats his shore. It is the source of the deceitfulness which we experience like a flood and which is more frightening than walking alone at the dead of night. Not only this: it is also an omen of our future exile from our homeland and of [our] departure from our homes and property.[22]

Open letters and telegrams protesting against Zionism had already been dispatched from Palestine on a number of occasions. This one was remarkable in that it was signed *al-Ḥizb al-Waṭani al-ᶜUthmani*—the Ottoman Patriotic Party.

In the summer of 1911 *al-Haqiqa* and *al-Mufid* (both published in Beirut) reported that the aims of this group were to oppose the Zionists.[23] One of its founders was named Sulayman al-Taji al-Faruqi,[24] a blind shaykh from Ramle who owned property near Jaffa and whose family was connected with the Nashashibis. After World War I, he was prominent in anti-Zionist politics and, *inter alia,* edited *al-Jamiᶜa al-Islamiyya,* an Islamic organ with strong anti-Zionist leanings.

In September 1911 Shimon Muyal, a Jewish doctor in Jaffa, wrote to the editors of *ha-Ḥerut* about the existence of another society in Jaffa called *al-Sharika al-Iqtiṣadiyya al-Tijariyya*—the Economic and Commercial Company. Muyal named Sulayman al-Taji, al-Ḥajj Ḥaydar (a trader from Nablus established in Jaffa), and Muḥammad Amin Ṣihyun (a Jaffa pharmacist) as the society's leading members. Muyal claimed that Jews were excluded from this society and that its object was also to oppose Zionism. It proposed that the local population should be induced to hate the Jews and compel them to depart.[25]

Muyal's letter to *ha-Ḥerut* was reproduced in *Falasṭin,*[26] where

22. *Ha-Ḥerut,* iii, 84 (24.5.1911), reprinting open letter from *Falasṭin* (relevant edition of *Falasṭin* not available).
23. Hochberg, p. 281.
24. *Loc. cit.*
25. Muyal to *ha-Ḥerut,* iii, 146 (4.9.1911).
26. *Falasṭin,* i, 69 (16.9.1911).

it sparked off an exchange with Muḥammad Ṣihyun.[27] From this correspondence it emerged that both the Ottoman Patriotic Party and the Economic and Commercial Company did exist and that both groups were very small. Muḥammad Ṣihyun confirmed that the object of the Ottoman Patriotic Party was to fight the Zionists, and the only point in dispute was whether the Economic and Commercial Company was purely a business organisation or was also concerned with religious and political issues.

These two societies had their counterparts in Haifa. Since the end of 1910 there had been reports of a group there whose aim was to resist Jewish immigration into Palestine.[28] After the second debate on Zionism, Najib Naṣṣar drew his readers' attention to the lax manner in which the Red Slip regulations were administered by the Ottoman authorities in the town. He persuaded them to set up a citizens' watch-committee, headed by himself, which succeeded in gaining permission from the Kaymakam of Haifa to supervise the disembarkation of Jews from all ships calling at Haifa.[29]

But Naṣṣar also began to shift the emphasis of his attacks. Having had only limited success in his campaign to prevent land sales to Jews, he started to pay more attention to their commercial activities in Palestine. For example, in February 1911 he accused them in *al-Karmil* of being economically exclusive and blamed them for rises in the cost of living, especially in basic commodities.[30] By the middle of the summer there were reports that he was trying to organise what was described as an "economic boycott" of the Jews in Haifa through his citizens' watch-committee.[31] Boycotts as such were not unknown in the Ottoman Empire, and indeed, later in 1911, when the war with Italy broke out, a boycott of Italian goods was called for. The originality in Naṣṣar's proposal lay in that it was directed against Jews. To give it substance, he suggested that local Arabs should not rent houses to Jews or trade with them. But apparently his proposal was none too successful, because, as one Hebrew journal put it, even "the most fanatical Christian" was happy to rent his house to a Jew who paid handsomely from year to year.[32]

27. *Falasṭin,* i, 69 (16.9.1911); 70 (20.9.1911); and 71 (23.9.1911); cf. also *ha-Ḥerut,* iv, 10 (20.10.1911).
28. *Ha-Ḥerut,* iii, 25 (19.12.1910); and *ha-ʿOlam,* v, 13 (12.4.1911), p. 23.
29. *Ha-Ḥerut,* iii, 132 (9.8.1911).
30. *Ha-Ḥerut,* iii, 48 (8.2.1911); and iii, 121 (19.7.1911).
31. *Ha-Poʿel ha-Ẓaʿir,* iv, 22 (1911), pp. 12–13.
32. *Loc. cit.*

Naṣṣar had still other ideas. On 7 June he published an open letter inviting all newspaper editors who shared his views to unite and present a common front against the Zionists.[33] With a few days, *al-Raᶜy al-ᶜAmm* in Beirut came out in favour of his suggestion,[34] but there is no evidence to show that anything was done about it. On the other hand, certain Arabic newspapers once again began attacking Najib al-Aṣfar and his project, mentioned in chapter four, to purchase all çiftliks in Syria and Palestine. In August, the British Consul in Damascus reported that al-Aṣfar had sent an agent, a certain Dr. Ḥaydar of Baalbek, to silence these papers by offering their editors shares in his project.[35] The attacks on al-Aṣfar accordingly ceased, but those on the Zionists did not. And, as will be seen, the number of newspapers taking an anti-Zionist line increased from this point on.

The first debate in March inspired Naṣṣar to write his booklet *al-Ṣihyuniyya.* Six months after the second debate, a young Arab wrote the first fictional work in Arabic about Zionism: *The Maid of Zion.* The author was Maᶜaruf al-Arnaᶜuṭ, who later became a member of the Arab Academy in Damascus. In 1911 he was nineteen years old and, having been educated in Beirut, was embarking on his literary career as a contributor to newspapers in that city.[36]

Ha-Ḥerut's Haifa correspondent detailed the story's chapter headings, which provide a clear outline of the plot:

The greatness of the Jews in early generations; the destruction of the First Temple; revolt amongst the nations; rebuilding the Temple; the children of Jacob; the destruction of the Second Temple; migration; Esther and Moses; feelings of love; the Tiberias incident and Dr. Ḥaydar and Dr. al-Aṣfar; Esther speaks at the Zionist Congress; the first kiss; the form of love; interview of the leader of the Zionists with Dr. Ḥaydar and Dr. al-Aṣfar; the Four-sided Covenant; the parties to the Covenant; a night in a German hostel; the sickness of the Maid of Zion; the uprising of the newspapers; the people arise; a wreath of flowers on the death-bed; the last kiss; Esther in the grave; cursed are ye, O Jerusalem; the voice of God; how pleasant is death; the sealing of the sorrow.[37]

33. *Ha-Ḥerut,* iii, 105 (16.6.1911); and *ha-Or,* ii (xxvii) 204/379 (9.7.1911).
34. *Ha-Ḥerut,* iii, 108/9 (21.6.1911).
35. *PRO* FO 195/2371, no. 41 (12.8.1911), G. P. Devey (Damascus) to Sir G. A. Lowther (Consple.).
36. *Al-Zirakli,* viii, 184.
37. *Ha-Ḥerut,* iv, 22 (9.11.1911(.

It is not difficult to reconstruct the gist of al-Arnaʿuṭ's story, which probably appeared in one of the newspapers to which he contributed. It began with some historical background, leading up to the second exile of the Jews from their Land. Moses (apparently the Jewish people) fell in love with Esther (the Land of Israel), who appealed to the Zionists at their Congress and was embraced by them. The unspecified "Tiberias incident" and the Zionist leader's talk with Ḥaydar and al-Aṣfar presumably related to the rumour that these Arabs were Zionist representatives. The "Four-sided Covenant" was the name given to the group of four newspapers which joined *al-Karmil* in 1910 in its anti-Zionist campeign: *al-Muqtabas, al-Mufid, al-Ḥaqiqa,* and *al-Raʿy al-ʿAmm* (see p. 87).[38] One cannot tell what happened in the German hostel, but Esther, the Land, contracted an illness, perhaps because Moses, the Jewish people, forced himself upon her. The Arabic press rose up and spoke out, whereupon the local population of the country also rose in protest. Esther, as a Jewish Land, died and ". . . how pleasant is death." God has passed judgement.

The author's hopes are barely concealed.

As befits a talented young writer, al-Arnaʿuṭ was ahead of his time. The Arabic press, though also in advance of the public, had certainly not "risen" as a body against Zionism. Moreover, the "Arab Revolt" in Palestine was still a quarter of a century away, and when it came, from 1936 to 1939, it was directed as much against the British administration as against the Jews. On the other hand, the Arabic press *was* devoting progressively more space to the Zionist question, and by 1912 the gap between it and its readers was contracting. Thus, al-Arnaʿuṭ's wishful thinking aside, it was becoming a useful indicator of Arab positions on the issue as they were developing.

Before examining the Arabic press in depth, certain preliminary observations are called for. First, a general *caveat*: the press must be approached with care. Newspapers throughout the Empire were usually small and shaky enterprises. There were a handful of Arabic newspapers with circulations in the thousands (for instance, *Lisan al-Ḥal* and *al-Naṣir,* the largest papers in Beirut in 1912, which put out ten to twelve thousand copies and six to eight thousand copies a

38. Malul, p. 466.

day respectively).[39] But they were exceptions. Circulations were more regularly limited to a few hundred copies, once or twice weekly. Consequently, editors looked for patronage and, in so doing, thought little of representing their backers' views for relatively small subsidies. The CUP "sponsored" many newspapers in this way, and foreign diplomats, not to speak of private individuals, often found it expedient to offer sweeteners to newspapers. However, if allowance is made for this fact and an "overview" is cautiously attempted, recognisable patterns do emerge concerning the treatment of Zionism in the Arabic press. The patterns are significantly different for Palestine, the surrounding provinces, and Egypt.

Second, "public opinion" in the sense in which the term is used today was nonexistent in the Arab provinces or, for that matter, in the Empire at large. Consequently, the press did not "reflect" opinion. If anything, the process was the other way round. The press helped to mould or form opinion, especially as its views tended to be in advance of those of its readers.

Even in this sphere, the moulding of opinion, the press's influence can be queried in view of the high rate of illiteracy prevailing. But apparently it cannot be discounted altogether, either among the educated élite or, what is more interesting, among non-élite groups in Palestine as well. In August 1911, Isaac Nahon, the director of the Alliance school in Haifa, noted that local Muslims, being little educated, accepted *al-Karmil's* allegations implicitly and identified with its point of view.[40] Similarly, Shimon Muyal of Jaffa observed a few months later that a "spirit of enmity" had begun "to gain a foothold among the masses because of the influence of the antagonistic press."[41]

Finally, the *function* of the press should not be overlooked. As suggested in Chapter Four, the press served as the principal medium through which Arab arguments against Zionism were worked out. Furthermore, it served as the vehicle by which detailed information about Zionism was conveyed far beyond Palestine to Arabs who might otherwise have remained uninformed. Periodicals appearing in Egypt, Constantinople, and Paris have already been cited in connection with Zionism. In 1910, *Mirᶜat al-Gharb,* an Arabic

39. *CZA* Z3/1448 (19.3.1912), Thon to ZAC.
40. *AIU* I C 1-2 (8.8.1911), I. Nahon (Haifa) to Pres., AIU.
41. *CZA* L2/167 (15.1.1912), S. Muyal (Jaffa) to Ruppin; cf. *Near East,* v, 77 (16.2.1912), p. 462.

newspaper produced by Syrian émigrés in New York, was also carrying anti-Zionist articles.[42]

In Palestine there were only two Arabic newspapers of consequence by 1912—*al-Karmil* in Haifa and *Falasṭin* in Jaffa. The first two newspapers to appear in the country after the Young Turk Revolution—*al-Quds* in Jerusalem and *al-Aṣmaʿi* in Jaffa—had gone out of existence; and although there were two other newspapers at the time—*al-Nafir* and *al-Munadi*—neither seems to have been taken seriously, even in Jerusalem where both were published. *Al-Nafir* received a small subsidy from the Zionist Office in Jaffa,[43] and during 1911 was managed by a Jew.[44] Not surprisingly, therefore, it was a consistent supporter of the Zionists.[45] *Al-Munadi,* on the other hand, was frankly anti-Zionist throughout its whole existence from the spring of 1912 to the autumn of 1913.[46]

But to return to *al-Karmil* and *Falasṭin.* Enough has been said about the former so that the mention of just one small, but illuminating, incident at this juncture will suffice. Although Najib Naṣṣar began to deploy economic arguments against the Zionists in 1911, he did not forsake his campaign against land sales to them.[47] In April 1912 he accused the Mutasarrıf of Acre of facilitating certain land purchases to Jews,[48] and the Mutasarrıf took him to court. But the Mutasarrıf lost his case and Naṣṣar was acquitted "on the grounds that he had written [his attacks on the Mutasarrıf] as a true and sincere Ottoman."[49] Apparently anti-Zionism on the basis of Ottoman loyalism was not a crime.

42. *Ha-Ḥerut,* iii, 6 (4.11.1910).
43. *CZA* L2/167 (2.8.1910), I. Lévy (Jerus.) to Thon; and L18/245/5 (20.1.1913), Thon to Lévy.
44. *CZA* L2/167 (11.4.1911), Lévy to Thon.
45. E.G. *ha-Ḥerut,* i 13 (22.6.1909); ii, 95 (25.5.1910); ii, 130 (8.8.1910); ii, 133 (16.8.1910); iii, 69 (27.3.1911); iii, 79 [= 80], (26.4.1911); iii, 83 (3.5.1911); iii, 104 (14.6.1911(; and *CZA* Z3/1448, press report of article in March 1912 (no date).
46. E.G. *ha-Ḥerut,* iv, 80 (21.2.1912); iv, 89 (11.3.1912); *CZA* Z3/1448, press reports re *al-Munadi* of 12.3.1912, of 20.4.1912, and of 4.6.1912; and *CZA* L2/167, press report re *al-Munadi* of 8.10.1912.
47. E.g. *ha-Ḥerut,* iv 18 (2.11.1911); *CZA* L2/167, press report re *al-Karmil* of 16.1.1912; *CZA* Z3/1447, press report re *al-Karmil* of 26.1.1912; *CZA* Z3/1448, press report re *al-Karmil* of 2.4.1912; *ha-Ḥerut,* iv, 116 (17.5.1912); and iv, 117 (19.5.1912).
48. *CZA* L18/246/2 (6.4.1912), J. Hankin (Haifa) to Ruppin.
49. *Near East,* iii, 55 (24.5.1912); cf. *CZA* Z3/1448 (8.5.1912), Thon to ZAC; and *ha-Or,* xxx 177 (17.5.1912).

Falasṭin began to appear in Jaffa in January 1911. Published twice weekly, it was owned and edited by two brothers, ʿIsa Daʿud al-ʿIsa and Yusuf al-ʿIsa. Greek Orthodox by religion, they were young, outspoken, and frequently at odds with the spiritual leaders of their Church. After World War I both brothers (but ʿIsa Daʿud especially) were active among Arabs in Palestine who opposed the British administration and openly favoured pan-Arab unity stretching beyond Palestine.

From its inception, their paper supported the CUP. Regarding Zionism, it did not seem to have an altogether firm position.[50] In its first year, it published anti-Zionist pieces, but it also printed articles inspired,[51] or submitted, by Jews.[52] During the General Elections in the spring of 1912 it tended to avoid the question,[53] a policy which brought it into line with pro-CUP papers outside Palestine (see below). But, with the Liberal Union's transition to power in the summer of 1912, it began to print articles which indicated that its editors had decided to take a strong stand against Jewish immigration and Zionist work in Palestine. The paper's opposition of Zionism mounted from that moment onwards, and by the spring of 1914 Jewish observers considered that it was more hostile than *al-Karmil.*[54]

Falasṭin's anti-Zionism differed from *al-Karmil's* in one notable respect. Its position was based more on grounds of local patriotism than of Ottoman loyalism. As befitted its name, *Falasṭin* regularly discussed questions to do with Palestine as if it were a distinct entity and, in writing against the Zionists, addressed its readers as "Palestinians."[55]

On the other hand, the themes of its attacks were similar to *al-Karmil's.* The Zionists, in addition to "grabbing up" land, were

50. *Ha-Ḥerut,* iii, 69 (27.3.1911).
51. *Ha-Ḥerut,* iii, 61 (6.3.1911), re article by Salim al-Salaḥi in *Falasṭin,* i, 13 [February, 1911]; CF. *CZA* Z2/635 (31.3.1911), Ruppin to ZCO.
52. *Falasṭin,* i, 54 (1911): article by S. Frumkin; ii, 8 (7.2.1912): letter from "Ottoman Jew"; also a series of articles in winter 1911 and spring 1912, entitled *"Rasaʾil al-fallaḥ"* and signed "Abu Ibrahim," which were written by M. Meirovitch, a settler at Rishon le-Ẓiyyon—see *CZA* Z3/1448 (6.6.1912), Ruppin to ZCO.
53. *Falasṭin,* vol. ii, nos. 1–39 (Jan. to May, 1912) contain almost no items on Zionism.
54. *Ha-Ḥerut,* vi, 155 (21.4.1914).
55. E.g. an editorial entitled "Palestine" in *Falasṭin,* ii, 66 (31.8.1912).

responsible for rises in the cost of living.[56] The Jews were exclusive socially, commercially, and in their schools.[57] Only on one point was *Falasṭin* noticeably original. It will be recalled that early in 1911, a Turkish writer in Salonika had claimed at the prompting of the local French Consul, that Zionism was a device to spread German influence in the Empire. In July of that year, a Jerusalem teacher, called Mustafa Tamr, argued in *Falasṭin* that it was the *Russians,* and possibly the British, who were trying to advance their interests in the Empire by directing Jews to Palestine and helping Zionist colonisation.[58] But two months later Yusuf al-ᶜIsa, the editor of *Falasṭin,* set his sights on Russia alone.[59] Since the majority of Jewish immigrants came from Russia and almost none from Britain, it is easy to understand why.

For *Falasṭin* and *al-Karmil,* Zionist activities in Palestine were news of genuine local interest which could not be ignored. This was not the case for most Arabic newspapers in the surrounding provinces. They were less involved in affairs in Palestine, and their stands on Zionism were, to a certain extent, a matter of party politics.

Turkish and Greek opponents of the CUP had found it convenient to depict the Committee as being pro-Jewish from 1910 onwards. Arab opponents of the CUP followed suit after the first debate on Zionism in Parliament in the spring of 1911. For example, Rashid Riḍa, the Islamic thinker mentioned in Chapter Two, supported the CUP for some time after the Young Turk Revolution. But in 1911 he joined its opponents, and in a brief report in *al-Manar* about the first debate on Zionism, he remarked that, when in Constantinople the previous year, he had indeed noticed "that the influence of the Jews in the CUP was great."[60] Muḥammad Kurd ᶜAli, the editor of *al-Muqtabas* in Damascus (anti-CUP from 1911 onwards), asserts in a historical work on Syria that in 1911 the CUP—or rather Jews and Dönmes in its ranks—intended to sell three million dunams of land in Palestine to the Zionists; however,

56. *Falasṭin,* ii, 39 (29.5.1912); and ii, 41 (5.6.1912).
57. *Falasṭin,* ii, 39 (29.5.1912); and ii, 41 (5.6.1912); ii, 60 (10.8.1912); ii, 67 (3.9.1912); ii, 69 (11.9.1912); ii, 73 (25.9.1912); ii, 75 (2.10.1912); and ii, 76 (5.10.1912).
58. *Falasṭin,* i, 53 (22.7.1911).
59. *Falasṭin,* i, 69 (16.9.1911).
60. *Al-Manar,* xiv, 2 (1911), p. 159.

Shukri al-ᶜAsali warned Parliament about the "danger of Zionism," and the proposed sale was abandoned.[61] Thus, in Palestine, both *al-Karmil* and *Falasṭin* were *pro*-CUP and anti-Zionist, whereas papers in the surrounding provinces tended to be *anti*-CUP and anti-Zionist. But if their opposition to Zionism was linked to their hostility to the CUP, it was also subordinate to it.[62]

This correlation was an important key to understanding the attitudes of most papers, but it was not the only one. In 1911 the Zionist Office in Jaffa began to monitor the Arabic press methodically, and in the first half of 1912 it made a careful analysis of twenty-four periodicals appearing regularly in Beirut and Damascus.[63] It discovered that the anti-CUP papers were almost invariably edited by Muslims and, besides being anti-Zionists, were also anti-Christian and anti-European. Papers edited by Christian Arabs were generally pro-CUP, and either friendly or neutral towards Jews and Zionists. In other words, Muslim editors in Beirut and Damascus tended to be averse to everything that was non-Muslim and non-Arab. Christian editors, on the other hand, perhaps worried about the mood among the Muslims, supported the CUP Government and, it seems, believing that "the enemies of my enemies are my friends," were willing to write in favour of the Zionists. Put differently, in Beirut and Damascus, a newspaper's stand in respect of Zionism was as much a function of its editor's religion as of his politics.

Thus another difference emerges between the press in Palestine and the press in the surrounding provinces. In Palestine, the Christian editors of *Falasṭin* and, within a short while of *al-Karmil* as well, could call on all Palestinians, both Muslim and Christian, to unite against Zionism on grounds of local patriotism, on the other hand, after the Arabic press outside Palestine had talked for a year or so about "Jewish influence" in the CUP, Ṭaha al-Mudawwar, the Muslim editor of *al-Raᶜy al-ᶜAmm* in Beirut (anti-CUP), called in

61. M. Kurd ᶜAli, *Khiṭaṭ al-Sham,* iii, 131.
62. Cf. *ha-Poᶜel ha-Ẓaᶜir,* v. 14–15 (1912).
63. Eleven periodicals from Beirut were analysed: *al-Naṣir, Lisan al-Ḥal, al-Raᶜy al-ᶜAmm, al-Mufid, al-Ḥaqiqa, al-Aḥwal, Ababil, al-Thabat, al-Ittiḥad al-ᶜUthmani, al-Ḥaris,* and *al-Ḥimara.* Thirteen periodicals (including eight humorous weeklies) from Damascus were analysed: *al-Muqtabas, al-ᶜAṣr al-Jadid, al-Mishkat, al-Muntakhabat, al-Muhajir, al-Nadim, al-Rawi, al-Bariqa, Juḥa, al-Damir, al-Raᶜy al-ᶜAmm, al-Ishtirakiyya,* and *Ḥuṭṭ bil-Khurj*—*CZA* Z3/1448 (19.3 and 24.6.1912), both Thon to ZAC.

1912 for specifically *Muslim* unity against the Zionists.[64] The first calls of a new trend in Arab anti-Zionism were being sounded.

The link between an editor's politics and religion and his attitude to Zionism can be illustrated for the years 1911 and 1912 without the need to enter into detailed content analysis. After the first debate, *Lisan al-Ḥal* and some other pro-CUP papers edited by Christians came out in favour of the Zionists. *Lisan al-Ḥal,* for example, quoted with approval a speech by Victor Jacobson made in Salonika in which he said that the Zionists did not want to establish an independent state in Palestine, but sought only to develop the country economically and as a cultural centre under Ottoman protection.[65]

In July, after the second debate, the Christian owner of *al-ʿAṣr al-Jadid,* an important CUP organ in Damascus, approached local Jews for subscriptions to his paper, as he was prepared to defend Zionism against the harsh attacks appearing in *al-Muqtabas* (anti-CUP).[66] In the summer of 1911, *Ḥuṭṭ bil-Khurj,* a humorous weekly in Damascus, was unsympathetic to the CUP Government and wrote against Zionism.[67] But during the elections in the spring of 1912 this paper, even though edited by a Muslim, shifted its support to the CUP, and its criticism of Jewish activities stopped.[68] *Al-Mishkat,* launched during the election campaign by a leading Christian supporter of the CUP in Damascus, fought the assaults on the Committee and, correspondingly, on the Zionists.[69]

During and after the elections, the CUP closed down a number of unfriendly Arabic papers.[70] As a result, articles on Zionism almost ceased to appear in Beirut and Damascus[71]—since the papers which would normally have carried them were either suspended or hesitant about speaking their minds. But when the Liberal Union

64. *CZA* Z3/1448 (10.6.1912), Ruppin to ZCO re *al-Raʾy al-ʿAmm* of 1.6.1912; and (26.7.1912), Thon to ZAC re *al-Raʾy al-ʿAmm,* no. 666 (no date).
65. *Ha-Ḥerut,* iii, 67 (22.3.1911).
66. *CZA L2/167 (6.7.1911),* [illegible signature] to "Cher Docteur" [Ruppin?] (Zionist Office, Jaffa).
67. *Ha-Ḥerut,* iii, 51 (11.9.1911).
68. *CZA* Z3/1448 (24.6.1912), Thon to ZAC.
69. *CZA* Z3/1448 (24.6.1912); cf. *ha-Poʿel ha-Ẓaʿir,* v, 14–15 (1912).
70. *Ha-Ḥerut,* iv, 155 (3.7.1912); cf. *PRO* FO 195/2427/1988, no. 21 (18.4.1912), Devey to Lowther.
71. *CZA* Z3/1448 (6.6.1912), Ruppin to ZCO; and *CZA* Z3/1448 (7. and 12.7.1912), both Thon to ZAC.

came to power in the summer, the familiar pattern was quickly re-established: anti-CUP papers (mainly Muslim) attacked the former Government violently for aiding the Zionists, while pro-CUP papers (mainly Christian) again tried to defend the Committee on that score.[72]

To complete this survey, newspapers in Egypt should also be reviewed. The majority of papers there were locally oriented and seldom referred to Zionism.[73] The exceptions were three large dailies in Cairo—*al-Maḥrusa, al-Muqaṭṭam* and *al-Ahram.* All were edited by Christian Arabs from the Vilâyets of Beirut and Şam and all maintained a concern for politics in the Arab provinces, where they were widely read. Beyond the reach of the Ottoman censor, they opened their columns to Arab grievances against the CUP, and by 1912 were sympathetic in varying degrees to Arab nationalism.

Al-Maḥrusa disliked the British occupation of Egypt, but was sympathetic to Europeans. It often mentioned the Zionists, and without actually supporting them, was prepared to recognise the benefits that they brought to Palestine.[74] *Al-Muqaṭṭam* was subsidised by the British to support them; it was neutral on Zionism.[75] Both papers were willing to publish pro-Zionist articles by Egyptian Jews and by Nisim Malul, a Palestinian Jew, who was *al-Muqaṭṭam's* correspondent in Jaffa.[76]

On the other hand, *al-Ahram* (still one of the leading newspapers in Egypt today) was anti-British and anti-Zionist.[77] More committed to Arab nationalism than *al-Maḥrusa* and *al-Muqaṭṭam* and close to Egyptian nationalists as well, it had manifested its feelings about Zionism even before the Young Turk Revolution.[78] In 1909, it claimed that the Jews had "a hidden, secret aim" of establishing an independent kingdom in Palestine.[79] They avoided service in the Ottoman army to concentrate on that objective. Pressure had to be

72. Cf. *ha-Poʿel ha-Ẓaʿir,* vi, i (1912).
73. *CZA* Z3/1447 (16.7.1912), Thon to ZAC.
74. *Ibid.*
75. *Ibid.*
76. *Ha-Ẓevi,* xxv, 240 (9.8.1909), re *al-Muqaṭṭam*; cf. *L'Aurore,* ii 37 (4.3.1910); *CZA* Z2/1447 (13.2.1912), press report re *al-Maḥrusa* of 21.1.1912 and 4.2.1912; also re *al-Muqaṭṭam* of 31.1.1912; and *CZA* L2/167 (17.10.1912), press report re *al-Muqaṭṭam* of 7.10.1912.
77. *CZA* Z3/1447 (16.2.1912).
78. *Ha-Ẓevi,* xxv, 240 (9.8.1909).
79. *Ha-Ḥerut,* i, 24 (23.7.1909).

put on the CUP Government to halt their activities,[80] otherwise the consequences would be unfortunate.[81]

In sum, therefore, these Christian-edited newspapers in Egypt handled Zionism differently from newspapers edited by Christians in Palestine and also Beirut and Damascus. *Al-Maḥrusa* and *al-Muqaṭṭam* were anti-CUP but neutral on Zionism. *Al-Ahram* was anti-CUP and anti-Zionist, and thus resembled newspapers edited by Muslims in Beirut and Damascus. As will be seen from subsequent chapters, the common denominator in this case was Arab nationalism.

The Liberal Union Cabinet held office from July 1912 to January 1913. Its brief spell in power was overshadowed by the first Balkan War, which broke out in October and was a disaster for the Ottoman Empire. When hostilities were halted on 3 December, "Turkey in Europe" was all but lost. Adrianople, about 150 miles from Constantinople, was the only major Ottoman city in Europe to hold out, surviving a siege by the Bulgarians whose forward advance had been checked at Çatalca, some 25 miles from Constantinople. Salonika had been lost to Greece, and Montenegro and Serbia (the other partners to the Balkan League) had also staked out claims to larger territories at the expense of the Empire.

This period proved to be a turning point in Arab relations with the Ottoman Turks. When the Liberal Union came to power, demands for administrative reforms in the provinces became the order of the day. And although the Liberal Union had advocated such reforms when in opposition, its tenure of office was too short and its preoccupations were too great for it to do much in the way of granting autonomy to the non-Turkish elements in the Empire. Arab expectations, therefore, like those of other groups, were disappointed. Some Arabs, who placed high hopes on reforms and on the possibility of greater self-administration, were completely disillusioned. From their point of view, the Liberal Union turned out to be no better than the CUP, which they had opposed so violently.

On the narrow plane of the Zionist issue, the Liberal Union's tenure of office was also a turning point for Arabs in Palestine.

80. *Ha-Ẓevi,* xxvi, 20 (22.10.1909).
81. *Ha-Ḥerut,* i, 24 (23.7.1909); cf. *ibid.*, iii, 60 (3.3.1911) and iii, 84 (24.5.1911).

Before coming to power, it had accused the CUP of being pro-Jewish and pro-Zionist. But the same reasons which prevented it from initiating administrative reforms in the provinces kept it from taking stronger action than the CUP against the Zionists. For Arabs in Palestine, the issue was dramatised by incidents involving a Mutasarrıf of Jerusalem named Muhdi Bey, who took up his post a few days after the Liberal Union Cabinet was formed.

Muhdi Bey was an Albanian who had studied law and written a book about the Capitulations.[82] He was a strong supporter of the CUP,[83] and before coming to Jerusalem he had been Mutasarrıf of Samsun, a province on the Black Sea coast. His appointment had been made shortly before the change of government, and within a fortnight of his arrival in Jerusalem he made a speech on a Jewish colony which disturbed local Arabs.

One of his first official engagements was to inspect possible sites for an agricultural school which the Government proposed to open near Ramle. Albert Antébi, who in 1912 was a leading representative of the Jewish community in Jerusalem, suggested that he might combine this tour with visits to Jewish colonies in the vicinity of Ramle.[84] The suggestion was accepted and the Mutasarrıf's party, which included the President of the Jerusalem Municipal Council and other Arab notables, set out on 6 August. They spent the night at Rishon le-Ẓiyyon, having passed through Reḥovot and New Ẓiyyona on the way. The following morning they viewed Nabi Rubin (on the Mediterranean coast, south of Rishon le-Ẓiyyon) as a possible location for the agricultural school. In the afternoon, the party returned to Rishon le-Ẓiyyon, inspected the wine cellars, and took part in a reception attended by representatives from all the Jewish colonies in the region.

At that gathering Muhdi Bey replied to appeals for greater public security in the Mutasarrıflık. His remarks, as published in *Truth* (an English-language newspaper in Jerusalem),[85] and reproduced in Arabic newspapers in Jerusalem,[86] Haifa and Damascus,[87] made it sound as if the new cabinet positively welcomed the Zionists in

82. *PRO* FO 195/2425/3806, no. 62 (31.7.1912), P. J. C. McGregor (Jerus.) to C. M. Marling (Consple.).
83. *PRO* FO 195/2452/6969, no. 97 (16.12.1912), McGregor to Lowther.
84. *Ha-Ḥerut,* iv, 180 (2.8.1912).
85. *Truth,* iii, 127 (9.8.1912).
86. *Q d'O* N.S. 134, no. 57 (2.9.1912), A. Guy (Jerus.) to Foreign Ministry (Paris).
87. *Ha-Poʿel ha-Ẓaʿir,* vi, 2 (1912).

Palestine and was willing to give them wider privileges of self-administration and defence than the local population. To make matters worse, Muhdi Bey seemed to have expressed himself in terms almost calculated to offend the Arabs.

He was reported to have denied that the Government objected to Zionism. The Government knew that the "holy associations" of Palestine attracted the Jews to the country—therefore it had "no reason to oppose Zionism." On the contrary, it was delighted to see Jewish progress in Palestine—"you [Jewish settlers] are an object lesson to your native neighbours, who can neither read nor write, that they may see the great possibilities of the land."[88]

To make the colonies more secure, Muhdi Bey was quoted as having said:

> Choose from among yourselves a municipal head, whose appointment will be ratified by the Government, to administer justice and execute judgement according to the rules and regulations of the Ottoman provinces.
>
> You will have to appoint guards and gendarmerie whose names will be registered in the books of the local government which will provide them with uniforms and all necessary accoutrements and invest them with authority.
>
> You must also install telephonic communication between colony and colony—village and village, so that any attack or outrage may at once be notified at headquarters and the marauders be apprehended and punished. . . .
>
> For my part, I will try to put you in possession of the sandhills bordering on the seashore and give you legal title-deeds for the same.
>
> A part of it I will allot you for a capacious Government Building which will serve as your central administrative premises.[89]

Fuller and probably more accurate versions of this speech (for instance, as reported a few days later in Hebrew in *ha-Or,*[90] and also as preserved in Rishon le-Ziyyon's archives[91]) show that it was probably a good deal less controversial than it must have seemed to readers of the Arabic press. Having been asked about public security, Muhdi Bey admitted that the policing of the Empire had

88. *Truth,* iii, 127 (9.8.1912).
89. *Ibid.*
90. *Ha-Or,* iii [xxx], 252 (15.8.1912).
91. Quoted in Dinur, I, i, 183.

always been inadequate and regretted that since 1908 the new régime had not carried out certain much needed reforms. He accordingly referred his audience to some old laws which were still in force and which were framed to protect the individual. Every permanent group of two hundred or more families was required by law to constitute itself as a township. Townships enjoyed certain privileges, among them the rights to elect a muhtar and a council of between five and ten elders, and also to appoint "policemen of the second grade" who were recognised by the local authorities. These "policemen of the second grade" received uniforms and arms and performed their duties under the supervision of the district chief of police.[92] But, Muhdi Bey stressed, the Jews had to become Ottoman subjects to enjoy these statutory prerogatives. He therefore concluded his remarks by appealing to the settlers to adopt Ottoman nationality.[93]

Even so, it is difficult to explain how he could have said that the Government did not oppose the Zionists and how he could have felt at liberty to promise land to the settlers at Rishon le-Ẓiyyon. All his immediate predecessors under CUP governments had been sent to Jerusalem with specific instructions to enforce the restrictions on Jewish entry and land purchase. It is not conceivable that the Liberal Union Government would have given him different instructions. In the absence of more detailed information, perhaps the easiest explanation is to suggest that, in the commotion surrounding the change of government, Muhdi Bey had not been fully briefed before taking up his post. Since arriving in Jerusalem, he had probably been impressed by what he had witnessed of Jewish achievements in his new province, and he saw no reason not to encourage so industrious an element in the population.[94]

By 1912 there was much in the Zionists' achievements to be impressed by. Muhdi Bey had visited three well-established colonies, thriving on land which not many years before had to a large extent been marshy and waste. He would have seen their modern agriculture and up-to-date equipment from Europe. In his search for a site for an agricultural school, he would have been told by Antébi and his hosts about the Miqve Yisraᶜel agricultural school (which

92. Cf. Young, i, 47–88.
93. Cf. *ha-Or,* iii [xxx], 263 (28.8.1912).
94. Cf. *ha-Or,* iii [xxx], 249 (12.8.1912); and iii [xxx], 263 (28.8.1912).

he visited the day after making his speech at Rishon le-Ẓiyyon) and also about other Jewish educational institutions. In addition to the Alliance school which Antébi directed, these included a teachers' seminary and an art school in Jerusalem, a new high school in Jaffa, an agricultural experimental station at ʿAtlit, and the beginnings of a technical school in Haifa. When Muhdi Bey said that the Arab peasants were illiterate and had much to learn from the Jews, he may have been somewhat tactless, but he was perfectly correct.

However, the damage had been done,[95] and pressure was soon put on the Government by local Arabs, supported by Liberal Union papers in Constantinople, to remove Muhdi Bey (a CUP appointee) from office.[96] In the middle of September, papers in Constantinople reported that he was to be replaced by Mehmed Sadık Bey, a Liberal Union journalist on the staff of *Sabah,* who had been educated in Berlin and who at one time had been an official in Jerusalem.[97] Arab notables in Jerusalem, who supported the CUP, promptly protested at this replacement, and, somewhat remarkably, the Liberal Union Minister of the Interior decided to keep Muhdi Bey at his post for the time being.[98]

The feelings of Arab anti-Zionists in Palestine could not have been soothed in the weeks immediately after Muhdi Bey's speech at Rishon le-Ẓiyyon. The local authorities were said to have been less stringent in applying the restrictions on land sales to Jews.[99] The coastal strip between Rishon le-Ẓiyyon and the sea was transferred to the colony as promised by Muhdi Bey.[100] And, at the end of October, he was informed by Constantinople that he could transfer a limited area of land at Dilb (near Jerusalem) to two Ottoman Jews.[101]

At the same time, however, Muhdi Bey received orders from the Grand Vezirate and the Ministry of the Interior to prohibit

95. Cf. *ha-Or,* iii [xxx], 253 (16.8.1912); iii [xxx], 264 (29.8.1912); and *ha-Poʿel ha-Ẓaʿir,* vi, 2 (1912).
96. *CZA* Z23/44 (23.9.1912), Neufach to ZCO (Berlin); and cf. *ha-Ḥerut,* v, 2 (16.9.1912).
97. *Q d'O* N.S. 134, no. 60 (20.9.1912), Guy to Foreign Ministry (Paris); cf. *CZA* Z3/44 (23.9.1912); and *ha-Ḥerut,* v, 6 (20.9.1912).
98. *CZA* Z3/44 (23.9.1912).
99. *Truth,* iii, 129 (23.8.1912).
100. Dinur, I, i, 184.
101. *CZA* Z3/1513 (27. and 30.9.1912), both Jacobson to ZAC.

absolutely both Jewish settlement in the Mutasarrıflık and land sales to foreigners.[102] Thereupon Muhdi Bey, well aware of the complaints against him, issued a circular to his subordinates, forbidding sales of rural land to all Jews, including Ottoman subjects; thenceforth, Ottoman Jews could only acquire buildings in towns for their own use—they could not buy land.[103] Since this went beyond Muhdi Bey's orders, Antébi had two long conversations with him and an agreement was reached.[104] Land transfers in process were to be concluded in the names of Ottoman Jews who were known not to be acting for Jewish immigrants. In return and in order to forestall protests, Antébi was to advise Muhdi Bey in advance of plans by Ottoman Jews to buy land.[105] Under this agreement the transfer of 4,800 dunams at Kafruriyya (near Latrun) was completed two or three weeks later.

With the outbreak of the first Balkan War in the middle of October, the tensions between Muslims and Christians in the Empire grew. The Muslims blamed Europe, especially Russia, for the war, and in various parts of the Empire, including the Arab provinces, they vented their anger on Christians who were suspected of sympathising with Europe. In Palestine, however, an opposite process was at work. Numbers of Muslim and Christian Arabs came closer to one another through their common opposition to Jewish immigration. Taking advantage of the discontent which Muhdi Bey had created, and exploiting the broader current of anti-Russian feeling,[106] they worked together against the Zionists and the Jewish community in Palestine in general.

Antébi described the working of this process in Jerusalem at the end of October.[107] Among Muslim Arabs there was an upsurge of "chauvinistic nationalism." Those affected were led by Ruḥi al-Khalidi and ʿUthman al-Nashashibi, the city's CUP deputies in the dissolved Parliament. With the object of working against the Zionists, they were allying themselves with Christian Arabs who were ill-disposed to Jews. Several delegations of local notables, both

102. *JCA* 268/enc. to no. 206 (1.11.1912), Antébi to Starkmeth.
103. *JCA* 268/enc. to no. 206: Circular, no. 467 [date omitted—probably 28.10.1912], Muhdi Bey (Jerus.) to the director of the Cadastre and kaymakams.
104. *JCA* 268/enc. to no. 206 (1.11.1912), Antébi to Starkmeth.
105. *JCA* 268/no. 206 (3.11.1912), Antébi to Pres., JCA; and encs.
106. *JCA* 268/no. 206 (3.11.1912), Antébi to Pres., JCA.
107. *JCA* 268/no. 205 (27.10.1912), Antébi to Pres., JCA; cf. *JCA* 268/enc. to no. 206 (30.10.1912), same to Starkmeth.

Muslims and Christians, had approached the Mutasarrıf "to injure and slander us."[108] Muslims and Christians in Jerusalem were signing "an anti-Semitic petition."[109] And, following the land sale at Kafruriyya in November, an article was published in *Falasṭin,* censuring the "duplicity" of the Mutasarrıf and the Jews.[110]

Arab efforts to have Muhdi Bey removed were answered in December when it was announced that he was to be replaced by Tahir Bey Hayreddin, the Liberal Union candidate who had defeated Memduh Bey twelve months earlier (see p. 119). Muhdi Bey left Jerusalem on 15 December, but Tahir Bey did not reach Jaffa until 12 January 1913. Eleven days later, Enver Bey led a coup d'état in Constantinople, restoring the CUP to power. And at the end of the month, Tahir Bey, a supporter and nominee of the Liberal Union, resigned his post as Mutasarrıf of Jerusalem.[111]

Tahir Bey arrived too late and stayed too briefly to prevent the transfer of 6,700 dunams of land at Abu Shusha (near Ramle) to the Zionists.[112] Before he was succeeded by Mecid Şevket Bey in March 1913, further land sales took place.[113] Almost inevitably, articles appeared in the Arabic press in protest.[114] One, in *Falasṭin,* was written by a young man called ᶜArif al-ᶜArif. Son of the deputy from Gaza, he later had a distinguished career in the British administration in Palestine and as Chief Secretary to the Government of Transjordan (before 1948). From 1950 to 1955 he was Mayor of Jerusalem, and in the latter half of the 1950s he wrote a six-volume work, entitled *The Disaster,* about the Arab–Israel War of 1948–49. In 1913, when he submitted his article to *Falasṭin,* he was twenty years old and a student in Constantinople. *Inter alia,* he wrote that "if this state of affairs continues . . . then the Zionists will gain mastery over our country, village by village, town by town; tomorrow the whole of Jerusalem will be sold and

108. *JCA* 268/enc. to no. 206 (30.10.1912); cf. enc. of 1.11.1912, M. Meierovitch (Rishon le-Ẓiyyon) to Antébi; and enc. of 1.11.1912, Antébi to Starkmeth; cf. also *ha-Ḥerut,* v, 44 (12.11.1912).

109. *JCA* 268/enc. to no. 206 (1.11.1912), Antébi to Starkmeth.

110. *Falasṭin,* ii, 92 (30.11.1912).

111. *Near East,* iv, 96 (1913).

112. *CZA* L2/26/III (26.1.1913), Thon to ZAC.

113. *Truth,* iii, 138 (21.2.1913).

114. *Falasṭin,* iii, 3 (22.1.1913); iii, 5 (29.1.1913); and iii, 7 (5.2.1913); cf. *CZA* Z3/115 press report [undated and unsigned] re articles in *al-Munadi* on 14. and 24.1.1913, and on 3., 6., and 20.2.1913; and in *al-Muqtabas* on 18.2.1913.

then Palestine in its entirety."[115] He also quoted back at Tahir Bey an article written a year earlier, with Tahir's help, by an "important Palestinian." Its author (possibly ᶜArif al-ᶜArif's father) had commented that the fellah was no longer secure on his land, given the Zionists' urge to acquire his property.

ᶜArif al-ᶜArif's article showed two things. First, local patriotism, involving a more distinctly articulated "Palestinian" consciousness, had advanced while the Liberal Union was in power. Second, the younger generation of Arabs in Palestine, who were to come into their own after World War I, were now alive to the Zionist question.

115. *Falasṭin,* iii, 4 (25.1.1913).

7

Alliance or Entente?

THE BALKAN WARS were a catalyst that led to many changes in the Ottoman Empire. They affected not only Arab attitudes to the Ottoman Government, but also, in a quite different way, the Government's attitude to the Zionists. Coming immediately in the wake of the war with Italy, the first Balkan War left the Empire penniless. In other circumstances, Britain or France might have considered extending significant credit facilities to the Empire. But fearing that further hostilities in the Balkans could lead to a Russian occupation of Constantinople and perhaps to a general conflagration in Europe, they were reluctant to provide the Sublime Porte with the means to continue fighting after the armistice of 3 December 1912. Consequently, Rothschilds of London withdrew a guarantee already given to the Ottoman Government for the purchase of two battleships from Brazil; and, arguing that new arrangements for international control of Ottoman finances were needed, the British Ambassador at Berlin secured Germany's consent to exchange views with Britain and France before any large sums were made available to the Ottoman Empire.[1] The Deutsche Bank accordingly agreed to shelve a loan which was being negotiated with the Ottoman Government in January 1913.[2] Denied

1. *PRO* FO 371/1783/4670, no. 23 (30.1.1913), Sir E. Goschen (Berlin) to Sir E. Grey (FO).
2. *PRO* FO 371/11783/4670, no. 23 (30.1.1913).

aid from the three Powers which traditionally had been its bankers, the Ottoman Government was prepared to seek financial help and other support from any quarter—Jews and Zionists not excepted. This changed position applied as of December 1912 to the Liberal Union Cabinet (under the influence of elder Ottoman statesmen), and with greater force to the CUP Cabinet which came to power in January 1913. With the Empire in dire military and financial straits, both parties were capable of moderating their opposition to Zionism.

Signs of a change in the Liberal Union's attitude came even before the end of the war with Italy, when the Treasury was already under strain. In September 1912, Victor Jacobson met Kâmil Paşa, the President of the Council of State. As an old-régime statesman, he had been familiar with the Zionist question for many years. He told Jacobson that he did not fear a "Zionist danger," that he valued Jewish settlement in Palestine, and that in the Council of State and in the Cabinet he would advocate that Jews, Ottoman and foreign, should be allowed to purchase land.[3] Shortly afterwards, Jacobson met Gabriyel Noradungiyan, the Minister of Foreign Affairs. He too was an old-régime statesman, and Jacobson also found him friendly and prepared to be helpful over land purchases by Jews.[4] Jacobson gained the impression that Kâmil and, to a lesser extent, Noradungiyan believed in the Zionists' "power" in Europe. Kâmil particularly wanted the German and Austro-Hungarian press to be influenced in favour of the still new Liberal Union Government.[5]

A few weeks later, in November, one of Jacobson's colleagues in Constantinople reported that Sami Hochberg, the editor of *Le Jeune-Turc* (which the Zionists sponsored), was having discussions with Turkish members of the Liberal Union. They claimed that the war in the Balkans had disabused them about the Greeks in the Empire. The Ottoman Greeks had previously taken a leading part in the Liberal Union, and had always accused the Zionists of seeking the downfall of the Empire. However, their role in the loss of Salonika to Greece had shown them to be "liars and hypocrites." The Turkish Liberal Unionists were now persuaded that the Jews

3. *CZA* Z3/1513 (27. and 30.9.1912), both V. Jacobson (Consple.) to ZAC (Berlin); and *CZA* Z3/1513 (7.10.1912), Zionist Executive minutes.
4. *CZA* Z3/1513 (7.10.1912).
5. *Ibid.*

and Zionists were in fact "genuine friends" of the Empire. "Now it was not a question of money, but of reciprocal services." If the Zionists could win over the European press for the Empire, the Liberal Union Government would favour the Zionists' wishes.[6]

At the end of November, Hochberg had a long conversation with the Minister of the Interior, Reşid Bey, who had been Mutasarrıf of Jerusalem from 1904 until 1906 and had earned a reputation for being unusually venal. After expressing his sympathy for the Zionists, Reşid Bey asked Hochberg to furnish him with a memorandum outlining Zionists aims, which he promised to examine with Kâmil Paşa (now Grand Vezir) before presenting it to the Cabinet.[7]

Hochberg reported on this meeting to Jacobson, who was in Berlin at the time. Having few illusions about what was behind the shift in the Liberal Union attitude, he stressed the Government's immediate need of considerable sums of money.[8] Jacobson was sceptical of Reşid Bey's sincerity, and also uncertain whether the Zionists could raise capital of the order required by the Ottoman Treasury. Nonetheless, he thought it worthwhile to try and win the sympathies of some European newspapers for the Ottoman Empire. Nahum Sokolow, a member of the Zionist Executive, was about to go to London and he agreed to do what he could there. Jacobson himself, claiming "some success" among German newspapers (including *Vossische Zeitung, Berliner Tageblatt, Frankfurter Zeitung,* and *Ullstein-Presse*), set out for Paris on 3 December on a similar mission.[9]

He returned to Constantinople towards the end of December, when he had what he considered a useful meeting with Reşid Bey. The latter, after repeating his request for a memorandum on Zionist aims, had promised to speak to Kâmil Paşa about the need to relax the Government's "campaign" against the Jews in Palestine.[10] On 6 January 1913, Jacobson sent Reşid Bey the memorandum he had requested.[11] However, four days later, Reşid Bey informed him that their business would have to wait until peace

6. *CZA* Z3/45 ("Zum Ende Nov. 1912" [sic], I Neufach (Consple.) to ZAC.
7. *Ibid.*
8. *CZA* Z3/45 (3.12.1912), [Jacobson (Berlin)] to S. Hochberg (Consple.).
9 *CZA* Z3/45 (3.12.1912); and *CZA* Z3/45 (4.12.1912), ZCO (Berlin) to Hochberg.
10. *CZA* Z3/45 (27.12.1912), Jacobson (Consple.) to ZAC.
11. *CZA* Z3/45 (6.1.1913), Jacobson to ZAC.

in the Balkans was achieved at the international conference then being held in London.[12]

In his talks with Reşid Bey, Jacobson seems to have volunteered a measure of tangible support for the Ottoman Empire in exchange for facilities to purchase twelve tracts of land in Palestine.[13] To that end, the Haham Başı was prevailed upon to speak to the Minister of Justice and also to the Secretary of the Council of State, who undertook to present the Zionist case favourably.[14] On being promised a commission, the Grand Vezir's secretary agreed to interest other members of the Countil of State in the transfers.[15] Said Paşa, another old-régime statesman who was now President of the Council, was reported to be sympathetic;[16] Kâmil Paşa was lobbying on behalf of the Zionists and so was Reşid Bey.[17]

The key to this spectacular change in the political climate in Constantinople lay in the military and financial straits facing the Government, as was made clear by Jacobson in his reports to the Zionist Executive in Berlin. On 18 January, the Great Powers sent a *Note Verbale Identique* to the Porte urging the cession of Adrianople to Bulgaria in return for certain territorial compensation and loans to tide the Empire over its difficulties. In Jacobson's view the Government's predicament was desperate—it was bankrupt and Adrianople would probably have to be relinquished.[18]

The Council of State was expected to consider the Zionist application to purchase lands in Palestine on 24 January.[19] However, one day before that, a Cabinet meeting was held at which, it was generally believed, the Powers' *Note* would be considered. The CUP deemed this to be the moment to overthrow the Liberal Union Government. Enver Bey (soon to emerge as one of the most powerful men in the Empire) led a small group into the Cabinet room. Having killed the Minister of War on the way in, he forced Kâmil Paşa and his ministers to resign. On 28 January, Mahmud Şevket Paşa, the new Grand Vezir, proposed that rather than relinquishing

12. *CZA* Z3/45 (10.1.1913), Jacobson to R. Lichtheim (Berlin).
13. *CZA* Z3/45 (16.1.1913), Jacobson to Lichtheim.
14. *Ibid.*
15. *Ibid.*
16. *Ibid.*
17. *CZA* Z3/45 (21.1.1913), Jacobson to Lichtheim.
18. *Ibid.*
19. *CZA* Z3/45 (16.1.1913), Jacobson to Lichtheim.

Adrianople, the frontier with Bulgaria be set at the River Maritsa, just to the west of the city. This was unacceptable to the Bulgarians, and the second Balkan War broke out on 3 February.

In January 1913 Jacobson had also discussed Zionism with members of the CUP's Central Committee, including Talât Bey. They, too, professed not to object to Zionism in principle, although Talât Bey stood firmly by the CUP's policy of Ottomanisation and the "denial of nationality" which it implied.[20] He also indicated that open CUP support for the Zionist Movement was impossible. He was very frank: "For us Zionism is a question of internal politics and of the struggle between parties."[21]

After the CUP coup d'état, Jacobson wrote to Jacobus Kann in The Hague, who although no longer a member of the Zionist Executive, continued to be responsible for the Anglo-Palestine Company. In his letter, Jacobson impressed upon him the Ottoman Government's immediate need for large sums of money.[22] Since the APC was registered in London, Leopold Greenberg, the editor of the *Jewish Chronicle* and one of APC's British directors, spoke to officials at the Foreign Office on 7 February. They explained the British Government's opposition to large loans to the Ottoman Empire at that juncture, and at the end of the month the APC agreed to wait "at least until the present war is brought to a close."[23]

At about the same time, Jacobson also pressed the Haham Başı into speaking once again to the President of the Council of State and others about the possibility of removing the restrictions against Jews in Palestine.[24] Having done so, the Haham Başı then submitted two *takrirs* (memoranda) to the Minister of Justice on 10 February. In these he urged that the old régime's restrictions be abolished on the grounds that they were unconstitutional (since they conflicted with the rights of Ottoman Jews) and contrary to the "vital interests" of the Empire.[25]

A few days later these takrirs were published in *L'Aurore,* a Jewish paper which supported the Zionists. With them appeared

20. *CZA* Z3/45 (6.1.1913), Jacobson to ZAC.
21. *Ibid.*
22. *CZA* Z3/45 (4.2.1913), Jacobson to J. Kann (The Hague).
23. *PRO* FO 371/1798/10065 (26.2.1913), L. J. Greenberg (London) to R. P. Maxwell (FO).
24. *CZA* Z3/45 (28.2.1913), Jacobson (Paris) to H. Frank (Paris).
25. *PRO* FO 371/1794/16925, no. 218 (17.3.1913), Sir G. A. Lowther (Consple.) to Grey, enclosing undated cuttings from *L'Aurore* [ca. 14.2.1913].

a leading article by the editor, Lucien Sciuto, which in the words of the British Ambassador at the Porte portrayed "a picture of what might be styled an alliance between Pan-Judaism and Pan-Islamism in Turkey."[26] Sciuto deplored the fates of the Ottoman Empire and Jewry: both, he said, had suffered from the Christian world. Then, as if thinking aloud, he wrote: "Our dearest dream—the dream of the whole of Jewry—is to see a great and strong Turkey marching resolutely towards its future, parallel with a powerful Jewry also going freely to its destiny."[27] World Jewry was not a power equipped with an army or a navy—it was more than that: "By its speakers, by its thinkers, by its politicians and, why not say it, by its financiers too, it is a great force of a different kind to be reckoned with, because it can lead all the others." Genuine friendship depended on mutual confidence. The Ottoman Government should therefore show its faith in world Jewry by abolishing the restrictions on Jews in Palestine.

Almost at once, two members of the CUP's Central Committee, Esad Paşa and Ahmed Agayev, approached Jacobson on behalf of Talât Bey. Recalling their conversations at the beginning of January, they now proposed a "Muslim-Jewish alliance."[28] Islam, they suggested, was in decline and must inevitably disappear unless knowledge, savoir-faire, and capital were injected from outside. The Jews could help on these scores, but they lacked a "field of action" for their own aspirations. "Would that the Jews come to our country to direct our affairs by forming an intimate alliance with us."[29] This proposal (which would have delighted Herzl) was not as utterly improbable as it may appear at first sight. Within the Empire the CUP was committed to a policy of Ottomanisation. But, from 1911 onwards, one element of its foreign policy was "Pan-Islamism," a policy which had been pursued by Abdülhamid before 1908 and which, by championing the cause of Islam, was aimed at rallying support for the Empire among Muslims beyond its borders. The primary purpose of a "Muslim-Jewish alliance" would almost certainly have been to canvass large sums of capital from

26. *PRO* FO 371/1794/16925, no. 218 (17.3.1913).
27. Cutting from *L'Aurore,* enclosed in *PRO* FO 371/1794/16925, no. 218 (17.3.1913).
28. *CZA* Z3/45 (28.2.1913), Jacobson to Frank.
29. *Ibid.*

Jews in Europe. But if, in addition to that, the Jews of the world, together with the Muslims of the world, could be brought to the Empire's side, then presumably so much the better in the difficult circumstances prevailing in the spring of 1913.

Jacobson recognised the naivety and hazards of the proposal if taken literally. Nonetheless, he immediately set out for Berlin and Paris, where he hoped to convince influential Jews of the need to seize this "slightly fantastic" opportunity.[30] And bearing a letter of introduction from the British Ambassador at St. Petersburg, Nahum Sokolow travelled to London to consult the Foreign Office about a loan to the Ottoman Empire and possible British help to put an end to the restrictions on the Jews in Palestine.[31]

These exploratory moves were unsuccessful. Everyone whom Jacobson hoped to contact was unavailable. Baron Edmond de Rothschild was cruising in the Mediterranean. Jacob Schiff, the American Jewish leader, was in North Africa. Dr. Paul Nathan, of the Hilfsverein der deutschen Juden, was absent from Berlin.[32] Nor did Sokolow meet with much encouragement at the Foreign Office. He was politely informed that the British Government did not favour loans to the Ottoman Empire at that time and could scarcely intervene on behalf of the Jews in Palestine, who were not British subjects.[33]

Accordingly, on 19 March, Jacobson wrote to Nisim Mazliah, a Jewish deputy in the Ottoman Parliament who was close to both the Zionists and Talât Bey, regretting that his mission had not been more fruitful. Not only were the most important Jews unavailable but, wherever he had presented himself, he had been told that it would be impossible to aid the Ottoman Empire until the exceptional measures against the Jews in Palestine were removed.[34]

The Haham Başı's takrirs on this question had not, however, been rejected out of hand. The Minister of Justice had taken a favourable view and had submitted them to the Grand Vezirate. The latter had passed them on to the Minister of the Interior for

30. *CZA* Z3/45 (28.2.1913).
31. *PRO* FO 371/1794/6584 (19. and 25.2.1913), both N. Sokolow (London) to Sir L. Mallet (FO).
32. *CZA* Z3/45 (18.3.1913), Jacobson [Berlin?] to Hochberg.
33. *PRO* FO 371/1794/10066 (3.3.1913) [minute—initials illegible].
34. *CZA* Z3/45 (19.3.1913), Jacobson (Berlin) to Nisim Mazliah (Consple.).

his comments before presenting them to the Council of State.[35] But the Minister was cautious and sent copies of the takrirs to the Vali of Beirut, asking for his views.[36]

On hearing of these bureaucratic procedures, Jacobson wrote to Ahmed Agayev on 27 March, informing him that the idea of a "Muslim-Jewish alliance" had found a "sympathetic, even enthusiastic, echo" in Jewish circles.[37] But now that the Haham Başı's takrirs had been referred to Beirut, the Jews sensed that the Government was procrastinating in the same way as the old régime. It could not expect any support from Jewish financiers until the restrictions against the Jews in Palestine were annulled.[38]

Accelerated by the first Balkan War, the trend towards Arab nationalism was gathering a certain momentum by the beginning of 1913. A detailed description of this movement is unnecessary for the purposes of this book. But the direction in which it was moving can be readily seen by comparing the names of the principal nationalist societies in 1908 and then in 1913. In the heady days following the Young Turk Revolution, Arabs in Constantinople founded the Ottoman Arab Brotherhood, a name which virtually speaks for itself. Its main aim was to try to ensure that the Arabs were accorded an equal place in the Empire along with other national groups. In the second half of 1912, when demands for reform in the Empire were mounting, Arabs in Beirut formed the Reform Society, and émigrés from the Arab provinces in Cairo formed the Decentralisation Party. There were Muslim and Christian Arabs in both these small societies. Most of their members were not nationalists in the full sense. Only a handful, mainly among the Decentralisationists, contemplated full Arab independence of the Empire. The remainder—the majority—sought what the names of their societies implied: administrative reform and decentralised government *within* the Empire. The programmes of both societies called for the establishment of local General Councils, which would control their own budgets and have the

35. *CZA* Z3/45 (6.3.1913), Haham Başı (Consple.) to Jacobson [Berlin?].
36. Cf. *CZA* L2/49/I (22.3.1913), Neufach to Zionist Office (Jaffa). The Ministry of the Interior only referred the takrirs to Jerusalem when the vacant post of mutasarrıf was filled later in March.
37. *CZA* Z3/45 (27.3.1913), Jacobson [Berlin?] to Ahmed Agayev (Consple.).
38. *Ibid.*

right to legislate for domestic affairs in the Arab provinces. And both insisted that Arabic should be recognised as an official language in those provinces, on a par with Turkish, which under the CUP's policy of Ottomanisation had been made the sole official language throughout the Empire.

In February 1913, at precisely the same time that Talât Bey proposed a "Muslim-Jewish alliance" to Zionists in Constantinople, members of the Decentralisation Party in Cairo were suggesting that an entente between the Arabs and the Zionists was "imperative." This suggestion, no less startling than Talât Bey's proposal, was first made in the course of an anti-Zionist polemic in the columns of *al-Ahram,* started by an anonymous writer who alleged yet again that the CUP relied on the Jews and Freemasons because it needed Jewish money.[39]

This accusation and others had been rejected by an Egyptian Jew, Robert Ghazi, writing in *al-Muqaṭṭam.*[40] On 19 February, the anonymous writer of the first article replied in *al-Ahram* to Ghazi's rejoinder. Now signing himself "E. Bey G.,"[41] he claimed that a secret agreement already existed between the CUP and the Zionists. Jews in the Empire were but a tenth of its Arab population, yet—according to E. Bey G.—they had two representatives in the new Cabinet: Nisim Mazliah and the Minister of Public Works, Batzariya Efendi. (In fact, Mazliah was not a Cabinet member, and Batzariya was not a Jew.) The Jews, E. Bey G. asserted, controlled the finances, the economy and the agriculture of the Empire. All loans and commercial concessions were made by or to Jews, through Jews, and to the advantage of Jews. Their advances in Palestine had been made over the heads of the local population. E. Bey G. therefore warned the Zionists that if they did not secure "the consent of the Syrians in particular and the Arabs in general, [Arab] hatred of the Zionists takes birth from today. [It is] a hatred which will fight with all means against the interests of Zionism to annul their achievements and to destroy all their hopes for the future." He advised the Zionists to obtain Arab assent to their activities and "to take into account the friendship of one's neighbour [that is, the

39. *CZA* Z3/752 (21.2.1913), S. Hasamsony (Cairo) to ZCO (quoting *al-Ahram* in French translation).
40. *CZA* Z3/752 (21.2.1913); Ghazi wrote under the pseudonym of "Ṭanṭawi."
41. "E. Bey G." are the writer's initials as transliterated into French by Hasamsony.

Arab] which is preferable to that of the distant stranger [that is, the Turk]."[42]

The editor of *al-Ahram,* Daᶜud Barakat, was a member of the Decentralisation Party. In view of his paper's long-standing antipathy to Zionism, he was considered by the French Vice-Consul in Haifa as a prominent Arab anti-Zionist, together with Najib Naṣṣar, Ruḥi Bey al-Khalidi, Shukri al-ᶜAsali, and Muḥammad Kurd ᶜAli (editor of *al-Muqtabas* in Damascus).[43] Nonetheless, Barakat was the first to suggest publicly that an agreement was needed between the Arabs and the Zionists. He did so in a comment which he appended to E. Bey G.'s article:

It is certain that the Syrians do not find it at all inconvenient to have their Jewish brethren as neighbours and to live among them. But what is reprehensible is that an agreement has been made [with the CUP] about [the Syrians'] land, without their knowledge or consent. It is absolutely imperative that an entente be made between the Zionists and the Arabs, because this war of words can only do evil. The Zionists are necessary for the country; the capital which they will bring, their knowledge and intelligence, and the industriousness which characterises them, will contribute without doubt to the regeneration of the country.[44]

On 21 February, Robert Ghazi answered this remarkable article and comment directly in *al-Ahram* with the retort that all the antagonism between the Zionists and the Arabs emanated from the latter. E. Bey G. should secure the friendship of the Arabs for the Jews.[45]

Four days later Ḥaqqi Bey al-ᶜAẓm, the Secretary of the Decentralisation Party, entered the polemic by publishing an article, again in *al-Ahram.*[46] He denied that all Syrians were opposed to the Zionists. On the contrary, they knew that Syria needed capital and energy to progress and that the Jews were best suited to that purpose. If the Arabs in Syria and Palestine were hostile towards the Jewish immigrants, it was because they retained their foreign

42. Cf. the proverb in colloquial Arabic *"Jarak al-qarib wala qaribak al-baᶜid"* ("Your next-door neighbour and not your relative who lives far away").
43. *Q d'O* N.S. 121 [no number] (30.4.1913), French Vice-Consul (Haifa) to F. Couget (Beirut).
44. *CZA* Z3/752 (21.2.1913).
45. *Ibid.*
46. *Al-Ahram* (25.2.1913)—details in Hebrew translation in *CZA* Z3/115, press report [undated and unsigned].

nationality or merely posed as Ottoman subjects, and also because they and many Ottoman Jews supported the CUP and its ruinous policies. The Arabs, wrote Ḥaqqi Bey, were willing to open their lands to the Jews, on condition that (1) they adopted the Arabic language, (2) they were not economically exclusive, (3) they became genuine Ottoman subjects, (4) they refrained from politics, and (5) they took into account the Arab people, which "today or tomorrow is bound to rise again." Otherwise, "a page of Arab history will be sullied by the acts which they will perpetrate against the Jews."

A little more than a month later, Ibrahim Sali Najjar, another member of the Decentralisation Party, sent a letter from Cairo to Sami Hochberg in Constantinople, officially inviting the Zionists to make an entente with the Decentralisationists. Najjar was a Syrian journalist connected with *al-Ahram.* At one time he had worked for *Le Jeune-Turc* and thus was well acquainted with Hochberg, its editor. He wrote:

> Mr. Hochberg, you are a friend and an intelligent man. Your interest obliges you to show agreement with us, hand in hand with the policy of decentralisation. Otherwise you will turn the Christians and the Muslims of Syria against your co-religionists. I say this to you as a friend and as a sincere friend. Repeat it to Dr. Jacobson. The [Decentralisationalists'] passage to power is very short and you will be obliged in the end to work with us. Should not [this co-operation] begin from now onwards? . . . Study the situation and plan your line of action. This is the moment to anticipate events. If you decide sincerely in favour of an entente between us, indicate to me here (in Cairo) the authorised representative of the Zionists to put us in contact with him.[47]

On 25 April an Egyptian Zionist in Cairo also reported to the Zionist Head Office in Berlin that representatives of the Decentralisation Party wanted to make an agreement "with us." Daʿud Barakat had informed him that some of the Decentralisationists, who were going to attend the "First Arab Congress" in Paris in June, would provavly try to have talks with Zionists in Europe with a view to reaching an entente. "But my personal impression is that they . . . take an [entente] in the sense of an *affaire.*"[48] Various considerations suggest that this assessment was wrong, and that

47. *CZA* Z3/45 (10.4.1913), Jacobson (Consple.) to Lichtheim.
48. *CZA* Z3/752 (25.4.1913), Hasamsony to ZCO.

the proposal of an Arab-Zionist entente was something other than just "an *affaire.*"

First, the Decentralisation Party was a very small group, with perhaps a score of members in the spring of 1913. As far as can be ascertained, few, if any, of the founding members in Cairo came from Palestine or had had direct contact with the Jewish immigrants there. Certainly, as the quotations above show, they spoke of themselves as *Syrians* and they took a broad, "non-Palestinian" view of the Zionist question. This point is all-important, for it was the hallmark of their relations with the Zionists during 1913 and in most, but not all, cases during 1914 as well. It allowed them to view the Zionists in a wide, almost "pan-Arab" context, and to see that the latter could benefit Syria and the Arab provinces generally, without impairing Arab unity as a whole.[49] This view differentiated the Decentralisationists, and other like-minded Arabs, from those Arabs in Palestine who were concerned about Zionism from the narrow standpoint of local patriotism. It also marked them off from Muslims outside Palestine who were beginning to oppose Zionism from another narrow standpoint: that of Muslim unity.

Some of the Decentralisationists were clearly impressed by Jewish achievements in Palestine. For example, Shaykh ʿAli Yusuf, editor of *al-Muʿayyad,* a paper in Cairo which supported the nationalists,[50] wrote in the autumn of 1912: "It is not for us to look askance at them with jealousy and vengeance because of their enlightenment and progress, lest we cause them ill instead of good and then we will lose a highly industrious element, so needed by us always but especially at this critical moment."[51] Daʿud Barakat's editorial comment in *Al-Ahram* on 19 February and statements of other nationalists in the next months indicate that some of them believed that the Zionists had much to offer, in terms of capital and know-how, to the Arabs in what they call "Syria." Moreover, the nationalists held the view that for the advancement of the Arab provinces

49. The Decentralisationists' concept of the area of "Syria" seems to have been vague, but it almost certainly included Palestine. After World War I, when the nature of an independent Arab state and its component parts were being discussed, the term "Greater Syria" was advanced to embrace the Fertile Crescent and its desert hinterland. Palestine, as an integral part of that area, was dubbed "Southern Syria." But these terms were not in use in 1913 and 1914, when very few nationalists contemplated complete Arab independence.
50. Saʿid, i, 12.
51. *Ha-Ḥerut,* v, 29 (25.10.1912).

help was needed from experts and advisers from countries in Europe which had no political interests in the Ottoman Empire. The Beirut Reform Society had included this point in its programme, and in *al-Ahram* on 25 February, Ḥaqqi Bey al-ᶜAẓm had specifically written that the Jews were best suited to this purpose.

The ground for Ḥaqqi Bey's view—and hence for a liaison with the Zionists—had been prepared by Rashid Riḍa, who was a founding member of the Decentralisation Party. In September 1911, Riḍa published an article in *al-Manar,*[52] which reflected his conviction that it was necessary to strengthen the *Dar al-Islam* (the "realm of Islam") to meet the challenge of a technically superior Europe.[53] He argued that the "Syrians" required large agricultural, industrial, and commercial projects to develop their country (*bilad*). To that end, the Syrians were not only greatly in need of European finance, but also had to come in contact with, and work alongside, Europeans and so acquire various technical skills from them. Riḍa referred the Syrians to the example of Egypt, which had progressed markedly through European investment. Since he asserted that the Jews controlled European finance, it followed that the Syrians must be prepared to accept aid from Jews. He held that the alternative—to reject this aid and to do without development—spelt poverty and ruin. The "Zionist danger" was, he believed, confined to the possibility of the Zionists' "taking possession of the Holy Land." The danger in employing foreign capital, Jewish or otherwise, was twofold: first, the local population and the Government could be drowned in debts; second, foreigners could gain a hold on the country (*bilad*) by acquiring most or much of its land (*arḍ*). But if the Zionist danger and the dangers inherent in foreign capital could be contained, Riḍa saw no objection to drawing on Jewish capital.

Given his theory that, besides needing European capital, the Syrians had to work with Europeans and so learn from them, it was not too big a step for Riḍa to reçoncile himself to a Zionist presence in Palestine—provided, of course, that the Jews could be prevented from taking over the country. He worked out this corollary to his original argument in the next year and a half and, by his own

52. *Al-Manar,* xiv, 9 (1911(, pp. 713-17, "Mashruᶜ al-Aṣfar" (as the title indicates, this article was occasioned by the renewed attacks on al-Aṣfar's project in summer 1911—see p. 124).
53. Cf. Hourani, *Arabic Thought,* pp. 235-36.

admission, came to the conclusion in spring 1913 that it was necessary for the Arabs to make an agreement with the Zionists.[54]

There is another possibility to be considered in connection with the proposal of an Arab-Zionist entente. The war with Italy and the first Balkan War had exposed how very weak the Ottoman Empire was. A few Arab nationalists, the more radical of them, probably drew the conclusion that the moment was ripe to work for Arab independence. Hence, in the winter of 1912 certain Druze and Muslims from the Lebanon and Damascus solicited the British and French Consuls-General in Beirut for the support of their countries in the Arab "struggle against the Turks."[55] At the same time, Syrian Muslims visited Lord Kitchener, the British Consul-General in Egypt, "petitioning Great Britain to annex Syria to Egypt and to give Syria an independent administration."[56] That the Decentralisationists may have approached the Zionists in this context in the spring of 1913 is a possibility which cannot be excluded.

Hochberg in Constantinople informed Jacobson about Najjar's letter as soon as he received it. Jacobson in turn relayed its contents to Berlin with the recommendation that Hochberg be dispatched to Cairo forthwith and perhaps to Beirut as well.[57] The recommendation was accepted at once and Hochberg arrived in Cairo at the end of April. From there he travelled to Beirut to meet members of the Reform Committee. His mission completed, he returned to Constantinople in the middle of May.

Hochberg's report is fascinating.[58] He had met twenty members of the Decentralisation Party and the Beirut Reform Committee. He mentioned only four by name: of the Decentralisation Party, Rafiq Bey al-ᶜAẓm (President) and Ibrahim Najjar; of the Beirut Reform Committee, Aḥmad Muḥtar Bayhum Bey (who arrived in Cairo independently but at the same time as Hochberg), and, in Beirut, Rizq Allah Arqash. Later evidence shows that, in Cairo, he also met Iskandar Bey ᶜAmmun and Ḥaqqi Bey al-ᶜAẓm

54. *CZA* L2/94/1 (6/7.6.1914), N. Malul (Cairo) to Zionist Office (Jaffa).
55. G. P. Gooch and H. Temperly (eds.), *British Documents on the Origins of the War: 1898-1914* (London, 1938), X, ii, 824; and cf. *La Vérité sur la Question Syrienne,* pp. 41-43, 50-54, 69-71, *et passim.*
56. Gooch and Temperly, X, ii, 825.
57. *CZA* Z3/45 (10.4.1913), Jacobson to Lichtheim.
58. *CZA* Z3/114 (17.5.1913), Hochberg (Consple.): "Le mouvement arabe."

(respectively Vice-President and Secretary of the Decentralisation Party)[59] and, in Beirut, Shaykh Aḥmad Ṭabbarah (editor of *al-Ittiḥad al-ʿUthmani*).[60] In all probability, he also talked in Cairo to Daʿud Barakat (as the first public advocate of an Arab-Zionist entente) and to Khalil Zayniyyah (a member of the Beirut Reform Committee who came to Cairo with Aḥmad Bayhum).[61] Thus is is possible to identify up to nine of the twenty nationalists whom Hochberg met, leaving eleven unknown.

On Jewish immigration into Palestine, Hochberg reported that there was "anxiety or at least uncertainty."[62] But as no official policy had been adopted by either the Decentralisation Party or the Beirut Reform Committee, the Arabs whom he met could only offer their personal views. Broadly speaking, these fell into four categories.

To Hochberg's surprise, those most favourably inclined towards Jewish immigration were Christians.[63] They explained that they were a minority element in Syria and, apart from economic arguments in favour of Jewish immigration, they welcomed the influx of Jews because it would help to counterbalance the Muslim majority. Indeed, according to Hochberg, some of them went so far as to say: "We even wish that the Jews would form the majority in Palestine and succeed in establishing there a Jewish autonomy properly speaking which would split in two that compact Muslim mass which peoples such vast contiguous regions as Iraq, Syria, Egypt, the Hijaz and Yemen."[64]

This was scarcely the authentic voice of Arab nationalism, but it was consonant with other contemporary evidence about Christian Arabs from Beirut. For instance, Rizq Allah Arqash and Khalil Zayniyyah, two of the Christians whom Hochberg met, had written with others on 12 March to the French Consul-General in Beirut,

59. *CZA* Z3/114 (10.6.1913), Hochberg (Paris) to Jacobson (Berlin); and *ha-Ḥerut,* v, 196 (18.5.1913).
60. *Le Jeune-Turc,* v, 150 (1.6.1913).
61. *PRO* FO 195/2451/2129, no. 36 (28.4.1913), and *PRO* FO 371/1775/26655, no. 47 (30.5.1913), both H. A. Cumberbatch (Beirut) to Lowther.
62. *CZA* Z3/114 (17.5.1913), Hochberg (Consple.); "Le mouvement arabe."
63. Hochberg did not indicate how many Christian Arabs he met or what their denominations were. Iskander Bey ʿAmmun was a Maronite; Rizq Allah Arqash and Khalil Zayniyyah were Greek Catholics; Ibrahim Najjar perhaps was a Greek Orthodox, and Daʿud Barakat possibly a Greek Catholic.
64. *CZA* Z3/114 (17.5.1913), Hochberg (Consple.), "Le mouvement arabe."

appealing for a French occupation of Syria and complete autonomy for the Vilâyet of Beirut under the protection and effective control of France. *Inter alia,* they explained that the equilibrium between Muslims and Christians was being upset on the one hand by the steady flow of Christians out of Syria and, on the other, by the resettlement in Syria of Muslims from Macedonia displaced by the Balkan Wars.[65] That summer, the Chairman of the "First Arab Congress," ᶜAbd al-Ḥamid al-Zahrawi, wrote to Rashid Riḍa, complaining bitterly that the Christian Arabs from Beirut who had attended the Congress were not Arab nationalists. "They had not once sipped from the fountain of Arab unity, no, nor from that of Syrian unity; their only interest was in Beirut and in Beirut alone."[66]

The other three positions vis-à-vis Jewish immigration were held by the Muslims whom Hochberg met. Some of them were willing to accept Jewish immigration without reserve. Others would only agree to it on certain conditions—for example, they wished to fix the annual number of immigrants, to limit the extent of land that Arab peasants could sell so that the fellah would never be wholly dispossessed, and to enact legislation similar to that in America requiring every immigrant to bring a certain sum of money to prevent him from becoming a burden on the country. Finally, still others declared themselves opposed to Jewish immigration. Their position was the reverse of that of the Christians who welcomed the influx of Jewish immigrants. They were opposed precisely because the Jews represented a foreign element, which would break the compact Arab mass whose strength derived from the very unity of its language and customs. The Jews may have had the same Semitic origins as the Arabs, but they were Europeanised in manners and mentality. They came to Palestine not to assimilate with the Arabs, but to preserve their own language and nationality. This view was expressed by only two Muslims, but in the course of the next year it was to gain more weight.

Some of those in favour of Jewish immigration had doubts of another kind. They felt that discussions with the Zionists should not take place before the Arab movement had consolidated itself, lest its leaders play into the hands of the CUP, which might accuse

65. See *La Vérité sur la Question Syrienne,* pp. 50–54.
66. Saᶜid, i, 43.

them (as they had previously accused the CUP) of "selling the country to the Jews."

Hochberg gained the impression that most members of the Decentralisation Party and the Beirut Reform Committee wanted to make an entente with the Zionists. But a formal agreement could not be signed on the spot. In the first place, Hochberg was not authorised to sign one.[67] Secondly, he had argued that an agreement would not be possible unless the Arabs accommodated the Zionists' demands into their own programme, since the Zionists were hardly likely to join forces with a movement that could turn against them. To take such a far-reaching step, the Arab nationalists needed to convene a meeting of "all the committees in Syria and Palestine" (presumably meaning the groups in various towns which had come out in support of the Beirut Reform Society, and also the Decentralisation Party's branches then being formed). A gathering of this kind could only be held after the First Arab Congress in Paris in June.

However, as a preliminary move aimed at attuning Arab opinion to the idea of a formal agreement with the Zionists, the Decentralisation Party and Hochberg made the following verbal agreement (*entente verbale*):

1. The Cairo Committee, being in principle in favour of Jewish immigration into Syria and Palestine and of an agreement with the Zionists, will make a point of working for a rapprochement between the Arab world and the Jewish world, and of dispelling by its word-of-mouth propaganda and by way of the Arabic press all the prejudices which have been current until now in the Arab world as regards Jewish immigration and which have prevented an Arab-Jewish rapprochement.

2. In exchange, *Le Jeune-Turc* will make a point of supporting the cause of the Arab movement while it remains compatible with the unity and the integrity of the Empire. *Le Jeune-Turc* will do all it can so that European newspapers (especially German ones), with which it has relations, will do the same.[68]

Rafiq Bey al-ᶜAẓm, the President of the Decentralisation Party (who had written an anti-Zionist article in *al-Ḥaḍara* at the end of 1910—see p. 84), then prepared a statement for the press, in which he declared that "we appreciate too well the precious

67. *CZA* Z3/45 (10.4.1913), Jacobson to Lichtheim.
68. *CZA* Z3/114 (17.5.1913), Hochberg, "Le mouvement arabe."

combination which Jewish capital, manpower and intelligence can bring us for the rapid development of our provinces to commit the error of refusing them."[69] Immigration laws would, he thought, be necessary, but not along the lines of the "exceptional measures" which were still in force from Abdülhamid's time. His statement was approved by other members of the Decentralisation Party. Ibrahim Najjar undertook to write a series of articles on the subject of an Arab-Zionist entente, which would appear in the Arabic press over the signatures of other members of the Decentralisation Party.

Aḥmad Bayhum from Beirut took part in the discussions in Cairo. Although the Government had ordered the dissolution of the Beirut Reform Committee and closed its premises earlier in April, Bayhum encouraged Hochberg to proceed to Beirut. Hochberg took this advice, and in Beirut the verbal agreement between himself and the Decentralisation Party was accepted by members of the Reform Committee as well. One of them, Rizq Allah Arqash, also prepared a statement for the press in which he, like Rafiq Bey al-ᶜAẓm, stressed the advantages to be gained from Jewish capital, culture and technical expertise.

In May and June, the parties to the verbal agreement took the first steps to implement it. The Decentralisation Party had passed a resolution on 30 April (while Hochberg was still in Cairo), assuring Ottoman Jews of equal rights in a decentralised administration. The resolution and the statements prepared by Rafiq Bey al-ᶜAẓm and Rizq Allah Arqash were incorporated into a long series of articles sympathetic to the Arab movement in *ha-Ḥerut* in Jerusalem.[70] On his return to Constantinople, Hochberg published a series of leading articles in *Le Jeune-Turc* entitled "Reforms in the Arab Provinces."[71] He too incorporated the statements by Rafiq Bey and Rizq Allah Arqash and also printed a further statement by Shaykh Aḥmad Ṭabbarah of Beirut assuring Ottoman Jews that the Reform Committee's programme guaranteed their rights.[72]

The Arab nationalists also began to do as they had promised. In

69. *CZA* 23/114 (17.5.1913), Hochberg, "Le mouvement arabe."
70. *Ha-Ḥerut,* v, 182 (1.5.1913); 183 (2.5.1913); 184 (4.5.1913); 185 (5.5.1913); 189 (9.5.1913); 190 (11.5.1913); 191 (12.5.1913); 196 (18.5.1913); 197 (19.5. 1913); 205 (28.5.1913); 212 (5.6.1913); 216 (10.6.1913); and 219 (15.6.1913).
71. *Le Jeune-Turc,* v, 145 (27.5.1913); 147 (29.5.1913); 150 (1.6.1913); and 154 (15.6.1913).
72. *Le Jeune-Turc,* 150 (1.6.1913).

June, the statements prepared in Cairo and Beirut were published in *al-Ahram* and *al-Iṣlaḥ* (which had begun to appear in Beirut in May under the editorship of Aḥmad Ṭabbarah).[73] And they seem to have used their influence with the Arabic press, for in July the Zionist Office in Jaffa reported that the tone of articles on the Zionist issue had become appreciably milder. Even *al-Muqtabas,* the report said, was showing "a certain restraint."[74]

The First Arab Congress was held in Paris from 18 to 23 June. While stressing Arab loyalty to the Empire, its aim was to focus European attention on Arab demands for reform and thereby put pressure on the Ottoman Government. It was attended by twenty-four official delegates and by a larger number of observers and others who kept in the background. One of these was Sami Hochberg, who arrived in Paris about ten days before the Congress opened.

The Chairman of the Congress was ᶜAbd al-Ḥamid al-Zahrawi. A former deputy from Hama, he had also been an editor of *al-Ḥaḍara* in Constantinople, which had published anti-Zionist articles. Hochberg had not met him previously, but Iskandar Bey ᶜAmmun of the Decentralisation Party, whom Hochberg does appear to have met in Cairo, spoke to al-Zahrawi and convinced him that Jewish immigration into Palestine was "not only desirable but necessary."[75]

On the agenda was an item called "Migration from and to Syria," which reflected two matters of concern to the Congress. For some decades Syrians, especially Christians, had been emigrating, mainly to Egypt, America and Australia; during and after the Balkan Wars, when Muslim-Christian tensions grew, the number of those leaving took an upward turn. Parallel with that, the Government was attempting to resettle in Syria Muslims from Macedonia who had been displaced by the Balkan Wars. Before the Congress opened, Hochberg discovered that almost all the delegates were opposed to the Government's policy vis-à-vis Muslims from Macedonia. Towards Jewish immigration he found the same four attitudes he had encountered in Cairo.[76] Shaykh Aḥmad Ṭabbarah

73. *Al-Ahram,* no. 10,718 (4.6.1913); and *al-Iṣlaḥ,* no. 24/1,419 (6.6.1913), both cited in Harran, p. 320, no. 80.
74. *CZA* Z3/115 (25.7.1913), Zionist Office (Jaffa) to [ZAC].
75. *CZA* Z3/114 (10.6.1913), Hochberg (Paris) to Jacobson; and *CZA* Z3/114 (16.6.1913), Hochberg to Jacobson.
76. *CZA* Z3/114 (10.6.1913).

of Beirut was to make the major speech about immigration. According to Hochberg, he was a little unsure about Jewish immigration at first,[77] but he had "changed his mind."[78] However, Hochberg felt that the Zionists had nothing to fear because the committee preparing Ṭabbarah's speech would edit out any unfavourable references to Jewish immigration.[79]

Ṭabbarah delivered his speech to the plenary session on 21 June. He took the Ottoman Government to task for failing in its obligations to the Syrians and causing many of them to leave the country of late. He avoided all direct reference to Jewish immigration (and related questions, such as land purchases by Jews). Instead he chose to adopt a somewhat ambiguous position. People, he said, differed over immigration into Syria. Some disapproved of "non-Arab" immigration, fearing its possible effects on the local population. Others did not share these fears and counted the immigration as a gain for Syria. Speaking personally, Ṭabbarah had no objection to the immigration—provided that "it has a special form of organisation [*niẓam khaṣṣ*]."[80]

A resolution was proposed in favour of immigration which could benefit Syria economically. In the ensuing discussion, a delegate representing the Arab group in Paris spoke against "Turkish" immigration (from Macedonia) and said that only immigrants with means of their own could be of value to the Arab provinces. At this Aḥmad Bayhum interjected "Jewish immigration: yes; but Turkish immigration: no!"[81] According to Hochberg, there were some murmurs at this remark from Arab students who had assisted in organising the Congress, but no one actually challenged it. All the speakers, however, were agreed in opposing Turkish immigration. Since the executive of the Congress wished to avoid any pronouncements which might anger the Ottoman Government, al-Zahrawi, as Chairman, deemed it wisest to close the discussion at this point. Hence the resolution, which might have amended

77. Ṭabbarah's *al-Ittiḥad al-ᶜUthmani* was regarded by the French Vice-Consul in Haifa as an anti-Zionist newspaper—see *Q d'O* N.S. 121 [no number], (30.4. 1913), French Vice-Consul (Haifa) to Couget.
78. *CZA* Z3/114 (16.6.1913).
79. *Ibid.*
80. *AL—Muᶜtamar al-ᶜarabi,* pp. 92–93; cf. *CZA* Z3/114 (24.6.1913), Hochberg to Jacobson.
81. *CZA* Z3/114 (24.6.1913).

to deplore Turkish immigration, was dropped.[82]

Two days after the Congress, ᶜAbd al-Karim al-Khalil, a leader of the Arab nationalist group in Constantinople, arrived in Paris with the draft of an agreement made between himself, on behalf of the Arabs, and Talât Bey, on behalf of the CUP. Although it did not meet all their demands, the draft promised the Arabs at least three Cabinet members, five valis, ten mutasarrıfs, and more senior posts in various ministries. Arabic would be the language of official correspondence in the Arab provinces as well as the language of instruction in elementary and secondary schools. As far as possible, Arab soldiers would do their service in their home provinces, and foreign advisers would be attached to all local administrations. Leading members of the CUP were expected in Paris within two or three days to discuss the draft in detail, and Hochberg was sure that it would be accepted.[83]

Al-Zahrawi and ᶜAbd al-Karim al-Khalil told Hochberg that they thought that an official entente should also be made with the Zionists.[84] A day later, on 26 June, al-Zahrawi said that he and his colleagues believed that Jewish immigration should be encouraged on two conditions: (1) that the immigrants become Ottoman subjects, and (2) that Arab peasants not be displaced from land sold to Jews.[85] However, "adversaries" of Jewish immigration had waged a campaign against Zionism.[86] Zahrawi and his friends wished either "to win over these adversaries by persuasion or to impose their views in the matter."[87] Attempts at persuasion could begin forthwith through the Arabic press. But nothing could be imposed until the nationalist leaders enjoyed genuine authority among the Arabs, which would only be theirs when the Ottoman Government started to satisfy Arab demands, thanks to their efforts.

At this stage, therefore, they preferred to make a secret entente with Hochberg. If Zionist leaders came to Paris, any official agreement would soon become public knowledge and this might

82. *CZA* Z3/114 (24.6.1913).
83. *CZA* Z3/114 (25.6.1913), Hochberg to Jacobson.
84. *Ibid.*
85. *CZA* Z3/114 (26.6.1913), Hochberg to Jacobson.
86. *Ibid.*; from the context, these "adversaries" seem to be Arab anti-Zionists who had voiced their opinions in the press for the last four years; but the allusion could also be to anti-Zionists among the Congress delegates.
87. *Ibid.*

prejudice both the Arab and Zionist causes. A secret entente would serve as the basis for a definitive agreement (*entente définitive*) to be made later in Constantinople with Zionist leaders. Hochberg accordingly wrote to Jacobson, who was then in Berlin, asking for instructions and for the Zionists' terms for a secret entente.[88]

Whilst awaiting a reply, Hochberg obtained a statement from al-Zahrawi in the form of an interview for *Le Jeune-Turc*. Al-Zahrawi associated himself with the published statements of Rafiq Bey al-ᶜAẓm, Rizq Allah Arqash and Shaykh Aḥmad Ṭabbarah on Jewish immigration. He then declared:

In the course of the Congress, I presented a new formula which had considerable success because it accorded perfectly with the mentality and the spirit of the delegates, namely: "The Jews of the whole world are but Syrian émigrés, like the Syrian Christian émigrés in America, Paris and elsewhere. Like them, [the Jews] are also nostalgic for the country of their birth." . . . We are quite sure that our Jewish brethren in the whole world will lend us their support to bring about the triumph of our common cause for the material and moral rehabilitation of our common land.[89]

This statement, more than any other, expresses the broad, "Syrian" view with which the nationalists regarded the Jews. It also reaffirms their desire for Jewish help to revive the Arab provinces which were called no less than "our common land." It was published on 16 July in *Le Jeune-Turc* (which had temporarily changed its name to *L'Union*).[80]

The Zionist Executive must have judged it inappropriate for Hochberg to make a secret entente with the Arab nationalists. Dr. Jacobson hurried to Paris and, having spoken to Hochberg on 28 June, reported back that an entente would probably not be discussed. Instead, he hoped to obtain declarations from the most important Arab leaders in Paris, which the Zionist representatives in Constantinople could use to influence the Ottoman Government to relax the restrictions on Jewish settlement and land purchases in Palestine.[91] He also mentioned that he was to meet al-Zahrawi and Aḥmad Bayhum on 30 June or 1 July. It is not clear if the meeting took place, but in the light of later events, it is clear that Jacobson did not succeed in getting the declarations that he wanted. After

88. *CZA* Z3/114 (25.6.1913); and Z3/114 (26.6.1913).
89. *CZA* Z3/114 (27.5.1913), Hochberg to Jacobson.
90. *L'Union*, i, 29 (16.7.1913).
91. *CZA* Z3/114 (29.6.1913), Jacobson (Paris) to ZAC.

some discussion, the draft agreement between the CUP and the Arabs, which ᶜAbd al-Karim al-Khalil had brought from Constantinople, was accepted by the Arabs assembled in Paris, and, it would appear, they were now unwilling to commit themselves to more than had already been said to Hochberg.

The first round of contacts between Arab nationalist leaders from Syria and the Zionists came to an end at this point. They originated in Cairo where the proposal of an Arab-Zionist entente was first made in the spring of 1913. And although the Egyptian Zionist who was contacted in April was sceptical, the Decentralisationists appear to have been serious about their proposal. Otherwise they would presumably not have made a preliminary agreement with Hochberg, encouraged him to have the agreement endorsed in Beirut, and taken steps to implement it by using their influence to moderate the Arabic press campaign against the Zionists.

But a change appears to have taken place in their position later in the summer. After the agreement with the CUP was accepted and the Arabs in Paris dispersed, Arab interest in an entente with the Zionists waned. Why then was Hochberg received so warmly in Paris? Judging by his letters, Hochberg inflated his own importance. He claimed, for example, to have acted as a mediator between the Arabs and Turks. He had introduced some of the Arab delegates to Batzariya Efendi, the Minister of Public Works, who had come to Paris before the Congress; and he had suggested to Cavid Bey, who was also in Paris, that ᶜAbd al-Ḥamid al-Zahrawi and Rafiq al-ᶜAẓm should be made Cabinet ministers to satisfy the Arabs.[92] He also reported that he had telegraphed this suggestion to Talât Bey through Ahmed Agayev in Constantinople.[93] He was convinced that the Zionists would be rewarded once the Turks and Arabs had been reconciled through his untiring efforts.[94]

In all his enthusiasm, Hochberg evidently misread the situation. The Arabs and the Turks did not need him, a Jewish newspaper editor, to act as their go-between. The Ottoman Government was well aware of the Arab demands, and the Arabs did not lack their contacts in CUP and Government circles. In all probability,

92. *CZA* Z3/114 (16.6.1913).
93. *CZA* Z3/114 (24.6.1913).
94. *CZA* Z3/114 (16.6.1913).

Hochberg also exaggerated the nationalists' interest in an Arab-Zionist entente. Their overriding interest was in an agreement with the CUP and the Government. Having achieved that, other proposed agreements were expendable. Seen in this light, it is even possible that the Arab nationalists purposely played along with Hochberg in Paris—and let the Turks see them doing so—to strengthen their negotiating position. Should Arab demands not be satisfied, they could hint that they would make an agreement with the Zionists, directing Jewish capital and influence in the European press against the Turks in exchange for some favours in Palestine. If this was so, then the proposal of an Arab-Zionist entente, genuine as it may well have been when first made, had become a clever political manoeuvre.

8

Apropos of a Muslim-Jewish Alliance: 1913–1914

Talat Bey's proposal of a Muslim-Jewish alliance, made in February 1913, did not get off to a good start. The Zionists had made their part of the bargain—financial support from Jews in Europe—contingent on the abolition of the restrictions on Jews in Palestine. The Haham Başı's takrirs supporting this demand on constitutional grounds had been fed into the Ottoman bureaucratic machine, and comments on them from Beirut and Jerusalem were not received until the summer. In the interval, the Government's attentions were wholly taken up with the second and third Balkan Wars on the external front and by worries such as the Arab demands for reform on the domestic front.

The Vali of Beirut, in commenting on the Haham Başı's takrirs, came out "categorically against the restrictive measures" imposed on the Jews.[1] Sami Hochberg had learnt that this reply was to be given when he visited Beirut in May, and hence on his return to Constantinople he published an article in *Le Jeune-Turc,* quoting the Vali as saying "I have studied these questions; my opinion can be summed up in the following manner. Jewish immigration

1. *CZA* Z3/114 (17.5.1913), S. Hochberg (Consple.), "Le mouvement arabe."

is useful to the Empire in general and favourable in particular to the rehabilitation of the provinces where it takes place. It is utterly inoffensive."[2]

The new Mutasarrıf of Jerusalem took somewhat longer to express a view. On his arrival in March from a post in Anatolia, he was, according to Albert Antébi, well disposed but apprehensive, because "his superiors, the Ministers, the [Grand] Vezir, the Committee, Parliament, are afraid of [Arab] public opinion."[3] Indeed, when Antébi had a further conversation with the Mutasarrıf in the middle of April, he sensed that ministers in Constantinople had recommended that the takrirs be shelved—again "for fear of Arab opinion."[4]

Considering Arab demands at the time and the fact that the Government had just ordered the dissolution of the Beirut Reform Committee, these were understandable fears. Moreover, in Jerusalem itself, Arab opponents of the Zionists, led by Ruḥi Bey al-Khalidi, were trying to persuade the Mutasarrıf to argue against abolishing the restrictions on the Jews.[5] As part of their campaign, Ruḥi Bey was writing a book, in the preface of which he spoke of "liberating his conscience before history."[6]

But these efforts were unsuccessful. At the beginning of June, the Mutasarrıf made a tour of Lydda, Ramle and Jaffa, visiting Jewish colonies on the way and attending a musical evening at the Hebrew high school in Jaffa. Like Muhdi Bey a year before, he seems to have been impressed by what he saw.[7] So, having consulted his kaymakams,[8] he sent a favourable reply to the takrirs in August.[9]

At the time the Government was going through the motions of celebrating the agreement with the Arabs. In the process, it was

2. *Le Jeune-Turc,* v, 154 (5.6.1913).
3. *AIU* X E 31 [n.d. (*ca.* 6.4.1913)], A. Antébi (Jerus.) to Haham Başı (Consple.).
4. *CZA* L2/44 (19.4.1913). Antébi to J. Thon (Jaffa).
5. *AIU* Z E 31 (11.4.1913), Antébi to Pres., AIU (Paris).
6. *AIU* X E 31 (5.5.1913), Antébi to Pres., AIU. Ruḥi Bey's book did not appear, for he died that summer. In the preface to Ruḥi Bey's posthumous *al-Muqadimma fi al-masʿala al-sharqiyya,* the title of his book is given as *"Tarikh al-umma al-israʿiliyya wa-ʿalaqatuha bil-ʿarab wa-ghayrihim min ul-umam."* Al-Zirakli, iii, 64 gives it as *"Tarikh al-ṣihyuniyya."*
7. *Falasṭin,* iii, 41 (11.6.1913); and iii, 42 (14.6.1913); *ha-Ḥerut,* v, 218 (13.6. 1913); and v, 222 (18.6.1913); and *Truth,* iii, 140 (15.7.1913).
8. *CZA* 268/no. 215 (18.8.1913), Antébi to Pres., JCA (Paris); cf *CZA* Z3/1450 (26.8.1913), Thon to AZC (Berlin).

reminded of how sensitive the Arabs had become to certain questions affecting the Zionists. Since the end of 1912 the sale of crown lands (*çiftliks*) in the Jordan Valley had been contemplated with a view to raising funds. A Syrian Christian, Ḥabib Luṭf Allah Paşa,[10] had put in a bid of T£200,000–T£250,000 for the çiftliks at Hula, Beisan and Jericho, while the Zionists had offered T£200,000 for the çiftlik at Beisan alone.[11] Both bids had been rejected as inadequate, and in April the Cabinet accepted in principle a revised proposal by Najib al-Aṣfar to acquire all the çiftliks in the provinces covering Syria, Palestine and Iraq.[12] Arabs at Beisan protested against the negotiations,[13] and the Arabic press took up the issue vigorously.[14] *Al-Muqtabas* insinuated that Luṭf Allah Paşa was a "Zionist agent" (Najib al-Aṣfar having been damned without reason on that ccount two years before);[15] and *Falasṭin,* which was particularly vocal, alleged that the fellahin living in the çiftliks would be dispossessed.[16]

In the midst of this outcry, which hampered the progress of al-Aṣfar's proposal, Talât Bey received a delegation of Arabs who came to express their gratitude for the announcement of a series of reforms connected with the agreement made in Paris. The delegation was led by ʿAbd al-Karim al-Khalil, and in his address of thanks he alluded obliquely but unmistakeably to Jewish immigration. Referring to the proposals to sell the çiftliks in the Arab provinces, and especially in Palestine, he suggested that Talât Bey—in his capacity as Minister of the Interior—could scarcely take a favourable view of the entry of "foreigners" (that is, Jews) and the displacement of the local population from those areas.[17]

In the middle of August, Albert Antébi discerned "a powerful upsurge" among "all the Syrian populations" against the sale of

10. *Q d'O* N.S. 134, no. 33 (21.11.1912), A. Guy (Haifa) to R. Poincaré (Paris).
11. *CZA* Z3/45 (13.2.1913), Jacobson to J. Kann (The Hague).
12. *CZA* Z3/45 (24.4.1913), Jacobson to ZAC.
13. *Q d'O* N.S. 121, no. 94 (6.5.1913), F. Couget (Beirut) to S. Pichon (Paris).
14. *CZA* Z3/115, press reports [undated and unsigned] re articles in *al-Karmil* and *al-Muqtabas* on 10, 13, 21, and 23.3.1913.
15. *CZA* Z3/115, press report [dated and unsigned] re *al-Muqtabas* of 23.3.1913.
16. *Falasṭin,* iii, 50 (12.7.1913); iii, 52 (19.7.1913); iii, 55 (30.7.1913); and iii, 59 (9.8.1913).
17. [A. Daghir], *Thawrat al-ʿarab,* p. 84.

çiftliks to foreigners and Zionists. The "Central Committee for Arab Reforms," he wrote, had issued a circular telegram calling for "vehement protests" to Constantinople.[18] And, in fact, there were reports of protest telegrams not only from village shaykhs and fellahin in Palestine and the surrounding provinces,[19] but also from notables as far afield as Baghdad.[20]

It is little wonder then that Talât Bey and Sulayman al-Bustani (a Maronite from Beirut and Minister of Commerce and Agriculture) told Dr. Jacobson a few days after ᶜAbd al-Karim's deputation that the restrictions on Jewish land purchase in Palestine could not be relaxed.[21] Indeed, the Government found it necessary to issue instructions on 3 September, reconfirming all earlier restrictions on foreigners seeking to buy land in Palestine.[22] Later that month, Jacobson went to Berlin, and the Haham Başı, who passed through the city shortly afterwards, informed him that the scheme to sell the çiftliks in Palestine had, for the moment at least, been relegated to "the realm of dreams and good intentions."[23] The Grand Vezir had told the Haham Başı that the Government must desist from such action in view of Arab opposition.[24]

But the Government was still in a quandary. Although France had permitted certain loans to the Empire over the summer, the Government still was in need of financial support and still prepared to see if Jews in Europe could supply it. On the other hand, the Arabs had high expectations of reforms in their provinces (which were going to be disappointed), and this was no time to aggravate matters by making concessions to the Jews in Palestine. In these circumstances, the Government recognized that one way around its difficulty was for the Zionists to make an agreement with the Arabs, and the Grand Vezir told the Haham Başı as much: "Before all, you must reach an understanding with the Arabs. We will do the rest."[25]

18. *JCA* 268/no. 215 (18.8.1913), Antébi to Pres., JCA.
19. *Near East,* v, 120 (1913), p. 448.
20. *Ha-Ḥerut,* v, 277 (22.8.1913).
21. *CZA* L2/49/I (12.8.1913), Jacobson to ZAC.
22. *CZA* Z3/1451 (20.10.1913), Thon to ZAC, enclosing text of order from Constantinople dated 3.9.1913.
23. *CZA* Z3/1642 (25.9.1913), Jacobson (Berlin) to H. Frank (Paris).
24. *CZA* Z3/47 (25.9.1913), same to R. Lichtheim (Consple.).
25. *Ibid.*

The argument presumably ran as follows. The Arabs and Zionists had already discussed an entente (a fact known to Talât Bey and other members of the CUP[26]). If they could reach an accord, the restrictions in Palestine could be removed without too great a risk of Arab complaint. And then it could be hoped that Jewish financial aid for the Empire would be forthcoming.

The flaw in the argument was that most Arab nationalists, having made their agreement with the CUP, had lost interest in an understanding with the Zionists. Accordingly, the matter was not advanced at this stage. Nonetheless, the Government began, very cautiously, to relax the restrictions on the Jews, trying to elicit Jewish support in Europe on the one hand, while not offending the Arabs on the other. The operation was a failure from both points of view. Jewish financiers were not induced to extend any aid to the Empire, and by the spring of 1914 Arabs, especially in Palestine, were alarmed.

The Government's first step was to abolish the "Red Slip"—in a highly ambivalent manner. This temporary residence permit had long been recognised as a totally ineffective measure. Indeed, in 1907 the Mutasarrıf of Jerusalem, Ali Ekrem Bey, had reported that the Jews welcomed the Red Slip because it guaranteed their entry into Palestine, whence it was all but impossible to expel them.[27] Since 1908, various figures, including Talât Bey,[28] and even Ruḥi Bey al-Khalidi,[29] had expressed the view that there was no point in issuing it.[30] Thus, when favourable comments were received from Beirut and Jerusalem on his takrirs, the Haham Başı approached Talât Bey, who referred the question to the CUP's Central Committee.[31] Within a short while it was back in the hands of the Grand Vezir,[32] and on his instructions an order was sent on 24 September from the Ministry of the Interior to Beirut and Jerusalem abolishing the Red Slip.[33]

The terms of the order were significant. Only the Red Slip itself

26. *CZA* Z3/114 (25.6.2924), Hochberg (Paris) to Jacobson.
27. *ISA (T)* no. 21 [n.d. (mid-August, 1907)], Mutas. (Jerus.) to SP.
28. *CZA* Z2/8 (8.11.1909), Jacobson to D. Wolffsohn (Cologne).
29. *Ha-Ẓevi,* xxvi, 29 (2.11.1909).
30. Cf. *CZA* Z2/8 (17.5.1909), Jacobson to Wolffsohn, re Ahmed Rıza; and *Jewish Chronicle,* no. 2,209 (4.8.1911), re Rıza Tevfık.
31. *CZA* Z3/47 (22.10.1913), Jacobson (Berlin [memorandum]).
32. *CZA* Z3/47 (25.9.1913), Jacobson to Lichtheim.
33. *CZA* Z3/47 (4.10.1913), Lichtheim to ZAC.

was done away with—"since it did not achieve the aim and benefit which had been intended but, on the contrary, led to numerous abuses."[34] However, all other restrictions on the Jews were to remain in force. Strict measures were to be taken with "redoubled vigilance" to ensure that Jewish pilgrims did not prolong their stay in Palestine or settle there. The Ottoman Government had abolished the Red Slip to please the Jews, and retained the other restrictions so as not to displease the Arabs.

To ensure that visiting Jews did not stay in Palestine more than three months, the authorities in Jaffa decided to take their passports from them on arrival.[35] In return the Jews were given a receipt—or, as they put it, a "white slip."[36] They therefore complained to the Kaymakam against this procedure, and in the middle of November he was instructed by the Mutasarrıf of Jerusalem to abandon it. Instead, the date of arrival was to be marked in every Jew's passport, and a passport officer was to note all the particulars in it. At the end of each month, a tally of all the Jews who had entered Jaffa was to be sent to Jerusalem.[37] The Kaymakam was reminded that the ban on Jewish settlement in Palestine was still in force and had to be implemented.[38] Thus the Jews were no longer given a Red Slip and were allowed to keep their passports, but for all practical purposes nothing else had changed.

In Constantinople, the Haham Başı again called on the Grand Vezir, Talât Bey and others.[39] They gave him and the Zionists to believe that the "prevarication" in Jaffa was merely a device employed by local officials to extract bribes from Jews entering Palestine.[40] But as the orders from Constantinople made clear, that was not the case. In December, Talât Bey assured the Haham Başı that he had instructed the authorities in Jerusalem not to

34. *CZA* Z3/1451 (21.10.1913), Thon to ZAC, enclosing German translation of no. 174 [= 175 (?)] (24.9.1913), Ministry of the Interior (Ĉonsple.) to Mutasarrıflık (Jerus.).
35. *CZA* Z3/1451 (19.10.1913), Thon to Jacobson; and *CZA* Z3/1451 (2.11. 1913), same to ZAC.
36. *Ha-Ḥerut,* vi, 17 (2.11.1913); and *CZA* L2/49/I (8.11.1913), Thon to ZAC.
37. Letter no. 326 (18.11.1913), Mutas. (Jerus.) to Kay (Jaffa), replying to enquiry from latter of 16.10.1913, enclosed in *CZA* Z3/1451 (25.11.1913), Thon to ZAC.
38. Cf. *US (T),* Reel 38, file 867.111/23, no. 681 (9.12.1913), S. Edelman (Jerus.) to Secretary of State (Washington).
39. *CZA* Z3/47 (3.11.1913), I. Neufach (Consple.) to ZCO; and (5.11.1913), Lichtheim to ZAC; plus many subsequent letters.
40. *CZA* Z3/47 (13.12.1913), Lichtheim to ZAC.

inconvenience Jews.[41] But three weeks later, the Zionist Office in Jaffa reported that the local authorities had not received any new orders.[42] Then, towards the end of January 1914, the Zionists in Constantinople were informed that the Cabinet had decided to lift the three-month limit on visits made by Jews to Palestine and also to remove the restrictions on Jewish land purchase after the next General Elections (to be held in April).[43] But once again, the latest instructions to Beirut and Jerusalem were found to go no further than repeating that the Red Slip had been abolished, while the restrictions on land sales to Jews were retained.[44] The Government, it seems clear, was trying to convince the Zionists of its good intentions by giving assurances and making promises, but was wary of carrying out its word for fear of Arab reactions.

The Government next tried a different approach to the problem. A major Arab—and Turkish—objection to the Jewish immigrants was that they held on to their foreign nationality after settling in Palestine. If more Jews could be induced to become Ottoman subjects, several difficulties would be eliminated at one stroke. The Arabs would no longer have this reason to object to Jewish settlers in Palestine. The parallel Turkish fear of the immigrants would be reduced, since Great Power influence through the Jews would be neutralised. And, finally, the way would be open for the Government to ease the restrictions on Jewish settlement and land purchase. Orders were accordingly sent to Beirut and Jerusalem on 2 March to grant special facilities to Jews wishing to become Ottoman subjects under Article 4 of the Nationality Law, whereby the five years' residence requirement could be waived in exceptional circumstances.[45]

The terms of this order are again of interest, as they illustrate the Government's predicament, which in this instance was complicated by an additional factor—the attitude of the Powers which, it was feared, might protest if large numbers of Jewish immigrants were made Ottoman subjects at any one time. The provincial governors

41. *CZA* Z3/47 (13.12.1913), Lichtheim to ZAC.
42. *CZA* L2/49 (5.1.1914), Zionist Office (Jaffa) to ZAC.
43. *CZA* Z3/48 (23.1.1914), Lichtheim to ZAC.
44. Order no. 1845/2217 (31.1.1914), Min. of the Interior (SP) to Governors (Beirut and Jerus.) enclosed in *CZA* Z3/48 (11.2.1914), Lichtheim to ZAC.
45. Order no. 88340/937 (2.3.1914), Min. of the Interior to Governors (Beirut and Jerus.), enclosed in *CZA* ZE/1454 (8.4.1914), A. Ruppin (Jaffa) to ZAC.

were therefore instructed to naturalise Jews in groups of three and four, and to avoid all correspondence with foreign representatives. The customary practice of seeking the approval of the applicant's consul was also to be dispensed with.[46]

There were other indications of the Government's efforts to convince the Jews of its good intentions. In February, a Zionist Society, called the Ottoman Zionist Union, was allowed to open in Constantinople[47]—no mean concession, because shortly after the Counter-revolution in 1909 the CUP had passed the "Law of Associations," under which a number of nationalist societies, including the Ottoman Arab Brotherhood, had been dissolved. In March, the Mutasarrıf of Jerusalem was interviewed by the editor of *al-Iqdam,* a weekly with strongly anti-Zionist views which had begun to appear in Cairo. The editor, a one-time Jaffa merchant who had gone bankrupt,[48] slanted his questions to evoke adverse comment about Jewish activities in Palestine. But the Mutasarrıf refused to be drawn and declared that the Government saw no harm in the Zionists. If it did, "it would certainly protest against them."[49] And although the restrictions on land purchases by Jews had been reconfirmed since September 1913, the Zionist Office in Jaffa reported in April and May 1914 that land was being transferred in the names of foreign Jews, quietly and without hindrance.[50] The British Vice-Consul at Jaffa was therefore justified in observing in April that "the Government have lately shown themselves extremely favourable to the Zionists."[51]

The net effect of this cautious change of policy was to strengthen local patriotism in Palestine. This had been the general trend since the summer of 1913. For example, in July *Falasṭin* criticised Shaykh Aḥmad Ṭabbarah for his "one-sided" treatment of the immigration issue at the First Arab Congress in Paris. Although his remarks about Turkish immigration into the Arab provinces won approval, his approach was questioned, because "he did not mention the

46. Order no. 88340/937 (2.3.1914).
47. *Ha-ᶜOlam,* viii, 8 (12.3.1914).
48. *CZA* Z3/116, press report [undated and unsigned].
49. *Al-Iqdam,* i, 12 (15.3.1914), reprinted in *ha-Ḥerut,* vi, 139 (25.3.1914).
50. *CZA* L2/34/II (22.4.1914), Zionist Office (Jaffa) to Jacobson; and *CZA* Z3/1455 (28.5.1914), same to J. M. Machover (Kiev).
51. *PRO* FO 371/2134/22036, no. 33 (29.4.1914), W. Hough (Jaffa) to P. J. C. McGregor (Jerus.).

dangers connected with the immigration of the Zionists to the country (*bilad*) and the problems for the future induced by the Government's leniency towards [the Zionists] at the present time—[problems] which an immigration of people from Macedonia would not create in any circumstances."[52]

At the end of July, *al-Karmil* proposed that another Arab Congress be held, this time in Nablus, to discuss means of combatting the "Zionist threat."[53] The proposal was seconded in *Falasṭin* by a contributor from Nablus,[54] and backed by *al-Mufid* (Beirut) and *al-Muqtabas* (Damascus).[55] At the beginning of September, *al-Muqtabas* explained that Nablus had been suggested because if offered an "enlightened Arab environment, youth with principles and ideals, the most zealous of nationalists," and also because "the Zionists have not succeeded in doing [to Nablus] what they have done to other towns in Palestine"[56]—a reference to the fact that, except for Kfar Saba (1903), there was no Zionist settlement in the whole of the Sancak of Nablus straddling the middle of Palestine. (The town of Nablus itself enjoyed a tradition of independence, and in 1910 local notables had even petitioned against a proposal to annex the Sancak to the Mutasarrıflık of Jerusalem "so as not to be infected by the Zionist germ."[57]) On 9 September *al-Karmil* published a telegram from "young Palestinians" in Constantinople, backing the proposal of an anti-Zionist Congress.[58] Two weeks later Muḥammad Salaḥ al-Ḥusayni, a notable in Jerusalem, voiced his support for the proposal in *al-Karmil.*[59] But for all this current of support, plans for the Congress were not advanced and it was not held.

Falasṭin, on the other hand, published a suggestion which did bear some fruit. On 12 July a correspondent from Nablus proposed the formation of a society made up of notables from the main towns of Palestine—Jerusalem, Jaffa, Haifa, Gaza, and Nablus—"to engage in the purchase of çiftliks before it is done by the Zionists."[60]

52. *Falasṭin,* iii, 49 (9.7.1913); cf. *ÇZA* Z3/116 (17.12.1913), press report re *al-Karmil* (26.10.1913).
53. Cf. *Falasṭin,* iii, 56 (2.8.1913).
54. *Falasṭin,* vi, 155 (21.4.1914).
55. *Ha-Ḥerut,* v, 278 (24.8.1913); and v, 280 (26.8.1913).
56. Reprinted in *ha-Ḥerut,* v, 288 (4.9.1913).
57. *AIU* IX E 28 [n.d. (*ca.* 1.2.1910)], Antébi to Frank (Jaffa).
58. *CZA* Z3/116 (21.9.1913), Thon to ZAC, enclosing press report.
59. *CZA* Z3/116 (12.9.[= 10.(?)]1913), Thon to ZAC, enclosing press report.
60. *Falasṭin,* iii, 50 (12.7.1913).

Very significantly, the writer described this society as a *Sharika Waṭaniyya Filasṭiniyya*—a *Palestinian* Patriotic Company (in contrast with the *Ottoman* Patriotic Party in Jaffa just two years earlier). On 2 August *Falasṭin* backed this proposal,[61] and at the end of the month Albert Antébi reported that an anti-Zionist group had in fact been set up in Nablus.[62]

In July an Arab from Zarnuqa and a Jew from Rishon le-Ẓiyyon were killed in a clash between Arab villagers and Jewish watchmen in the vineyards at Reḥovot. The incident provided Arab anti-Zionists with a pretext to step up their activities. *Falasṭin* expanded its coverage of the affair with each issue until, by the end of August, its format was enlarged by an extra page.[63] A rumour was purposely put about "accusing the Jews of systematically persecuting the peasants."[64] The muhtars of several villages around Reḥovot were encouraged to petition the Mutasarrıf of Jerusalem to protect their lives and property against the young Russian Jews who guarded the settlement and who, it was alleged, "kill, pillage and violate Muslim women and girls."[65] When a Jewish delegation came to deliver a petition to the Mutasarrıf countering these charges, "the Governor did not hide that every day he receives complaints and reports against Jewish activity and the colonies"[66]—complaints which, according to the Zionist Office in Jaffa, were being made by "various respected citizens."[67]

A leader of this campaign was Shaykh Sulayman al-Taji, a founder of the Ottoman Patriotic Party in Jaffa (which had not been heard of since the end of 1911). He was by no means a disinterested party because, to acerbate his known anti-Zionist views, he was at odds with a group of Jews in the summer of 1913 over some land he owned near Tel Aviv.[68] Moreover, as the campaign proceeded, he also found himself bidding against Jews for a plot of land, again in

61. *Falasṭin,* iii, 56 (2.8.1913).
62. *JCA* 268/no. 217 (26.8.1913); and no. 218 (31.8.1913), both Antébi to Pres., JCA; cf. *Truth,* iv, 145 (26.8.1913).
63. *Falasṭin,* iii, 57 (6.8.1913); iii, 59 (13.8.1913); iii, 61 (20.8.1913); iii, 63 (27.8.1913); and iii, 64 (30.8.1913).
64. *JCA* 268/no. 215 (18.8.1913), Antébi to Pres., JCA.
65. *JCA* 268/no. 215 (18.8.1913); and no. 219 (1.9.1913), Antébi to Pres., JCA; cf. *ha-Ḥerut,* v, 268 (11.8.1913); and *CZA* Z3/1450 (25.8.1913), Thon to ZAC.
66. *JCA* 268/no. 217 (26.8.1913), Antébi to Pres., JCA.
67. *CZA* Z3/1450 (2.9.1913), Thon to ZAC.
68. *CZA* Z3/116 (16.9.1913), Thon to ZAC.

the vicinity of Tel Aviv. At the end of August he addressed an open letter to the Mutasarrıf and the Prosecutor General in Jerusalem, which was published in *Falasṭin* under the caption "Freedom or Slavery: Justice or Tyranny?"[69] His contention was that the Jews had almost "conquered" Palestine, and that their settlements near Zarnuqa despised the village and had waited for an opportunity to destroy it, which, in the event, was provided by a bunch of grapes in the vineyards. In October he addressed another open letter to the Mutasarrıf, which was distributed in the form of a leaflet,[70] and in November he published a poem, entitled "The Zionist Danger," in *Falasṭin.*[71]

Political poems of its kind have been a fashionable mode of expression among Arabs since the middle of the nineteenth century, but, as far as is known, this was the first poem to be penned in Arabic against the Zionists. Although Palestine is not mentioned by name, al-Taji's repeated reference to "our country" and his remonstrances against the authorities show him to be a local patriot first and an Ottoman loyalist second. As befits a Muslim shaykh, there are distinctly Islamic elements in his poem. For example, in keeping with the Quran and certain *hadiths* (Islamic oral traditions), the Jews are a weak and humiliated people, who achieve their ends by deceit. And appeals could still be addressed to the Caliph, even though the Caliphate was impotent as an institution by this time.

> Jews, sons of clinking gold, stop your deceit;
> We shall not be cheated into bartering away our country!
> Shall we hand it over, meekly,
> while we still have some spirit left?
> Shall we cripple ourselves?
>
> The Jews, the weakest of all peoples and the least of them,
> are haggling with us for our land;
> how can we slumber on?
> We know what they want
> —and they have the money, all of it.
>
> Master, rulers, what is wrong with you?
> What ails you?

69. *Falasṭin,* iii, 64 (30.8.1913).
70. *CZA* Z3/116 (10.11.1913), Thon to ZAC, enclosing details of leaflet.
71. *Falasṭin,* iii, 84 (8.11.1913).

It is time to awake, to be aware!
Away with this heedlessness
—there is no more time for patience!

While you said nothing,
our enemies were encouraged.
Now you must speak
—to put them to flight and us at ease!
The danger is clear;
can no one resist it?
Is there not an eye left
to shed a tear for our country?

Send the rulers a message for me,
to alarm and dismay the bravest of hearts:
if they do not do their duty as leaders,
why do they hold power,
and why do they sit so high?

And you, O Caliph, guardian of the faithful,
have mercy on us, your shield.
Ours is a land whose frontiers God has blessed,
we are a people rejoicing in the merit of religions;
we are worthy of the mercy you can show.
Without it, the faithful will lie wounded
  and afflicted in their holy places.
Bearer of the Crown, does it please you
that we should witness our country
being bought from us, wrenched from us?

The Government's easing of the restrictions against the Jews over the winter months of 1913–14 did not pass unnoticed by the Arab press, particularly in Palestine. Although the abolition of the Red Slip was taken relatively lightly by *Falasṭin* and *al-Karmil* (since both papers considered its existence "a farce"),[72] the other steps were viewed more seriously, and by April the protests were louder than ever before.[73]

As has been seen, the Government was wary of Arab sensitivities, and if the press is now taken as a more direct reflection of Arab opinion by this time, it scored certain successes from its point of

72. *Falasṭin,* iii, 77 (15.10.1913); and 78 (18.10.1913); *CZA* L2/70 (5.11.1913), Thon to ZAC, enclosing press report re *al-Karmil* of 24.10.1913.
73. *Ha-Ḥerut,* vi, 155 (21.4.1914).

view. Apart from limiting the Government's freedom to manoeuvre in general, three specific examples will serve to illustrate the point. First, in the face of continued pressure against the sale of çiftliks in Palestine,[74] the Government was constrained in the winter of 1913 not only to make a further public announcement that no such sales were contemplated,[75] but also to reverse its decision of April to accept Najib al-Aṣfar's offer.[76] In January 1914 the General Council in Beirut awarded a concession for the draining of the Hula swamps (north of the Sea of Galilee) to Aḥmad Bayhum and a member of the Sursuq family, who were at once accused of acting on behalf of Jewish interests,[77] even though this was not the case.[78] Press and other protests (mainly from Beirut) forced the Government to overrule the General Council's decision by the end of February.[79] Finally, the Zionists had tried for a number of years to obtain a concession to develop a health and tourist resort around the hot springs at Tiberias.[80] When negotiations were reopened at the end of 1913, *al-Karmil* and other papers took issue,[81] and in June 1914 the Government granted the concession to an Arab group.[82]

Falasṭin and *al-Karmil* also closely followed Zionist affairs in Palestine and abroad. The eleventh Zionist Congress was held in Vienna in September 1913. *Al-Karmil* suggested that Arabs should attend as observers,[83] and although this proposal was not acted upon, the arrangements for the Congress and its proceedings were

74. *Near East,* v, 127 (1913), p. 660.
75. *CZA* Z3/116 (5. and 24.11.1913), both Thon to ZAC, re articles in *al-Karmil* of 24. and 28.10.1913, both discussing the announcement.
76. *CZA* Z3/47 (22.12.1913), Jacobson and Lichtheim to ZAC; reporting that al-Aṣfar was prepared to help the Zionists to buy land now that the Government had rejected his offer!
77. *US (T),* Reel 62, file 867.52/14, no. 653 (17.2.1914), American Consul-General (Beirut) to Secretary of State (Washington), enclosing translation of an article from *Le Réveil* (Beirut) of 5.2.1914; and *CZA* Z3/116, press report [undated and unsigned], re articles in *al-Ahram* of 21.2.1914 and *al-Qabas* of 24.2.1914.
78. *CZA* L18/246/II (24.1.1914), Lichtheim to Ruppin.
79. *US (T),* Reel 62, file 867.52/15, no. 664 (17.3.1914), American Consul-General (Beirut) to Secretary of State (Washington); and *CZA* Z3/116, press report [undated and unsigned] re article in *al-Karmil* of 27.2.1914.
80. E.G. *CZA* W/125/II (5.11.1906), D. Levontin (Jaffa) to Wolffsohn (London); and *CZA* L18/246/II (14.7.1912), J. Hankin (Haifa) to Thon.
81. *CZA* Z3/116, press report [undated and unsigned], re article in *al-Karmil* of 27.2.1914.
82. *Ha-Ḥerut,* vi, 207 (22.6.1914).
83. *CZA* Z3/115 (16.7.1913), Thon to ZCO.

reported in detail by both papers.[84] The use of Arabic for official business and in schools, a basic demand of the Arab nationalists, had roused strong feelings in the Arab provinces. Thus *Falasṭin* and *al-Karmil* could not fail to take a lively interest in the debate which raged within the New Yishuv in the winter of 1913–14 over the proposed language of instruction at the new technical school in Haifa. The school's sponsors, the Hilfsverein der deutschen Juden, wanted it to be German, whereas teachers in Palestine wanted it to be Hebrew. *Falasṭin* and *al-Karmil* correctly took the latters' position as an expression of Jewish nationalism and regarded their eventual victory as a triumph for Zionism, as was evident, for instance, in an article by ᶜArif al-ᶜArif in *al-Karmil* in March 1914.[85] German influence in the Empire had been growing steadily and in May 1913 the Government had turned to Germany for help to modernise the Ottoman army. In September, *Falasṭin* and *al-Karmil* contended that Zionism was an instrument of German policy in Palestine,[86] even though *Falasṭin* had previously been inclined to see a Russian hand behind the Zionists (see p. 129) and *al-Karmil* cited an article to the same effect from an English periodical called the *New East* in the winter of 1913.[87] And whether or not some European Power was behind the Zionists, the growth of Jewish institutions in Palestine continued to be attacked. Thus in the autumn of 1913 *Falasṭin* campaigned against the law courts set up by the Zionist Office in Jaffa in 1910 (the "Hebrew Court of Peace"), which, it claimed, were evidence of Jewish "self-government."[88] Such was *Falasṭin's* concern with Zionist activities that in the first three months of 1914 scarcely an edition appeared without one or more articles on the subject. Small items were grouped under a column headed "The Jewish Week," and on

84. *Falasṭin,* iii, 47 (2.7.1913); 56 (2.8.1913); 58 (9.8.1913); 68 (13.9.1913); 73 (1.10.1913); and 74 (4.10.1913); *CZA* Z3/116 (28.9.1013), Thon to Zac, enclosing press report, re article in *al-Karmil* of 16.9.1913.
85. E.G. *Falasṭin,* iii, 91 (27.12.1913); iii, 93 (3.1.1914); and iii, 94 (7.1.1914); and *CZA* L2/94/I, press report [indated and unsigned] re articles in *al-Karmil* of 10 and 17.3.1914 (the second by ᶜArif al-ᶜArif).
86. *Falasṭin,* iii, 35 (21.5.1913); and iii, 71 (24.9.1913); and *Q d'O* N.S. 123, no. 37 (20.9.1913), French Vice-Consul (Haifa) to Pichon, re *al-Karmil* of 9.9.1913.
87. *Hashqafat ha-ᶜitonut ha-ᶜaravit,* vol. i (1913), re *al-Karmil,* no. 382.
88. *Falasṭin,* iii, 78 (18.10.1913); and iii, 80 (25.10.1913); cf. *CZA* Z3/116 (5.11.1913), Thon to ZAC, enclosing press report re *al-Karmil* of 24.10.1913.

11 April a special supplement was published on the Zionist Movement.[89]

A telling note of self-criticism crept into this stream of reporting. In December 1913 an editorial on "The Zionist Danger" appeared in *Falasṭin* signed by a "patriot" (*waṭani*), who argued that the Zionists were not to be reproached for their advances; those at fault were local notables who sold land to the Zionists. "The work of a criminal who hands over his country to the enemy in wartime is no different from their work."[90] And in April 1914 *al-Karmil* published an article entitled "The Newspapers Are Not Guilty, but We Are." The "thousands" of Arab opponents of Zionism in Palestine were to be blamed for their lack of leadership and organisation.[91]

But the greater part of the strictures were still directed against the Government for its policies towards the Zionists. And, with newspapers outside Palestine still pressing for reforms in the Arab provinces, the Government seems to have been ill at ease about the press criticism from Palestine. Having closed down *al-Muqtabas* (Damascus) in October for printing an article in support of renewed demands for reforms emanating from Baghdad and Basra,[92] it appears to have decided that the time had come to take disciplinary action against *al-Karmil* and *Falasṭin.* Najib Naṣṣar, who in recent months had withdrawn his support from the CUP, was taken into custody for a few days,[93] but his paper was not suspended. *Falasṭin,* on the other hand, was closed down on 14 November, ostensibly because of an article two days earlier severely criticising the Mutasarrıf of Jerusalem.[94] However, it continued to appear, first as *al-Akhbar* and then as *al-Dustur,* until it was permitted to revert to its former name a month later when its editors were reprieved from Constantinople in view of their record of loyalty to the CUP.[95]

Shaykh Asʿad Shuqayr (the CUP deputy from Acre) and Tawfiq

89. *CZA* Z3/116 and *CZA* L2/94/I, enclosing press reports re articles in *Falasṭin* of 21, 28 and 31 January; 4, 7, 11, 14, 18, 21, and 28 February; 28 March; 4 April and the special supplement of 11 April on the Zionist Movement. Other articles have also been cited in preceding notes.
90. *Falasṭin,* iii, 91 (27.12.1913); cf. iii, 85 (12.11.1913).
91. *CZA* Z3/116, press report [undated and unsigned], re *al-Karmil* of 24.4.1914.
92. *Ha-Ḥerut,* vi, 3 (7.10.1913).
93. *Near East,* vi, 137 (1913), p. 232.
94. *Falasṭin,* iii, 85 (12.11.1913); cf. iii, 89 (17.12.1913).
95. *PRO* FO 371/2134/22036, no. 33 (29.4.1914), Hough to McGregor.

ʿAbd Allah (the President of the CUP branch in Acre) exerted pressure on Naṣṣar, and from the beginning of 1914 his attacks on the Government and the Zionists grew somewhat milder.[96] *Falasṭin,* however, did not relent, and on 20 April it was suspended a second time on orders from Constantinople, because of an article which appeared on 4 April, containing "a fulminating and vague threat that when the eyes of the nation were opened to the peril towards which it was drifting it would rise like a roaring flood and a consuming fire and there would be trouble in [store] for the Zionists."[97]

After this suspension, *Falasṭin* issued a circular to its readers[98] which, according to both the British Vice-Consul in Jaffa and the Britisn Consul in Jerusalem, "faithfully mirrors the growing resentment among the Arabs" against the Zionists.[99] Its emphasis was on the fact that the Zionists sought to establish an exclusively Jewish state in Palestine, and its thrust was against the Government for going out of its way, in *Falasṭin's* view, to help them.

It seems that in the opinion of the Central Government we have done a serious thing in drawing the attention of the nation to the danger threatened by the advancing tide of Zionism, for in the course of last week the Local Authorities received a telegram from the Ministry of the Interior ordering the suppression of our paper "Palestine" and our committal for trial as having committed in our campaign against Zionism and our appeal to the national spirit an offence which they term "sowing discord between the elements of the Empire."

This is mighty well; still better is the acknowledgement by the Government of the Zionist Society as one of the elements of the Empire, in which she shows more devotion to their cause than the Zionists themselves.

They cry in their meetings, declare in their conferences, and announce in the highways and byways of Palestine, nay from the very housetops, that they are a *political party* whose aim is to restore Palestine to their nation and concentrate them in it, and to keep it exclusively for them. Then comes the Government saying, "No, you are on the contrary one of the elements of our happy empire, and he who opposes you is in our sight a criminal bent on causing strife between those elements."[100]

96. *CZA* Z3/1453 (3.2.1914), Zionist Office (Jaffa) to Jacobson.
97. *PRO* FO 371/2134/22036, no. 33 (29.4.1914).
98. Issued on or about 27.4.1914—see *CZA* L2/94/II (27.4.1914), B. Ibry (Jerus.) to Ruppin.
99. *PRO* FO 371/2134/22036, no. 31 (30.4.1914), McGregor to Mallet.
100. *PRO* FO 371/2134/22036, no. 33 (29.4.1914); cf. *CZA* Z3/1455 (1.5.1914), Thon to ZAC.

"Zionist," the circular asserted, was not synonymous with "Jew." Until a few years ago, the Jews were a "fraternal Ottoman element," but then a wave of immigrants (the Second Aliya), "composed of German revolutionaries, Russian nihilists and vagabonds from other nations," arrived. They proclaimed that the Jews were not a religion but a nation, and that they sought national autonomy in Palestine. They cautioned the Jews against mixing with the Muslim and Christian Arabs, and built separate quarters. They only spoke Hebrew, "which is useless to the world except as a weapon of Zionism," and they announced that they would only give up their foreign nationalities when they could replace them by "the Zionist nationality." The Government, the circular went on, could ask us "to be blind and deaf," and could even close our newspaper. "But what it cannot do is restore our trust in it, or alter our belief that we are a nation going to its death before the Zionist stream in this land of Palestine."

According to the circular, Henry Morgenthau, the American Ambassador at the Porte, had promised to help the Zionists and had demanded the closure of *Falasṭin* during a visit to Palestine earlier in April. The circular suggested that Morgenthau (who was Jewish) would do better to prevent Zionists from making provocative remarks than to stifle *Falasṭin.* The Government had to be made to realise that the Zionists were not an "apparition." Even if *Falasṭin* were permanently suppressed, the local population could produce scores of papers like it. The youth of the country and the press in Egypt (that is, beyond the authorities' reach) could not be silenced by the Government.

Muslim and Christian notables in Jaffa used their influence to have *Falasṭin* reopened. As a result, the closure order was soon annulled by a local judge, who gave a ruling upholding the freedom of the press.[101]

In April 1914 General Elections were held once again for the Ottoman Parliament. In the Mutasarrıflık of Jerusalem, the CUP was as weak as it had been during the last elections two years earlier; and when the CUP's Central Committee notified its branch in Jerusalem in January 1914 to select candidates for the forthcoming elections, instructions were given to take local opinion and trends

101. *CZA* L2/34/II (10.5.1914), Zionist Office (Jaffa) to Jacobson.

into account.[102] The successful candidates were Raghib Bey al-Nashashibi (the District Engineer of Jerusalem before his election and, as Mayor of the city from 1920 to 1934, a prominent figure throughout the Mandatory period), Fayḍi al-ʿAlami (President of the Municipal Council in Jerusalem from 1906 to 1909, and father of Musa al-ʿAlami, a senior Arab official during the Mandate), and Saʿid Bey al-Ḥusayni (a deputy in the first Parliament). *Truth* (Jerusalem) called the new deputies "inveterate judeophobes," and reported that they had promised to do their utmost to restore the restrictions against the Jews which the Government had recently relaxed.[103]

In the Vilâyet of Beirut the Zionist issue played its part in the elections as well. On 2 April a petition (apparently from young Arabs in Nablus) appeared in *Fatat al-ʿArab* (the new name of *al-Mufid* in Beirut) reminding the candidates of the Zionists' aims.[104] After the election, this paper published an article headed "A clear word to our deputies," warning them of Zionism's political ambitions, which, it claimed—as had often been claimed before—were not confined to Palestine.[105] At the end of April, *al-Iqdam* (Cairo) reported a speech made by Hadi Tawfiq Ḥammad, a notable in Nablus, in honour of the newly elected deputy from that town, Saʿid Shahin. The speaker asserted that the local population had no money or protector to save it from the Zionists who, he said, were attacking "with infantry and cavalry" to force it from its land. He therefore admonished Saʿid Efendi "in the name of the homeland" to make it his primary concern to apprise the Ottoman Parliament of these matters.[106]

Before the elections *Falasṭin* interviewed Ḥafiẓ Bey al-Saʿid in Jaffa and reprinted conversations which had appeared in *al-Iqdam* between its editor and candidates in Jerusalem. After the elections the editor of *al-Iqdam* published interviews with notables from Gaza as well. Those concerned came exclusively from the traditional leadership, the group which until recently had been most loyal to

102. *CZA* Z3/1453 (29.1.1914), I. Lévy (Jerus.) to Zionist Office (Jaffa).
103. *Truth*, iii, 164–165 (8.5.1914).
104. *Fatat al-ʿArab* (2.4.1914)—details in *CZA* Z3/116, press report [undated and unsigned].
105. *Fatat al-ʿArab* (19.4.1914)—details in *CZA* Z3/116 (7.6.1914), Thon to ZAC, enclosing press report.
106. *Al-Iqdam* (26.4.1914)—details in *CZA* Z3/116 (7.6.1914), Thon to A ZAC, enclosing press report.

the Empire. They all expressed their views on Zionism, which compared with those being voiced in the anti-Zionist press and elsewhere (see Chapter Ten) were relatively moderate. Nonetheless all were distinctly concerned about the future of Palestine and its peasant population. Each notable criticised the Government in his own way and called for firmer measures against Jewish immigration and land purchase.

Ḥusayn al-Ḥusayni, the President of the Municipal Council of Jerusalem, had always been regarded by the Jews in Palestine as well disposed towards them. He was by far the mildest of all those interviewed, saying that he saw no danger in the Zionist Movement, because it was not a political movement, but was concerned with settlement. Even so, he had his reservations.

I am certain that the idea of founding a Jewish state in Palestine does not occur to any reasonable and rational Zionist, as people say. The Zionists come to this country to live. They are educated, cultured people; they do not inflate their importance and they are united amongst themselves. It is not just or humane that we should hate or despise this people. On the contrary, we should imitate them and learn from their activities, which can give us a good and appropriate lesson and thereby we can give an important impetus to the progress of our husbandry and agriculture.

But . . . despite all this, we must keep an open eye on them, for if we continue in our way and they in theirs, then all our lands will pass into their possession. Our fellah is poor and impoverished, and the poor man is liable to surrender his land to keep himself alive. Therefore, the Government must pass a new law concerning the sale of land in Palestine, setting up known conditions and limiting them according to our position in the country.[107]

Ḥafiẓ Bey al-Saᶜid, of Jaffa, had also been thought by the Jews to be well disposed but, it will be recalled, he was the first Arab deputy to raise the Zionist issue in the Ottoman Parliament (see p. 72). "Zionist immigration," he believed, "can be both harmful and useful." However:

Were the Zionist danger not great, I would be the first to declare that we need Zionism here in this country. [But] it is otherwise, if the matter proceeds unrestricted, if the immigrant is entitled to buy [land] wherever he pleases. . . . If the Government does nothing against the danger of Zionist immigration, it is quite possible that the new settlers will attract to

107. *Ha-Ḥerut,* vi 143 (30.3.1914), reprinting interview from *al-Iqdam* [date and number not given].

themselves the lion's share of trade and land [in Palestine], and that they will outnumber the local population, nine-tenths of whom are ignorant of what knowledge and education are. . . . I do not share the view of some people that the local population can benefit from having Zionist neighbours, that they can learn agriculture, trade and building from them. Rather, I believe that the object lesson of the Zionists through their fine buildings, modern plantations, new machines, their founding agricultural companies and schools has no significance for the local population, because for these things one needs money and education, which is possessed only by the Zionists. . . . I ask God that the people at the helm of government will take measures which will benefit the inhabitants of the country.[108]

After the elections, an unsuccessful candidate, Aḥmad al-ᶜArif of Gaza, who had been elected in 1912, told the editor of *al-Iqdam* that "the sole topic of conversation among Palestinians at present . . . is the Zionist issue; all are frightened and afraid of it,"[109] The Government welcomed the Zionists with open arms, but it forgot that this would bring "disaster" to the local population, thus cancelling out any gain in revenue from the colonies. The fellahin were poor and suffering; the Zionists were rich and would therefore be victorious.

The Zionist question, although at first glance economic, is in fact an important political question. If we examine ancient history and that of the countries which have been taken from our hands, it is proven that all political events are built on economic foundations. The Government looks upon Zionism as an economic issue, but there is no doubt that with the passage of time, short or long, the issue will prove to be an important political one. Changes and modifications will take place in the geography of Palestine, if things continue in the future as they are [at present]. The Zionists' zeal in preserving their language, customs and nationality confirms this conclusion.[110]

The views of the two successful candidates from Jerusalem are, of course, of special interest. They both made the most vigorous appeals for measures against the Zionists; at the same time, they both spoke in Ottoman loyalist terms, as was proper for CUP candidates. Saᶜid Bey al-Ḥusayni declared that if he were elected he would continue to act as he had done in the first Parliament. In particular he

108. *Falasṭin,* iv, 24 (4.4.1914)—details in *CZA* Z3/116, press report [undated and unsigned].
109. *Al-Iqdam* (14.6.1914), reprinted in *ha-Ḥerut,* vi, 210 (25.6.1914).
110. *Ha-Ḥerut,* vi, 210 (25.6.1914).

stressed that land questions had to be tackled and that the fellah had to be helped, so that "the remnant of land which remains in our possession will not pass into the hands of the Zionists."[111] Zionism was a danger to the Empire from both the political and the economic points of view.

I am very surprised at how the Government passes over this movement in silence, since the Zionists have retained the protection of [their] foreign nationality. Therefore, the Government must bestir itself and awake from its sleep and recognise the danger facing it.[112]

Raghib Bey al-Nashashibi said that he was only opposed to foreign Jews. However:

If the foreign Jew truly wishes to win our sympathy for him, then he must accept Ottoman nationality and must learn the language of the country so that he will understand us and we shall understand him, and both [our peoples] will work for the good of the country. But if the foreign subject comes to fight us with the weapon of his foreign nationality and despises our sons and brethren and breaks our statutes and laws, then it is our duty not to pass over this in silence. If I am elected as a deputy, I will dedicate all my energies day and night to remove the harm and danger awaiting us from Zionism and the Zionists—without, as has been said, harming the rights of our Ottoman [Jewish] brethren.[113]

He then recommended that the Government should adopt "the methods of Rumania" in dealing with the Zionists—that is to say, treat them as Rumania treated its Jews: as aliens, and deny them political and civic rights in certain areas.

In sum, the proposal of a Muslim-Jewish alliance did not come to anything. But the Government's cautious moves to relax the restrictions on the Jews had various effects on the Arabs. Arabic newspapers, particularly *Falasṭin* and *al-Karmil,* were more critical of the Government than ever on this score. The political élite in Palestine, in addition to being Ottoman loyalists, had become local patriots. And, as will be shown in Chapter Ten, certain Arab nationalists had come to the conclusion that the CUP had made an alliance with the Zionists in order to weaken the Arab cause.

111. *Ha-Ḥerut,* vi, 143 (30.3.1914), reprinting interview from *al-Iqdam* [date and number not given].
112. *Ha-Ḥerut,* vi, 143 (30.3.1914).
113. *Ibid.*

9

Apropos of an Arab-Zionist Entente: 1913–1914

Although the Arab nationalists' interest in an Arab-Zionist entente waned after they made their agreement with the CUP in the summer of 1913, the idea did not die completely. It was kept alive, independently, by Zionists in Constantinople and Decentralisationists in Cairo. However, nothing of a serious nature was done about it until May 1914, by which time it had become patently clear that the Ottoman Government had no intention of implementing the reforms which the Arabs had been promised.

In Constantinople, Victor Jacobson was of the opinion that "the first article of our work-programme ought to be an entente with the Arabs."[1] In the latter half of 1913 he and his colleagues had several long discussions with leaders of the Arab group in the capital.[2] But although the talks were amicable enough, they went no further than what Jacobson called "entente pleasantries."[3]

ʿAbd al-Ḥamid al-Zahrawi (who had been President of the First Arab Congress in Paris) reaffirmed his view that the Arabs "must maintain good relations with the Jews and work together."[4] He then

1. *CZA* Z3/1642 (10.10.1913), V. Jacobson (Berlkin) to H. Frank (Paris).
2. *CZA* Z3/46 (23.8.1913), I. Neufach (Consple.) to ZCO (Berlin); and (26.8.1913), Jacobson (Consple.) to ZAC (Berlin).
3. *CZA* Z3/48 (11.1.1914), R. Lichtheim (Consple.) to ZAC.
4. *CZA* Z3/47 (8.11.1913), Lichtheim to ZAC.

accepted an appointment as an Ottoman senator in January 1914, thereby discrediting himself in the eyes of many Arab nationalists and giving up his contacts with the Zionists in the process. Sulayman al-Bustani, the Minister of Commerce and Agriculture (from Beirut), was unfavourably disposed towards Zionism. He regarded "Syrian Jews" as *Syrians,* who should merge with the general population. On the other hand, "he did not wish to know about foreign Jews."[5] Younger Arab nationalists, who spoke to Asher Sapir, a Jewish student from Palestine, emphasised that the Jewish immigrants must become Ottoman subjects and "good Syrians."[6]

The broad picture which emerges from these discussions is one of indifference on the part of the Arabs and a tendency to look at the Zionists from a "Syrian," rather than a Palestinian, perspective (probably reflecting the background of most Arabs in Constantinople). Consequently, the Zionists were not sanguine about the prospects of reaching a formal agreement. Richard Lichtheim, for example, who had joined Jacobson's staff in September 1913 and who was to become a respected figure in the Zionist Movement, came to the conclusion that the Arabs "do not care a rap about the 'common Semitic spirit'" which the Zionists had mentioned in connection with an Arab-Zionist agreement. At best, they wanted the Jews to promote the Arab movement with "specifically European things: money, organisation, machines."[7]

In Cairo, the position was rather different, since the entente proposal was kept going not by Zionists but by the Decentralisationists, who, as the originators of the idea, were the Arab group most committed to it. In September, *al-Ahram* accepted two pro-Zionist articles from Egyptian Jews.[8] The editor, Daᶜud Barakat, spoke to local Zionists, reminding them that, in principle, an entente already existed between the Decentralisation Party and the Zionists. But since the matter was still "equivocal," the Zionists should delegate someone to discuss the matter with Rafiq al-ᶜAẓm (President of the Decentralisationists) "to obviate misapprehensions as well as unfortunate consequences."[9]

5. *CZA* Z3/47 (3.10.1913), Lichtheim to ZAC.
6. *CZA* Z3/47 (9.10.1913), same to same.
7. *CZA* Z3/47 (20.11.1913), same to same.
8. *CZA* Z3/753 (1.10.1913), H. Hasamsony (Cairo) to ZCO.
9. *CZA* Z3/753 (1.10.1913) and (10.11.1913), both Hasamsony to ZCO.

Victor Jacobson was in Berlin at this time. Acknowledging the report from Cairo, he replied that Arthur Ruppin, the director of the Zionist Office in Jaffa, would interest himself in the question when he visited Egypt in December.[10] Ruppin did visit Cairo, but the matter does not appear to have been advanced, because in January 1914 another Zionist in Cairo reported that leading members of the Decentralisation Party had recently contacted him twice about an Arab-Zionist entente. On the first occasion, he was approached by Rashid Riḍa and, on the second, by both Rafiq Bey al-ᶜAẓm and Ḥaqqi Bey al-ᶜAẓm (Secretary of the Decentralisationists) who wanted to be put in touch with the Zionist Executive "with the object of laying the foundations of an entente and of mutual collaboration for the realisation of the reciprocal aims of both [the Decentralisation and Zionist] organisations."[11]

Again the Zionist Head Office in Berlin did not act promptly, and the question was not raised by the Decentralisationists for another two months, perhaps because they were deeply engaged in the agitation to secure the release of ᶜAziz ᶜAli al-Miṣri, an Egyptian involved in Arab nationalist affairs, who was arrested in Constantinople on 9 February.[12] However, on 27 March, Rashid Riḍa wrote an article in *al-Manar* in which he speculated that the CUP was actually helping the Zionists in Palestine. He went on to suggest that there were two courses open to the Arabs: either they could make an agreement with the Zionists or—striking a completely new note—they could take up arms against them.

> The leaders of the Arabs—the local population—must do one of two things. [Either they must] make an agreement (*ittifaq*) with the leaders of the Zionists to settle the differences between the interests of both parties in the country (*bilad*) . . . [or] gather all their forces to oppose the Zionists in every way, first by forming societies and companies, and finally by forming armed gangs that will oppose [the Zionists] by force. Some [Arabs] say that this is the first thing to be done, because cauterisation is the only way—and cauterisation is the ultimate remedy, as it is said.[13]

10. *CZA* Z3/753 (10.11.1913), Jacobson (Berlin).
11. *CZA* Z3/753 (10.1.1914), J. Caleff (Cairo) to Pres., ZAC (Berlin).
12. Cf. *CZA* Z3/116 (29.4.1914), Ḥaqqi Bey al-ᶜAẓm (Heliopolis) to N. Malul (Jaffa).
13. *Al-Manar,* xvii, 4 (1914), p. 320. Cf. Burckhardt, p. 9, *"Akhir al-ṭibb al-kayy"* ("The ultimate remedy is a cautery").

At the beginning of April a Zionist Executive delegation arrived in Palestine. One of its members, Nahum Sokolow, was charged *inter alia* with the task of examining Arab-Zionist relations. On 10 April, *al-Muqaṭṭam* published an interview which he gave its correspondent, Nisim Malul, on arrival in Jaffa.[14] In reply to a question about the possibility of an Arab-Zionist mutual understanding (*tafahum*), Sokolow suggested that the Arabs should regard the Jews, not as foreigners, but as fellow-Semites "returning home," equipped with European skills which could be of immense worth to the local population. If Jewish immigration was hindered, the land would remain desolate and of no value to anyone. If it went ahead, Arabs and Jews would prosper together. To that end Arabic would be taught in Jewish schools; a health campaign would be begun; social services, including hostels for the poor of all creeds, would be launched; and new branches of the Anglo-Palestine Company would be opened to offer the local population long-term credit at low rates of interest.

This interview triggered off a remarkable discussion in the Cairo press about an Arab-Zionist entente. It began on 14 April when Rafiq Bey al-ᶜAẓm commented, also in *al-Muqaṭṭam,* that Sokolow's words were fine—"on the surface."[15] But the Zionists did not act on them. They did not, for example, mix with the local population of Palestine. Instead, they endangered it economically and, according to some, politically as well, since unwittingly they were liable to bring about a Great Power occupation of the country. Rafiq Bey hoped that the happy future which Sokolow envisaged would be realised. But curing physical ailments (as Sokolow suggested) would not heal wounds of the heart, and simply to teach Arabic was not enough. The Zionists must actively pave the way to integration by becoming Ottoman subjects, by opening their schools to Arab children, and by cooperating economically with the local population. The Zionists had to act—not just talk.

Parallel with these articles, there was a sharp exchange between Ibrahim Najjar in *al-Ahram* and Nisim Malul in *al-Muqaṭṭam.*[16] A year before, Najjar had written to Sami Hochberg about an Arab-Zionist entente, but now he launched a lengthy attack on

14. *Al-Muqaṭṭam,* no. 7,613 (10.4.1914).
15. *Al-Muqaṭṭam,* no. 7,616 (14.4.1914).
16. *Al-Ahram* (11.4.1914); details in *CZA* Z3/116, press report [undated and unsigned]; and *al-Muqaṭṭam,* nos. 7,623 and 7,624 (23. and 24.4.1914).

the Zionists. Malul, on the other hand, was concerned to point out some obvious misrepresentations in Najjar's broadside. Then on 29 April, Ḥaqqi Bey al-ᶜAẓm wrote an angry letter to Malul, who, although a Jew, had been a founding member of the Decentralisation Party branch in Jaffa in 1913. Ḥaqqi Bey was annoyed by the renewed polemic in *al-Ahram* and *al-Muqaṭṭam* which, he said, could only harm both the Arabs and the Zionists.[17] But he was more angry at what Sokolow had said in his interview with Malul, for he understood him to mean that the Zionists would return to Palestine, whether the Arabs liked it or not. This was the same sort of "mocking language" as that used by the CUP, which also ignored the Arabs' wishes. Moreover, Sokolow had advocated the use of Hebrew by the Jewish immigrants—this, wrote Ḥaqqi Bey, meant "death" to Arabic. And, finally, Sokolow had not said a word about the Jews' foreign nationality—which, according to Ḥaqqi Bey, implied that they did not intend to become loyal Ottomans. The Arabs were still prepared to make an entente with the Jews, on two conditions: (1) the Arabic language did not suffer, and (2) the immigrants became genuine Ottoman subjects.

Malul did not reply at once to Ḥaqqi Bey's letter because Sokolow was on an extended tour of the Jewish colonies in Palestine. Nor did the Arab-Zionist polemic, which worried Ḥaqqi Bey, stop. Quite the reverse: more Arabic newspapers in Egypt joined in, publishing articles which were generally anti-Zionist in tone.[18] The pace quickened in the second half of May when ᶜIsa al-ᶜIsa, the proprietor of *Falasṭin,* visited Cairo and placed articles in local newspapers.[19]

In the midst of all this, *al-Muqaṭṭam* printed two articles from Constantinople, entitled "A Zionist Leader Answers Rafiq Bey al-ᶜAẓm, and Stresses the Need for an Arab-Jewish Agreement (*ittifaq*)."[20] The "Zionist leader" (Victor Jacobson) denied that the Zionists relied on the Ottoman Government at the expense of the Arabs, as Rafiq Bey had alleged in his criticism of the Sokolow

17. *CZA* Z3/116 (29.4.1914), Ḥaqqi Bey al-ᶜAẓm to Malul.
18. *Q d'O* N.S. 124, no. 231 (15.5.1914), A. Defrance (Cairo) to G. Doumergue (Paris): cf. *CZA* Z3/116, press reports for many examples.
19. E.G. *Le Journal du Caire* (27.5.1914); *al-Muqaṭṭam,* no. 7,655 (30.5.1914); and *al-Iqdam* (31.5.1914); details in *CZA* Z3/116, press report [undated and unsigned].
20. *Al-Muqaṭṭam,* no. 7,652 (27.5.1914).

interview. He accepted Rafiq Bey's demand for mutual cooperation and urged an Arab-Zionist entente. When *al-Muqaṭṭam's* correspondent pointed out to the "Zionist leader" that most Arabs were opposed to the Zionists, Jacobson said that he believed that an agreement was possible because educated and enlightened Arabs whom he met did not object to an entente, and leaders, such as Rafiq Bey himself, advocated one.

On 27 May, Malul sailed from Jaffa to Egypt, where he met Rafiq Bey and Ḥaqqi Bey together with other members of the Decentralisation Party in a journalists' café in Cairo the following evening.[21] After a discussion about the recent General Elections, Rafiq Bey left the group. Then Ḥaqqi Bey asked Malul what he thought of the "Zionist leader's" reply to Rafiq Bey in *al-Muqaṭṭam*. Malul remarked that it answered the questions about the Zionists' attitude to the Hebrew language and Ottoman nationality which Ḥaqqi Bey had raised in his letter of 29 April. This prompted Ḥaqqi Bey to comment that when Malul had not responded to that letter as requested, the Decentralisationists had reacted unfavourably against the Zionists. His silence, it was felt, showed that the Zionists did not want an entente with the Arabs and that they were supporting the CUP. Indeed, it was believed to substantiate a rumour that the Jews were trying to bring about a rift between Turks and Arabs. Consequently, Rafiq Bey had that very day prepared a circular to all their branches, describing their disillusionment with the Zionists. Ḥaqqi Bey mentioned that the idea of convening an Arab-Zionist conference in Cairo had been mooted, but their current suspicions had put an end to that.

Malul protested against the construction which had been put on his failure to reply to Ḥaqqi Bey's letter, explaining that the reason lay in Sokolow's absence from Jaffa. He therefore suggested that, instead of issuing Rafiq Bey's circular, (1) preparations for an Arab-Zionist meeting should be put in hand; (2) Sokolow should be informed so that he might come to Cairo to make the necessary arrangements; and (3) Arab journalists should be prevailed upon not to write about Zionism, because their articles tended to widen the differences between Arabs and Jews at a time when both sides were seeking an agreement. Ḥaqqi Bey was prepared to accept this alternative course and sent Malul in search of Rafiq Bey.

21. *CZA* A18/14/6 (29.5.1914), Malul (Cairo) to N. Sokolow and A. Ruppin (Jaffa).

On the following day, *al-Muqaṭṭam* printed a third and final part of the "Zionist leader's" reply, in which Jacobson also suggested that the best way of dispelling Arab misapprehensions about Zionism would be to hold a meeting of representatives of both groups.[22] In the same issue, an article appeared by Rafiq Bey himself, headed—somewhat ominously—"The Zionist Question and How to Ward Off Its Danger."[23] Rafiq Bey was mainly concerned with protecting the fellahin in Palestine (by land reform, legislation, agricultural companies and loans), and although he urged the Arabs in Palestine to take all possible legal action against the alleged "Zionist danger," his programme was not cast in a form that precluded an entente with the Zionists.

Malul took credit for persuading Rafiq Bey to submit a further article to *al-Muqaṭṭam*,[24] which appeared on 30 May to the effect that he had now read the whole of the "Zionist leader's" reply, and he thought an Arab-Zionist entente was possible "if both sides gave a little" to align their interests. He had no doubt that an Arab-Zionist conference would be helpful. If requested by the Zionists, the Decentralisation Party was prepared to convene this meeting in Egypt, and to persuade notables in Palestine to attend. He himself was going to stop writing about Zionism for the time being, as polemics were sterile "when there is the idea of work and not [just] talk."[25]

It soon became clear that Rafiq Bey's thinking about an Arab-Zionist entente had advanced in the last months. A year previously, he had talked about the benefits which the Zionists could confer on the Syrians in general. By writing on 29 May about ways to safeguard the fellahin in Palestine, and by indicating the next day that the Decentralisationists were prepared to invite notables from Palestine to a meeting in Egypt, he was making an important distinction.

On 1 June, at Malul's request,[26] *al-Muqaṭṭam* announced that it was closing its columns to articles on Zionism until the proposed conference had taken place.[27] A few days later *al-Ahram,* also at

22. *Al-Muqaṭṭam,* no. 7,654 (29.5.1914).
23. *Ibid.*
24. *CZA* L2/94/I (31.5.1914), Malul to Ruppin.
25. *Al-Muqaṭṭam,* no. 7,655 (30.5.1914).
26. *CZA* L2/94/I (31.5.1914).
27. *Al-Muqaṭṭam,* no. 7,656 (1.6.1914).

Malul's prompting,[28] followed suit. Thus the extraordinarily open exchange about an Arab-Zionist entente came to an end, and the stage was set for less public negotiations. To prepare the ground still further, Malul called on the editors of all the other newspapers in Cairo, and asked them not to write about the Zionist question "until it was solved." He felt sure that they would comply with his request,[29] and his confidence was all but justified for, with one exception, Egyptian newspapers stopped publishing articles about Zionism after the beginning of June. Only *al-Iqdam* continued to write, and to write bitterly, on the topic, even though its editor and secretary had assured Malul that, in principle, the Arabs were not opposed to the Zionists—they were antagonistic to the Ottoman Government and, therefore, to the Zionists who were at present being protected by it.[30] Were it not for the persistence and tenor of *al-Iqdam's* attacks, this explanation might have been credible (see Chapter Ten).

In Cairo, Malul also spoke to Rashid Riḍa, who not only supported the proposal of an Arab-Zionist entente but also was very candid about the nationalists' aims at this point and the difference in approach between Muslim and Christian Arabs.[31] It was certainly the case that the Zionists brought benefit to Palestine but, Riḍa insisted, they must let "the Arabs" share it. Palestine, being large and desolate, needed industrious people and could contain both the Arabs and the Jews. The Arabs knew that the Government and the Jews patronised each other. However, the Arabs were opposed to the Government and had to detach their land from the Ottoman Empire. They were positive of victory, since there were only "three to four million" Turks against "at least twenty million" Arabs. Riḍa then distinguished between Muslim and Christian Arabs. The Christians were the Zionists' greatest enemies; moreover, they wanted the Great Powers to occupy Palestine, which was contrary to the interests of both the Muslims and the Jews. Therefore the Muslims and the Jews should make an agreement to support one another to free the country from the Turks and work together for its progress.

28. *CZA* L2/94/I (31.5.1914).
29. *Ibid.*
30. *CZA* L2/94/I (4/5.6.1914), Malul to Ruppin.
31. *CZA* L2/94/I (6/7.6.1914), same to same.

Independently of these developments in Cairo, the Zionist Office in Jaffa was informed by local Arabs in May that "Arab leaders", especially in Beirut and Damascus, wished to meet authorised Zionist representatives to discuss a "programmatic understanding."[32] These approaches led to a separate series of contacts between Zionists and Arab nationalists, which resulted in plans to hold an Arab-Zionist meeting in a village near Beirut, unconnected with the conference in Cairo contemplated by the Decentralisationists.

Central to these contacts was Naṣif Bey al-Khalidi, a native of Jerusalem and a cousin of Ruḥi Bey al-Khalidi.[33] An engineer by profession, he had worked on the construction of the Hijaz Railway.[34] In 1908 he had stood, unsuccessfully, for Parliament, promising to improve the supply of drinking water in Jerusalem and to link the city by rail with Damascus and the Egyptian border.[35] In 1913 he had worked with a British team of archaeologists in the Mosque of ᶜUmar;[36] and in 1914 he was Chief Engineer in Beirut.[37]

In March of that year, the Vali of Beirut, accompanied by Naṣif Bey and others, visited the Jewish settlement at Rosh Pinna (near Safed), which was administered by the Jewish Colonization Association. At lunch, the question of Arab-Jewish relations was raised, and Chaim Kalvarisky, the local JCA administrator, remarked that the Jews and Arabs should try to reach an understanding. The suggestion apparently met with some approval from the Arabs in the party; and, according to notes written by Kalvarisky in 1919, the Vali took him aside and in effect repeated the point made by the Grand Vezir to the Haham Başı in September 1913. "Your idea is excellent; without an understanding, our assistance will be of very little use to you. We cannot, in order to favor [*sic*] you, go against an entire population."[38]

Kalvarisky wrote to the Zionist Office in Jaffa about this conversation,[39] and in May introduced Naṣif Bey to Soiolow (who was on

32. *CZA* Z3/65 (4.5.1914), Zionist Office (Jaffa) to Lichtheim; and *CZA* L2/34/II (10.5.1914), Zionist Office (Jaffa) to Jacobson (Consple.).
33. *Near East,* iv, 101 (1913), p. 642.
34. *Q d'O* N.S. 132, no. 17 (8.10.1908), G. Gueyraud (Jerus.) to S. Pichon (Paris).
35. *Ibid.*
36. *Near East,* iv, 101 (1913), p. 642.
37. *CZA* Z3/1456 (1.7.1914), Ruppin to ZAC.
38. *CZA* L4/276/II B (1.6.1919), C. Kalvarisky (notes).
39. *CZA* Z3/65 (4.5.1914), Zionist Office (Jaffa) to Lichtheim.

his tour of Palestine).[40] In his turn, Naṣif Bey introduced Sokolow to Arab leaders in Beirut,[41] and then took him to Muḥammad Kurd ᶜAli's house in Damascus,[42] where he met Shukri al-ᶜAsali, ᶜAbd al-Wahhab al-Inklizi, ᶜAbd al-Raḥman al-Shahbandar and Jurji Bey al-Fakhuri.[43] The anti-Zionist views of Kurd ᶜAli and Shukri al-ᶜAsali have been discussed in preceding chapters. Al-Inklizi, a former deputy who was hanged by Cemal Paşa in 1915, was also a known anti-Zionist, having made Arab nationalist speeches in Damascus in 1913, in which—uniquely for the period—he branded the Zionists as "colonialists" in the modern sense of the word (as distinct from forerunners of German or Russian imperialism).[44] On the other hand, al-Shahbandar, a doctor who from 1918 to his murder in 1940 was a prominent Syrian politician, appeared well disposed.[45] Al-Fakhuri was described as a freethinking Christian and an Arab nationalist;[46] nothing is known of his views on the Zionist question.

Despite the anti-Zionist views of some of them, Sokolow found these Arabs responsive to the idea of an entente, presumably because of their almost total estrangement from the Ottoman Government by this time.[47] An Arab-Zionist meeting, to be attended by ten delegates from each side,[48] was accordingly projected for some time in June,[49] no exact date or place being fixed.[50] Al-Fakhuri undertook to write to Christian and Muslim Arabs, belonging to both the CUP and the Liberal Union, to gain their support for the meeting.[51] It was not suggested that Sokolow or other members of the Zionist Executive should attend, since at this stage the Arab and Zionist representatives were only to become acquainted. No commitments or undertakings were envisaged, as this meeting was was seen as a preliminary to subsequent ones.[52]

40. *CZA* Z3/399 (5.7.1914), Sokolow (London) to J. Tschlenow [Berlin?].
41. *CZA* Z3/399 (23.5.1914), Sokolow (Damas.) to same.
42. *CZA* L4/276/II B (1.6.1919), Kalvarisky (notes).
43. *CZA* L2/34/II (3.6.1914), Zionist Office (Jaffa) to Jacobson.
44. *CZA* L2/94/II [n.d. (spring, 1913)], A. Almaliᵓaḥ, *"ha-Tenuᶜa ha-ᶜaravit besuriyya."*
45. *CZA* L2/34/II (3.6.1914).
46. *Ibid.*
47. Cf. Kalvarisky, "ha-Yaḥasim . . . lifne ha-milḥama," pp. 54–55.
48. *CZA* L4/276/II B (1.6.1919), Kalvarisky (notes).
49. *CZA* Z3/399 (23.5.1914), Sokolow to Tschlenow.
50. *CZA* Z3/399 (5.7.1914), Sokolow (London) to Tschlenow.
51. *CZA* L2/34/II (3.6.1914), Zionist Office (Jaffa) to Jacobson.
52. *CZA* Z3/399 (5.7.1914).

At the end of May Sokolow returned to Jaffa, where he instructed the Zionist Office to prepare a list of local delegates for the meeting. Then, returning to Beirut, he again saw Naşif Bey al-Khalidi, who now requested that Zionist leaders from Europe should attend the meeting. Naşif Bey also added that the meeting would take a long time to arrange (which led Sokolow to write a few weeks later that it was then expected to take place "*possibly* in July").[53] Thereafter, Naşif Bey set out for Jerusalem, Jaffa, Nablus and Haifa to make up the list of Arab delegates,[54] while Sokolow sailed for Constantinople.

Sokolow's arrival was preceded by that of the Vali of Beirut, who had come to Constantinople in the middle of May. At a dinner given in his honour by Jacobson, the Vali pronounced himself absolutely in favour of Jewish immigration into Palestine, but demanded that the immigrants become Ottoman subjects. He stressed the need for the Zionists to devote great attention to the Arabs and suggested that Arabic be introduced in the new technical school at Haifa so that the local population could benefit from it. On the other hand, he dismissed the Arab nationalists as being of little consequence—"leaders without an army" who, he maintained, could all be bought for cash. At the same time he admitted, apparently without embarrassment, that the Government still needed financial support, and if the Zionists could provide enough money for the purchase of one "Dreadnought" battleship, he could guarantee that their requirements would be satisfied.[55]

By the time that Nahum Sokolow reached Constantinople, Jacobson had left for a meeting of the Zionist General Council in Berlin. In his absence, Sokolow contacted the Vali of Beirut and told him of the proposed Arab-Zionist meeting which he had planned with Naşif Bey al-Khalidi. The Vali insisted "in most precise and very categorical terms" that Zionist leaders from Europe should attend. He believed that serious negotiations could only take place if the "real leaders" participated and that the "proper place" for the meeting was "Syria".[56]

53. *CZA* Z3/399 (5.7.1914).
54. *PJCA* 79/319 (8.6. and 1.7.1914), both Nazif el-Khaledy [sic] (Beirut) to C. Kalvarisky (Rosh Pinna).
55. *CZA* Z3/49 (28.5.1914), Lichtheim to ZAC.
56. *CZA* Z3/399 (5.7.1914), Sokolow to Tschlenow.

In Constantinople, Sokolow did not hear from any of the Arabs whom he had met in Beirut and Damascus. But he was approached by Najib Bey Shuqayr, a Druze from the Lebanon connected with the Arab nationalists, who told him, on behalf of Rafiq al-ᶜAẓm, that the Decentralisation Party now wished to meet the Zionists in Cairo (as a result of Nisim Malul's recent visit there).[57] It appears that Sokolow, on hearing this, made some indiscreet remarks to Najib Bey about the apparent lack of coordination between the Arabs in Syria and in Egypt.[58] However, the matter was left in abeyance, since—it may be assumed—Sokolow thought that he should consult Jacobson before coming to a decision.

Sokolow arrived in Berlin in the middle of June, where he and Jacobson discussed the proposed Arab-Zionist meeting in Syria and the invitation from the Decentralisation Party in Cairo. Regarding the meeting in Syria, there were various considerations to take into account. Naṣif Bey had told Sokolow that it would take a long time to arrange. As Sokolow had still not heard from Beirut or Damascus, he suspected that the Arabs were beginning to procrastinate. Moreover, the Vali of Beirut—like Naṣif Bey—had insisted that Zionist leaders from Europe should attend. Sokolow and Jacobson therefore came to the conclusion that the meeting in Syria could not be held until the autumn when all the interested parties would be in a position to assemble the appropriate delegates.[59]

As for Rafiq Bey's invitation to come to Cairo, the Vali's advice that "Syria" was the proper place for any Arab-Zionist meeting, coupled with the fact that arrangements for such a meeting were already in hand, had to be borne in mind. It was accordingly decided not to go to Cairo at that stage.[60] However, Jacobson—presumably with Sokolow's help—did work out a list of proposals to put to the Decentralisation Party. He sent them to a young Arab in Constantinople called Asᶜad Daghir, who worked for *Le Jeune-Turc* and had been instrumental in introducing Jacobson to a number of Arab leaders.[61] In turn, perhaps at the beginning of

57. *CZA* Z3/399 (5.7.1914); and *CZA* Z3/49 (3.7.1914), Lichtheim to ZAC.
58. Letter no. 68 (30.7.1914), Rafiq Bey al-ᶜAẓm [Cairo] to Asᶜad Daghir [Consple.], published in *Le Journal de Beyrouth,* iii, 414 (2.9.1915).
59. *CZA* Z3/399 (5.7.1914), Sokolow to Tschlenow.
60. Letter no. 68 (30.7.1914), Rafiq Bey al-ᶜAẓm to Asᶜad Daghir.
61. *CZA* Z3/49 (7.6.1914), Lichtheim to Jacobson.

July, Daghir forwarded the proposals to Cairo. According to Daghir, they were as follows:

1. The Arabs and Jews are from one stock (*jins*), and each [people] possesses attributes complementary to the other. The Jews have knowledge, funds and influence; while the Arabs have a vast land (*bilad*), awesome power, cultural treasures and inexhaustible material wealth. Therefore a reconciliation (*tawfiq*) between both [peoples] will be to the good of both and to the good of all the Orient.

2. The Arabs will receive the Jews in Arab lands as their brethren, on condition that the Jews become Ottoman subjects and that Palestine will not be exclusively theirs.

3. In exchange, the Jews pledge to put their cultural and material power at the service of the Arab cause; they will support the Arab groups (*aḥzab*) and place at their disposal three million guineas.

4. An Arab-Jewish conference will be held in Egypt when the Syrian and Iraqi deputies return from Constantinople to their lands [that is to say, during the summer parliamentary recess].[62]

Nothing else is known about these proposals. But their substance, if not their language, sounds authentic, fitting well into the context of the events preceding them. If Lichtheim and Daghir worked over Jacobson's draft proposals in Constantinople before transmitting them to Cairo, their idiomatically Arabic formulation becomes intelligible, and only the offer of "three million guineas" remains suspect: Jacobson might have indicated the possibility of financial support for the Arabs, but he is unlikely to have named a specific sum.

Daghir's account in his memoirs of his part in these affairs is apologetic and confused—perhaps intentionally so.[63] However, the most convincing proof of the existence of some proposals from Jacobson is that Rafiq Bey wrote a letter to Daghir on 30 July acknowledging them.[64] In it, Rafiq Bey expressed surprise that Sokolow had been able to persuade Jacobson to decline the invitation to meet the Decentralisation Party, especially as Jacobson had been one of the promoters of the idea. He was also displeased at Sokolow's remarks to Najib Bey Shuqayr about the Arab nationalists' lack of coordination. The Zionists had to realise that

62. Daghir, *Mudhakkirati,* p. 43.
63. *Ibid.,* pp. 42–44.
64. Letter no. 68 (30.7.1914), Rafiq Bey al-ʿAẓm to Asʿad Daghir.

the Decentralisationists could do nothing that was not approved by authorised representatives of all Arab groups, despite the fact that Sokolow thought the Arab nationalists disorganised.

Rafiq Bey explained that he viewed the Zionist question at two levels. First, it concerned the local population in Palestine; and, secondly, it related to the "Arab question" in general. The Decentralisation Party had wanted the Zionists to come to Cairo to discuss the Palestinian aspect "so that [the meeting] would not take on a political colouring capable of angering [the Ottoman Government]." It had also paved the way for "genuinely interested" individuals in Palestine to come to Cairo, since it was very important for the Palestinians to be satisfied. "If from the outset we mix the two aspects into a single question and if the local population [of Palestine] declare themselves dissatisfied, then all our efforts will go to waste—[the Zionists] must recognise this".

On the more general aspect, the relationship between Zionism and the wider Arab nationalist cause, Rafiq Bey wrote that "the discussions must not be public," indicating that they would be of a highly confidential political character. Jacobson's proposals, and others "emanating from Palestine", were "good and acceptable." But, he emphasised, nothing could be done until the Zionists came to Cairo.

Unknown to Sokolow and Jacobson (and, judging by Rafiq Bey's letter, unknown to him as well), things had been moving on apace in Palestine through the whole of June. At the beginning of the month, Naṣif Bey al-Khalidi, like Nisim Malul in Cairo, made efforts to stop the Arabic press in Beirut from writing about Zionism until the proposed Arab-Zionist meeting was held.[65] On 19 June, the Zionist Office in Jaffa invited ten delegates to attend a meeting (at this stage planned for 1 July) at Brummana, near Beirut.[66] At the Arabs' request,[67] none of these delegates had been directly involved in land purchases on behalf of the Zionists. A week or so later, Naṣif Bey passed through Jaffa on his mission to gain the support of prominent Palestinians for the meeting. He was reluctant to disclose the names of the Arabs who would attend, as his list was

65. *PJCA* 79/319 (8.6.1914), Naṣif Bey to Kalvarisky.
66. *CZA* L2/516 for copy invitations, signed by Ruppin and dated 19.6.1914.
67. *PJCA* 79/319 (8.6.1914).

not yet complete, but he did say that the editors of *Falasṭin* and *al-Karmil* might be invited to be present.[68] On 25 June, Kalvarisky wrote to Dr. Ruppin, saying that he had still not been informed of all the Arab delegates, but they would certainly include Naṣif Bey himself, as well as Muḥammad Kurd ʿAli and ʿAbd Allah Mukhliṣ (the owner of *al-Karmil*).[69] In reply, Ruppin commented that the presence of men who had been campaigning for some years against Zionism was undesirable, since it could only lead to an acrimonious discussion. He requested that the Zionists be advised of the names of all the Arab delegates in advance, and enclosed the names of the Jewish delegates for the Arabs' information.[70] On 1 July, Naṣif Bey informed Kalvarisky that everything was now arranged on the Arab side and suggested that someone, preferably Kalvarisky himself, come to Beirut to make the final preparations for the meeting, which he believed could not be held before 15 July.[71]

It was only now, at the beginning of July, that reports of these developments reached Sokolow in Europe. Although he had helped to initiate them, he was surprised at how far the arrangements for the meeting had advanced in the last month, in view of Naṣif Bey's warning that they would take a long time.[72] He believed, however, that the progress was all to the good. The meeting at Brummana would make "still more actual" the major conference in Syria which he hoped would take place that autumn.[73] With this in mind, he saw to it that the Zionist Office in Jaffa was reminded that the initial meeting was to be of a "private, preparatory" character, at which no commitments were to be made.[74]

In the first week of July, word reached the Zionist Office in Jaffa that the meeting would have to be postponed for at least a month, as an earlier date was not convenient for some of the Arab delegates.[75] To clarify the situation, Dr. Thon of the Zionist Office set

68. *PJCA* 79/319 (30.6.1914), Ruppin to Kalvarisky.
69. *PJCA* 82/322 (25.6.1914), Kalvarisky to Ruppin.
70. *PJCA* 79/319 (30.6.1914). The Zionist delegates were J. Abrévaya, C. Chissin, M. Dizengoff, A. Eisenberg, C. Kalvarisky, S. Levi, I. Lévy, Dr. Moscowitz, J. Thon and D. Yellin; cf. *CZA* Z3/1456 (1.7.1914), Ruppin to ZAC, giving a slightly amended list.
71. *PJCA* 79/319 (1.7.1914), Naṣif Bey to Kalvarisky; cf. *PJCA* 82/322 (6.7.1914), Kalvarisky to Ruppin.
72. *CZA* Z3/399 (5.7.1914), Sokolow to Tschlenow.
73. Cf. *CZA* Z3/49 (6.7.1914), Tschlenow to Jacobson.
74. *CZA* Z3/399 (5.7.1914).
75. *CZA* Z3/1456 (9.7.1914), Ruppin to ZAC.

set out on 9 July for Rosh Pinna to accompany Kalvarisky to Beirut and meet Naşif Bey. Meanwhile Kalvarisky's involvement in these Zionist affairs had come to the attention of his superiors in the JCA office at Haifa.[76] JCA's head office in Paris was consulted and feeling unable to approve of Kalvarisky's involvement, it ordered him to desist.[77] In consequence, Dr. Thon was obliged to proceed to Beirut by himself.[78]

The Vali of Beirut had returned from Constantinople at the beginning of July. On 14 July, he instructed Naşif Bey not to take any steps without letting him know first.[79] On that or the next day, Naşif Bey saw the Vali again, in the company of two Jewish land-agents, Hankin and Rosenheck (representing the Zionists and JCA), who had come to discuss land purchases in the Valley of Jezreel. When the forthcoming Arab-Zionist meeting was mentioned, the Vali announced that he was absolutely opposed to it. The meeting was unnecessary; he did not know whom Naşif Bey and his colleagues represented or in whose names they could speak; such negotiations between Arabs and Jews were superfluous; the Government had ordered him to protect the Jews, whose advocate he undertook to be; the level of the press in the Orient was low and the Syrian press ranked lowest of all—it could be bought and was not to be taken seriously.[80] As it happened, Hankin and Rosenheck also had their doubts about the way in which the proposed meeting was shaping, and therefore they did not take issue with the Vali but indeed supported him.[81]

The Vali's volte-face is not hard to understand. His statement that he was acting on instructions from the Government may be believed. In September 1913 CUP had concluded its agreement with the Arabs and apparently reckoned that, if the Arabs could settle their differences with the Zionists through some form of entente, Jewish financial aid for the Empire would be assured. For that reason, the Government had encouraged the Zionists to seek an entente with the Arabs at that time. But, by the summer of 1914, Arab grievances against the Government had risen to

76. *PJCA* 82/322 (26.6.1914), Kalvarisky to J. Rosenheck (Haifa).
77. *PJCA* 82/322 (13.7.1914), Kalvarisky to Rosenheck.
78. *Ibid.*; cf. *PJCA* 82/322 (13.7.1914), Kalvarisky to Naşif Bey.
79. *PJCA* 79/319 (14.7.1914), Naşif Bey to Kalvarisky.
80. *CZA* Z3/1457 (23.7.1914), Ruppin to ZAC.
81. *Ibid.*

unprecedented heights, and there was cause to fear the growing Arab movement, especially if general war in Europe was imminent. Hence the Government now had no wish for the Arabs to ally themselves with the Zionists and with the capital imagined to be at their command—capital which the Government still wanted for itself. It may therefore be assumed that the Vali had been instructed during his recent visit to Constantinople to do his utmost to prevent the conclusion of an Arab-Zionist entente.

A day or so later, Thon arrived in Beirut. Naṣif Bey was indignant at the stand taken by Hankin and Rosenheck and blamed them for the Vali's volte-face.[82] Nevertheless, it appears that he and Thon did not jettison the idea of an Arab-Zionist meeting. Naṣif Bey furnished Thon with a proposed agenda and the names of the Arab delegates. They were Aḥmad Bayhum Bey and Rizq Allah Arqash (both of the former Beirut Reform Committee), Ḥasan Asir (a supporter of the CUP from Beirut), Muḥammad Kurd ᶜAli and ᶜAbd al-Raḥman al-Shahbandar (both from Damascus, the first a committed anti-Zionist, the second not), Aḥmad Ḥabash (also from Damascus, described as a Reformist), ᶜAbd Allah Mukhliṣ (the owner of *al-Karmil*), Yusuf al-ᶜIsa (the editor of *Falasṭin*), Jamil al-Ḥusayni (a young Arab from Jerusalem who was politically active during the Mandate), and Naṣif Bey himself.[83] As Thon took his leave, Naṣif Bey cautioned him: "Governments are transient and fluctuate; the people are the constant factor, and one must come to an agreement with the people."[84]

Dr. Thon passed through Haifa on his way back to Jaffa. Meetings of Zionist representatives were held in both towns, on 20 and 30 July respectively, to consider the situation. Besides the Vali's opposition, which could not be ignored, the Zionists were loth to negotiate with the Arabs whom Naṣif Bey had nominated. Three of them (two newspaper editors and a newspaper owner) were strongly anti-Zionist. Six of them came from Beirut and Damascus, while there was not a single Palestinian of any standing on the list. Moreover, according to the agenda proposed by Naṣif Bey, "(1) [The Zionists] should explain, as far as possible by producing documentary evidence, the aims and methods of Zionism and of the

82. *CZA* Z3/1457 (23.7.1914).
83. *Ibid.*; Jamil al-Ḥusayni was marked as a "doubtful."
84. *CZA* L2/44 (30.7.1914), Zionist Standing Committee (Jaffa), minutes.

colonisation in Palestine connected therewith. (2) Thereafter, the Arabs will formulate their demands, acceptance of which would determine whether the [Zionist] Movement could be considered harmful to the Arabs or not."[85]

The Zionists were unhappy about this agenda, which hardly sounded as if it were geared to reaching an entente. As it stood, they feared that it was liable to worsen, rather than better, their relations with the Arabs.

The general view, therefore, was that a way should be found of avoiding a confrontation with the Arabs for the time being, without severing all contact with them. The Zionists accordingly decided to send a small delegation, consisting of Kalvarisky and two or three others, to confer with Naṣif Bey during the first week of August and find an acceptable way of postponing the meeting.[86] In the event, however, something far removed from Palestine put an end to all thoughts of meetings between Arabs and Zionists, in either Brummana or Cairo, to explore the possibility of an Arab-Zionist entente. World War I broke out in Europe on 4 August 1914.

The series of Arab-Zionist contacts which took place in the summer of 1914 was extremely complicated. Two separate sets of arrangements were put in motion, one centred on Cairo, the other on Palestine and the surrounding area. As they developed, each came to involve "two-stage" meetings.

In Cairo, the Decentralisationists foresaw the need for the Zionists to meet first with Arab notables from Palestine and then, on a confidential level, with Arab nationalists from all groups. And they expected the meetings at both stages to take place in Cairo.

The arrangements centred on Palestine and the surrounding area advanced furthest. At first, Sokolow and his Arab acquaintances planned to hold a low-level meting. Then, at the insistence of Naṣif Bey al-Khalidi and the Vali of Beirut, the nature of this meeting also changed—in Sokolow's mind, at least. Though still to be held in "Syria," it would take place in the autumn and would be attended by Zionist leaders from Europe. When, at the beginning of July, Sokolow heard of the plans for the meeting at Brummana, he had no objections, because in his view it could serve as

85. *CZA* Z3/1457 (23.7.1914), Ruppin to ZAC.
86. *Ibid.*, and *CZA* L2/44 (30.7.1914), Zionist Standing Committee minutes.

a preliminary to the larger gathering which he envisaged for the autumn.

Rafiq Bey al-ᶜAẓm in Cairo and Naṣif Bey al-Khalidi in Palestine seem to have been unaware of each other's efforts. There were, perhaps, two reasons for this lack of coordination. First, the Arab nationalists had lost much of their organisational cohesion after making their agreement with the CUP in 1913. Second, by the spring of 1914, when many Arabs were thoroughly disenchanted with the Ottoman Government and the idea of complete Arab independence had gained ground, more of them in different centres were willing to explore the possibility of an Arab-Zionist entente.

The ways in which the Arabs concerned viewed such an entente varied, and in some cases their motives were not entirely clear.[87] Certain Arabs in Constantinople wanted what Lichtheim termed "specifically European things" to strengthen the Arab movement. Rafiq Bey al-ᶜAẓm in Cairo appears to have sought an entente to advance the well-being of the Syrians in general, provided that the prior agreement of the Arabs in Palestine could be secured. Rashid Riḍa advocated an entente, not only to work towards Arab independence of the Ottoman Empire but also, as he told Malul, to frustrate the designs of certain Christian Arabs who, he believed, wished the Great Powers to occupy the Arab provinces.

It is more difficult to explain a report from Kalvarisky at the end of June that ᶜAbd Allah Mukhliṣ, the owner of *al-Karmil,* was Naṣif Bey's "supporter and motivating spirit."[88] It is no easier to comprehend why anti-Zionists such as Muḥammad Kurd ᶜAli and Yusuf al-ᶜIsa, the editors of *al-Muqtabas* and *Falasṭin* respectively, should have been willing to meet the Zionists at Brummana. The anti-Zionist papers which they represented had come out firmly against an Arab-Zionist entente in the autumn of 1913. In October, *al-Karmil* had asked, rhetorically, what basis could possibly exist for an agreement of this kind.[89] In November, Sayf al-Din al-Khaṭib, an Arab from Haifa who was hanged in 1915 by Cemal Paşa for Arab nationalist activities, expressed incredulity in *al-Karmil* that any patriotic Arab could contemplate an entente with the

87. Cf. *CZA* Z3/49 (3.7.1914), Lichtheim to ZAC.
88. *PJCA* 82/322 (25.6.1914), Kalvarisky to Ruppin.
89. *CZA* Z3/116 (5.11.1913), Thon to ZAC, enclosing press report re *al-Karmil* (10.10.1913).

Zionists.[90] *Al-Karmil's* comment was to revive its proposal of an anti-Zionist congress in Nablus.[91] In the spring of 1914 other papers wrote against an Arab-Zionist entente, and in April Yusuf al-ʿIsa of *Falasṭin* joined in the chorus by sending a letter to *al-Raʾy al-ʿAmm* (Beirut), in which he argued that an entente with the Zionists would still not prevent them from achieving their "secret aims."[92]

Perhaps the clue to the willingness of Mukhliṣ, Kurd ʿAli and Yusuf al-ʿIsa to go to Brummana is to be found in the proposed agenda. The way in which it was formulated suggests that, far from wanting an Arab-Zionist entente, these men may have been using Naṣif Bey to seek a "show-down" with the Zionists. Why else, for example, should they have asked the Zionists to produce documentary evidence of their aims? Ever since Najib Naṣṣar had published his translation of Richard Gottheil's article on Zionism in the *Jewish Encyclopedia* in 1911, the Arabic press had followed Zionist statements and publications closely,[93] and had found it a relatively simple matter to condemn the Zionist Movement of separatism, despite its official policy of seeking no more than a "home" in Palestine—within, and not independent of, the Ottoman Empire. As recently as 30 May, ʿIsa al-ʿIsa, the owner of *Falasṭin,* had tried to demolish the arguments used by Jacobson in *al-Muqaṭṭam* by comparing them, also in *al-Muqaṭṭam,* with writings and statements by Herzl, Nordau, Ussishkin, Ruppin and other Zionists.[94] And then, was not a show-down almost inevitable if, as the agenda laid down, Arab judgements of Zionism depended on Zionist acceptance of Arab demands—which would only be formulated *after* the Zionists had set out their aims? If this suspicion is warranted, the three prominent anti-Zionists concerned were not taking part in the Arab delegation to discuss an entente. They had joined it to put the Zionists on trial.

The other seven Arab delegates were probably going to Brummana with much more positive views about an entente. Their basic positions are unknown (only Riza Allah Arqash and Aḥmad

90. *CZA* Z3/116 (17.11.1913), Thon to ZAC, enclosing press report re *al-Karmil* (4.11.1913).
91. *CZA* Z3/116, press report [undated and unsigned] re *al-Karmil* (13.2.1914).
92. *CZA* Z3/116, press report [undated and unsigned], re *al-Raʾy al-ʿAmm* (23.4.1914).
93. E.G. *Falasṭin,* i, 63 (26.8.1911); ii, 77 (9.10.1912); and iii, 2 (5.1.1913); and *CZA* Z3/1448 (19.5.1912), Ruppin to ZAC re *al-Karmil* [no date], all quoting various Zionist leaders including Nordau, Warburg and Tschlenow.
94. *Al-Muqaṭṭam,* no. 7,655 (30.5.1914).

Bayhum had been involved in the "verbal agreement" of 1913, and their views might have changed thereafter). On the other hand Sokolow, helpfully from the point of view of the record, observed in June that the basic demands of the Arabs whom he met in Beirut and Damascus were the same as those of Arabs in Constantinople[95]—and the demands of the latter are known.

In April and May (that is, before Sokolow came to Constantinople), Jacobson had spoken to several Arabs representing different groups in the capital and had attempted to summarise their views. Among them were Saᶜid al-Ḥusayni, Raghib al-Nashashibi, and Saᶜid Shahin (the CUP deputies for Jerusalem and Nablus), Faris al-Khuri (a Protestant and a deputy for Damascus who, after a long political career, was Prime Minister of Syria in 1944–45 and 1954–55), Aḥmad Bayhum (formerly of the Beirut Reform Society), Najib Shuqayr (the Druze connected with the Decentralisation Party), and Shukri al-Ḥusayni (a notable from Jerusalem, long resident in Constantinople).[96]

Generally speaking, these Arabs tended to look unfavourably on the Jewish immigrants into Palestine, who were blamed for failing to integrate with the local population and for building "a state within a state."[97] Moreover, the Arabs entertained fears for the future. Although he came from Damascus, Faris al-Khuri endeavoured to look at the question from the viewpoint of Arabs in Palestine and argued: "A small immigration of Jews is indeed very good . . . , but, in the future, [the Jews] must have an interest to dislodge the Arabs."[98]

Jacobson had countered this argument by pointing out that Palestine was only a small part of the Arab lands, and if the Arabs aspired to eventual autonomy, it would be folly for them to hinder Jewish immigration and thus deprive the whole Arab world, far beyond Palestine, of the benefits which could be derived from it.[99] This line of reasoning was said to have impressed the Arabs, especially the non-Palestinians, who were able to view the question in a wider

95. *CZA* Z3/449 (7.6.1914), Zionist General Council minutes.

96. *CZA* Z3/48 (28.4.1914), Lichtheim to ZCO; *CZA* L2/34/II (3.5.1914), Jacobson to Ruppin; *CZA* Z3/49 (28.5.1914), Lichtheim to ZAC; and *CZA* Z3/49 (7.6.1914), Lichtheim to Jacobson (Berlin).

97. *CZA* Z3/49 (28.5.1914), Lichtheim to ZAC; and *CZA* Z3/449 (7.6.1914), Zionist General Council minutes.

98. *CZA* Z3/49 (7.6.1914), Lichtheim to Jacobson.

99. *Ibid.*; *CZA* Z3/48 (28.4.1914), Lichtheim to ZCO.

context. But, like Rafiq Bey al-ᶜAẓm in Cairo, the non-Palestinians in Constantinople also believed that the agreement of the Arabs in Palestine was absolutely essential. They therefore urged the Zionists to interest themselves in the wishes of the Arabs in Palestine so that an Arab-Zionist understanding would not be resisted.[100]

Jacobson realised that the Arabs whom he met were associated with groups that were not necessarily in agreement with one another.[101] Nevertheless, he felt able to summarise their basic demands for an understanding with the Zionists as follows: "(1) The 'Ottomanisation' of the Jews in Palestine. (2) [Jewish immigration and] settlement should not be restricted only to Palestine. (3) A common social life. (4). Certain benefits for [the Arabs'] national development."[102]

As to the last requirement, Jacobson was horrified by the sums which the Arabs seemed to expect the Zionists to provide.[103] In another report he mentioned that the Arabs wanted the Jews to open their schools to Arabs and also to support Arab educational institutions.[104] All these points would presumably have been aired at Brummana, had the meeting taken place.[105]

One group refused to take part in the proposed meeting at Brummana—the one group which, in the opinion of both Rafiq Bey al-ᶜAẓm and the Arabs in Constantinople, mattered most and on which all else hinged. No prominent member of the political élite in Palestine (for example, a parliamentary deputy or an important member of a leading family) was prepared to go to Brummana. It is impossible, on the evidence available, to know why this should have been so. Perhaps the prominent notables felt that it would be more appropriate for them to see what happened at Brummana and then attend any subsequent meetings. Or perhaps they had undertaken to go to Cairo and were awaiting instructions from the Decentralisation Party. But whatever the reason, their absence was noteworthy and, consciously or not, a precedent had been set for the practice of not negotiating with the Zionists adopted by Arabs in Palestine after World War I.

100. *CZA* Z3/449 (7.6.1914), Zionist General Council minutes.
101. *CZA* L2/34/II (3.5.1914), Jacobson to Ruppin; cf. Z3/49 (3.7.1914), Lichtheim to ZAC.
102. *CZA* Z3/449 (7.6.1914), Zionist General Council minutes.
103. *CZA* L2/34/II (3.5.1914), Jacobson to Ruppin.
104. *CZA* Z3/449 (7.6.1914), Zionist General Council minutes.
105. Cf. *CZA* L2/34/II (3.6.1914), Ruppin to Jacobson.

10

Towards Collision: 1914

IN THE SUMMER of 1914 the Ottoman Government reimposed the restrictions on Jews which it had so cautiously begun to relax over the previous nine months. The first signs of this reversion to former practice came in June when Ottoman consuls reinstituted three-month visas for Jews wishing to visit Palestine, and when the authorities at Jaffa began to demand a cash deposit guaranteeing departure before giving Jews their passports back on entry.[1] On 18 June, the Mutasarrıf of Jerusalem reminded the Kaymakam of Jaffa that although the Red Slip was abolished, strict measures were to be taken to prevent foreign Jews from settling in Palestine.[2] And at the same time difficulties were made for Jews, bearing valid papers, seeking to land at Haifa.[3]

The Haham Başı and Nisim Mazliah approached Talât Bey (the Minister of the Interior) and Midhat Şükri (the Secretary-General of the CUP) on the subject. At first, it was denied that any new orders had been issued.[4] But, by the end of July, when it was clear that the restrictions had definitely been reimposed, both Talât Bey and Midhat Şükri argued that the Jews had only themselves to blame.

1. *CZA* Z3/449 (7.6.1914), Zionist General Council (Berlin) minutes.
2. *CZA* L2/69 (9.7.1914), Haham Başı (Jaffa) to A. Ruppin (Jaffa), enclosing Hebrew translation of order (18.6.1914), Mutas. (Jerus.) to Kay. (Jaffa).
3. *CZA* Z3/1457 (16.7.1914), Ruppin to ZAC.
4. *CZA* Z3/49 (17.7.1914), R. Lichtheim (Consple.) to ZAC.

The Government, they said, had relaxed the procedures for Jews to become Ottoman subjects, and they had not shown any eagerness to take advantage of this privilege.[5] This was true—not only because the Jews enjoyed far greater privileges as foreign nationals, but also because the authorities in Palestine had been visibly hesitant to act over the heads of the foreign consuls as instructed.[6] Thus, in the three months during which the naturalisation procedures were eased, only twenty Jews chose to become Ottoman subjects.[7]

Be that as it may, it was not the real reason for the restoration of the restrictions. The truth was that Zionist representatives in Constantinople had not been impressed by the Government's ambiguous measures and had therefore made no efforts to raise capital for the Empire. (Even if they had tried, there is no guarantee that they would have succeeded.) Thus, all that the Government had achieved by relaxing the restrictions was to provide the Arabs with yet another grievance, by convincing many of them that the CUP had made a secret agreement with the Zionists. Hence, since the General Elections in April Arab deputies had pressed the Government to enforce the restrictions once more.[8] In agreeing to do so, the Government's efforts to court the Zionists—and, through them, the Jews of Europe—had come to an end.

On 2 August, the Ottoman Empire and Germany signed a secret treaty. Total mobilisation in the Empire began immediately. Every Ottoman subject who was eligible for military service was called up. In Palestine, foreign Jews no longer in possession of their travel papers were treated as Ottoman subjects and made liable for service.[9] During August, the outbreak of World War I absorbed the attentions of the Arabic press, and according to the Zionist Office in Jaffa, nothing of importance was written about the Zionist issue.[10] At the beginning of September, the authorities suspended a number of newspapers (including *Falasṭin*), and others stopped appearing of their own accord. Those which continued reported almost exclusively on the war in Europe.[11] And, on 11 November,

5. *CZA* Z3/49 (28.7.1914), Lichtheim to ZAC.
6. *CZA* L2/34/II (21.6.1914), Zionist Office (Jaffa) to V. Jacobson (Consple.).
7. *CZA* Z3/449 (7.6.1914), Zionist General Council minutes.
8. *CZA* Z3/49 (28.7.1914).
9. *CZA* L2/39 (3.9.1914), Zionist Standing Committee (Jaffa) minutes.
10. *CZA* Z3/116 (10.9.1914), J. Thon (Jaffa) to ZAC, enclosing press report.
11. *CZA* Z3/116 (8.10.1914), Thon to ZAC, enclosing press report.

the Ottoman Empire entered the war on the side of Germany and Austro-Hungary.

Many questions remain, but one is particularly intriguing. If, for the sake of argument, either of the proposed meetings between Arabs and Zionists had been held in the summer of 1914, is it likely that a meaningful Arab-Zionist entente would have emerged? The answer must surely be in the negative.

Arab notables in Palestine were opposed to Zionism on grounds of Ottoman loyalism and local patriotism. Those Arabs in Palestine who were involved in the nationalist movement were opposed to the Zionists, and moreover several members of the Decentralisation Party had changed their minds about an Arab-Zionist entente. Finally, there seems to have been a new mood abroad in Palestine by the summer of 1914, and both the peasant population and the younger elements in the towns were affected by it.

The first of these obstacles had been dealt with in depth. If notables in Palestine had agreed to meet the Zionists, they would no doubt have put forward their demands for an end to Jewish immigration and land purchase. It is fair to say that these were not demands which the Zionists could easily have met.

The other obstacles in the way of an Arab-Zionist entente by 1914 need some elaboration. The Arab nationalist movement had touched Palestine to a similar degree as the other Arab provinces. In February 1913 the Decentralisation Party set up a branch in Jaffa, and later in the year other branches were established in Nablus and Jenin, towns in the middle of Palestine.[12] Likewise, in March 1913 a group sympathising with the Beirut Reform Society was formed in Jaffa, headed by Ḥafiẓ Bey al-Saʿid, the former deputy to Parliament.[13] Less organised groups of notables in Jerusalem and Gaza sent telegrams to Constantinople seeking permission to hold talks similar to those conducted in Beirut about administrative reform.[14] And in Haifa *al-Nafir* (which had moved there from Jerusalem in the spring) supported the Beirut Reform Society as well.[15]

12. *La Vérité sur la Question Syrienne,* p. 89.
13. *PRO* FO 195/2451/1795, no. 27 (12.4.1913), W. Hough (Jaffa) to P. J. C. McGregor (Jerus.).
14. *PRO* FO 195/2451/1823, no. 35 (12.4.1913), McGregor to Lowther.
15. *CZA* Z3/1449 (8.4.1913), Thon to ZAC.

Young nationalists from Palestine at this time included ᶜArif al-ᶜArif (then a student in Constantinople and in the years after World War I a proponent of the view that Palestine was part of "Greater Syria"); ᶜAwni ᶜAbd al-Hadi (one of the student organisers of the First Arab Congress in Paris and a political leader under the Mandate); Jamil al-Ḥusayni (a former member of the nationalistically oriented "Literary Club" in Constantinople and a prospective delegate to the proposed meeting at Brummana); Sayf al-Din al-Khatib (mentioned in the previous chapter as opposed to an Arab-Zionist entente and hanged by Cemal Paşa in 1915 for nationalistic activities); and ᶜAli al-Nashashibi (hanged by Cemal Paşa in 1915 for the same reasons).

Except for ᶜArif al-ᶜArif and Sayf al-Din al-Khaṭib, whose anti-Zionist articles have already been discussed, the views of these and other nationalists in Palestine are unknown. But it is reasonable to assume that they would have sympathised with another of their contemporaries, Khalil al-Sakakini, a leading radical in Jerusalem before and after World War I.[16] He kept a diary and in February 1914 made some important entries in it about his attitude to Zionism. Although a Greek Orthodox Christian, his views were close to those of the two Muslim nationalists who, when Hochberg met them in Cairo in 1913, argued that Jewish immigration into Palestine would break the compact Arab mass whose force derived from a unity of language and customs. In his entry for 23 February 1914, al-Sakakini added the territorial element:

> [The Jewish people's] conquest of Palestine is as if it had conquered the heart of the Arab nation (*umma*), because Palestine is the connecting link which binds the Arabian Peninsula with Egypt and Africa. If the Jews conquer [Palestine], they will prevent the linking of the Arab nation; indeed, they will split it into two unconnected parts. This will weaken the cause of Arabism (*shaʾn al-ᶜarabiyya*) and will prevent its solidarity and unity as a nation.[17]

A few days later, he wrote:

> If the Arabs are asked by what right they possess this country (*bilad*), they would say that it is a natural part of the Arab lands. Yes, it was not the cradle of Arab civilisation—but it is not debarred from a share in it. This sacred precinct [in Jerusalem] and these schools are eloquent signs that

16. Kedourie, "Religion and Politics," pp. 85-86.
17. Al-Sakakini, pp. 64-65.

the country is Arab and Islamic. The Arabs have settled in this country from very ancient times; and if this country is the cradle of the Jews' spirituality and the birthplace of their history, then the Arabs have another undeniable right [to Palestine], which is that they propagated their language and culture in it. [The Jews'] right had died with the passage of time; our right is alive and unshakeable.[18]

Not a man to mince words, al-Sakakini had written earlier in February:

What I despise is this principle which [the Zionist] Movement has set up, which is that it should subjugate another [national movement] to make itself strong, and that it should kill an entire nation so that it might live, because this is as if it is trying to steal its independence and to take it by deceit out of the hand of destiny. . . . And what glory does it have if it acquires its independence in this way? This independence, which is acquired by cash, whereby the opportunity of other nations' lethargy, weakness and indolence is exploited, is indeed a feeble independence, founded on sand. What will the Jews do if the national feeling of the Arab nation is aroused; how will they be able to stand up to [the Arabs]?[19]

And these Arab nationalists in Palestine are not the only ones who might have resisted an Arab-Zionist entente. Even within the Decentralisation Party there was a distinct trend against such an agreement, despite the efforts of Rafiq Bey al-ᶜAẓm to arrange meetings between Arabs and Zionists. Ibrahim Najjar's attack on the Zionists in *al-Ahram* on 11 April was mentioned *en passant* in the previous chapter.[20] In it, he revealed that a verbal agreement had been made between the Arabs and Zionists in 1913. But both sides had failed to fulfil their commitments and now, he asserted, the Zionists had made an alliance with the Government. That was why the Government ignored the economic challenge of the Jews in Palestine, the threat of Hebrew to Arabic, the self-government and virtual self-sufficiency of the Jewish colonies. The answer, according to Najjar, was not an entente with the Zionists, but the formation of a Christian group in Europe, "perhaps in France," to help the local population in Palestine to withstand the Zionists.

Other Decentralisationists were opposed to an Arab-Zionist entente. Muḥammad al-Maḥmaṣani, another of the student organisers

18. Al-Sakakini, p. 68.
19. *Ibid.*, p. 63.
20. *CZA* Z3/116, press reports [undated and unsigned] re *al-Ahram* (11.4.1914).

of the First Arab Congress and in 1914 a lawyer in Beirut,[21] had written a series of articles in *Fatat al-ᶜArab* (Beirut) in which he argued that an entente with the Zionists was impossible.[22] And Muḥammad al-Shanṭi, who edited *al-Iqdam* in Cairo,[23] was an implacable enemy of Zionism, attacking it remorselessly in June and July, when other newspapers in Cairo had agreed to keep silent until an Arab-Zionist meeting had been held.[24]

More significantly, Ḥaqqi Bey al-ᶜAẓm withdrew his support for an entente by the beginning of the summer, and by the end of the summer Rashid Riḍa did likewise. Both accused the Zionists of seeking a Jewish state that would stretch from Palestine to Iraq ("to the Euphrates," as Riḍa put it). Ḥaqqi Bey al-ᶜAẓm went as far as advocating violence against the Zionists.

On 20 June, he wrote to Maḥmud al-Maḥmaṣani in Beirut, a relative of Muḥammad al-Maḥmaṣani and also a Decentralisationist,[25] saying that he did not share Rafiq Bey's opinion about an Arab-Zionist meeting. If he was not working against the suggestion, it was because such a meeting could do no harm, even though it could not achieve anything.

Understand, dear brother, that [the Zionists] are marching towards their objective at a rapid pace, thanks to the help of the Government and the indifference of the local population. I am sure that if we do nothing which is demanded by the present situation, they will achieve their objective in a few years in [Palestine], where they will found a [Jewish state]. Then they will gravitate towards Syria, next towards Iraq and thus they will have fulfilled their political programme. . . . But by employing means of threats and persecutions—and it is this last means which we must employ—by pushing the Arab population into destroying their farms and setting fire to their colonies, by forming gangs to execute

21. For his membership in the Decentralisation Party, see *La Vérité sur la Question Syrienne,* p. 99.

22. *CZA* Z3/116, press reports [undated and unsigned] re *Fatat al-ᶜArab* (4. and 5.5.1914; and 4.6.1914).

23. For his membership in the Decentralisation Party, see *La Vérité sur la Question Syrienne,* p. 96.

24. *CZA* Z3/116, press reports [undated and unsigned] re *al-Iqdam* (21. and 28.6.1914; and 12. and 27.7.1914); also *ha-Ḥerut,* vi 121 (25.6.1914); 235 (24.7.1914); 236 (26.7.1914); 237 (27.7.1914); and 241 (31.7.1914).

25. For his membership in the Decentralisationist Party, see *La Vérité sur la Question Syrienne,* pp. 98–99.

these projects, then perhaps [the Zionists in Palestine] will emigrate to save their lives.[26]

Shortly after word was received that the Zionists had declined to come to Cairo for the time being, Ḥaqqi Bey contributed an article to *al-Iqdam* in which he disclosed his conviction that the Government was helping the Zionists against the local population. Obliquely, he warned the Government that the Arabs were beginning to think about ways of combating the Zionists by force, so that:

One day [the Zionists'] hair will stand on end and their knees will knock, and then that alliance and those relations [with the Government] will be of no use to them. Then they will turn back from Palestine with great losses; and as for [Arabs] who have sold land [to the Zionists], they are about to discover the abyss into which they will plunge.[27]

About a month and a half later, Rashid Riḍa publicly joined the Decentralisationist opposition to the Zionists. During the summer *Falasṭin* translated Ussishkin's *Our Programme,* and towards the end of August an abridged version of the first eight parts of it was published in *al-Manar.* Riḍa commented that this résumé was sufficient to show that if the Zionists achieved what they desired, not one Muslim or Christian would remain in the "Promised Land," which in Jewish tradition extended as far as the River Euphrates. In the Book of Deuteronomy, God had commanded the Jews to destroy the inhabitants of the Promised Land; today they would do so again, not by fire and the sword, but by money and deceit, so that Jews alone would live in their "new kingdom." To combat the "Zionist danger," Riḍa prescribed "deliberation, determination, communal strength, . . . promptitude in organising means of defence . . . acts and deeds, not talk and words."[28]

Indirectly, Ḥaqqi Bey's call for violence against Jewish colonies and Rashid Riḍa's call for action were already on the way to being answered in Palestine. On the one hand, attacks on Jewish settlers by fellahin had multiplied over recent years and, on the other,

26. Letter no. 70 (20.6.1914), Ḥaqqi Bey al-ᶜAẓm (Heliopolis) to Maḥmud al-Maḥmaṣani [Beirut], published in *Le Journal de Beyrouth,* iii, 413 (1.9.1915).
27. *CZA* L2/94/I, press report [undated and unsigned] re Ḥaqqi Bey al-ᶜAẓm, "The Ottoman Government and the Zionist Question," in *al-Iqdam* ([ca.12.]7. 1914).
28. *Al-Manar,* xvii, 9 (1914), pp. 707–08.

younger elements in the towns were taking steps in the months before World War I to oppose the Zionists in an organised fashion.

The attacks on Sejera in the spring of 1909 appear to have been unique, insofar as they were inspired by outsiders and bore some marks of a conscious protest against Jewish colonisation in the north of Palestine. On the other hand, the harassment of Jewish settlers and their colonies did not stop. Alongside the generally good relations, there were also frequent instances of fellahin molesting Jews in their fields, uprooting their saplings, damaging their crops, and stealing their livestock. On occasion, colonies were raided, granaries set on fire, and thefts committed.

No doubt many of these incidents occurred because they were part and parcel of contemporary village life in Palestine. At the same time, the special factors affecting the Jewish colonies which were described in Chapter Two must also have come into play. The peasants often harboured grudges against the settlers over land questions, and the Jews, largely ignorant of Arabic and local customs, did not always ease things. Moreover, as has been noted, the peasants were not insensible to what was being written in the anti-Zionist press from 1910 onwards, and thus, as the attacks on Jewish colonies multiplied, the British Consul-General in Beirut was led to conclude in November 1911 that "the local fellaheen in general . . . regard the steady influx of Jews as a menace to their own rights and privileges."[29]

Moreover, the situation of the Jewish settlers was different from that of other elements of the rural population, and the peasants were aware of this. They knew full well that the Ottoman authorities disapproved of Jewish settlement in Palestine and restricted it. It can hardly have helped to tell some of them that "the Jews are traitors and every act of violence committed against them is a patriotic act," as Şakir Ertugrul, the Kaymakam of Tiberias, is reported to have announced at a meeting of his Administrative Council in 1910.[30]

There were other ways in which the peasants could draw conclusions from the official attitude towards the settlers. For example,

29. *PRO* FO 371/1263/4715, no. 64 (6.11.1911), H. A. Cumberbatch (Beirut) to Sir G. Lowther (Consple.).

30. *CZA* L2/50/I, "Note sur l'état d'insécurité dont souffre la population israélite agricole dans les [*sic*] Caza de Tibériade" [undated and unsigned (ca. end 1911)].

from May 1909 (after the incidents at Sejera) until July 1911, six Jews from various colonies in the region of Tiberias were murdered. No convictions were made in any of these cases.[31] By contrast, when a German Templer was killed by Arabs near Haifa in 1910, the Vali of Beirut hurried to Haifa in person (probably in deference to Germany) and within a few months one Arab had been sentenced to death, one to fifteen years and others to four years imprisonment.[32] Also by way of contrast, when a Jewish guard killed an Arab during an attack on Merḥavya in 1911, the authorities stood by idly while fellahin from several villages pillaged two colonies in reprisal.[33] The Jewish guard was arrested, together with ten other Jews who were not present when the Arab was killed.[34] Four of them were quickly set free, but the other seven were held without trial for eleven months. They were only released when Asʿad Shuqayr, the CUP deputy for Acre, intervened on their behalf in gratitude for services rendered by a Jewish doctor who had successfully set a broken leg for him![35]

Most of the more violent acts committed against Jewish colonies in the first years after the Young Turk Revolution took place in the north of Palestine. Again, this was principally for the reasons mentioned earlier—the mixed, unruly population in the north, and the fact that public security was better in the compact Mutasarrıflık of Jerusalem than in the outlying districts of the Vilâyet of Beirut. But it was not long before the violence spread south. The turning point seems to have been the latter half of 1911, after the second debate on Zionism in Parliament. As will be recalled, Albert Antébi observed at that time that accounts of the Arab deputies' speeches had reached the peasants, and anti-Jewish feeling had widened. That autumn there were persistent reports that the Ottoman Patriotic Party in Jaffa was planning some large-scale anti-Jewish action after Ramadan (the month of fasting and religious devotion in the Muslim year).[36] The reports were taken seriously by the Mutasarrıf, who

31. *CZA* L2/50/I, "Note."
32. *Ha-Ḥerut,* iii, 53 (17.2.1911).
33. *CZA* Z2/636 (3.6.1911), Ruppin to ZAC; *JCA* 271/no. 324 (17.7.1911), E. Krause (Sejera) to JCA (Paris); and *CZA* L2/50/I, "Note."
34. *CZA* Z2/636 (3.6.1911), Ruppin to ZAC.
35. *CZA* L18/246/2 (25.4.1912), J. Hankin (Haifa) to Ruppin; and *CZA* Z3/1448 (21.5.1912), Ruppin to ZAC.
36. *AIU* X E 29 (14.9.1911), A. Antébi (Jerus.) to Pres., AIU (Paris).

dispatched senior police officers from Jerusalem to Jaffa and alerted the military garrison there.[37] The alleged plan, further molestation by peasants, and the murder of three Jews, were the background to the appeal for greater security made in August 1912 by representatives of various colonies to the new Mutasarrıf, Muhdi Bey.

In the summer of 1913 two more Jews were killed in the Mutasarrıflık, and in the winter of 1913–14 there was an upsurge of violence against Jewish settlers in the north. It was only then, in January 1914, that the Government, wishing to show its—temporarily—more favourable disposition towards the Zionists, responded to complaints from the Haham Başı in Constantinople, and for the first time posted soldiers at main crossroads and in Arab and Jewish villages.[38] Also for the first time, the local authorities made earnest efforts to apprehend those responsible for the last two murders in the north.[39] But the effects of this action were transitory, and by the end of April 1914 the British Consul in Jerusalem reported that "the assaults upon Jews in the outlying districts are increasingly frequent."[40]

It should be noted that, despite their growing frequency, these attacks were not "political" in the sense of being organised and part of a definite campaign. Quite the opposite: although they reflected peasant resentment of the Jewish settlers, they were sporadic and their causes essentially local. But, in the longer run, they did take on political significance. The foundation had been laid for the organised attacks launched against the Jewish colonies in the early 1920s.

Of a more specifically political nature was the activity among younger elements in the towns in 1914. According to Rafiq Bey al-ᶜAẓm, a new spirit was gripping them: they wanted to organise educated people to resist the Zionists, and had recently sent a long telegram to the Government protesting against the Zionists' aims and work.[41] A month later, ᶜAbd al-Qadir al-Muzghar, a well-known

37. *AIU* X E 29 (13.10.1911), Antébi to A. Brill et al. (Jaffa).
38. *CZA* L2/69 (12.1.1914), Haham Başı (Jaffa) to Zionist Office (Jaffa).
39. *CZA* L18/246/II (28.11.1913), Hankin to Thon; *CZA* Z3/1451 (2.12.1913) and Z3/1452 (31.12.1913), both Thon to ZAC.
40. *PRO* FO 371/2134/22036, no. 31 (30.4.1914), MacGregor to Sir L. Mallet (Consple.).
41. *Al-Muqaṭṭam,* no. 7,616 (14.4.1914).

shaykh in Jerusalem, also spoke of the new mood. He told Dr. Isaac Lévy, the manager of the Jerusalem branch of the Anglo-Palestine Company, that he was perturbed at attitudes held by Arab and Zionist youth, both of whom harboured extremely chauvinistic and potentially dangerous elements.[42] And, on 27 May, ʿIsa al-ʿIsa, the proprietor of *Falasṭin,* mentioned in an interview with *Le Journal du Caire* that there was "a very important movement afoot among [young Muslims] to put an end to the Zionist invasion."[43]

These observations were corroborated by reports reaching the Zionist Office in Jaffa that young Arabs were organising anti-Zionist societies. In April, Muslims in Jerusalem told Dr. Lévy that Jewish immigration into Palestine had become a special topic of discussion "at the meetings of their secret societies."[44] Towards the end of that month, the director of the Zionist Office in Jaffa received a letter from another correspondent in Jerusalem who was convinced that an organisation of young Muslims and Christians existed in Jerusalem and Jaffa to fight the Zionists by every means throughout Palestine.[45]

In fact, several anti-Zionist societies were formed during this period, not only in Jerusalem and Jaffa, but also in Constantinople, Haifa, Beirut and Cairo. Detailed information is not available about them, but judging from their names and the references to them, they were small and of two types.

First, there were anti-Zionist groups *per se,* like the anti-Zionist society founded in Nablus in August 1913 (which, incidentally, seems still to have been in existence in the spring of 1914[46]). Thus, in February 1914, *al-Karmil* reported that young Arabs in Constantinople had founded an anti-Zionist society.[47] In May, Albert Antébi received a letter from a Turkish friend in Constantinople, saying that its aim was "to study means of stopping land sales in Syria and Palestine to foreigners and Zionists."[48] According to *al-Raʾy al-ʿAmm* (Beirut), most of its members were Muslims, and its

42. *CZA* L18/245/5 (13.5.1914), I. Lévy (Jerus.) to Ruppin.
43. *Le Journal du Caire* (27.5.1914).
44. *CZA* L18/245/5 (9.4.1914), Lévy to Ruppin.
45. *CZA* L2/94/II (27.4.1914), B. Ibry (Jerus.) to Ruppin.
46. *CZA* Z3/116, press report [undated and unsigned] re petition in *Fatat al-ʿArab* (2.4.1914).
47. *CZA* Z3/116, press report [undated and unsigned] re *al-Karmil* (24.2.1914).
48. *PJCA* 39/168 (21.5.1914), Antébi to Bril.

President was Amir ᶜAli Paşa al-Jazaᶜiri, a deputy from Damascus and one of the Chamber's two vice-presidents.[49] References in *al-Karmil* and a telegram of support from Jerusalem and Beirut suggest that it was Ottoman Loyalist in orientation.[50]

In June, two more anti-Zionist societies were reported to have been formed, under the influence of Najib Naṣṣar (who, having now abandoned the CUP completely, had added Arab nationalism to his local patriotism). One, in Beirut, was made up of about a hundred students from Nablus and called *al-Shabiba al-Nabulsiyya*—the Nablus Youth [Society][51]. Its aims—"to protect the rights of the Arabs, to agitate for the good of the Arab people and for the good of Syria"—suggest it was nationalist in orientation. Over the summer, it planned to stage a play written by Najib Naṣṣar, called "The Pride of the Arabs" and dealing with "every Arab's duty to defend his land and birthplace with all his might."[52] The other society, in Haifa, was headed by Naṣṣar in person, and it had both Muslim and Christian members. Called *al-Muntada al-Adabi*—the Literary Club—its aims were said to be overtly nationalist and secretly anti-Zionist.[53]

Finally, in July, more details were published about an anti-Zionist society which had been formed at al-Azhar, the great centre of Islamic learning in Cairo, and which was first mentioned in the press in May.[54] Its members were students from Palestine,[55] and its name was the Society for Uprising against the Zionists.[56] Its official programme follows:

1. To oppose the Zionists by all possible means, by awakening public opinion and uniting views on this point, and by spreading the Society's programme among all avenues of the Arab nation in general and in Syria and Palestine in particular.
2. To found branches and societies in all the towns of Syria and Palestine for this purpose alone.
3. To try to spread unity among all the elements making up the [Arab] nation.

49. *CZA* L2/39 (30.7.1914), S. ᶜAbbadi (Haifa) to Ruppin.
50. *Ibid.*
51. *Ha-Ḥerut,* VI, 192 (4.6.1914).
52. *Ibid.*
53. *Ha-Ḥerut,* vi, 207 (22.6.1914).
54. *Le Journal du Caire* (27.5.1914).
55. *Ibid.*
56. *Ha-Ḥerut,* vi, 237 (27.7.1914).

4. To help economic, commercial and agricultural ventures and to develop the farmer and the peasant so that they may be able to save themselves from the hands of the Zionists.
5. To make representations to all those interested in this question to halt the stream of Zionist immigration.[57]

In private correspondence, however, Ḥaqqi Bey al-ʿAẓm said that the society secretly called for the same violent methods of "threats and persecutions" as he advocated himself.[58]

The second type of anti-Zionist society was economic. Such organisations reflect the fear of Jewish economic competition and recall the existence of the Economic and Commercial Company alongside the Ottoman Patriotic Party in Jaffa in 1911, and Najib Naṣṣar's attempt to launch an economic boycott against the Jews, also in 1911. The names of two of these societies are known, both of them in Jerusalem. The first was called *al-Sharika al-Waṭaniyya al-Iqtiṣadiyya*—the Patriotic Economic Company.[59] The "patriotic" element in its name suggests that it had Ottoman loyalist leanings. By sharp contrast, the other society was called *Sharikat al-Iqtiṣad al-Falasṭini al-ʿArabi*—the Arab Palestinian Economic Company.[60] This group may have been formed by members of the anti-Zionist society in Nablus, because in April a petition in *Fatat al-ʿArab* announced that some of its members were setting up a "Palestine Economic Company" with its headquarters in Jerusalem.[61]

The "new spirit" among the youth of Palestine ran forcefully through a "General Summons to Palestinians," distributed in Jerusalem at the end of June. Headed "Beware of the Zionist Danger," it was signed anonymously by "a Palestinian,"[62] and managed to combine local patriotism with a call for Muslim unity and Arab nationalist elements. It began:

Countrymen! We summon you in the name of the country which is in mourning, in the name of the homeland which is lamenting, in the

57. *Ibid.*, reprinting programme from *al-Iqdam* (19.7.1914).
58. Letter no. 70 (20.6.1914), Ḥaqqi Bey al-ʿAẓm to Maḥmud al-Maḥmaṣani.
59. *Falasṭin*, iv, 34 (27.6.1914).
60. *Ibid.*
61. *CZA* Z3/116, press report [undated and unsigned] re *Fatat al-ʿArab* (2.4.1914).
62. Published in *al-Iqdam* on 5.7.1914 and in *al-Karmil* on 7.7.1914—see Hebrew translation in press report in *CZA* Z3/116; also published in *Fatat al-ʿArab* (date not known)—see *ha-Ḥerut*, vi, 225 (13.7.1914).

name of Arabia, in the name of Syria, in the name of our country, Palestine, whose lot is evil, in the name of everything which is dear to you.

Claiming that the moment of death was at hand, it invoked the names of ʿUmar ibn al-Khaṭṭab and Ṣalaḥ al-Din, and urged the Palestinians to hold on "with their teeth" to the land that these Muslim heroes had conquered in the seventh and twelfth centuries. "Will you leave the country, and God has not commanded you to depart?"

If indeed you do so—if you are not Muslims—God, His Messenger and Angels, and all men will be obliged to punish you. [Therefore] observe the laws of your faith and your language. Have pity on your land, and do not sell it as merchandise. Otherwise you will live to regret it. At least let your children inherit the country which your fathers gave you as an inheritance.

History had come full circle. Once a nation blessed and privileged by God, the Palestinians were now weak and divided, and were being dealt grievous blows. "Who of our noble ancestors, from the day that Islam appeared or from the day that the Arabs were known in history," would have dreamt that their offspring would one day "scatter this dear heritage and throw it to the winds, leaving it to their enemies."

Men! do you want to be slaves and servants to people who are notorious in the world and in history? Do you wish to be slaves to the Zionists who have come to you to expel you from your country, saying that this country is theirs? Behold, I summon God and His Messenger as witnesses against them that they are liars. They dwelt in this holy land in former times and God sent them from it and forbade them to settle in it. Therefore why are they now craning their necks towards it, wishing to conquer it, after having deserted it for two thousand years? The Zionists desire to settle in our country and to expel us from it. Are you satisfied with this? Do you wish to perish?

The danger was said to be "immense." The Zionists had already purchased most of Palestine. "Over 300,000" had arrived at a time when the local population are leaving the country in thousands for America and other countries. The Jewish immigrants had already taken over trade and industry. Soon they would control the country's agriculture, "and thereafter conquer the whole country."

It is not merely that they wish to have dominion over us, but [they also wish] to expel us from the country. Are you, Muslims, content with this? Are you, Palestinians, Syrians, Arabs, happy at this? They have to learn that there is a nation in the country and that they cannot enter so long as we are in it.

The "General Summons" also spelt out a plan of action for the Arabs in Palestine. They should agitate for an end to Jewish immigration so that the Government would be forced to take account of "public opinion" in Palestine. They should demand the reinstitution of the Red Slip and the enforcement of the land purchase restrictions. Local industry should be encouraged, and Arabs should only trade amongst themselves, as did the Zionists who, it was alleged, "do not trade with the 'Goy'—the unbeliever, that is, the Muslim and the Christian." Land should not be sold to Jews, and Arab land-agents should be reviled; one day they would pay dearly for their crimes. Efforts should be made not only to stop the influx of Jews, but also to stem the emigration (to America and elsewhere) on the part of the local population. Religious trusts should be devoted to the creation of religious, technical, and agricultural schools. Youth should be encouraged to engage in agriculture and industry, and not to swell the ranks of bureaucracy. Arabic should be the language of instruction in institutes of higher learning, "because the Zionists are vying with you in language as well."

Above all, "trust in God and in yourselves; do not trust in the Government because it is occupied with other things. . . . Strive, act, and God will favour your deeds."

11

Conclusions

THE CONCLUSIONS to this study can be stated simply.

1. The Arabs knew of both the Lovers of Zion and the Zionist Movement from the outset.

In 1882, an Arab wrote to *al-Muqtaṭaf* about the increased flow of Jews through Beirut on their way to Palestine, and both that journal and *al-Manar* discussed the Zionist Movement within a few months of its formation. In Palestine itself, the Jewish newcomers immediately made themselves known, not only to fellahin near the colonies which they established, but also to Arabs in the towns, especially landowners and merchants in Jerusalem and Jaffa.

2. By 1914, the Arabs were well aware of Zionist aims and activities in Palestine.

In 1902, Rashid Riḍa discerned that the Zionists sought national sovereignty in Palestine. In 1905, Négib Azoury predicted that Zionism was likely to conflict with the cause of Arab nationalism. From 1909 onwards, Arabic newspapers in several important centres, including Constantinople and Cairo, began to write with increasing frequency about Zionism. Thereafter, Zionism statements and publications, the progress of the Zionist Movement and its practical work in Palestine were followed closely. In the light of all this, the Arabs were sceptical, to say the least, about the official Zionist position that the Movement merely sought a "home" for the

Jewish people within the Ottoman Empire, rather than a completely independent Jewish state.

3. Because of the administrative divisions of the Arab provinces, Arabs outside Palestine were familiar with the question from the beginning.

Official correspondence about Jewish immigration and settlement in Palestine was copied to Beirut and Damascus, and Arabs in the lower and middle ranks of the local administration were familiar with it. Thus, for example, in 1901 Arab officials in Jerusalem collected signatures to protest against the consolidated regulations on Jewish entry and land purchases which they considered too favourable to the Jews. Likewise, Arab officials in Beirut withheld publication of those regulations for the same reason.

The involvement of Arabs outside Palestine was intensified by the presence of an important group of Syrians in Cairo, and also by the reportage in the Arabic press which brought information about Zionist activities in Palestine to Arab émigrés as far afield as New York.

4. Arab reactions to the Zionists can only be fully understood in the light of the Ottoman Government's response to modern Jewish immigration into Palestine.

The Government was opposed to this influx, mainly because it did not want to encourage another national problem or to have more Europeans with special privileges under the Capitulations resident in a sensitive part of the Empire. It announced its opposition to Jewish immigration into Palestine already in 1881, before the flow began in earnest. Theodor Herzl brought his ideas about a Jewish state to the direct attention of both the Porte and the Sultan in 1896, a year in advance of the first Zionist Congress, and they were firmly rejected by Abdülhamid.

But, despite the official restrictions on Jewish entry into Palestine (from 1882 onwards) and on land purchase (from 1892 onwards), Ottoman policy was a failure. Thus, from 1882 to 1908, the Jewish community in Palestine grew from about twenty-four thousand to between seventy and eighty thousand, and twenty-six colonies were founded.

5. By 1908, a decade after the first Zionist Congress, anti-Zionism as such still had not emerged among the Arabs. On the other hand, there was unease about the expanding Jewish community in Palestine, and relations between Arabs and Jews were deteriorating.

Economic fears lay behind the protest telegram sent to Constantinople in 1891 by Arab notables in Jerusalem. Soon after the Zionist Movement was founded, there were signs of increasing discontent over Jewish immigration, and Arab attitudes to Jews, which traditionally were unfavourable among both Muslims and Christians, were being affected by European anti-Semitism.

6. At the same time, most notables in Jerusalem seem to have been prepared for Jews to settle in Palestine, provided that they became Ottoman subjects.

This view was expressed in a report written in 1899 which recommended that either the entry restrictions be made to work, or Jews be allowed to settle on the condition mentioned above. It was repeated on many subsequent occasions, but after 1901 there was no legal framework for Jewish newcomers to become Ottomans, while there were strong disincentives to their attempting to take that step. When the naturalisation requirements were relaxed for three months in 1914, only a score of Jews applied to become Ottoman subjects.

7. The Young Turks were as opposed to the Zionists as Abdülhamid's régime.

Leading Young Turk politicians made this clear to Zionist representatives in the months after the Revolution in 1908. The official opposition hardened in 1909 when the CUP, the dominant wing among the Young Turks, began enforcing its policy of Ottomanisation. This opposition was relaxed for only a few months between the autumn of 1913 and the summer of 1914, when the Government angled for the financial support it believed to be at the command of Jews in Europe. Although the old régime's restrictions against the Jews were retained, they continued to be ineffective. By the outbreak of World War I, the Jewish community in Palestine had risen to about eighty-five thousand, and over forty colonies had been established.

8. The Arabs distinguished carefully between "foreign Jew" and "Ottoman Jew." They were also aware of the difference between "Jew" and "Zionist," but often blurred it in practice, sometimes on purpose.

The first distinction was maintained throughout, and explicitly stated on many occasions. Thus, the resolution passed by the Decentralisation Party in April 1913 assured *Ottoman Jews* of equal rights in a decentralised administration; and Raghib Bey al-Nashashibi who, as a CUP candidate in Jerusalem in 1914, advocated the "methods of Rumania" against foreign Jews, was careful to explain that he was not opposed to Ottoman Jews.

On the other hand, while Arab members of the CUP branch in Jerusalem differentiated between "Jew" and "Zionist" in 1908, the distinction was seldom made by others. This was because most Arab anti-Zionists were opposed to *all* Jewish immigration from Europe into Palestine. In addition, Najib Naṣṣar, Shukri al-ᶜAsali and others argued that the difference between the Zionist Movement and other Jewish groups interested in settlement in Palestine was immaterial because, it was claimed, they all had the same object in mind, namely, the founding of an autonomous Jewish state.

9. Arab anti-Zionism proper emerged between 1909 and 1914. Various trends can be distinguished in it, the main ones being anti-Zionism on grounds of Ottoman Loyalism, local patriotism and Arab nationalism.

Ottoman loyalism was deeply ingrained in most of the traditional Arab élite. They objected to Zionism for much the same reasons as Ottoman ministers from the 1880s—that is to say, they saw the Zionist Movement as yet another nationalist "separatist" movement and as the vanguard of increased Russian or German influence in Palestine.

Local patriotism grew largely out of Ottoman loyalism. Having been regarded as a danger to the Empire as a whole, the Zionists came to be seen as a "threat" to Palestine in particular, and from 1910 Arabs in the country began to protest against their activities, without reference to their implications for the Empire at large. From that point onwards, local Arabs increasingly spoke of themselves as "Palestinians" in the context of Zionism. A graphic illustration of this trend is that in 1911 the first anti-Zionist group to be formed in Palestine was called the *Ottoman* Patriotic Party; two years later, an Arab in Nablus, writing in *Falasṭin,* proposed the formation of a *Palestinian* Patriotic Company. In 1914, a "General Summons to Palestinians," signed by "a Palestinian," was distributed in Jerusalem. At about the same time, members of the traditional élite in Palestine were interviewed by two Arabic newspapers, and from their replies to questions about Zionism, it is clear that they, once the most loyal of Ottoman loyalists, had also become local patriots.

The Arab nationalists were by no means of one mind about the Zionists. In 1913 and 1914, the majority view favoured some form of agreement with the Zionists, a proposal which originated with the Decentralisationists in Cairo. Partly because the early Decentralisationists came from areas outside Palestine, and partly because they included Christian Arabs, they tended to view the Zionist question in a broad, almost "pan-Arab" contest. Consequently, in 1913, a "verbal agreement" was reached between a Zionist representative and the Arab nationalists; and in 1914, separate attempts, centring on Cairo and Palestine, were made for Arabs and Zionists to meet with the object of laying the foundations for a formal agreement. The outbreak of World War I interrupted these attempts.

In 1913, only a small minority of the nationalists objected outright to Jewish immigration into Palestine as likely to erode the compact Arab mass whose strength derived from a unity of language and customs. But in 1914 nationalist opposition to the Zionists grew. In Palestine, Khalil al-Sakakini argued that if the Jews "conquered" Palestine, the territorial unity of the Arabs would be broken and their cause weakened. In Cairo, leading Decentralisationists took note of the recent relaxation of the restrictions against the Jews and came to the conclusion that the CUP had made an alliance with the Zionists, also to weaken the Arab cause. Ḥaqqi Bey al-ʿAẓm called for violence against Jewish colonies in Palestine, and Rashid Riḍa likewise declared that the time for action had come.

10. Local patriotism, by definition, was confined to Arabs in Palestine. After World War I, it developed into Palestinian Arab nationalism, which was soon locked in violent conflict with the Jewish national movement.

On the other hand, Ottoman loyalism and Arab nationalism were the two great ideologies competing for the support of all politically aware Arabs on the eve of World War I. The fact that neither of these ideologies had a genuine place for Zionism did not bode well for the New Yishuv (even though Ottomanist loyalism ceased to exist after 1918).

11. In addition to these three main categories of Arab anti-Zionism, there was also fear of economic competition from the Jewish newcomers, the anti-Zionism of Arabs affected by anti-Semitism and that of Arabs who believed in Muslim unity.

Although these can scarcely be called "ideological" positions (insofar as they related to Zionism), they each played a distinct role.

Fear of economic competition led to the formation of the Economic and Commercial Company in Jaffa in 1911, and of both the Patriotic Economic Company and the Arab Palestinian Economic Company in Jerusalem in 1914—in addition to Najib Naṣṣar's unsuccessful attempt to organise an economic boycott against the Jews in 1911.

Arab anti-Semitism expressed itself in various ways—for example, in the press (witness the cartoon facing page 90); in Rashid Riḍa's conviction (shared by many others) that the Jews controlled the finances of Europe; in representations made against the Zionists in the Mutasarrıjflık of Jerusalem in the autumn of 1912, and in Sulayman al-Taji's poem, the "Zionist Danger," which referred to the Jews as the "sons of clinking gold." Arab anti-Semitism was sufficiently pervasive for Ruḥi Bey al-Khalidi to think it necessary to preface his speech in Parliament in 1911 by declaring that he was not an anti-Semite but an anti-Zionist.

The call for Muslim unity against the Zionists was sounded in Beirut in the summer of 1912, after the notion that the CUP was dominated by Freemasons and Jews had gained ground among the Arabs. This trend, already prevalent among Arabs on wider issues, was probably given added momentum by the Balkan Wars when Muslims in the Arab provinces reacted against local non-Muslims and Europeans. It can be seen in the formation of an anti-Zionist society at al-Azhar in Cairo in 1914, and in the distinctly Islamic features running through the "General Summons to Palestinians."

12. Many arguments against the Zionists were elaborated in the years between the Young Turk Revolution and the outbreak of World War I. Indeed, it can be suggested that the essentials of the Arab "case" against Zionism, as the world came to know it in the 1920s and 1930s, were worked out during those years.

The main Arab arguments were that the Zionists sought a Jewish state in Palestine (which might extend as far as Iraq); that they retained their foreign nationality and did not become loyal Ottomans; that they did not integrate with the local population; that they were establishing independent institutions of self-government and self-defence; that they preferred Hebrew to Arabic; that they possessed vast financial resources and thus the capacity to achieve their aims; that they stood behind the CUP; and that they were flagbearers of Great Power influence in Palestine.

13. Not all the Arab arguments against Zionism were valid, but they go some distance to make their fears intelligible.

The Zionists did not seek a state extending from Palestine to Iraq. They did not possess vast financial resources, any more than the Jews controlled the finances of Europe. They did not dominate the CUP, nor were they in league with it (even though the idea was mooted in 1913 and 1914). And neither the Russians nor the Germans were using them as a device to extend their respective interests.

14. Arab anti-Zionists showed a marked tendency to exaggerate the numbers of Jewish newcomers in Palestine and the anount of land which they had acquired.

From 1882 to 1914, an average of two to three thousand Jewish immigrants a year might have entered Palestine, of whom many departed after a short while. At the end of the period, the total Jewish population of Palestine numbered about eighty-five thousand. In 1910, however, a protest telegram from Haifa spoke of "about 100,000" Jewish immigrants who had arrived "recently." and the "General Summons to Palestinians" mentioned "over 300,000" Jewish newcomers. Newspaper articles frequently suggested that the Jews had bought up the larger part of Palestine, whereas in reality they possessed only about 2 per cent of the total area in 1914.

15. The basic Arab demands were an end to Jewish immigration into Palestine and an end to land purchases by them.

Although these demands were first made by telegram from Jerusalem in 1891, the dispatch of that telegram seems to have been an isolated event. However, after the Young Turk Revolution, the same demands were pressed vigorously, not only by the Arabic press, but also by Arab parliamentary deputies, who worked for new legislation to put them into effect.

In 1913 and 1914 the increasing exodus of Arabs from Syria and Palestine and the belated recognition that Arab landowners and agents were also responsible for the sale of Arab land added to the anxiety of the anti-Zionists. It is worth noting that in subsequent years the Arabs never abandoned the same basic demands: an end to Jewish immigration and an end to Jewish land purchases.

16. Against this, there was a marked absence of any significant body of opinion in support of the Zionists.

It is true that articles in favour of the Zionists sometimes appeared in the Arabic press outside Palestine. But almost always those articles were published by pro-CUP papers, trying to defend the CUP for its alleged pro-Jewish and pro-Zionist inclinations. On the other hand, no arguments in support of Zionism for its own sake ever took root among the Arabs—despite some Zionist attempts to implant them through articles sent to the Arabic press or in discussions with Arab leaders.

Likewise, while Arab notables in Palestine were often friendly with Jews, it was usually on a personal, non-political basis. Asʿad Shuqayr (the CUP deputy from Acre) owned a debt of gratitude to a Jewish doctor, and Ḥusayn al-Ḥusayni (the President of the Municipal Council in Jerusalem in the years before World War I) called for new legislation against Jewish land purchases in his interview with *al-Iqdam* in March 1914, despite his respect, clearly stated, for Jews and Zionists. A better indicator of opinion—and omen for the future—was that no prominent Arabs from Palestine were prepared to meet Zionists at Brummana in the summer of 1914.

17. The Arabs took political action against the Zionists before 1914.

Ḥafiẓ Bey al-Saʿid's parliamentary question about Zionism in June 1909 was followed by prolonged, if unsuccessful, efforts by Arab deputies from Palestine and beyond to persuade the Government to adopt the new legislation mentioned above. The second parliamentary debate on Zionism in May 1911 clearly was coordinated Arab political action, and during the General Elections in 1912 and 1914 the Zionist question was an issue for Arabs in Palestine. During the first Balkan War, the former CUP deputies in Jerusalem tried to bring together Arab anti-Zionists, both Muslim and Christian; and after the killing of an Arab and a Jew near Reḥovot in the summer of 1913 an anti-Zionist campaign was mounted, involving petitions and deputations to the Mutasarrıf of Jerusalem. But perhaps more telling in the long run was the existence by 1914 of small anti-Zionist societies in Jerusalem, Jaffa, Nablus, Haifa, Beirut, Constantinople and Cairo.

18. Although Arab political action did not achieve tangible results, it limited the Government's freedom to manoeuvre in relation to the Zionists.

Most notably, it deterred the Government from openly relaxing the restrictions on Jews in Palestine in the autumn of 1913. But it also made the Government reverse its decision to sell crown lands to Najib al-Aṣfar in 1913, and the local authorities withdrew concessions from individuals accused of acting for the Zionists in 1914. Recognising that the Government was beginning to take Arab opinion on the Zionist issue into account, some Arabs urged that they should adopt means of making their voice more felt.

19. In all this, Arabs outside Palestine were actively involved. Thus, when the Arab list of delegates was presented for the proposed meting at Brummana, it contained six Arabs from Beirut and Damascus, and only four from Palestine itself. After World War I, Arabs outside Palestine continued to be involved in the Arab-Zionist conflict, and indeed at later stages overshadowed the Palestinians themselves.

20. Nonetheless, by 1914, some Arabs had begun to distinguish between the Zionist question, first, as it affected Arabs in Palestine and, second, as it related to the wider Arab cause.

This distinction was most clearly drawn in the early summer of 1914 by Rafiq Bey Al-ᶜAẓm, the President of the Decentralisation Party in Cairo, but it was also well understood by Arab leaders who met Zionist representatives in Constantinople at that time.

21. Finally, the younger generation of Arabs were also involved. The members of the anti-Zionist societies in Beirut, Cairo and Constantinople were students—mainly, it appears, from Palestine.

Only a few of the Arabs mentioned in this study were prominent in Arab politics after World War I. Some of them died, and some were hanged by Cemal Paşa during the war. But most were overtaken by a new generation of leaders, more attuned to the changed circumstances of the interwar period. But it should not be forgotten that the war, cataclysmic as it was for Turks and Arabs, lasted only four years; that the new leadership—the younger generation—grew up in the prewar period; and that it emerged from exactly the same social and political élites as have been the main concern of this book.

22. The period before 1914 therefore takes on new importance in terms of the Arab-Zionist conflict. The roots of Arab antagonism, and perhaps of the conflict itself, stretch back to it. Indeed, it may even be argued that the Balfour Declaration was not so much the starting point of the conflict as a turning point which greatly aggravated an existing trend.

Notes on Sources

The following is a brief description of the unpublished diplomatic and Jewish material employed in this study.

A. Diplomatic Material

Austria, *Haus- Hof- und Staatsarchiv, Politisches Archiv* (Vienna). Cited as *CZA (A).*

The Central Zionist Archive of Jerusalem possesses a number of documents on microfilm, mainly from the former Austro-Hungarian Embassy at Constantinople to Vienna. These despatches (from files J IV and P I) deal mainly with Great Power intervention against Ottoman restrictions on Jewish immigration and settlement in Palestine. Being very incomplete, they are of limited value.

France, *Archives du Ministère des Affaires Etrangères* (Quai d'Orsay, Paris). Cited as *Q d'O.*

Within the *"Nouvelle Série"* (which begins at 1896), seven volumes are devoted to Palestine (N.S. vols. 129–135) and three volumes to Zionism (N.S. vols. 136–138). These and other selected volumes on the internal affairs of the Ottoman Empire were examined in detail. They were not found to be as useful as the material in the British and German archives—for two reasons. First, French representatives in Palestine were little interested in the Jewish immigrants (as scarcely any were French subjects), while they were greatly concerned with the Holy Places, which absorbed most of their attentions. Second, the documents in the *Nouvelle Serie* have been severely weeded, and there are still certain despatches which have probably not yet been declassified. However, the French lack of interest in the Jewish immigrants is compensated for by a certain detachment when writing about them, which is not always maintained in the British and German despatches.

Germany, *Archiv des Auswartigen Amtes* (Berlin). Cited as *PRO (G).*

The Public Record Office in London possesses a large collection of German documents on microfilm from the German Foreign Ministry Archives. Film K 692 ("Die Juden in der Türkei: 1897–1920") contains despatches from German representatives in Constantinople, Jerusalem, Beirut and elsewhere.

In addition, the Israel State Archive in Jerusalem houses a collection of files from the former German Consulate in Jerusalem. Cited as *ISA (G).*

This collection proved more valuable than *PRO (G).* The latter was filmed selectively, while in *ISA (G)* there are internal files from the Jerusalem Consulate, which preserve the drafts of reports sent to Berlin, and details omitted from the final text. Moreover, these files contain memoranda, press cuttings, circulars and correspondence with the Ottoman authorities in Jerusalem and Jaffa, upon which the consuls' reports were based. The files are arranged according to subject, and all relevant ones for the years 1880 to 1914 were examined.

Great Britain, *Foreign Office Archive* (Public Record Office, London). Cited as *PRO.*

All volumes of reports from Constantinople, Jerusalem and Beirut were examined for the years 1880 and 1914. Reports from other posts, such as Cairo and Damascus, were consulted where relevant. Almost all these volumes fell under the classifications of FO 78, FO 195 and FO 371'. The information contained in them is rich but widely scattered because most of the volumes are arranged chronologically and not by subject. These volumes were also employed to provide much of the background information required for this study which could not be found elsewhere.

Ottoman Empire, *Archive du Ministère des Affaires Etrangères* (Sublime Porte, Istanbul). Cited as *OFM.*

A limited number of files from this archive were examined. Files, the titles of which indicated that they had direct bearing on this study, were put at the disposal of the author, who was not permitted, however, either to consult files of a more general nature or to inspect the catalogues to this archive himself. The files employed contain correspondence between the former Ottoman Foreign Ministry and its representatives abroad as well as exchanges between the Sublime Porte and the Foreign Missions at Constantinople. These files are by no means complete, especially for the period after 1908, and one important file, concerning Jewish immigration from Russia into the Ottoman Empire during the 1880s, could not be found by the archive officials. The correspondence in these files between the Foreign Ministry and its representatives abroad confirmed all other evidence that the Ottoman Government kept a very watchful eye on Jewish affairs in Europe after 1881.

Under this heading should be mentioned a collection of Turkish documents housed in the Israel State Archive. Cited as *ISA (T).*

These documents came from the papers of Ali Ekrem Bey, who was Mutasarrıf of Jerusalem from December 1906 to August 1908. They comprise personal letters and, more important, copies of documents from the Archive of the Mutasarrıflık of Jerusalem which Ali Ekrem Bey utilised to prepare reports sent to Constantinople. Copies of some of these reports are also available, as well as orders received from various ministries at the Porte. The serial numbers ascribed to these documents by the Israel State Archive bear no relation to their chronological order.

United States, *National Archives* (Department of State, Washington). Cited as *US (T).*

The American National Archives have published a series of microfilms entitled *Records of the State Department Relating to the Internal Affairs of Turkey: 1910–1929* (Washington, 1961). The index to the films was used to locate likely material, but the despatches obtained were disappointing and reflect America's lack of interest in the Ottoman Empire prior to 1914.

B. Jewish Material

Alliance Israélite Universelle Archive (Paris). Cited as *AIU.*

This vast collection of material consists mainly of reports sent by the directors of Alliance Israélite Universelle schools in various parts of the world to the head office in Paris. Since the Alliance was opposed to the

Zionist Movement, a number of special files were opened on Zionist questions. The archive is well catalogued, and files, mainly from Constantinople and Jerusalem, were examined.

By far the most important reports were those sent by Albert Antébi, who directed the Alliance school in Jerusalem after 1900. Born in Damascus, he came to Jerusalem in 1896, where he worked both as an employee of the Alliance and as the representative of the Jewish Colonization Association (JCA) in Jerusalem. He was a highly political individual, and his letters, even when dealing with routine educational matters, frequently contain valuable information about his contacts with the local authorities and influential Arabs.

Central Zionist Archive (Jerusalem). Cited as CZA.

This archive, by far the most important of those researched, houses all official Zionist correspondence as well as many collections of private papers and a large library of Zionist literature, periodicals and pamphlets. Most of the files employed were classified as follows:

ZŁ = Correspondence of the Zionist Central Office, Vienna, 1897–1905.
Z2 = Correspondence of the Zionist Central Office, Cologne, 1905–11.
Z3 = Correspondence of the Zionist Central Office, Berlin, 1911–14.
L2 = Correspondence of the Zionist Office, Jaffa, 1908–14.
L5 = Correspondence of Zionist representatives, Constantinople, 1908–14.
KKL = Correspondence of the Jewish National Fund.
H = Theodor Herzl's papers.
W = David Wolffsohn's papers.
A18 = Nahum Sokolow's papers.

The most rewarding reports were those from Zionist representatives in Constantinople and Jaffa. From 1908 onwards Dr. Victor Jacobson was the principal Zionist representative in Constantinople, and he relied on prominent Ottoman Jews to gain his information and to introduce him to Young Turk leaders of all groups. Through them, there was hardly an Ottoman politician of distinction whom Jacobson did not meet at some state between 1908 and 1914.

The Zionist Office in Jaffa was opened in 1908. It was directed by Dr. Arthur Ruppin, who was seconded by Dr. Jacob Thon. Both talented, they reported in detail on events in Palestine. From time to time they were informed about local feeling by Arabic-speaking Jews, and in December 1911, arrangements were made to follow the Arabic press in a systematic fashion. Nisim Malul, who came to Jaffa in 1911 as the correspondent of *al-Muqaṭṭam* (Cairo), was engaged to read the Arabic press extensively and translate all important articles on Zionism; he also contributed pro-Zionist articles to the Arabic press. Although detailed press reports were sent regularly from Jaffa to the Zionist Central Office in Berlin, no cuttings of the Arabic originals were preserved. However, whenever it was possible to compare the translation of an article with the original Arabic (which might be available elsewhere) or with an alternative rendering published in *ha-Ḥerut* (the newspaper of Sephardi Jews in Jerusalem), the version prepared by Malul and his colleagues was found to be reliable.

Jewish Colonization Association Archive (London). Cited as *JCA.*

This archive used to be housed in Paris. During World War II part of it was transferred to London; the remainder fell into Nazi hands and has not been recovered. Although incomplete, it is still by no means inconsiderable. JCA began to interest itself in colonisation in Palestine in 1896, and the documents utilised in this study are today kept in Boxes 254–280. These include reports from Albert Antébi in Jerusalem (mentioned above), from the directors-general of the colonies in the north and south of Palestine, and from administrators on individual colonies founded or supported by JCA. Once again, the reports written by Albert Antébi were immensely valuable. The other reports concern themselves rather narrowly with the day-to-day administration of the JCA colonies. They therefore throw light on relations between the settlers and their fellahin neighbours, but contribute little to the political questions of major concern in this study.

Palestine Jewish Colonization Association Archive (Haifa). Cited as *PJCA.*

At the end of 1899 Baron Edmond de Rothschild handed over to JCA the administration of all the colonies in Palestine which he had supported for almost two decades. JCA kept the records of these colonies separate from those of its own colonies, setting up a special administration which it dubbed the "Commission Palestinienne." Access to this vast archive, located in Haifa, is severely restricted, and the author was permitted to use only a few important files.

Selected Bibliography

*1. Periodicals**

L'Aurore. Constantinople, vols. i–iii, 1909–11.
Falasṭin. Jaffa, vols. i–iii, 1911–13.
Ḥavaẓẓalet. Jerusalem, vols. x–xx, 1880–90.
Hashqafa. Jerusalem, vols. i–ix, 1897–1908.
Ha-Ḥerut. Jerusalem, vols. i–vi, 1909–14.
Al-Hilal. Cairo, vols. i–xxii, 1892–1914.
L'Indépendence Arabe. Paris, vols. i–ii, 1907–8.
Le Jeune-Turc. Constantinople, vols. iv–vi, 1912–14.
Al-Manar. Cairo, vols. i–xvii, 1897–1914.
Al-Mashriq. Beirut, vols. i–XVII, 1898–1914.
Ha-Mevasser. Constantinople, vols. i–ii, 1909–11.
Mècheroutiette. Paris, vols. i–vi, 1909–14.
Al-Muqtabas. Cairo-Damascus, vols. i–viii, 1906–13 (monthly review).
Al-Muqtaṭaf. Beirut-Cairo, vols. i–xlv, 1876–1914.
Near East. London, vols. i–vii, 1908–14.
Ha-Or. Jerusalem, vols. vi–ix, 1889–93; and vols. xxvi–xxviii, 1910–12.
Ha-Poᶜel ha-Ẓaᶜir. Jaffa, vols. i–vi, 1908–14.
Revue du Monde Musulman. Paris, vols. i–xxviii, 1906–14.
Ha-Shiloᶜaḥ. Berlin-Krakow-Odessa, vols. i–xxxi, 1897–1914.
Times. London, [no volume numbers], 1908–14.

*Complete sets of some of the periodicals listed were not always available; accordingly the years of the volumes used are indicated.

Truth. Jerusalem, vols. iii–v, 1912–14.
Ha-Ẓevi. Jerusalem, vols. xxv–xxxi, 1908–12.

2. Works in Hebrew and Arabic

Almaliᶜah, Avraham. "Avraham Albert Antébi." *Ha-Mizraḥ,* i, 3 (1942), pp. 6–7; 4, pp. 6–7; 5, pp. 6–7; 6, p. 6.

Alsberg, P.A. "Ha-Sheᶜela ha-ᵓaravit bi-mediniyyut ha-hanhala ha-ẓiyyonit lifne milhemet ha-ᶜolam ha-rishona." *Shivat Ẓiyyon,* vol. iv (1956–57), pp. 161–209.

______. "Ha-Oryenṭaẓya shel mediniyyut ha-hanhala ha-ẓiyyonit ᶜerev milḥemet ha-ᶜolam ha-rishona: 1911–1914." *Ẓiyyon,* vol. xxii (1957), pp. 149–76.

Ariᶜel, Dov. "Ha-Moshava Gedera." *Luᶜah ereẓ yisraᶜel,* vol. vi (1900), pp. 73–126.

Asaf, Michael. *Ha-Tenuᶜa ha-ᶜaravit be-ereẓ yisra₈ el umeqoroteha.* Tel Aviv, 1936.

______. *Toldot ha-ᶜaravim be-ereẓ yisraᵓel.* 2 vols. Tel Aviv, 1935 and 1941.

Bein, Alex. *Toldot ha-hityashshvut ha-ẓiyyonit.* Tel Aviv, 1954.

Braslawski, Moses. *Poᶜalim ve-jirgunehem ba-ᶜaliyya ha-rishona.* Tel Aviv, 1961.

Brill, Jehiel. *Yesud ha-maᶜala.* Mayence, 1883.

Chissin, Chaim. *Miyyoman aḥad ha-biluyim.* Trans. S. Herberg. Tel Aviv, 1925.

Cohen, Aaron. *Yisraᵓel veha-ᶜolam ha/ᶜaravi.* Merḥavya, 1964.

Cohn-Reiss, Ephraim. *Mizzikhronot ish yerushalayim.* Jerusalem, 1934.

[Daghir, Asᶜad]. *Thawrat al-ᶜarab.* Cairo, 1916.

Daghir, Asᶜad. *Mudhakkirati.* Cairo, 1959.

Dinur, Ben Zion, et al. (eds.). *Sefer toldot ha-haganna.* 7 vols. Tel Aviv, 1954–72.

Druyanow, A[lter], (ed.). *Ketavim letoldot ḥibbat ẓiyyon ve-yishshuv erez yisraᵓel.* 3 vols. Odessa and Tel Aviv, 1919, 1925 and 1932.

______. *Pinsker uzemano.* Jerusalem, 1953.

Epstein, Isaac. "Sheᵓela neᶜelama." *ha-Shiloᵓaḥ,* vol. xvii (1907), pp. 193–206.

Farḥi, David. "Teᶜudot le-toldot ᶜha-sheᵓela ha-ᶜaravitᵓ." *ha-Mizraḥ he-Ḥadash,* vol. xxii (1962), pp. 230–32.

Freidlander, Nili. "ha-Qaᵓimmaqam miyyafo nilḥam ba-ᶜaliyya." *Maᶜariv* (10.11.1964).

Ginsberg, Asher [Aḥad ha-ᶜAm]. *Kol kitve Aḥad ha-ᶜAm.* Tel Aviv, 1961.

Habbas, Berakha (ed.). *Sefer ha-ᶜaliyya ha-sheniyya.* Tel Aviv, 1947.

ben Ḥananya, Joshua. "Sifrut ᶜaravit anṭi-ẓiyyonit." *ha-Shiloᵓaḥ,* vol. xliii (1924), pp. 272–79.

______. "ha-Yehudim besifrut ʿarav." *Moznayim,* vol. xviii (1944), pp. 34–38, 305–9, and 393–97.

Ḥaviv-Lubman, Dov. *Missipure ha-rishonim le-ẓiyyon.* Tel Aviv, 1934.

Ḥermoni, A. "ha-Tenuʿa ha-ʿaravit umegamoteha." *ha-Shiloʾaḥ,* vol. xv (1905), pp. 377–90.

______. "ha-Tenuʿa ha-ʿaravit ve-qudmat asya." *ha-Shiloʾaḥ,* vol. xvi (1907), pp. 257–69 and 454–64.

______. "ʿAravi bizekhut ha-ʿaravim." *ha-Shiloʾaḥ,* vol. xvii (1907, pp. 360–65.

Hitaḥdut ha-moshavot bihuda. Hashqafat ha-ʿitonut ha-ʿaravit ʿal ha-yishshuv. Vol. i, Rishon le-Ẓiyyon, 1913.

______. *Zikhron devarim shel yeshivat majlis ha-ʿumumi birushalayim.* Rishon le-Ẓiyyon, 1914.

Hiẓb al-Lamarkaziyya. al-Muʾ tamar al-ʿarabi al-awwal. Cairo, 1913.

Hochberg, S[ami]. "ha-Yishshuv veha-ʿaravim." *ha-Mevasser,* ii, 13–14 (1911), pp. 146–48; 18, pp. 205–6; 19, pp. 218–19; 23, pp. 281–82.

Joffe, H[illel]. *Dor ha-maʿapilim.* Eds. Y. H. Ravnitsky et al. Tel Aviv, 1939.

Kaḥḥalah, ʿUmar Riḍa. *Muʿjam al-muʾallifin.* 15 vols. Damascus, 1957–61.

Kalvarisky, Chaim Margalit. "ha-Yaḥasim ben ha-yehudim veha-ʿaravim lifne ha-milhama." *Sheʾifotenu,* vol. ii (1931), pp. 50–55.

______. "ha-Yahasim ben ha-yehudim weha-ʿaravim bizeman ha-milhama." *Sheʾifotenu,* vol. ii (1931), pp. 88–93.

al-Khalidi, Ruḥi. *al-Muqaddima fi al-masʾala al-sharqiyya.* Jerusalem, n.d.

Klausner, Israel. *Ḥibbat ẓiyyon berumanya.* Jerusalem, 1958.

Kurd ʿAli, Muḥammad. *al-Mudhakkirat.* 4 vols. Damascus, 1948–51.

Landau, Jacob M. "Teʿudot min ha-arkhiyyonim ha-beriṭiyyim ʿal nissayon ha-hityashshvut ha-yehudit be-midyan bi-shenot 1890–1892." *Shivat Ẓiyyon,* vol. i (1950), pp. 169–78.

Levontin, Z[alman] D[avid]. *Le-ereẓ avotenu.* 2 vols. Tel Aviv, 1924 and 1928.

Lewin-Epstein, Elija Zeʾev. *Zikhronotai.* Tel Aviv, 1932.

Lichtheim, Richard. *Sheʾar yashuv.* Tel Aviv, 1953.

Lunz, Joseph, "ha-Megaʿim ha-diplomaṭiyyim ben ha-tenuʿa ha-ẓi yonit veha-tenuʿa ha-ʿaravit ha-leʾumit ʿim siyyum milḥemet ha-ʿolam ha-rishona." *ha-Mizraḥ he-Ḥadash,* vol. xxii (1962), pp. 212–29.

L[uria], J[oseph]. "ha-Tenuʿa ha-ʿaravit." *ha-ʿOlam,* vii, 13–14 (18.4. 1913); and 15 (6.5.1913).

Malul, Nisim. "ha-ʿItonut ha-ʿaravit." *ha-Shiloʾaḥ,* vol. xxxi (1914), pp. 364–74 and 439–50.

Medzini, H. *ʿEser shanim shel mediniyyut ereẓyisraʾelit.* Tel Aviv, 1928.

Naṣṣar, Najib al-Khuri. *al-Ṣihyuniyya: taikhuha, gharaḍuha, aham-miyyatuha.* Haifa, 1911.

Netanyahu, B. (ed.). *Max Nordau el ʿamo.* Vol. ii. Tel Aviv, 1937.

Porat, Joshua. *Ẓemiḥat ha-tenuʿa ha-leʾumit ha-ʿaravit ha-palestinaʾit, 1918–29.* Jerusalem, 1971.

Rabinovitz, Jacob. "Ṭurḳiyya ḥadasha, ha-yehudim veha-ẓiyyonut." *ha-Shiloʾaḥ,* vol. xix (1908), pp. 280–88, 456–61, and 548–57.

Roʾi, Jacob. "Yaḥas ha-yishshuv el ha-ʿaravim: 1880–1914." Unpublished M.A. thesis. Jerusalem, 1964.

______. "Nisyonotehem shel ha-mosdot ha-ẓiyyoniyyim le-hashpiʿa ʿal ha-ʿitonut ha-ʿaravit be-ereẓ yisraʾel ba-shanim 1908–1914." *Ẓiyyon,* vol. xxxii, 3–4 (1967), pp. 201–27.

Ruppin, Arthur. *Pirqe ḥayyai.* Tel Aviv, 1947.

Sabba, Solomon. "Tiqo ha-peraṭi shel Ekrem Bey." Weekly supplement to *Davar,* no. 11,651 (27.9.1963).

al-Safari, ʿIsa. *Falasṭin al-ʿarabiyya bayn al-intidab wal-ṣihyuniyya.* Jaffa, 1937.

Saʿid, Amin.. *al-Thawra al-ʿarabiyya al-kubra.* 3 vols. Egypt, [1934].

al-Sakakini, Khalil. *Kadha ana ya dunya.* Ed. H. al-Sakakini. Jerusalem, 1955.

Samsonow, Aryeh. *Zikhron yaʿaqov: parashat divre yameha, 1882–1942.* Zikhron Yaʿaqov, 1943.

Sapir, [Elija]. "ha-Sinʾa le-yisraʾel ba-sifrut ha-ʿaravit." *ha-Shiloʾaḥ,* vol. vi (1899), pp. 222–32.

Shimʿoni, Jacob. *ʿArave ereẓ yisraʾel.* Tel Aviv, 1947.

Shuv, D[avid]. *Zikhronot levet david.* Jerusalem, 1937.

Smilanski, Moses. *Reḥovot: shishshim shenot ḥayyeha, 1890–1950.* Tel Aviv, 1950.

______. *Nes ẓiyyona: shivʿim shenot ḥayyeha, 1883–1953.* Nes Ẓiyyona, 1953.

Wissotski, Kalonimus Zeʿev. *Qevuẓat mikhtavim.* Warsaw, 1898.

Yaʿari, Y., and Charizman, M. *Sefer ha-yovel petaḥ tiqva.* Tel Aviv, 1929.

Yavneʾeli, Samuel (ed.). *Sefer ha-ẓiyyonut: tequfat ḥibbat ẓiyyon.* 2 vols. Tel Aviv, 1961.

Yellin, Joshua. *Zikhronot leven yerushalayim.* Jerusalem, 1924.

ben Ẓevi, Isaac. *Ereẓ yisraʾel ve-yishshuveha bime ha-shilṭon ha-ʿotomani.* Jerusalem, 1955.

al-Zirakli, Khayr al-Din. *Aʿlam.* 10 vols. No place, 1954–59.

3. Works in other languages

Aaronsohn, Alexander. *With the Turks in Palestine.* London, 1917.

Adler, Cyrus, and Margalith, Aaron M. *With Firmness in the Right: American Diplomatic Action Affecting Jews: 1840–1945.* New York, 1946.

Ahmad, Feroz. *The Young Turks: The Committee of Union and Progress in Turkish Politics, 1908-1914.* Oxford, 1969.

Amery, L[eopold] S. *My Political Life.* London, 1953.

Antonius, George, *The Arab Awakening: The Story of the Arab National Movement.* London, 1961.

Azoury, Bégib. *Le Réveil de la Nation Arabe dans l'Asie Turque.* Paris, 1905.

Bambus, W. *Die jüdishchen Dörfer in Palästina.* Berlin, 1896.

Barron, J. B. *Palestine: Report and General Abstracts of the Census of 1922.* Jerusalem, [1923].

Bein, Alex. *The Return to the Soil.* Trans. I. Schen. Jerusalem, 1952.

Bergman, Judah. "Jews and Moslems in their Popular Beliefs." *Edoth,* vol. iii (1948), pp. 126-36.

Böhm, Adolf. *Die Zionistische Bewegung.* 2 vols. Tel Aviv and Jerusalem, 1935 and 1937.

Burckhardt, John Lewis. *Arabic Proverbs: or the Manners and Customs of the Modern Egyptians, illustrated from their proverbial sayings current at Cairo.* London, 1830.

Burstein, Moshé. *Self-Government of the Jews in Palestine since 1900.* Tel Aviv, 1934.

Canaan, T. *Conflict in the Land of Peace.* Jerusalem, 1936.

Cuinet, Vital. *Syria, Liban et Palestine: Geographie Administrative; Statistique, Descriptive et Raisonée.* Paris, 1896.

Dalman, G. H. "Gegenwärtiger Bestand der jüdischen Colonien in Palästina." *Zeitschrift des deutschen Palaestin-Vereins,* vol. xvi (1893), pp. 193-201.

Davidson, Roderic H. "Turkish Attitudes concerning Christian-Muslim Equality in the Nineteenth Century." *American Historical Review,* vol. lix (1953-54), pp. 844-64.

______. *Reform in the Ottoman Empire: 1856-1876.* Princeton, 1963.

Dawn, C. Ernest. "From Ottomanism to Arabism: The Origin of an Ideology." *Review of Politics,* vol. xxiii (1961), pp. 378-400.

______. "The Rise of Arabism in Syria." *Middle East Journal,* vol. xvi (1962), pp. 145-68.

Devereux, Robert. *The First Ottoman Constitutional Period: A Study of the Midhat Constitution and Parliament.* Baltimore, 1963.

Elazari-Volcani, I. *The Fellah's Farm.* Tel Aviv, 1930.

Emin, Ahmed *The Development of Modern Turkey as Measured by its Press.* Studies in History, Economics and Public Law edited by the Faculty of Political Science of Columbia University, vol. lix, no. 1, New York, 1914.

Erskine, Beatrice Steuart. *Palestine of the Arabs.* London, 1935.

ESCO Foundation for Palestine, Inc. *Palestine: A Study of Jewish, Arab, and British Policies.* 2 vols. New Haven, 1947.

Farhi, David. "Documents on the Attitude of the Ottoman Government towards the Jewish Settlement in Palestine after the Revolution of the Young Turks (1908-1909)." Unpublished paper given at Jerusalem, 1970.

Feldman, J. "Unsere Arabische Frage." *Die Welt,* xvii, 33 (1913), pp. 1057-59.

Finn, E. A. "The Fallahheen of Palestine." *Palestine Exploration Fund Quarterly Statement* (1879), pp. 33-48 and 72-87.

Franco, Moise. *Essai sur l'Histoire des Israélites de l'Empire Ottoman depuis les Origines jusqu'à Nos Jours.* Paris, 1897.

Fraenkel, Josef. "Paul Friedmann's Midian Project." *Herzl Year Book,* vol. iv (1961-2), pp. 67-117.

Friedfeld, Joseph, "Zur Geschichte der arabischen Nationalbewegung." *Jüdische Rundschau,* (28.4.1925), pp. 303-4, and (22.5.1925), pp. 366-67.

Galanté, Abraham. *Turcs et Juifs: Etude Historique, Politique.* Istanbul, 1932.

______. *Abdul Hamid II et le Sionisme.* Istanbul, 1933.

______. *Le Juif dans le proverbe, le conte et la chanson orientaux.* Istanbul, 1935.

Gelber, N[athan] M. "An Attempt to Internationalize Salonika: 1912-1913." *Jewish Social Studies,* xvii, 2 (1955), pp. 105-20.

______. "Philipp Michael de Newlinski: Herzl's Diplomatic Agent." *Herzl Year Book,* vol. ii (1959), pp. 113-52.

George-Samné. *La Syrie.* Paris, 1921.

Gibb. H. A. R., and Bowen, Harold. *Islamic Society and the West: A Study of the Impact of Western Civilization on Moslem Culture in the Near East.* Vol. I, parts i and ii. London, 1950 and 1957.

Goitein, S. D. *Jews and Arabs: Their Contacts Throuth the Ages.* New York, 1955.

Gottheil, Richard. "Zionism." *Jewish Encyclopedia,* xii, 666-86. New York and London, 1905.

von Grunebaum, Gustav E. *Medieval Islam.* Chicago, 1961.

ben-Gurion, David *Rebirth and Destiny of Israel.* Trans. Mordekhai Nurock et al. London, 1959.

Gutman, Edwin Emmanuel. "The Development of Local Government in Palestine: Background to the Study of Local Administration in Israel." Unpublished Ph.D. dissertation, 1958. Columbia University.

Haddad, G. *Fifty Years of Modern Syria and Lebanon.* Beirut, 1950.

Haim, Sylvia G. " 'The Arab Awakening.' A Source for the Historian?" *Die Welts Des Islams,* N.S. ii, 4 (1953(, pp. 237-50.

______. "Arabic Antisemitic Literature." *Jewish Social Studies,* xvii, 4 (1955), pp. 307-12.

———. "Islam and the Theory of Arab Nationalism" *The Middle East in Transition,* pp. 280–307. Ed. Walter Z. Laqueur. London, 1958.

Halpern, B. *The Idea of the Jewish State.* Harvard Middle Eastern Studies, 3. Cambridge, Mass., 1961.

Harosin, J. *La Palestine et les Etats arabes-unis: Sionisme, Panarabisme, Panislamisme, Antisémitisme.* Paris, 1939.

Harran, T. E. A. M. "Turkish-Syrian Relations in the Ottoman Constitutional Period (1908–1914)." Unpublished Ph.D. dissertation. University of London, 1969.

Haslip, Joan. *The Sultan: The Life of Abdul Hamid.* London, 1958.

Haycraft Commission. *Palestine: Disturbances in May 1921.* Cmd. 1540, London, 1921.

Henderson, Philip. *The Life of Laurence Oliphant: Traveller, Diplomat and Mystic.* London, 1956.

Herzl, Theodor. *The Jewish State: An Attempt at a Modern Solution of the Jewish Question.* Trans. Sylvie d'Avigdor. London, 1946.

———. *Altneuland.* Trans. Paula Arnold. Haifa, 1960.

———. *The Complete Diaries of Theodor Herzl.* Ed. R. Patai and trans. H. Zohn. 5 vols. New York and London, 1960.

Heyd, Uriel. *Foundations of Turkish Nationalism: The Life and Teachings of Ziya Gokalp.* London, 1950.

Hocking, W. E. "Arab Nationalism and Political Zionism." *Muslim World,* vol. xxxv (1945), pp. 216–23.

Hourani, Albert. "Race, Religion and Nation-State in the Near East." *A Vision of History,* pp. 71–105. Beirut, 1961.

———. *Arabic Thought in the Liberal Age: 1798–1939.* London, 1962.

———. "Near Eastern Nationalism Yesterday and Today." *Foreign Affairs,* vol. xlii (1963), pp. 123–36.

Howard, Harry N. *The King-Crane Commission: An American Inquiry into the Middle East.* Beirut, 1963.

Jeffery, Arthur. "The Political Importance of Islam." *Journal of Near Eastern Studies,* i, 4 (1942), pp. 383–95.

Jung. Eugene, *La Révolte Arabe.* Paris, 1924.

Kan, J[acobus] H[enricus]. *Erets Israël—le Pays Juif.* Brussels, 1910.

Kassab, Farid [Georges]. *Le Nouvel Empire Arabe.* Paris, 1906.

Keddie, Nikki R. "Symbol and Sincerity in Islam." *Studia Islamica,* vol. xix (1963), pp. 27–63.

Kedourie, Elie. "Religion and Politics: The Dairies of Khalil Sakakini." *St. Antony's Papers,* iv, 77–94.

———. "Young Turks, Freemasons and Jews." *Middle Eastern Studies,* vii, i (1971), pp. 89–104.

———. "The Politics of Political Literature: Kawakibi, Azoury and Jung." *Middle Eastern Studies,* viii, 2 (1972), pp. 227–40.

Khairallah, K. R. "La Syrie." *Revue du Monde Musulman,* vol. xix (1912), pp. 1-143.

Kohn, Hans. *The Ideas of Nationalism.* New York, 1961.

Lammens, Henri. "Le 'Sionisme' et les colonies juives de Palestine." *Études,* vol. lxxiii (1897), pp. 433-63.

Landau, Jacob, and Maᶜoz, Moshe. "Jews and Non-Jews in Nineteenth-century Egypt and Syria." Unpublished paper given at Jerusalem, 1974.

Laqueur, Walter. *The Israel-Arab Reader.* London, 1969.

______. *A History of Zionism.* London, 1972.

Lewis, Bernard. *Notes and Documents from the Turkish Archives: A Contribution to the History of the Jews in the Ottoman Empire.* Oriental Notes and Studies, vol. iii. Jerusalem, 1952.

______. *The Emergence of Modern Turkey.* London, 1961.

Lybyer, Albert H[owe]. "The Turkish Parliament." *Proceedings of the American Political Science Association at its Seventh Annual Meeting,* pp. 65-77. Baltimore, 1910.

Mandel, Neville. "Turks, Arabs and Jewish Immigration into Palestine: 1882-1914." *St. Antony's Papers,* xvii, 77-108. Oxford, 1965.

______. "Attempts at an Arab-Zionist Entente: 1913-1914." *Middle Eastern Studies,* i, 3 (1965), pp. 238-67.

______. "Ottoman Policy and Restrictions on Jewish Settlement in Palestine: 1881-1908." *Middle Eastern Studies,* x, 3 (1974), pp. 312-332.

______. "Ottoman Practice as regards Jewish Settlement in Palestine: 1881-1908." *Middle Eastern Studies,* xi, 1 (1975), pp. 31-46.

Mandelstam, André. *Le Sort de l'Empire Ottoman.* Paris, 1917.

Manuel, Frank E. *The Realities of American-Palestine Relations.* Washington, 1949.

Mardin, Şerif [Arif]. *The Genesis of Young Ottoman Thought: A Study in the Modernization of Turkish Political Ideas.* Princeton, 1962.

Margalith, Israël. *Le Baron Edmond de Rothschild et la colonisation juive en Palestine, 1882-1899.* Paris, 1957.

Miller, William. *The Ottoman Empire, 1801-1913.* Cambridge, 1913.

Montagne, Robert. "Les Arabes et la colonisation juive en Palestine." *Politique Etrangère,* vol. ii (1936), pp. 54-66.

Morawitz, Charles. *Les Finances de Turquie.* Paris, 1902.

Morgenthau, Henry, *Secrets of the Bosphorus.* London, 1918.

Moussalli, Negib. *Le Sionisme et la Palestine.* Geneva, 1919.

Nazly, Férid. "L'immigration juive en Palestine." *La Correspondance d'Orient,* no. 84 (1912), pp. 265-68.

Nordau, Anna and Nordau, Maxa. *Max Nordau: A Biography.* New York, 1943.

Nuseibeh, Hazem Zaki. *The Ideas of Arab Nationalism.* Ithaca, New York, 1956.

Oliphant, Laurence. *The Land of Gilead.* London, 1880.

Ongley, F., and Miller, Horace E. *The Ottoman Land Code.* London, 1892.

Pears, Edwin. *Life of Abdul Hamid.* London, 1917.

Perlmann, Moshe. "Chapters of Arab-Jewish Diplomacy: 1918–1922." *Jewish Social Studies,* vi, 2 (1944), pp. 124–54.

______. "Arabic Antisemitic Literature. Comment on Sylvia G. Haim's Article." *Jewish Social Studies,* xvii, 4 (1955), pp. 313–14.

______. "Paul Haupt and the Mesopotamian Project, 1892–1914." *Publications of the American Jewish Historical Society,* xlvii, 3 (1958), pp. 154–75.

Rabinowicz, Oskar K. "Herzl and England." *Jewish Social Studies,* xiii, 1 (1951), pp. 25–46.

Ramsaur, E. E. *The Young Turks—Prelude to the Revolution of 1908.* Princeton, 1957.

Roʾi, Yaacov. "The Zionist Attitude to the Arabs, 1908–1914." *Middle Eastern Studies,* iv, 3 (1968), pp. 198–242.

Ruppin, Arthur. *The Jews of Today.* Trans. Margery Bentwich. London, 1913.

Saab, Hassan. *The Arab Federalists of the Ottoman Empire.* Amsterdam, 1958.

Saad, L[amec]. "Die jüdischen Kolonien und Niederlassungen in Syrien und Palästina." *Dr. A. Petermanns Mitteilungen,* xlix, 11 (1903), pp. 250–54.

Schmidt, H. D. "The Nazi Party in Palestine and the Levant 1932–1939." *International Affairs,* vol. xxviii (1952), pp. 460–69.

Sereni, Enzo, and Ashery, R. E. *Jews and Arabs in Palestine: Studies in a National and Colonial Problem.* New York, 1936.

Seton-Watson, R. W. *The Rise of Nationality in the Balkans.* London, 1917.

Simon, Ernst. "Zur Geschichte des Zionismus: Der Zionismus und die Jungtürken." *Judische Rundschau,* xxxiv, 101–102 (24.12.1929).

Slousch, N. "Musulmans et Juifs." *Revue du Monde Musulman,* vol. i (1907), p. 406.

S[lousch], N. "Antisémitisme et Sionisme en Turquie." *Revue du Monde Musulman,* vol. ix (1909), pp. 174–77.

Sokolow, Nahum. *History of Zionism: 1600–1918.* 2 vols. London, 1919.

Stein, Leonard. *The Balfour Declaration.* London, 1961.

Straus, Oscar S[olomon]. *Under Four Administrations: From Cleveland to Taft.* Boston, 1922.

Sykes, Christopher. *Cross Roads to Israel: Palestine from Balfour to Bevin.* London, 1965.

Szajkowski, Z[osa]. "Jewish Emigration Policy in the Period of the Rumanian 'Exodux' 1899–1903." *Jewish Social Studies,* xiii, 1 (1951), pp. 47–70.

Trietsch, Davis. *Palaestina Handbuch.* Berlin, 1912.
Tunaya, Tarik Z. "Elections in Turkish History." *Middle Eastern Affairs,* v, 4 (1954), pp. 116-19.
Vadja, Georges. "Juifs et Musulmans selon le Ḥadit." *Journal Asiatique,* vol. ccxix (1937), pp. 57-127.
Vambéry, A. "Personal Recollections of Abdul Hamid II and his Court." *The Nineteenth Century and After,* lxv, 388 (1909), pp. 980-93; and lxvi, 389 (1909), pp. 69-88.
La Vérité sur la Question Syrienne. Istanbul, 1916.
Weltmann, Saadia E. "Germany, Turkey and the Zionist Movement, 1914-1918." *Review of Politics,* vol. xxiii (1961), pp. 246-69.
Whitman, Sidney. *Turkish Memories.* London, 1914.
Yale, William. "Ambassador Henry Morgenthau's Special Mission of 1917." *World Politics,* i, 3 (1949), pp. 308-20.
Young, George. *Corps du Droit Ottoman.* 7 vols. Oxford, 1905-6.
Zeine, Zeine N. *The Emergence of Arab Nationalism.* Beirut, 1966.

Index